D1602257

THE CHINESE DEBATE
ABOUT SOVIET SOCIALISM,
1978-1985

GILBERT ROZMAN

THE CHINESE DEBATE
ABOUT SOVIET SOCIALISM,
1978-1985

PRINCETON UNIVERSITY
PRESS

Copyright © 1987 by Princeton University Press

Published by Princeton University Press, 41 William Street,
Princeton, New Jersey 08540
In the United Kingdom: Princeton University Press, Guildford, Surrey

All Rights Reserved

Library of Congress Cataloging in Publication data will be found
on the last printed page of this book

ISBN 0-691-09429-2

Publication of this book has been aided by a grant from
The Andrew W. Mellon Foundation

This book has been composed in Linotron Aldus type

Clothbound edition of Princeton University Press books are printed
on acid-free paper, and binding materials are chosen
for strength and durability. Paperbacks, although satisfactory
for personal collections, are not usually suitable
for library rebinding

Printed in the United States of America by Princeton
University Press, Princeton, New Jersey

CONTENTS

LIST OF TABLES

PREFACE

Under the leadership of Deng Xiaoping, China can be characterized as pragmatic in its economic policy, independent in its foreign policy, and unmistakably socialist in its political and ideological policy. Aware of potential contradictions among these policies, observers in and out of China have been asking which is the true enduring face of China. In the long run, will the balance of economic management shift further toward family-based operations and market forces, or will it tilt back toward centralized planning? Will cooperation expand with the United States and Japan, or will China gravitate toward the socialist bloc and the Soviet Union? Will political centralism and ideological orthodoxy be relaxed to match economic pragmatism, or will they be shored up to withstand "spiritual pollution"? On the basis of information on the policy changes and leadership shifts observed in the first half of the 1980s these questions have been difficult to answer. Other evidence exists, however. This book extends the search for answers to the central questions concerning China's future into a different arena—into the literature published in China on the Soviet Union.

As recently as 1977-1978 there would have been no point in delving deeply into Chinese publications about the Soviet Union. Not many were appearing, and those that did conveyed a monolithic message of hostility. How different is the state of Chinese publications in the mid-1980s! There are now more than twenty specialized journals in the social sciences and humanities on the Soviet Union and no fewer than forty others that regularly carry articles on that country.[1] These publications are rich in content, varied in interpretation, and informative about internal debates. According to China's *National Periodical Index*, by 1983 approximately 2,000 articles a year in the social sciences and humanities, including translations, were focused on the Soviet Union.[2] Suddenly an arena has developed that makes it possible to explore the thinking of Chinese officials and academics concerning sensitive themes of Soviet history and contemporary Soviet life.

Although the number of publications on the Soviet Union has expanded rapidly from 1979, foreign awareness of this literature was delayed by China's *neibu* system. *Neibu* means restricted to internal circu-

---

[1] Publications in this field are reviewed in Gilbert Rozman, "China's Soviet-Watchers in the 1980s: A New Era in Scholarship," *World Politics* 37, no. 4 (July 1985): 435-74.

[2] *Quanguo baokan suoyin* (Shanghai: Shanghai Library, 1973-   ).

lation within China. Normally this label has been interpreted to deny access to foreigners. In early 1985, American library collections carried no more than a single Chinese journal (*Sulian wenyi*, or "Soviet Arts") on the Soviet Union, while the other twenty or more journals were not available for export. Even the *National Periodical Index* is classified *neibu*, making it difficult for foreigners to read it and thus to determine the scale and range of publications in a field such as Soviet studies.

Fortunately, I was able to see a considerable number of *neibu* publications as well as the less numerous publications in Chinese on the Soviet Union. Although I remain handicapped by not gaining complete access to these materials, the more than one thousand articles and books that I have scanned or read include many from the more important journals and on the most sensitive subjects discussed in *neibu* publications. I believe that my access was sufficient for me to be able to summarize and assess the lively Chinese discussions about Soviet socialism with more than a fair degree of accuracy. A rich treasure house of previously inaccessible materials has the potential to open our eyes to an intriguing debate within China that may have important consequences for international relations and for the future of Chinese socialism.

As a sociologist interested in how internal debates about social change are reflected in perceptions of other societies, I have two goals in this book. First, because many of the Chinese sources cited in this text have not readily been available to foreigners, and because relations among the world's great nations have long been plagued by misinformation and distorted fragments of information, I consider it my responsibility to present the Chinese views in detail. My primary goal is to convey, as accurately and fully as one could expect within the limits of a single book, the Chinese views on the Soviet Union. In this regard, it is necessary to alert the reader to the less-than-ideal circumstances of my research undertaking. In using Chinese sources, I was not always able to work as a researcher should, with ample time for use of a dictionary and note-taking, and with an opportunity to recheck the original sources when reviewing my notes. As a result, I use quotation marks sparingly. There are many instances of rough translations in which I try to stick closely to the author's text, but because of the possibility that the meaning has not been captured precisely, it would have been inappropriate to use quotation marks. Owing to the problem of verification, I have deemed it advisable to err on the side of sticking too closely to the sources rather than on the side of liberally restating in my own words the meaning of what I have read. This should not pose any special problems for the reader because the Chinese sources with which I was working are eminently readable, and, I believe, my notes capture more than a little of the colorful language used in referring to the Soviet Union.

The other goal for this book is to assess the meaning of Chinese debates about the Soviet social system and, in a preliminary way, to make comparisons with Soviet perceptions of Chinese society. The evidence shows that these Chinese debates are important not only for understanding developments in the Soviet Union, but also for understanding differences of opinion about the history and prospects of socialism more generally, including inside China. Above all, we learn from this literature about the Chinese worldview on sensitive matters critical to domestic and international affairs.

The organization of the chapters largely parallels the arrangement in my prior book on Soviet views of China.[3] Separate chapters examine each of the four social classes or strata into which socialist societies can be readily divided: peasants, workers, the intelligentsia, and officials. The one exception to the parallel study of social groups is the omission of a chapter on national minorities in this book; in recent years China's Soviet specialists have not been publishing much on this topic. Because Chinese views have been changing quite dramatically during the decade since Mao Zedong's death, I have added a chronological treatment in Chapter Two, which was unnecessary in the study of the more static Soviet views to 1983. With the completion of this second stage of research on Sino-Soviet mutual perceptions, it is possible to look simultaneously at both sides of the relationship: to draw comparisons and to examine the interrelations between changing perceptions and developing relations between Beijing and Moscow.

The first half of the 1980s witnessed a remarkable relaxation of tensions between China and the Soviet Union. To be sure, it is not a complete rapprochement. There was no reestablishment of the Sino-Soviet alliance that prevailed in the 1950s, and the Chinese remain critical of Soviet foreign policy near China's borders. Nevertheless, the improvement in relations was dramatic and largely unanticipated, and it shows signs of continuing, as Mikhail S. Gorbachev tightens his grip on power in Moscow, and his Chinese contemporaries, many of whom were Soviet-trained, rise to the top in China's leadership.

It requires only glancing back to the beginning of the decade to appreciate how much Sino-Soviet relations and mutual perceptions have changed. The 1980s began with continued intense hostility between China and the Soviet Union; Brezhnev's status-quo leadership remained

---

[3] Gilbert Rozman, *A Mirror for Socialism: Soviet Criticisms of China* (Princeton: Princeton University Press, 1985).

entrenched in Moscow while Deng Xiaoping's reform-oriented leadership was consolidating power in Beijing. Vitriolic accusations flew back and forth, and there seemed to be little prospect for a substantial improvement in relations. Suddenly in the fall of 1982 came the much-ballyhooed beginning of Sino-Soviet negotiations directed at "normalization" and the widespread speculation about a new reform course in Moscow following the end of Brezhnev's eighteen years in power, both of which raised a host of uncertainties about the future of the socialist world. Hostility and seemingly diametrically opposed courses of development had given way to uncertainty and prospects for some convergence in reform strategies.

Through the ups and downs of negotiations in 1983 and 1984 and the short illness-plagued terms in office of Andropov and Chernenko, these doubts were not quickly resolved. Observers became accustomed to a state of limbo, in which a surfeit of talk did not result in much change of course. Moscow and Beijing discussed normalization, but could not reconcile fundamental differences. Moscow promised domestic reforms, but would not dare to dismantle the mainstays of its socialist system, which were the real barriers to reform. Beijing kept on its successful reform course, but paid lip service to its unbroken adherence to socialism. These were the common perceptions of observers of the socialist world, most of whom, as in prior decades, projected the recent past well into the future.

Another interpretation of the developments from 1982 to 1984 was also forming. It found substantial improvements in Sino-Soviet relations and perceptions despite short-term ups and downs in the negotiations and the absence of a dramatic breakthrough. This view recognizes the existence of a power struggle in Moscow, but sees the reformers, led by Andropov and Gorbachev, gaining ascendancy. When Brezhnev fell seriously ill in 1982, the reformers pushed ahead and led Moscow into negotiations toward "normalization." When Chernenko took office, there was a temporary setback in relations. But his incapacitation later in 1984 brought Gorbachev to the fore, which helped to propel binational relations and Soviet domestic reforms forward. Simultaneously, China's leaders were pulling back from discussions that seemed to threaten socialism, gaining confidence from the success of their economic reforms and gradually refining a new socialist worldview more favorable to the Soviet Union on most domestic matters and even on some foreign policy matters. Given these developments in negotiations, in Soviet internal affairs, and in Chinese internal affairs, the period from 1982 to 1984 should be perceived as a time when conditions were ripening for closer Sino-Soviet ties.

In the winter of 1985 came new reminders that the fate of the socialist world, and perhaps the equilibrium between socialism and capitalism, hung in the balance. Additional pieces were falling in place to resolve the principal uncertainties about the future of socialism. The tone of Sino-Soviet communications grew appreciably warmer not long before Gorbachev's accession to the top post in the Soviet leadership brought a healthy vigor and urgency to the momentum for domestic reform. The interconnection between the two themes became more apparent when the Chinese press referred to "Comrade Gorbachev," and the Soviet press began to write more positively, although still with circumspection, about China's reforms. One could detect a new spirit of mutual admiration of each other's socialist reforms. A mood of expectancy mounted about how far Sino-Soviet relations would develop in the process of normalization and how comprehensive the Soviet reform of socialism would be. In 1985 it was becoming increasingly clear that a strikingly different socialist world was emerging from that which had existed in the 1970s.

How far Sino-Soviet relations have come, from the depths of border clashes in 1969-1970 and the intense name-calling in 1975-1976, to the uncertainties about whether the Soviet Union is socialist of 1978-1979, and finally to the upbeat, but still indecisive, mood of 1985! How much further are relations likely to improve, as "normalization" of state-to-state ties transforms into party-to-party contacts? The answer to this question must not be sought simply in some preconceptions about geopolitical differences, on the assumption that bonds of ideology and memories of a close alliance count for little. As the Chinese under Deng Xiaoping's leadership constantly remind us, it is necessary "to seek truth from practice"—to focus on the direct evidence of what the Chinese have been writing in recent years. These writings on the Soviet Union tell us that socialism retains deep roots in China, restraining reforms in some spheres more substantially than many foreign observers have indicated. Chinese sources also argue that Soviet reforms will be more substantial and more similar to Chinese developments than most observers have anticipated. Understandably, differences of opinion within China can be detected concerning the timing of Soviet reforms and, by implication, the rate of improvement in Sino-Soviet relations. Only by appreciating the differences in viewpoint and focusing on the evolution of the prevailing views can we make the most of the valuable Chinese materials on Soviet socialism. Through these materials our eyes can be opened to the possibilities that loom ahead for socialism in a reform era and for relations between the two great powers of the Eurasian mainland.

December 1985   G.R.

ACKNOWLEDGMENTS

This volume is a product of research conducted in 1984-1985, supported by funds provided by the National Council on Soviet and East European Research, The Committee on Scholarly Communication with the People's Republic of China, and the Center of International Studies at Princeton University. The Institute of the Soviet Union and Eastern Europe of the Chinese Academy of Social Sciences served as my host in China. I wish to gratefully acknowledge the assistance given to me by each of these organizations. In particular, I want to thank Xu Kui, director of the institute, for his help in arranging meetings with Chinese specialists. Above all, I am indebted to the many Chinese scholars who took the trouble to meet with me and to answer my many questions about their field of study.

The book was written under the auspices of the Center of International Studies, Woodrow Wilson School, Princeton University.

Neither the American organizations that supported my research nor the Chinese scholars who assisted me should be held responsible for the conclusions I have reached. This book represents my own attempt to bring together the available information.

I want to thank Patricia Zimmer for her assistance in preparing my manuscript. Her energy and the support of Gladys Starkey helped speed this book to publication. Margaret Case and Sherry Wert also deserve credit for moving the book rapidly into production.

THE CHINESE DEBATE
ABOUT SOVIET SOCIALISM,
1978-1985

ONE

INTRODUCTION

When Chinese write about the Soviet Union—its history, its recent conditions, and its prospects for reform—they are not engaged in some obscure academic controversy. They are, in fact, at the behest of China's leaders, consciously contributing to an ongoing national debate that has potentially far-reaching consequences for redirecting both the domestic and the foreign policies of the People's Republic. Discussions of the Soviet Union are of such importance because China's communist leaders have continuously measured their country against the yardstick of their neighbor to the north; their worldview has been intimately related to their view of Soviet socialism, and their foreign policy has taken shape in the shadow of Soviet relations. Even when Mao Zedong and Deng Xiaoping have doubted the benefits of close links with Moscow, statements by them and others close to them about the Soviet Union have served as a critical guide to the Chinese people.

In three separate periods, three contrasting images of the USSR have taken hold. In the 1950s the Soviet Union was "big brother," whose example should be followed. Through almost the entire two decades of the 1960s and 1970s, the Soviet Union became synonymous with "revisionism," the dreaded fate that China must avoid at all costs. Finally, in the 1980s, such extremes were avoided. The Soviet Union came to represent the common starting point for socialism, from which China and other socialist countries (the Soviet Union included) must shift, in steps, through carefully planned reforms. This recent, third image has produced by far the most interesting scholarship, which is the subject of our study. Even now, in the second half of the 1980s, Chinese authorities and academic specialists continue to be obsessed with the country whose military power, communist ideology, and program for building a socialist economy have left an indelible imprint on their own. Soviet socialism looms very large above its socialist neighbor in East Asia.

NOTE: Many of the sources cited are *neibu* publications normally restricted to internal circulation. The two principal *neibu* journals used are *Shijie jingji yu zhengzhi neican* and *Sulian dongou wenti*. Also, all the journals cited with *Sulian* (Soviet Union) in the title are *neibu* publications. It may be helpful to keep in mind whether the journal is *neibu* or not in using these notes.

Unlike the monochromatic criticisms leveled against Moscow in the Maoist era, a well-informed, up-to-date literature now explores the twists and turns of Soviet policy and the fundamental turning points of Soviet history. The burning question that initially smoldered within these writings at the end of the 1970s and the start of the 1980s was "what is Soviet socialism?" This one question led to numerous others. Is Soviet socialism really socialism? Is it what Marx, Engels, or Lenin conceived of in their classics about communism? Is it specifically a product of Stalin's rule, and, if so, did alternatives exist no less socialist in nature? Was Mao correct in arguing that Moscow turned away from the essence of socialism under the successive leadership of Khrushchev and Brezhnev?

By 1981 attention was shifting to the relevance of Soviet socialism for Chinese socialism. Chinese specialists were simultaneously reexamining many periods of Soviet history to uncover the implications for China's new economic reform and continued adherence to socialism. Do the NEP and the moderate approach to socialism taken by Lenin in his last years establish a model of value for present-day China? Is Stalin's model, which had been influential during China's First Five-Year Plan, of continued importance as a guide for domestic policy? Does the contemporary Soviet system under Brezhnev's leadership offer much that China should borrow? Whatever the answers proposed to these questions, all Chinese sources ruled out the two extremes: China must not copy the Soviet Union uncritically, and it must not repeat the error of trying to become self-reliant without borrowing from other socialist countries.

Recently Chinese have been asking what they should make of the Andropov-Gorbachev reform spirit of the 1980s. A few harsh critics of Soviet policies, whose views in recent years are stated with great circumspection, may wonder if recent reforms are stoking the embers of a socialist system that had been allowed to fade to a flicker. Many others who are more positive in their assessments see the Soviet reforms as consistent with a powerful reform wind that is blowing across the socialist world. Still others contend that as of 1983, 1984, or even 1985, the reforms were too hesitant to revitalize the Soviet system. Perhaps no other question is as important as the concern about whether the new Soviet reform agenda will again demonstrate the superiority of a socialist system.

Under Deng Xiaoping's leadership, China's leading circles have been genuinely curious about the nature of the Soviet system and the meaning of the Soviet experiences for socialism in China. No less a goal than to find their own roots—and in the process to figure out how much to nourish them and how much to try to move away from them—is what Chinese are striving for.

Studies in China of the Soviet Union are important for at least four reasons. First, more than perceptions of any other society, views of this country *are informative about the evolving worldview of China's leadership and its community of foreign affairs specialists.* They provide valuable insight into China's official understanding of the past, present, and future of socialism as well as into the struggle between the socialist and capitalist systems in the twentieth century. This literature may be one of the best places to turn to understand Chinese thinking that will help decide in the decades ahead the balance between the Soviet bloc and the American-led Western and Japanese bloc. It is here that we can gain a general impression of the battle for the minds of the Chinese people as well as the debate within the minds of their leaders.

Second, perhaps more than any other subject discussed in publications appearing in China, views of the Soviet Union and of Marxist-Leninist ideology that developed in that country *reveal differences of opinion* on issues critical to the balance between reform and orthodoxy in China. Why else would Chinese publications on the Soviet Union be less accessible to foreigners than those on any other country?[1] It is not a coincidence that the most open clash between orthodoxy and reform in the first half of the 1980s—the campaign against spiritual pollution—centered on writings about the history of Marxism. Divergence in thinking about Soviet Marxism and its application are central to the battle over how far reforms should take China away from the old Soviet model of socialism.

Third, writings on the Soviet Union in Chinese are of direct value for specialists on the Soviet Union because, among other reasons, of the shared frame of reference that attunes Chinese researchers to mistakes by Soviet leaders and to the problems of Soviet socialist reforms. Increasingly China's experts are taking a wide-ranging, comparative perspective on socialism as well as following closely the most recent reform currents in Moscow. Their studies *contribute to international awareness of the nature of the Soviet Union.*

Fourth, this subject *offers background material valuable for understanding and predicting the course of Sino-Soviet relations.* Foreign relations should be examined against the backdrop of mutual perceptions. Important changes in bilateral relations during the first half of the 1980s can be related to what Chinese have been writing about the Soviet Union for domestic readers.

Given these wide and varied implications, it is understandable that Chinese writings on the Soviet Union do not simply reflect the evolving realities of Soviet life. They serve many objectives and are of potential

---

[1] Gilbert Rozman, "China's Soviet-Watchers in the 1980s: A New Era in Scholarship," *World Politics* 37, no. 4 (July 1985): 437-38.

value to researchers who study Chinese domestic conditions, Soviet domestic conditions, and international relations.

Changes in Chinese perceptions appear to reflect three powerful historical forces, each of which has been in considerable flux during the years 1978 to 1985. On the most fundamental level, they reflect China's domestic needs. Changes in China's ideology and reform program have steered Soviet studies along a new course, which remains carefully guided by awareness of China's own priorities and alternatives. On the next level, Chinese attitudes about the Soviet Union have not failed to take into account the development of China's foreign relations—above all, bilateral ties between the two giant communist-led nations, but also, the overall international environment including Chinese and Soviet relations with third parties such as the United States and Vietnam. Finally, Chinese attitudes have also been deeply affected by changes in actual conditions inside the Soviet Union; the rapid succession in the 1980s of four Soviet leaders, two of whom have launched substantial reform programs, have given Chinese specialists ample opportunity to highlight new trends on the Soviet scene.

Attention to political landmarks over the past decade can guide our search for how and why Chinese perceptions of the Soviet Union have changed. First, in September and October 1976 came Mao's death and the downfall of the radical faction known as the "Gang of Four." Intense, personal hostility between Chinese and Soviet leaders now stood a better chance of being reduced. Second, in December 1978 there occurred the decisive Third Plenum of the Eleventh Central Committee of the Chinese Communist Party, which under the leadership of Deng Xiaoping launched a massive reform program. The leftist line of opposing most post-Stalin reforms in the Soviet Union could now be replaced by appreciation for reforms in a socialist system. Third, in the fall of 1982 came the beginning of Sino-Soviet negotiations aimed at normalization and, shortly afterwards, the death of Brezhnev and his replacement by Andropov. Chinese could now more closely identify Moscow's new reform agenda with their own reforms and predict improvements in relations. Fourth, in the winter of 1984-1985 a warm reception was given to Ivan V. Arkhipov, the first Vice-Chairman of the USSR Council of Ministers, and then, at the time of the replacement of Chernenko by Gorbachev, signals from China heard around the world announced the acceptance of the Soviet Union as a fellow socialist country. There was no longer any doubt that two socialist neighbors with some nostalgic memories were working to resolve their serious differences.

Old leaders (except Deng Xiaoping, who led the 1963 delegation to Moscow but presumably was acting under Mao's instructions) who were personally identified with poisoned relations were gone, China had entered a reform era, the Chinese and Soviets had sat down to discuss their differences, and the Soviet Union, more hesitantly to be sure, had begun its own reform program. These were the fundamental historical forces that steered Chinese scholarship on the Soviet Union in a new direction. In turn, that scholarship, arising out of the needs of China's reforms and reporting on Soviet reforms, shaped perceptions in China that could influence the development of Sino-Soviet relations.

THE CHINESE WORLDVIEW[2]

Economic growth is the key to satisfying the official aspirations of China's current leadership. These leaders seek prosperity for their people and national strength to protect the interests of their country. With a flourishing economy the Chinese people can overcome the malaise wrought by the Cultural Revolution, and China can assume its rightful place among the rich and powerful nations of the world. Without it China will be doomed to backwardness—its people poor and ignorant and its leaders unable to defend against the hegemonistic ambitions of the two superpowers. Modern history, in this view, proves that economic growth is the most pressing need and the basic precondition from which other blessings flow. It is both the immediate goal of socialism and the means to achieving socialism in its other dimensions.

Feudalism

Chinese draw their lessons largely from the experience of their own country. Their deepest impressions are of a weak and divided country suffering humiliations one after another in the nineteenth and first half of the twentieth century. While roundly condemning rapacious foreign states, including Russia, for their imperialist behavior, the Chinese also find fault with their own country's internal shortcomings. Internal divisions and backwardness "invited" aggression.

There are limits on the form this debate over what went wrong in Chinese history can take. By 1984 a brief discussion on the Asiatic Mode of Production had been quieted. As one review commentary phrased it, on this subject "there were previously two points of view."[3] The first

[2] The primary guide to the Chinese worldview is Deng Xiaoping's writings. See *Selected Works of Deng Xiaoping (1975-1982)* (Beijing: Foreign Languages Press, 1984); and for his later views, *Jianshe you Zhongguo tese de shehuizhuyi* (Beijing: Renminchubanshe, 1984).
[3] "Yinianlai ruogan xueshu wenti taolun zongshu," *Xueshu yuekan*, no. 1 (1984): 65-66; Yang Zijing, "Wunianlai woguo shijieshi ruogan wenti taolun zongshu," *Shixue*

opinion, which was widespread, held that the Asiatic, the ancient, and the feudal modes of production were three different social forms of the same stage of social development. The second opinion, which seems scarcely distinguishable, held that the three types were parallel; Marx did not refer to one type coming before or after another. In any case, the review adds, the recent consensus is that the three types are variations of the same feudal, economic form. They have some commonalities and some peculiarities that are qualitative differences, but they are not basically different with regard to such important indicators as the level of development of the forces of production and the extent of the division of labor. The review fails to mention any recent differences of opinions. It leaves the clear impression that the Asiatic Mode of Production theme has ceased to be a subject of controversy and, even more, does not provide any answers to questions about modern China or the Soviet Union. In short, it is sufficient to treat China as a feudal society.

Much more attention has centered on the prolongation of feudal society. The discussion on Chinese feudalism incorporates such themes as the role of the state, the demographic structure, Confucian theory, family and kinship relations, the impact of foreign elements, the relationship between the landlord class and the middle peasants, the development of market relations among the people, the success of the peasants in developing their material and spiritual resources, and the independence of cities. Increasingly, comparisons with Western Europe (albeit not systematic ones) are introduced to explain China's slow development, but studies of Russia rarely mention these themes, and Russia is not included in the comparative study of feudalism.

In the eyes of modern Chinese, Chinese feudalism suffered from at least three pervasive weaknesses that proved to be the cause of modern backwardness. First, the Confucian ideology held back the advancement of science and receptivity to modern knowledge. The people were burdened with a way of thinking, and an educational tradition, not at all conducive to a modern transformation, even by feudal standards. Chinese needed to liberate their thinking, which occurred to an appreciable degree only at the time of the May Fourth Movement from 1919. Second, Chinese historians insist that China's social structure was unusually stagnant. Many explanations have been offered for historical stagnation. For the most part, they point to the social class system, with its fluid forms of exploitation, and to the slow development of the bourgeoisie. Finally, China's retardation is also deemed to have been a failure of its political system, beginning with poor leadership at the top by the alien

yuekan, no. 1 (1984): 114-16; Tian Jujian, "Zhongguo fengjian shehui changqi yanxu yuanyin taolun zongshu," Wenshi zhishi, no. 11 (1983): 121-28.

Manchu rulers before 1912 and the dissolute and insufficiently anti-imperialist warlords and Guomindang in the following decades. Looking back to these experiences before 1949, Chinese communists find, almost exclusively, negative examples to be avoided. In their view, successful modernization requires, most of all, the repudiation of a country's feudal and colonial (or, in the case of China, semi-colonial) heritage.

Feudalism still figures importantly in explanations of the present. In the view of China's leaders, it persists as an obstructionist legacy in the minds of the people and even of many of the country's leaders. Much that has gone wrong in the People's Republic is associated with remnants of feudalism.[4] In recent years, these errors are largely attributed to leaders and officials, whose abuse of the people and mistaken policies somehow stemmed from their feudal ways of thinking. Without the impact of capitalism and its democratic aspects, China (and the Soviet Union as well, as we learn in Chapter Six) was burdened with a despotic political heritage. The prevailing message is that more must be done to provide people with a scientific education and with information about the modernized world in order to eradicate these vestiges of a 2,000-year era in China's history. Marxist-Leninist education as well as modern scientific knowledge are weapons in the battle against negative traditions in such fields as politics and education. They can show the way out of feudalism and its legacy.

Given this one-sided view of the past, Chinese have felt little need to examine the continuities that link past and present. It is sufficient to condemn the past and to seek its eradication in the present. This requires devising policies that take into account the special characteristics inherited from the feudal era.

The issue of the consequences of enduring feudalism has been incorporated into the Chinese worldview through the efforts of Deng Xiaoping and other reform-oriented leaders eager to bring sweeping changes in the 1980s. Feudalism is an attractive target for the reformers because it is associated with governing through ignorance and with closing China off to world progress. The old, undereducated revolutionary veterans who remain in high posts are the obvious bearers of feudalist thoughts. Recognition of the need to combat feudalism calls for turning instead to well-educated intellectuals and to the capitalist world, where science and technology are most developed.

Capitalism

Chinese historians portray capitalism as a short-lived and minor force in their country's history. Along with imperialism from outside, it emerged

[4] Ding Xueliang, "Qieshi gaige: suqing fengjianzhuyi canyu yingxiang," *Renmin ribao*, August 24, 1983, p. 5; "Lishi xuejia tan rendaozhuyi," *Shijie lishi*, no. 2 (1984): 1-3.

in the late Qing dynasty and especially in the decades after the revolution of 1911. Its impact was important in creating the conditions for the communist revolution, but after 1949 there was scarcely any capitalist foundation on which to build a socialist society. Under these circumstances, greater difficulties existed in establishing a socialist society in China than elsewhere. Weakness in capitalist development complicates a country's transition to socialism.

From 1979 to 1981 a debate raged in China over the implications of passing over the independent capitalist stage. An article in the newspaper *Guangming ribao* on May 4, 1981 took one position in the debate and, with its strongly worded conclusions, helped to stifle the view that China was not fully socialist due to its economic backwardness.[5] The article, which appeared at a time when China's leaders were demanding more ideological conformity, refers to some people, both inside and outside the country, who doubt that China is socialist—who say that China is in the transition to socialism or is half-socialist because of its low level of development of the forces of production. As a result, they contend, the country must rely on the New People's Democracy or on compromises with capitalism to develop these forces. The newspaper article also makes note of some foreigners who assert that only when the vast majority of the population are in the proletariat can there be a proletarian dictatorship, that China now only has a party dictatorship. Recognizing that there are some differences between internal and external advocates, the article nevertheless concludes that both agree that a low level of economic development cannot give rise to socialism.

The 1981 article rejects this viewpoint. It notes that China was more backward economically than Russia was when it was building socialism, but Russia had also been backward. Even so, Lenin was correct in arguing that socialism could be built first in that country. Lenin's conclusion applies also to China. China was pushed off the normal track of historical development by the invasion of capitalist imperialism, making China a semi-colonial, semi-feudal society. This opened the way to revolution; the very close ties of China's working class and vast peasantry were a sign of the superiority of China's proletariat and helped it form a broad revolutionary united front capable of leading the country to socialism.

Advantages for the revolutionary movement were not necessarily advantages for building socialism. The article notes that many complications resulted from China's backwardness. To a great extent, errors committed after 1949 were due to not having passed through an independent, capitalist stage and to continuing to have a backward economy with

---

[5] "Lun xian jieduan Zhongguo de shehui xingshi," *Guangming ribao*, May 4, 1981, p. 1.

eighty percent of China's huge population still peasants. It takes longer
to build socialism in a backward economy. China erred in not realizing
this for a long time and paid a heavy price. In politics too, the absence of
experience with an independent stage of capitalism created special problems, for example, in building socialist democracy and socialist legality,
and in perfecting the socialist system of management.

Although admitting that there were difficulties due to China's negligible experience with capitalism, the article rejects the conclusion that the
timetable for socialism was incorrect: it says that China's mistakes should
not be exaggerated, admonishing that those youths who regard Lin Biao
and the "Gang of Four" as monsters never before seen in history only
need look back to the history of capitalism to gain a proper perspective
and realize that all new social systems experience complications. The economic results of China's first seventeen years prove that China could accomplish the transition to socialism and build socialism with impressive
achievements.

Those who argue that because of the absence of an independent capitalist stage, China should have relied on a mixed capitalist and socialist
economy and on capitalists while waiting for a high level of development
of the forces of production, are in error, insists the newspaper article.
That is an illusion. The socialist and capitalist economies cannot long coexist. There would be internal conflict in the economy, which would damage the forces of production. The article cites the "five-anti" campaign of
the early 1950s in China as fully persuasive evidence on this point.

Even the critique that the socialist transformation went too quickly is
denied. If it went faster than anticipated, that was because industry grew
rapidly and made appropriate demands for agricultural collectivization,
and because the motivation of the peasants was very high. Even in the
period 1957-1966, when mistakes were committed, the building of socialism remained fundamentally correct. The forces of production developed rapidly. Despite the Cultural Revolution, the socialist system persisted. Backwardness caused problems and led to policy twists and turns,
but it did not mean that the relations of production did not correspond to
the forces of production or that another approach would have accelerated
the development of the forces of production. After the 1981 article appeared, reform criticisms mounted against negligence in the development
of the forces of production in 1957-1966, yet the basic argument stood:
the bypassing of capitalism could be cited as an excuse for mistakes made
from the 1950s to 1970s, but not as a basis for arguing that collectivization was premature (earlier accompanied by the accusation that China
ended up with "agrarian socialism") or that China is not yet socialist.

Which is the greater obstacle to reform in China: feudalism or capitalism? The architects of China's opening to the West and Japan apparently consider feudalism to be the principal danger. Deng Xiaoping has spoken often of the effects of feudalism, observing for example that "any capitalism is superior to feudalism."[6] Zhao Ziyang, Hu Yaobang and *People's Daily* take feudalism seriously. They have led China into an era of striking reforms in economic and foreign relations in an effort to reduce its backwardness, to wipe out feudalism. In contrast, Chen Yun, Hu Qiaomu, Deng Liqun, and others with responsibility for ideology and propaganda seem to treat capitalism as the more serious enemy. They have apparently tried to restrict discussions of feudalism. A striking example is the omission of any mention of feudalism in the synopsis of Deng Xiaoping's collected writings of 1975-1982 that appeared in *Hongqi*.[7]

The image within China of capitalism abroad has improved dramatically in the decade following Mao Zedong's death. Capitalist countries are now greatly admired for their prosperity and scientific achievements. Chinese believe that there is much to learn from these countries and that there are great benefits to be gained by expanded trade and foreign investments. At the same time, capitalism continues to be portrayed as inferior to socialism. The old vices of excessive inequality, unemployment, racism, spiritual depravity, and imperialism are still part of the litany of criticisms. Chinese publications also point to the inferiority of capitalist economies. In comparison to the economies of socialist countries, they grow slowly. Planning is insufficient. Economic waste is excessive. In the final analysis, socialism will defeat capitalism because it will continue to prove that it achieves higher rates of economic development.[8] This is one of the core assumptions in the official Chinese worldview.

Socialism

Of course, in recent years the most fundamental reconsideration has come in Chinese thinking about socialism itself. Less emphasis is given to the long-term ends of socialist development, while more is given to the means for realizing them. The "four modernizations" in agriculture, industry, defense, and science and technology are the means with which Chinese leaders are largely concerned. At least, through the year 2000, China is to concentrate on building its economy in these areas. In accord

---

[6] *Selected Works of Deng Xiaoping (1975-1982)*, 333.

[7] *Hongqi*, no. 13 (1983): 40-44.

[8] Negative views of capitalism are conveyed, in the use of the term "imperialist" (*diguozhuyi*) to discuss the internal affairs of capitalist countries, e.g. "Diguozhuyi guojia zhong de jingji xingshi," *Gongyun ziliao*, no. 10 (1983), and "Longduan zibenzhuyi guojia jiushi diguozhuyi guojia," *Shijie jingji yu zhengzhi neican*, no. 10 (1984). *Shijie jingji yu zhengzhi neican*, no. 11 (1984): 14, repeats the goal of socialism defeating capitalism.

with Deng Xiaoping's views, leaders propose pragmatism as the way to realize these short-term goals. They hold that economic growth can best be achieved by planning without disregard for market forces, by experimentation to see what works. A quadrupling of the national income in two decades with living standards rising in tandem is the primary promise that socialism now holds for the Chinese people.

A secondary, but occasionally resurgent motif is that socialism provides advantages missing in more prosperous capitalist societies. It is an appeal to order over anarchy, to community over individualism, to spiritual civilization over depravity. Crime, divorce, pornography, consumer waste, and other evils of the capitalist world can be diminished, if not avoided, under socialism, the Chinese people are told. This worldview assumes that along with economic growth Chinese can maintain and strengthen a family-centered, community-oriented, morally superior way of life. To be sure, Chinese officials do not have in mind the old style of family relations and community solidarity, but new patterns that have emerged since 1949—in the case of family relations, more in the cities than in the villages.

In response to doubts expressed about whether China is socialist, writers insist that it must be. It relies primarily on public ownership of the means of production, despite contracts that give individuals the right to use land and various facilities for specified periods and within certain guidelines. It applies the principle of "to each according to his labor," both by eliminating exploitation and by equitably rewarding people for their labor. China is led by the Communist Party and follows the scientific writings of Marxism-Leninism, even if it follows these more flexibly now that it has discarded a dogmatic approach that developed under Stalin. The workers, peasants, and intelligentsia and other working people are designated the masters of the state.

In response to the questions of foreigners about whether reform will lead China toward capitalism, the required answer is "no." China's reforms are said to maintain the fundamental features of socialism, although diverse conditions in a big country and unequal development of the forces of production lead to variations in ownership practices. Acknowledging that China needs to draw on foreign capitalists to speed its modernization, Chinese leaders insist that this does not mean China cannot keep its socialist system.[9]

Within the spectrum of socialism, feelings of great intensity are aroused against a target disturbingly familiar to the Chinese people. The

[9] Su Shaozhi, "Zhongguo zai zou xiang zibenzhuyi ma?" *Liaowang*, no. 49 (1984), foreign edition, 46-47.

consensus of the Third Plenum signified a repudiation of much that had preceded over the previous two decades. It was a rejection of control at the expense of initiative, of campaign movements and class struggle at the expense of legal predictability, of egalitarianism at the expense of incentives. In place of continuous revolution and class struggle, the new approach called for the acceptance of everyone as a potential contributing citizen. The consensus that developed at the end of the 1970s formed the foundation of the official Chinese view of socialism in the 1980s. Leaders have now declared that socialism must prove itself in China by raising living standards and maintaining a high rate of economic growth, and by satisfying and involving the people.

The familiar socialist concepts of "forces of production" and "relations of production" figure importantly in current thinking. To achieve the goals of socialism, the forces of production, including modern technology, must be built up greatly, but that can only be accomplished if the relations of production, primarily the economic management system, are appropriate for the current stage of development of the economy. An experimental approach to such fundamentals of managing the economy as ownership, planning, and income distribution is required, say China's leaders. Missing from this interpretation is any detailed discussion of social class relations. In this respect, the current Chinese worldview is more focused on the economic aspects of production than the earlier Maoist worldview or even than the Soviet worldview of the Brezhnev era.

Despite the increased emphasis on economic determinism, China's spokesmen do not show any lack of appreciation for the impact of ideas on behavior. Often they can be found saying that if only they can change the way people—especially those in responsible positions—think, all kinds of obstacles to progress will be overcome. This is not the extreme ideological determinism that raised Mao Zedong's hopes for the Great Leap Forward and the Great Proletarian Cultural Revolution; the post-Mao leaders do not regard consciousness as a substitute for material incentives and scientific management. Today, reform of the ideology is seen as having been in the late 1970s a requirement to improve incentives and management. The chief danger in socialism is dogmatism or the rigid adherence to old ways of thinking, as if they were universal truths applicable to all times and circumstances.[10] Such narrow-minded theory slows the march of history, preventing a socialist system from realizing its superiority, especially in economic growth.

Ideology, similar to the legacy of feudalism, now figures in discussions

[10] This point was mentioned in many of my interviews in China in December 1984 and January 1985.

mostly for the harm it brings. For a long time China is alleged to have suffered from a triple dose of ideological constraints: the negative weight of Confucian thinking, the continued impact of erroneous ideas about socialism from Stalin's writings, and the serious errors in Mao Zedong Thought during Mao's later years.[11] To remove these brakes on modernization, communists must reform Marxist theory to increase its flexibility. Deng Xiaoping's slogan "to seek truth from practice" meets this need by shifting the emphasis from a deductive approach starting from the ideology to an empirical approach rooted in observations of actual conditions. Pragmatism will bring out the superiority of communist ideology as measured, above all, in the superior performance of socialist economies. As long as the ideology is not allowed to rigidify into a barrier to concrete investigations and reforms, the superiority of socialism will be manifest.

Chinese use the euphemism "traditional views" (*chuantong guannian*) for the ideological restraints imported from the Soviet Union under Stalin. A report issued on June 1, 1985 of a conference on the theory of China's socialist economy points to the great significance of breaking through the barriers of traditional views on such subjects as socialist ownership, socialist distribution "to each according to his work," the combination of a planned and a commercial economy, relations of enterprises owned by the entire people to the state, and the model for a socialist economy.[12] Theory, the report asserts, has long remained backward, imposing a rigid model not suitable for the development of the forces of production and failing to change in accord with evidence on actual conditions. Continued updating and open debate about economic theory are the only ways to ensure timely and effective reforms. Chinese acknowledge that the goal of reconstructing socialist theory is a staggering task; their writings on philosophy and the social sciences treat it as a very high priority.

Controversy has surrounded the prospects for continued reform of ideology in the 1980s. Orthodox officials consider the shift in ideology in the late 1970s, that is, the repudiation of the "two whatevers" (Hua Guofeng's attempt to treat Mao's writings and policies as unalterable), to be sufficient. They are mainly concerned about preventing further deviations on the right, which threaten to undermine the socialist system. While the orthodox group grants the need for some opening of the economy (the image of a birdcage is often heard; let the bird fly freely as long as the cage remains closed), the prevailing view is that it would be unde-

[11] This view was expressed by Su Shaozhi in a lecture at Princeton University on April 8, 1985.

[12] Ma Biao, "Ruiyi gaige kaituo qianjin: 'Zhongguo shehuizhuyi jingji lilun de huigu yu zhanwang' xueshu taolunhui ceji," *Guangming ribao*, June 1, 1985.

sirable to pursue both economic reform and political-ideological reform
simultaneously. The visible reform stance is to push for continued
change in ideology, but only in a limited sense. Where ideology can be
shown to be an obstacle to economic reform, it must be changed. At the
same time, where ideology consists of the fundamental principles of
Marxism-Leninism, it must be upheld. Following Zhou Enlai's earlier
wording, these two meanings of ideology are called the two frameworks
(*liangge kuangkuang*). One must not be against both. Thus Chinese are
not permitted to write about ideological reform in a general sense, and
rarely can one find any linkage between ideological and political reform.

In the 1980s, the phrase "socialism with Chinese characteristics" has
been popularized throughout China. This is a repudiation of the idea that
there is a single model (i.e. a Soviet-developed model), that applies without substantial change to socialism everywhere. Chinese explain that
they erred from 1949 in ignoring the particular circumstances of their
country, such as its great population pressure. They assign some blame
to both the United States, which forced China into isolation, and the Soviet Union, whose theory of socialism narrowly defined what is permissible within this kind of system. The current worldview allows for considerable diversity in response to national traditions and circumstances.

Deng Xiaoping's collection of essays covering the period from the
Twelfth Party Congress in September 1982 to November 1984 is entitled,
"Building Socialism with Chinese Characteristics."[13] In these presentations, Deng sets forth the goal of combining the general truths of Marxism with the specific realities of China. Deng faults earlier socialist plans
and programs adopted by party congresses in China for erring on the side
of not taking Chinese conditions sufficiently into account. Although in its
revolutionary movement China had eventually learned the lesson of
charting a distinctive Chinese path (Mao led the way in this direction),
this lesson had to be relearned after 1949. China's modernization can
benefit from studying foreign experiences, but it would lead only to failure to follow another country's model closely. Deng notes that China has
had not a few lessons in this area. Clearly the significance of Deng's message is that after rejecting the discredited path of the Cultural Revolution,
China will not now follow the Soviet model; it must find its own path to
socialism.

Articles in Chinese journals from 1983 have sought to elaborate on
China's special characteristics, implicitly comparing China with the So-

---

[13] Deng Xiaoping, *Jianshe you Zhongguo tese de shehuizhuyi*, 3, 34; Yong Wenyuan
and Luo Zong, "Chuangjian you Zhongguo tese de shehuizhuyi jingji moshi," *Shehuikexue*, no. 3 (1983): 10-25; Dong Fuqi, "Guanyu jianshe you Zhongguo tese de shehuizhuyi de jige wenti," *Xuexi yu sikao*, no. 1 (1984): 3-10.

viet Union—long the standard for any comparisons of socialism. Deng led the way by identifying two characteristics: 1) poverty and backwardness, and 2) a large population with little arable land. Others expand on these points, even if they normally add little about historical differences and offer few if any explicit comparisons. Mostly they proceed directly to the current socialist period and discuss what about the Soviet model of old is not suitable to China. Not coincidentally these features, such as a highly centralized planning system, are also seen as problematic in the Soviet Union and have already been rejected in China's reforms of recent years.

The concept "socialist spiritual civilization" was introduced in the early 1980s to provide a positive alternative to the implicit, but secretly admired ideals of "bourgeois humanism." This new concept implies the superiority of socialism in the spiritual realm.[14] To many, it is a call for stepping up political education. Teachers, even in the field of Soviet and Russian literature, should inspire their students to stand on the side of socialism and recognize the advanced spiritual civilization that it can bring.[15] Through this concept and others, the official worldview has been reshaped to continue to highlight what is distinctive and superior about socialism.

Both "socialism with Chinese characteristics" and "socialist spiritual civilization" are vague concepts. Voices of reform and orthodoxy have sought to give more specificity to them. The reformers hope for a democratically oriented interpretation of "socialism with Chinese characteristics" to establish a reform blueprint that would steer China away from leftist ideology in the future. Without this, they fear that existing shortcomings cannot be eliminated and, after Deng's departure from the leadership, controls are likely to tighten. The forces of orthodoxy also seek a blueprint. In its absence, they ask if China is to give up everything Mao stood for and if China can hold the line against reformers who would undermine China's political and ideological foundation. The concept of the "socialist spiritual civilization" serves up a bone to the orthodox critics. It offers them an ideological focus for distinguishing socialism and capitalism. Yet this concept has two dimensions: ideology and politics, which the orthodox group has seized; and science and education, which the reformers prefer to emphasize. While Deng Xiaoping speaks of the "socialist spiritual civilization," his primary focus is on a different dimension altogether—material civilization, the other of the two civilizations

[14] Wang Chi, *Shehuizhuyi jingshen wenming shilun* (Hunan: Hunan renminchubanshe, 1983).
[15] Editor's response to a letter, *Sulian wenxue*, no. 4 (1984): 95-96.

(*liangge wenming*). In 1978-1979, when an emergency was being faced, Deng, Chen Yun, and other top leaders agreed that the material civilization required first priority; the economy had to be developed quickly and living standards needed to be promoted or the Communist Party was in danger of losing power. This consensus on developing the forces of production at almost any cost has relegated themes like the "socialist spiritual civilization" to a secondary level and allowed Deng to lead with an ideology that gives China wide scope for flexibility in economic reforms.

In short, socialism has come to be interpreted as a system distinct from and more just than capitalism, serving the people's democratic dictatorship, led by the Communist Party, guided by Marxism-Leninism and Mao Zedong Thought. It stands out for the pragmatic application of theory in accord with national characteristics and for the continuous reform of the relations of production to speed the development of the forces of production. It emancipates the mind and rewards workers justly on the basis of the labor they perform. It achieves a superior spiritual civilization. Socialism is the trend of the past and the wave of the future as long as dogmatism is overcome and a realistic assessment of problems is made. This is the core of the official Chinese worldview.

Soviet Socialism

Writings on the Soviet Union and Soviet Marxism-Leninism provide an application of this worldview and also an unparalleled opportunity to amend and extend it. Since 1949, Chinese thinking about the Soviet Union has been central to their own worldview. As part of Mao's struggle for the minds of the Chinese people, he first encouraged the enthusiastic emulation of "big brother" for its socialist model. Thousands of Soviet writings were translated, and Chinese eyes focused on the more advanced socialism in the USSR. Barely a decade later Mao harshly condemned the revisionist failure of socialism in that country. Alleged deviations from the correct path in the USSR were held up as the justifications for policy changes in China. After the Third Plenum the position of the Soviet Union became more ambiguous. Was it socialist? Should the Stalinist model still be seen as mostly a positive contribution to socialism? Did recent Soviet policies offer lessons useful for China's reforms? Answers to these questions about the Soviet Union could help China's leaders chart a new and difficult course at home and abroad. In the uncertain conditions at the end of the seventies and in the eighties, answers could help Chinese figure out what socialism has meant and what it should mean on a national and global scale.

While Mao Zedong attached great weight to ideological reeducation, his emphasis on self-reliance downplayed the gains to be achieved from

studying the experiences of other countries. In contrast, the Deng Xiaoping leadership has insisted that learning from the experiences of other
countries—both nonsocialist and socialist ones—is vital to reform. The
nonsocialist models, especially Japan, may attract considerable interest in
closed discussions, and in publications it may be acceptable to focus on
Hungary as the foremost socialist model, but the Soviet Union is now
probably the most widely studied case, from which, authors inform their
readers, China is expected to learn something of use for its further reforms. In this spirit of learning from the Soviet example, Chinese specialists have examined Soviet history and current conditions in considerable detail. Particularly because much of the history of the Chinese
communist movement is virtually off-limits to scholars and public debates over current reforms are confined within narrow limits, the opportunity to discuss Soviet history in depth is one of the most open forums
for reconsideration of issues central to the Chinese worldview. Answers
to difficult questions about Soviet socialism have been sought since 1978
as a vital element in reshaping the thinking of the Chinese people.

For some of China's reform leaders, such as Hu Yaobang and Zhao Ziyang, the main purpose of studying the Soviet Union may be to find out
how to break away from the Soviet model. This goal can be best realized
by learning what has prevented the Soviet economy from moving rapidly
forward in the 1970s and 1980s. For other leaders, such as Peng Zhen,
who hold a nostalgic view of China's "golden age" in the 1950s, the main
purpose of study may be to draw closer to the Soviet model. In either
case, the Soviet example figures importantly in thinking about policies
for China.

In comparison to the slowly evolving Soviet worldview in the Brezhnev era, the Chinese worldview under Deng became a powerful force for
reform. Deng stripped socialism of many of the characteristics associated
with it since Stalin became the foremost arbitrator of its meaning. Deng
brought socialism and capitalism together within one world-system of
economic relations and political alliances. Nevertheless, recurrent tightening of ideological controls made it clear that China's leaders insist on
drawing a line to keep reformers, potential sympathizers with foreign
countries, and Maoists in check. The line that has been drawn closes off
debates about many aspects of foreign policy. The approved point of view
is that historically, in relations with imperialist and socialist countries, in
pursuit of power, and later in power, the Chinese communists have never
been the international transgressor. Studies of world events, including
Soviet foreign relations, are tightly circumscribed by these restrictions.

The line drawn by China's leaders also leaves no room for ambiguity
about the overall struggle between socialism and capitalism. There can be

no convergence! Capitalist countries do not gradually transform into socialist ones, and socialist ones, regardless of what Chinese wrote in the sixties and seventies, remain socialist. Socialism is the superior system even when it is not functioning as it should, and when it functions properly, it provides a basis for continuous reforms that reveal its clear advantages over capitalism. This is the context for studies of the Soviet Union.

Soviet socialism occupies an important place in Chinese efforts to bolster their own citizens' belief in socialism. In 1978-1981 morale was low in China; apathy or hostility toward the socialist system was widely reported. Chinese leaders adopted a two-fold strategy: 1) to make changes that would improve the system's popularity and enable it to work better, especially through increasing living standards and offering rewards to persons who work harder; and 2) to explain previous mistakes within a context of the history of socialism that would minimize the damage to the continuation of communist rule. Strong criticisms of Soviet socialism would have threatened the second objective. Much effort in Soviet studies from 1979 went into turning Chinese understanding of the Soviet experiences over more than sixty years to the advantage of the emerging Chinese view of socialism. Like China, the Soviet Union is socialist, has made serious mistakes, and is demonstrating the importance of reforms away from the old (Stalin) model of socialism. This is the consensus about Soviet socialism.

No Convergence Between Capitalism and Socialism

Chinese insistence that capitalism and socialism are two separate entities rules out theories of convergence. While accepting the need to replace traditional theories and consciousness with scientific explanations suitable to new conditions, spokesmen draw the line at questioning fundamental distinctions between socialist and capitalist countries. Simultaneous development of capitalist and socialist countries may occur, but the latter will: keep to the socialist road, uphold a form of dictatorship, uphold the leadership of the Communist Party, and uphold Marxism-Leninism. The four cardinal principles of 1979, although modified in 1982 and 1984, persist. As Hu Qiaomu explained in January 1984, even if socialist humanism has inherited something from capitalist humanism, the two types of humanism are mutually exclusive; they serve different property systems. Capitalist countries cannot escape the existence of capitalist relations of production. No amount of theorizing about the growth of the middle class can hide the persistence of the contradiction between the proletariat and the capitalists. The proletariat cannot become part of the middle class. Its historical mission remains, in the final analysis, to overthrow the capitalist system. (I should add that Hu Qiaomu's position is not representative of the entire leadership, or even, it seems, of Hu Yaobang, the party secretary; yet there is no open contradiction of his viewpoint on this issue.) Claims about the emergence of a new type of society, found in writings on the technological revolution and the information society, must be opposed by Marxist-Leninists, concludes an article published in June 1984. Another article in February 1984 refutes the view that Japan has shed capitalism by insisting it still has capitalist exploitation of workers. Even if, through the use of scientific principles of management and psychological methods to deceive workers, there has been some success in keeping class conflict from becoming open class opposition, this is not grounds for asserting that Japan is not capitalist.[16]

Statements and actions by the United States have on occasion helped the Chinese perceive their commonality of interests with the Soviet Union. One example is the reaction to Ronald Reagan's address before the British parliament on June 8, 1982. A Chinese article called Reagan's proposal to throw Marxism-Leninism in the dustbin of history a direct attack on Marxism-Leninism. The article catalogues other programs of the Reagan administration to use propaganda to advance the "democratization" of the world, including an international congress in the fall of 1982 involving 34 countries and a propaganda campaign in the first half of 1983. It lumps these programs together with Reagan's hegemonistic military policies in producing resistance among America's allies and Third World countries, and concludes that the strategy had not changed into 1984. The article sees the Soviets as countering Reagan's intensification of the political and ideological struggle. The result has been a worsening in state-to-state relations. The article concludes by agreeing with the Soviet view that this American offensive constitutes interference in the internal affairs of another country.[17] It should be noted that this article and some of the other sources that I cite are not normally available to foreigners and are even not available to many Chinese (as *da cankao* they are less accessible than ordinary *neibu* publications known as *xiao cankao*); Chinese have no desire to damage bilateral relations through strongly worded articles about foreign leaders and their views. Chinese have debated, but only for internal audiences, whether Reagan's aggressiveness is harmful to China's interest or, in some sense, has served those interests.

[16] Huo Shishou, "Shilun zhongchanjieji," *Shijie jingji yu zhengzhi neican*, no. 6 (1984): 19. Zhu Jianrong, "Riben shehui de xingshi gaibian le ma?" *Shijie jingji yu zhengzhi neican*, no. 2 (1984): 58-61.
[17] "Ligen zhengfu cujin minzhu yundong shuping," *Shijie jingji yu zhengzhi neican*, no. 7 (1984): 37-40.

Mao Zedong Thought

The Chinese worldview still credits Mao Zedong with an original and important input into Marxist thought. He is said to have applied Marxism to China's development, creating a basis for what is now termed socialism with Chinese characteristics. This is not a blanket endorsement of Mao's thought; rather, he is said to have made serious errors. Mao Zedong Thought is now separated from the thought of Mao himself and treated as the crystallization of the collective wisdom of the Chinese Communist Party. Essentially, what is left as the new guiding philosophy of China is: 1) "to seek truth from practice," which Deng has borrowed from Mao; 2) the mass line, which retains the meaning of learning from the masses and then giving guidance to the masses, but now places more emphasis on democracy and material incentives; and 3) independence and self-reliance in foreign policy, which means no alliances but does not exclude large-scale foreign trade and investment. Implicitly Mao's creative application of Marxism indicates differences from the Soviet model. The Soviets are, in fact, criticized for failing to accept independent paths of socialism, for interfering in the internal affairs of other parties, and for not accepting equality among parties. The principle of "seeking truth from practice" is cited as Mao's legacy in rejecting Stalin's orders for the revolutionary movement and resisting Soviet control in the 1950s. Much of Mao's thought, according to the current interpretation, has acquired the meaning of the theory of China's departure from Stalin's model.[18] The experience of socialist creativity in the past—for which Mao is praised—is the basis for an undogmatic, independent, trial-and-error search for reform in the present day.

There is no cult of Deng Xiaoping, but he is given major credit for the recent emancipation of the mind, finally freeing Chinese from overreliance on quotations and deductive thought, turning attention to reliance on facts and investigation of concrete conditions, and carrying on what Mao had left undone. Deng's major contributions are rooted in Mao Zedong Thought, according to Chinese publications.

A Scholarly Tightrope

Conclusions in studies of the Soviet Union must be sufficiently negative to support China's foreign policy positions vis-à-vis that country, but sufficiently positive to attest to the long-term superiority of socialism. Instructions to specialists warn that their research must not attack social-

[18] Yong Wenyuan and Luo Zong, "Chuangjian you Zhongguo tese de shehuizhuyi jingji moshi," 11.

ism.[19] Yet it is also clear that unequivocally positive views of Soviet domestic policies could be interpreted as opposition to China's reform agenda of the 1980s; strong approval of the Soviet Union is limited by existing restrictions. These factors make it likely that the Chinese will write about Soviet domestic conditions without taking an extreme position. A mixed assessment of the Soviet Union is called for by China's thinking in the Deng Xiaoping era. Combined with the official creed of "seeking truth from practice," this worldview, in comparison to the views in the first three decades of the PRC, opens the way to relatively balanced, although not unfettered, research and scholarly debate. The Soviet Union poses the most sensitive challenge for the Chinese worldview; yet the only way to meet that challenge is to present a mixed appraisal of pros and cons supported by factual evidence. Much room is left in this worldview for difference of opinion about the strengths and weaknesses of the Soviet system. Changes in the exact mix of views are a window on changes in China's political climate and expectations. Conditions in the 1980s have been ripe for serious scholarship on the Soviet Union, with implications for China's understanding of socialism and the fate of its own social system.

On the whole, the Chinese official view of world history sees socialist revolution as possible in a country that is still economically backward, but then explains what follows the revolution largely in terms of economic determinism. The development of technology and other forces of production led historically to the appearance of the proletariat and other progressive class elements, which in turn became the basis of a scientific interpretation of society known as Marxism. Marxism is a valuable guideline for action and revolution; however, to be successfully applied it must constantly be updated and related to concrete conditions specific to a country's circumstances and the changing international environment. Lenin and Mao realized these requirements and succeeded. Socialist revolution, whether under Lenin's leadership or Mao's, required the creative application of Marxism to a specific environment. For revolution to succeed, the existence of a large proletariat is not sufficient; imperialism and a particular internal political climate may also be necessary. The existence of a communist party and Marxist-Leninist writings is not sufficient; much depends on the creativity of the national communist leadership.

Once the party is in power, faithful observance of the ideology and strong leadership at the party congresses cannot ensure success. As in the revolutionary struggle, pragmatic leadership is required. In order to develop theory, leaders need practical experience and in-depth information

[19] Liu Keming, "Fakanci," *Sulian dongou wenti*, no. 1 (1981): 1-2.

about actual conditions. They should draw heavily on the experiences of other socialist countries, acknowledging that there are many models of socialism rather than only one that fits all countries and periods. They should not be attached to particular interpretations of the ideology, but should be aware of the need for continuous reform. In pursuit of modernization, communist leaders should be prepared to cooperate with capitalist governments. These are the views that predominate in China during the 1980s.

Comparisons of Chinese and Soviet Worldviews

How does this recent worldview in China compare to the Soviet worldview of the Brezhnev era? China's is less deterministic, particularly on the question of what makes things go right in a socialist country. Although the Chinese also claim to accept the existence of objective laws of social relations, they consider these laws to be more variable and less self-evident in the writings of Marx and Lenin. The Chinese also are less confident that party leaders can provide the answers. They say that only if leaders are pragmatic, eager to rely on social scientific evidence and open to borrowing from other socialist countries, will they charter the correct course. In the post-Brezhnev era, the Soviet worldview has been changing in the direction of Chinese views under Deng, but the Chinese continue to find rigidities in Soviet theory that they contrast to their own positions.[20]

Table 1.1 summarizes the major differences between the two worldviews at the beginning of the eighties. Under Gorbachev, the Soviet column is changing and, as we will see in Chapters Five and Six, Chinese debate the extent to which it is converging with their own approach to socialism.

REFUTATIONS OF DIFFERING OPINIONS

Chinese scholarship lacks a tradition of citations and refutations. In writings on the Soviet Union, there are no indexes, no bibliographies, and often no footnotes. No historiographical section can be found that summarizes the views of previous sources on the subject. While occasional articles mention that they present a direct response to a prior article (often in the same journal), there is no indication that specialists are responding to an international literature. Translations and infrequent brief review articles may be informative about foreign thinking on a given sub-

---

[20] Tang Zhuchang, "Andeluopofu shiqi de Sulian jingji wenti," *Sulian dongou wenti*, no. 4 (1984): 21-22.

TABLE 1.1

Contrasts in Chinese and Soviet Worldviews (Under the Deng and Brezhnev Leaderships)

	China	The Soviet Union
Judgment of the Communist Party Leadership	qualified trust; fallible leaders	unlimited trust; collective leadership is a guarantee
Validity of Marxist-Leninist Ideology	a guide, not a dogma; needs constant updating	a complete, scientific system; Lenin's views fully apply today
Importance of Social Sciences	experience is the test; pragmatism requires facts	theory cannot be challenged; truth is in the theory
Models of Socialism	multiple models exist; borrowing is for mutual benefit	there is one model; little interest in borrowing
Necessity of Reform	continuous reform needed; need to respond to conditions of time and place	cautious, occasional reform; uniform approach despite time and place

ject,[21] but subsequent Chinese articles on that very subject make no reference to them. Even when an article is part of an ongoing Chinese discussion of a disputed topic, there is unlikely to be any mention of other contributions to the discussion. Only articles that summarize the proceedings of a conference and sections of recent historiographical yearbooks compensate to a small degree for the atomized state of scholarship by discussing differences of opinion (without normally listing any of the names of those whose opinions are reported), or by grouping the articles published during the past year on one theme or another.[22]

Whereas some aspects of scholarship fail to meet world standards, others have notably improved in a short span of time. Chinese writings on domestic conditions in the Soviet Union have become less one-sided and more factual. Not a few articles in the most recent two or three years have eschewed any praise or blame. In such cases one must look closely at the list of pros and cons in the argument to see if the balance differs

[21] Sun Chengmu, "Sulian jinxiandai shi," *Zhongguo lishixue nianjian 1982* (Beijing: Renminchubanshe, 1982), 225-31; Fan Guizhen, "Guanyu Sulian '40 sui yidai zuojia' de taolun shuping," *Sulian wenxue*, no. 5 (1983); Zhang Shen, "Sulian jingji lilun wenti taolunhui zaijing zhaokai," *Jingjixue dongtai*, no. 9 (1983).

[22] "Shijieshi suo zhaokai Sulian zaoqi duiwai zhengce wenti xiaoxing zuotanhui," *Shijieshi yanjiu dongtai*, no. 11 (1984): 45-46.

from that in comparable writings. Some Chinese claim that the fact that
authors and reporters now sign their articles proves that they are the individual's responsibility and reflect only one person's views.

Chinese Sources in the Middle

In conversations, and to a lesser extent in publications, the impression is
of Chinese writings on the Soviet Union steering a middle road between
the excessively rosy picture of Soviet life painted in Russian sources and
the one-sidedly negative picture conveyed in Western, capitalist sources.
Chinese specialists remark that their Western counterparts are unable to
be objective about the Soviet Union because they start with negative
premises about socialism. They are out to prove that socialism does not
work. To this end, Westerners play up Stalin's errors while awarding little credit to his achievements. They give too much credit to Khrushchev
because of his repudiation of Stalin and encouragement of so-called anti-
socialist elements without adequately assessing his shortcomings. They
stress the deteriorating conditions of Brezhnev's final years while overlooking the substantial economic growth and political stability of most of ·
his time in office. Finally, some Chinese specialists note that Westerners
eagerly embrace pessimistic forecasts for the Soviet economy in the 1980s
and beyond, downplaying the prospects for reform. In one conversation
I was told that Yugoslavian press coverage of the Soviet Union tends to be
more objective than Western coverage. In short, Chinese argue that
Western specialists, biased by their desire to prove the superiority of capitalism to socialism, fail to provide objective, well-rounded evaluations of
the Soviet Union.[23] Despite these criticisms, in conversation Chinese specialists frequently acknowledge the valuable information and scholarly
analyses in Western sources. Many express the desire to learn from the
West through academic exchanges and access to publications unavailable
in their own libraries.

Rarely do Chinese refer to émigré sources on the Soviet Union. In conversation many express suspicion of such sources, doubting the objectiv-
ity of the information. A few Chinese specialists told me that they do not
write about purges and related subjects because they do not trust émigré
sources and the Soviets themselves have not provided much information.
When reporting internal Soviet shortcomings, Chinese specialists rely
heavily on Soviet self-criticisms, rarely on Western and even less on
émigré writings. It is reported, however, that *neibu* bibliographies are incomplete: they omit émigré sources that have been translated for the

---

[23] This view was expressed at many of my interviews with Soviet specialists in China in
December 1984 and January 1985.

benefit of small numbers of high officials and highly placed academics; such sources on the Stalin era may be numerous.

The Chinese have not written much about inadequacies in Soviet sources and statistics. They tend to accept Soviet economic data at face value, although sometimes they will mention a contrasting Western (or CIA) estimate. There is scarcely any comparison of different viewpoints in foreign schools of Soviet studies or in and out of the Soviet Union. Because Soviet sources in recent years have tended to be self-critical and the Chinese are familiar with the art of weeding out hard information from sanctimonious statements, Chinese writers tend to be skillful in their analysis of Soviet conditions despite the inattention to methodology.

Although there are a few Chinese translations of Western writings about Soviet criticisms of China,[24] the Chinese themselves do little research on this. They are somewhat more active in refuting Western criticisms of China, but this is also not a major preoccupation. There is no equivalent to the large Soviet literature in refutation of so-called anti-communism. Unlike Brezhnev and Chernenko, China's leaders do not talk of the intensification of the ideological struggle. Yet they too are concerned that the literature on the Soviet Union should serve their cause, which includes not only support for the "four modernizations" and China's independent foreign policy, but also support for socialism and adherence to the four cardinal principles set forth by Deng in 1979. With this in mind, China's leaders have indicated that it is wrong to criticize the internal affairs of other socialist countries; criticisms should be restricted to foreign affairs. To some extent, Chinese have even extended the same principle to capitalist countries, although any restriction is undermined by the continued approval for general criticisms of capitalism. Even for socialist countries, as the following chapters demonstrate, criti-

[24] Luosiman [Rozman], "Sulian Zhongguo wenti zhuanjia dui Zhongguo gaige de fanying," *Guowai shehuikexue dongtai*, no. 1, (1984): 1-6. The major publication that covers Soviet studies of China is *Guowai Zhongguo jindaishi yanjiu* (Beijing: CASS jindaishi yanjiusuo), which is a collection of articles that appears about once a year. Volume 5 was published in 1983, with many translations from Russian. Volume 4 (369-73), also published in 1983, includes an introduction to the Institute of the Far East by Wu Yongqing followed by a bibliography of roughly 100 items. A short article in *Shehuikexue*, no. 12 (1982) describes Soviet studies of China from the 1960s as leaning to research on the history of Chinese literature with results that far surpassed those of the 1950s. It praises the direct reliance on primary sources and related materials, the deep theoretical questions studied, the creative realism of separate authors, the comparative studies involving world literary history, and the specialists who work on subjects very rarely studied outside of China. Review articles in *Guowai shehuikexue dongtai*, no. 6 (1984): 48-51, summarize a conference establishing a new association of Soviet China scholars and another Soviet conference on American studies of China.

cisms of domestic matters continue to appear, although they tend to be found largely in *neibu* publications and not to address recent decisions by Soviet leaders.

An overview of Chinese research on Soviet history by Chen Zhihua published in the middle of 1984 leaves no doubt of the restraints in this field, especially to make sure it does not stray over to the side of rejecting the socialist system. Another article by Zhou Xincheng and Li Jun that appeared later in 1984 calls for comparative research including the Soviet Union, and argues that it will be superior to Western comparative studies, which are aimed at slandering the socialist system.[25] The next two sections present the views found in these articles.

Do Not Reject the Socialist System

"In recent years research work in Soviet history has had the following notable features: First, researchers energetically attempt to use Marxism as a guide, to support the four cardinal principles. The Soviet Union under the leadership of Lenin and Stalin was transformed from a country dominated by small peasants to a powerful socialist state. In this developmental process various complications were encountered, there appeared shortcomings and mistakes of one kind or another, all of which historical researchers ought not to obliterate and avoid. But, research on these problems is in order to generalize about historical experiences and lessons, and not to reject the socialist system, or to prove that socialism is inferior to capitalism, or that the collective economy is inferior to the individual one. Second, researchers energetically attempt to undertake independent investigations based on concrete historical materials, not limited to preexisting conclusions, but daring to liberate thinking, vigorously to study new circumstances, to resolve new problems, not to fail to pay heed to the research results of foreign scholars, nor to follow them blindly. Third, research topics are continually expanding, topics of comparatively great real significance are assigned priority. This explains why researchers of the study of Soviet history have already established the viewpoint of serving the building in our country of two civilizations of socialism. Fourth, in research the tendency is steadily growing of cooperation of a national and local character and cooperation between various disciplines. Multi-disciplinary, comprehensive research is just beginning to be carried out for some topics. . . . Now there is a new situation of Soviet historical research and the basic corps of Soviet historical researchers

---

[25] Chen Zhihua, "Sulian xiandaishi yanjiu de xin jumian ye yi xingcheng," *Shijie lishi*, no. 5 (1984): 7; Zhou Xincheng and Li Jun, "Shiying woguo jiakuai chengshi tizhi gaige de xuyao jinyibu kaizhan Sulian, dongou guojia jingji tizhi gaige de yanjiu gongzuo," *Shijie jingji yu zhengzhi neican*, no. 11 (1984): 15-19.

has already been formed; it is only necessary to have the cooperation of the entire group of comrades, to study hard without fear of hardship, then we certainly can realize greater achievements on our existing foundation."[26]

The World Economic Olympics

Articles appearing in some internally circulated journals and in openly circulated textbooks, speak of socialism and capitalism as systems opposed to each other and engaged in a struggle. They predict the eventual victory of socialism. The essence of the struggle is economic competition. Beginning with Marx and Engels, the promise of socialism has been to liberate the forces of production. Socialism can develop them faster than previously thought possible. The message of Lenin was of the same order: socialism, with its greater labor productivity, will win out against capitalism.

The 1984 article by Zhou Xincheng and Li Jun, which reviews these assertions, comments that over the sixty-odd years of socialist development, one needs to say honestly that for the past thirty years the results have not completely realized the prophecies of Marx, Engels, and Lenin. While over the first three decades, through the period of recovery from World War II, the socialist economic system demonstrated its great superiority to the extent that even reactionary, imperialist elements could not deny the successes, and thus assured its salvation, from the mid-fifties things have turned around greatly. The Soviet Union and Eastern European countries have each met with difficulties; gradually their rate of development has slowed, economic efficiency has been lowered, the living standards of the people have not risen rapidly. At the same time Western capitalist countries have taken advantage of technological advances and the special environment of the post-war era to increase their economic growth. Zhou and Li find that the superiority of socialism has not been so evident, and some people have come to have doubts. Why has this situation arisen? The authors immediately rule out the possiblity that socialism is not superior. No, the problem was that times changed while the "system" of economic management remained the same. A highly centralized "system" is inappropriate for the demands of socialist forces of production that grow more developed; the "system" increasingly becomes a barrier to expressing the superiority of socialism. When discussing shortcomings in a socialist system, Chinese use the word "tizhi"

---

[26] Shu Yan, "Ba dui Sulian dongou wenti de yanjiu xiangqian tuijin yibu: zaijing bufen Sulian dongou wenti zhuanjia, xuezhe zuotanhui zongshu," *Shijie jingji yu zhengzhi neican*, no. 11 (1984): 3.

(sometimes translated as "institutions") for "system," and often mention the term *"juti"* ("concrete"). While concrete institutions may work poorly, the fundamental system (*"zhidu"*) is good. Criticisms of the Soviet economic *tizhi* contrast to criticisms of the American capitalist *zhidu*. Behind this terminological distinction is the decision not to permit challenges to China's own fundamental socialist *zhidu*.

In recent decades socialist countries have faced a common problem of reform. Through reforms, Zhou and Li conclude, countries will find a new model that will speed up the development of the forces of production and lead to victory for socialism. The more varied the reform experiences in the socialist bloc, the easier it is to find appropriate models for a particular country's reforms.

The two authors go into some detail in their comparisons of socialist and capitalist economies over the past thirty years. In overall economic development, the socialist countries are intermediate between Japan and some Third World countries on the one hand and most of the countries of the world on the other. Socialist countries have scored successes in the growth of some important products, including oil, steel, coal, machinery, fertilizer, and cement. They have experienced relatively stable growth of national income. In speed and quantitative indices, they still maintain a certain degree of superiority.

What Zhou and Li term inferior in the socialist world (i.e. the Soviet Union and Eastern Europe) are product quality, scientific and technological progress, and the living standards of the people. High rates of investment bring low returns; economic efficiency is one-half that of the United States and certain Western European countries. The quality of products is even more deficient. Not one country in the socialist world ranks in the first twenty in the world in per capita annual income. Furthermore, new technologies are slow to be applied. In these respects, the Soviet Union and its Eastern European neighbors are losing their position and influence.

The authors conclude that the four factors of efficiency, quality, modern technology, and living standards are even more important than the positive factors of growth rates and quantitative measures of various products. For this reason, the socialist corner of the world is daily losing its influence and ability to absorb developments elsewhere. According to Zhou and Li, Chinese comrades notice that if one proceeds from west to east, conditions grow worse step by step—from Western Europe to Eastern Europe to the Soviet Union. This refers primarily to market supplies, but to a certain degree can also be said of economic conditions generally. The situation is equated to the Olympics: those who do not succeed must find out why and make the necessary changes to emerge victorious.

For three decades, Zhou and Li add, the goals of reform have not been realized. There still exists a serious struggle to prove the superiority of the socialist system. The main barrier is ideological. Soviet theoretical orthodoxy takes individual utterances of Marx and Lenin as unchangeable dogma. Citing particular classical writings and speeches, leaders block fundamental reform. They tie their own feet by refusing to act if Marxism-Leninism does not say it should be done, if current socialist theory would be contradicted. While throughout the world all countries that are developing rapidly import foreign capital and technology on a large scale, the Soviet theoretical insistence on the existence of two world markets makes it hard for that country to open to the outside.

Finally, Zhou and Li argue that the lack of success in socialist reforms also stems from insufficient research. They call for a new research area: the comparative study of the economic management systems of the Soviet Union and Eastern Europe on the one hand and the capitalist countries on the other. Acknowledging that Western scholars already have engaged in comparative research of East and West, Zhou and Li disparage their work as directed at slandering the socialist system and praising capitalism. Westerners use one-sided materials and present erroneous conclusions. The two authors conclude that Chinese scholars will do the opposite. They will apply the basic principles of Marxism-Leninism in their comparative work and will uncover the real reasons for inadequate reforms and slow growth, thus identifying the means for a reassertion of the superiority of socialism.

Zhou and Li emphasize how valuable the study of Soviet and Eastern European reforms has already been for China's recent reforms. Study of these experiences has provided "very great guidance" for China's economic theorists. Very many suggestions have already been adopted by the Central Committee and by separate ministries. Especially in 1983, when the State Council made decisions about reforms in the planning system, prices, taxes, wages, etc., the concrete reforms of the Soviet Union and Eastern Europe were discussed in detail and borrowed. The authors credit this contribution to China's reforms to five years of achievements and hard work by research specialists, and explain that demands are now even higher following the late 1984 decision to reform the urban economic system.[27]

The Sociology of Socialism

When the Chinese people were released at the end of the 1970s from their nightmarish two decades of recurrent campaigns and grand experiments

---

[27] Zhou Xincheng and Li Jun, "Shiying woguo jiakuai chengshi tizhi gaige," 15-19.

to remake mankind, they could not help but look back to the Soviet experience over the same period. The criteria they would use in judging the Soviet experience were naturally their indelible impressions of China's own failures and missed opportunities. The tortuous course of political intrigues and instability over this period made Chinese appreciate stable, continuous leadership. The impact of undereducated leaders intolerant of intellectuals led Chinese to value professional management of society with respect for experts. Stagnant living conditions and inconsistent economic growth were reflected in admiration for rapid growth in consumption and in the economy as a whole. The widespread state of depression and apathy heightened interest in a different social psychological state allegedly marked by optimism and long-term expectations and a stable system of political education. Chinese have applied to the Soviet Union the standards of national strength, economic development, political stability, material well-being, personal satisfaction, and political education that arose from personal anguish or the realization that party and state leadership had failed.

Educated Chinese are curious about these and other aspects of Soviet society. Whether they are seeking to salvage their belief in socialism, looking for further evidence of socialism's shortcomings, or simply searching for ways to make improvements in the only system that is acceptable to those in power, they have reason to examine the Soviet Union closely.

Themes in Soviet Studies

Chinese Soviet specialists and a wider community of officials and intellectuals seek to understand and inform the Chinese people about the Soviet Union. Altogether, close to 10,000 publications on the Soviet Union appeared in Chinese from 1979 to 1985 in the various fields of the humanities and social sciences. Approximately 40-50 percent examined some aspect of the Soviet economy, including historical and theoretical topics. Others in such fields as politics, law, and education also can be grouped under the general theme of "socialism and modernization." Chinese authors have been less concerned with technical economics than with the organization and management of the economy, less with leadership struggles and traditional views of politics than with the selection and implementation of policies affecting modernization. Disciplinary boundaries are easily crossed in this purposive, question-oriented approach to research. Chinese specialists study social relations and organizations with an emphasis on their economic consequences. They do so, for the most part, in short articles that raise general questions.

A second theme in the Chinese literature on the Soviet Union is "socialism, control, and participation." Authors seek to explain the nature of socialism, what is permissible and impermissible. In the arts, the social sciences, international relations, and politics, what is consistent with socialism and what threatens its existence? Studies of Marxist-Leninist ideology, when they are not centered on the priority topic of "socialism and modernization," often have this objective. Debates about alienation and humanism actually refer to social class relations in a socialist society and the prospects for convergence between socialism and capitalism.

Under Mao, Chinese used to write about the sensitive subjects of bureaucracy, privilege, class conflict, and, in a limited way, violations of human rights in the USSR. With China's change in course under Deng, these subjects generally became too hot to handle. Before, total disregard for standards of scholarly argumentation allowed Chinese to write even about the topics that might have been turned against the abuses in their own system. After 1978, the increased need to focus on actual circumstances and to argue realistically, paradoxically, made coverage of some sensitive subjects more complicated. Nevertheless, many topics remain open to critical treatment. Calls for "emancipation of the mind" and, in early 1985, "literary freedom" provide an opening for discussions of some problems faced by the intelligentsia. Stress on the need for payment according to work performed encourages studies of workers and peasants. Continuing efforts to reform China's bureaucracy create opportunities for analyses of officials. Studies of Soviet society are both restricted and encouraged by the political climate in China.

What Is the Major Contradiction?

Just as in May 1981 the Chinese newspaper *Guangming ribao* fixed firm limits on the discussion about whether economic backwardness means that China is somehow not yet fully socialist, an article in the paper *Heilongjiang ribao* in that same month sought to narrow the discussion on other favorite themes of the reformers.[28] It focuses on the question of what is the major contradiction in a socialist society—a question widely raised in studies of the Soviet Union in the 1960s and 1970s. The article draws attention to the view that the major contradiction is between the masses and the bureaucratic class, arguing that this is essentially not a fresh view, and accusing those who advocate it of being poisoned by the anti-Marxism of Lin Biao and the "Gang of Four." The article then affirms that the principal contradiction is no longer between classes but between the relations of production and the forces of production, between

[28] "Ping yizhong guanyu shehui zhuyao maodun de guandian," *Heilongjiang ribao*, May 20, 1981, p. 3.

the superstructure and the economic base. For this reason, the primary task for the dictatorship of the proletariat remains (as it was identified at the Eighth Party Congress in 1956, which recognized that China had made the transition to socialism), to develop the forces of production through the peaceful labor of the whole people. Bureaucratism exists in party and state organs, but it is not the main problem.

The article also criticizes the old view that the socialist system is the origin of bureaucratism, claiming that this pernicious problem results instead from cultural backwardness, a low level of development of the forces of production, the continued force of petty-bourgeois habits, remnants of feudalism, and capitalist influences. The analysis states that those who trumpet the existence of contradictions with a "bureaucratic class" as the major contradiction also call for a struggle for democracy and freedom and against bureaucracy and privileges. These too are discredited as old opinions and, at the end of the article, are portrayed as destabilizing elements that interfere with the need to maintain the four cardinal principles and to strengthen efforts on behalf of the "four modernizations."

Sociology Creeps In

In a way, sociology is a misnomer for Chinese studies of the Soviet Union since 1978. There are no book-length studies of social classes or comprehensive explanations of relations between classes in Soviet history. In these respects, Chinese studies of the Soviet Union are well behind Soviet studies of China. Leaders in Beijing remain concerned about the danger of opening up for study the subject of social classes in the history of socialism. They have not authorized a fundamental reevaluation of class differences in China after 1949, and this has ramifications for Soviet studies. It is safer to write about aspects of the economic management system, with the obvious justification that this can contribute—both through positive and negative examples—to China's pressing urban reforms.

The overall restrictions do not prevent sociology from creeping into Chinese publications, especially those written for internal circulation (*neibu*). Under the rubric of economic management, much is written about the motivation of workers and peasants. Are they creative in their labor? What effects can be attributed to low living standards and excessive egalitarianism? There are also occasional articles on the intelligentsia. Such sensitive topics are normally treated briefly, not as part of a systematic and detailed historical review of Soviet socialism. Nevertheless, opportunities arise to raise some controversial issues, for example on the relationship of officials and the intelligentsia. Reform figures manage on occasion to insert more sweeping condemnations of Stalin. To the extent that writers succeed in escaping the narrow, applied focus of the literature on economic management and in expanding the scope of coverage of Soviet history, they appear to be groping for a sociological approach to Soviet society based on an analysis of the distribution of power and income among social classes and groups.

In April 1985, the organization of Soviet history was systematized with the establishment of a seventeen-member committee to represent specialists in the field. The first conference of the association of Chinese historians of the Soviet Union and Eastern Europe met in Xian and included representatives from thirty-three research organs and institutions of higher education. The conference split into groups, which focused on topics that clearly signified new departures for the field. The group of Russian historians discussed problems in the modernization of Russia, including the contents of modernization and the period of its origins in Russia. The Soviet history group discussed Soviet socialist construction in the Khrushchev period.[29] Taboos were falling in Soviet studies; new items appeared on the agenda for research in this field. While still heavily concentrated on economic subjects, Chinese studies of the Soviet Union are being called on to diversify and at the same time to integrate—to become multi-disciplinary comparative research that links historical and contemporary questions.

Types of Publications

Books in Soviet studies have largely been translations. In 1979 a crash program of translations on the Soviet Union was launched. The results would not have been as impressive if some buildup had not taken place earlier. In 1975-1976, there was an outpouring of critical newspaper articles on the Soviet Union. In 1977 and 1978, compilations of Soviet economic statistics began appearing; one that was sent to press in August 1977 was 790 pages long. Even before 1978-1979, when normalcy was returning to the academic world, Soviet studies were reviving.

It was 1980 when the new approach to information-gathering began to bear fruit on a large scale. In January a 573-page translation of A. C. Sutton's book on Western technology and the Soviet economy from 1930 to 1945 arrived at the press. In April a 269-page book on the economy of Siberia and the Far East went to press in Heilongjiang. In June there arrived a 230-page compilation of recent Soviet economic reforms. In October a 610-page volume on the economic history of the NEP and a 611-page book on economic reforms and debates in the period 1965-1969 were simultaneously sent to press. Then in February 1981 there arrived a 1169-page, two-volume translation of the compilation of American arti-

[29] "Zhongguo Sulian dongou shi yanjiuhui chengli," *Renmin ribao*, June 28, 1985.

cles on the Soviet economy issued by the Joint Economic Committee of the United States Congress. Card catalogues of Chinese libraries listed many more translated books on the Soviet Union—indicating both the date they went to press and the official publication date—as they rolled out at a rate of almost one a month from 1980.

In addition to the publications listed in bibliographies—those accessible to all and the *neibu* ones with restricted circulation—other types of writings are omitted altogether. These are *baomi* (secret) writings targeted for select readers. The Central Committee produces documents known as *zhongyang wenjian* (Central Committee documents), which, at the rate of several each month, provide the frankest discussion of policy alternatives and explanations of the changing rules for what is or is not permissible. Newspapers also maintain their tradition of filing dispatches on international developments (*neibu jianbao*) not available to the public. The Chinese Academy of Social Sciences distributes administrative newsletters (*yuanbu tongbao*)with details on personnel matters. Reports on academic meetings are also circulated as drafts. The Soviet Union figures more prominently in *neibu* than in open sources, and may figure even more importantly in the *baomi* materials.

Under Mao, because of impatience with the time-consuming and sometimes unsuccessful procedure of arranging distribution through *zhongyang wenjian*, the radicals turned to communicating directly via *liangbao yikan*, consisting of two papers and one journal (*People's Daily, Liberation Army Daily,* and *Red Flag*). In this way Mao could bypass the party and the government and reach his audience directly. Articles in these publications can still be influential, but they do not have the same binding authority for cadres at all levels as do the sixty or so *zhongyang wenjian* issued each year after passing through strict review procedures, including conferences.

Information is carefully rationed. Apart from the *baomi* system for state secrets, there is a distinction between truly sensitive *neibu* writings and less sensitive ones. The former are differentiated according to various levels of audiences; some are intended only for officials above a certain rank and perhaps selected academics, and are omitted altogether in the available bibliographies that list most *neibu* publications. It is said that just as Chinese are likely to be more outspoken before a small gathering than a large conference, they will be less cautious in a white paper or restricted article than writing for a wide audience (*xiao cankao*). Greater frankness is clearly evident in accessible *neibu* than in open publications, and also seems to characterize the more sensitive *da cankao*. Both the most positive and the most negative (including translations of Soviet émigré sources) observations are found in the sensitive *neibu* sources.

Scholarly Convictions

Both bureaucratic and academic types can be found in Soviet studies. The former—most previously employed by the Central Committee's Liaison Department, the Foreign Ministry, or some other official organ—have long been accustomed to writing from a policy point of view. Numerous in the institutes of the Chinese Academy of Social Sciences, they respond quickly in their writings to changes in state policy. The latter are likely to adhere more consistently to deep-seated convictions. The views of quite a few specialists can be construed variously as optimistic or pessimistic depending on the current frame of reference. If they take China as the standard, which is common when domestic policy in China is more conservative, they tend to emphasize positive qualities of Soviet economic, political, or intellectual life. If they take the West as the standard, they tend to be more critical of the Soviet Union. What counts most is the possible impact of the article on the Chinese domestic scene.

Even if authors vary the message in response to domestic goals, there are consistent long-term differences observable between individuals who, I think, can be properly labeled voices of orthodoxy or reform. On the whole, the reformers fear that praise of the Soviet Union will be used to take the pressure off the call for reforms in China, while the orthodox group seeks in writings relatively favorable to the Soviet Union to reassert the superiority of what it regards as socialist principles that might be in danger of attack. Particularly on issues that range beyond narrow economic themes, one finds the discrepancy between orthodox and reform viewpoints most noticeable.

Is Soviet socialism a forum for debate in China? The answer that many Chinese give is "no." In their opinion, this subject was discontinued as an arena for debate some time ago—some say late 1979—when the Chinese stopped criticizing Soviet internal policy as "revisionism." They point to the disparity between continued Soviet criticisms of China's internal policies and their own silence about Soviet society. Some Chinese advised me to drop any plans to study China's views of social classes in the Soviet Union because Chinese do not write about this subject. Their opinions have a degree of validity, but it is necessary to introduce three qualifications. First, they are talking about open publications, not the *neibu* internal circulation writings. Second, they apparently exclude Chinese repetition of Soviet self-criticisms, particularly concerning economic shortcomings. Third, they underestimate the number of critical observations about Soviet policies, past and present, toward workers, peasants, officials, and intellectuals scattered in diverse writings. Whatever their motive, some Chinese academics have erred in undervaluing the substantial and informative Chinese literature on the Soviet Union. It is my impression, however, that there are many other specialists and officials who consider these writings of considerable value and sensitivity.

Why Study the Soviet Union?

Research on the Soviet economy and certain social conditions is justified by the widely proclaimed need to emancipate thinking. In five years it has served well China's reforms of the economic system. Not long after the Third Plenum, economic circles raised the question of which model to choose for China's own reform. At first, for political reasons, Chinese emphasized the Yugoslavian reforms and Romania; many strongly endorsed the Yugoslavian experience and some interest in Yugoslavia continued, while Romania, which had been selected for foreign policy reasons, was quickly dropped from attention. Later, according to the November 1984 article by Zhou Xincheng and Li Jun, some comrades also approved the ways and experience of Soviet reforms, advocating that the direction of the First Five-Year Plan in the mid-fifties ought to be restored to China's economic system. After comparative research began to expand, the majority perceived Yugoslavia as excessively fragmented and the Soviet Union as excessively centralized and decided that neither was very appropriate for China. Attention gradually concentrated on Hungary's reforms, mixing planning and market, centralization and dispersal. Of course, Zhou and Li add, China's reforms must start from its own concrete circumstances; no single foreign model will be copied. Nonetheless, study of differing Soviet and Eastern European reforms and reform models has been advantageous for borrowing and setting the direction of China's economic reforms. Now that China, as of October 1984, has entered the stage of reform of its urban economic system, even higher demands are being placed on this comparative socialist research. For success in urban reforms, they say, much more than in the case of rural reforms, research on foreign countries will play a vital role.[30]

The purpose of research on the Soviet Union and the relative standing of that country among models of socialism is discussed in a 1983 article entitled "To Create a Distinctive Chinese Socialist Economic Model."[31] The article states, "We cannot start from books, taking as dogma the conceptions of Marx and Engels in those years, we also cannot take socialist society as a fixed, unchanging thing." Already in the first decade of Soviet

[30] Zhou Xincheng and Li Jun, "Shiying woguo jiakuai chengshi tizhi gaige," 16.

[31] Yong Wenyuan and Luo Zong, "Chuangjian you Zhongguo tese de shehuizhuyi jingji moshi," 10-14.

rule two kinds of different models for the transition to socialism had emerged: War Communism and the NEP, the former based on administrative and military coercion to make a direct transition and the latter relying on economic measures to make an indirect transition. History proves that the latter corresponds to the objective conditions of small-scale peasant producers. Stalin relied primarily on administrative methods to develop a socialist economic model. He accomplished a great deal and demonstrated the superiority of the socialist system, but the system also revealed notable shortcomings, such as low efficiency and growing bureaucratism. This model was far from perfect. Yugoslavia devised a new economic model in the 1950s, creating worker self-management enterprises and relying primarily on market regulation. Later, Eastern European countries carried out reforms. Hungary's combination of planning and market regulation was comparatively effective and can be considered another model. The Soviet Union also launched reforms. The lesson from these experiences is that each nation must draw on its distinctive characteristics to follow its own path to socialism.

There are also common characteristics among socialist countries, which call for systematic research and learning from each other. This demands comparative study. Research on the strengths and weaknesses of various models can be useful in establishing China's distinctive economic model. Yet Deng Xiaoping has correctly pointed out that this cannot be successful if it leads to blind copying of another country.

The article continues by noting that in the past China copied the Soviet model, while in recent years many Chinese theorists have taken a critical attitude toward that model, especially its highly centralized planning system and weak market system. In the past year there also have been some comrades who advocate borrowing from Soviet experience. Their reason is that conditions in China and the USSR are quite similar, our original economic system was sent from the Soviet Union, now the Soviet system is having its own reforms. We recognize that if one seeks truth from practice, one cannot unconditionally find fault with a high degree of centralization and ignore later advances and, of course, cannot also ignore continuing shortcomings. The 1965 Soviet reforms had a great role in sustaining economic growth. The reformed system no longer, as in the past, rejected market structures in general. Nevertheless, because of such factors as excessive centralization and rigid planning and rejection in theory of a self-regulating market, the economy operated inefficiently, enterprises lacked incentives, the achievements of science and technology were applied slowly, and goods were of low quality and little variety. In the process of borrowing, Chinese must adopt what is effective and start from China's own needs, definitely not again copying the Soviet system exactly.

As for the Yugoslavian model, a few years ago quite a few theorists proclaimed its superiority, yet in the past two years, because certain difficulties have appeared in it, there also have been quite a few who talk about its shortcomings, even to the point of rejecting it in theory and practice. Over the past thirty years, Yugoslavia has had not a few good results from encouraging socialist democracy and using the market system, but in controlling the macro-economy there apparently exist shortcomings due to relative fragmentation. Even so, Yugoslavian theory and practice is worth our systematic and deep research, the late-1984 article adds.

In the past few years the appeal of the Hungarian economic model has sounded quite loudly. Hungary's reforms were comparatively thorough and successful, and there is much to learn. Yet Hungary's population is small and China's is large. From this alone, it is clear that China must not copy Hungary closely. Hungary's enterprises are few, foreign trade is relatively large. Chinese circumstances are not suitable for proceeding as far as Hungary did in abolishing command planning. China must strengthen enterprise democratic management, but absolutely cannot overlook the correct handling of central and local relations.

The article concludes with the suggestion that Yugoslavia's present problems stem from reform steps that were too large, exceeding the present stage of development of the forces of production and the level of consciousness of the people. It leans to the Hungarian model, yet finds reasons for regarding at least some of it as irrelevant. It casts doubt on the old Soviet model, yet indicates that there is much to learn from Soviet reforms. On the whole, this article captures the balance that seems to prevail in Chinese publications from 1982 to the present: Yugoslavia has fallen to third place as a model, the Soviet Union is in second but may actually be seen as the most relevant, and Hungary is in first place but somehow seems of limited relevance.

Some specialists of either reform or orthodox persuasion put the case for studying the Soviet Union even more strongly. They say the Soviet Union has reference value. In the past, China erred by failing to study the Soviet case deeply, by paying little heed to Soviet theoretical discussions when, in fact, their problems are largely China's problems. When Chinese scholars and officials are struggling to resolve these problems, how could China fail to benefit from Soviet experience? Naturally, reformers and orthodox thinkers part company on some of the lessons to be drawn from the Soviet experience. As we shall see in the following chapters, there are disagreements on what they study, how they interpret it, and where they see the Soviet Union heading in the near future.[32]

ORTHODOX AND REFORM VIEWS

Organizational divisions account for only a part of the observed differences between orthodox and reform advocates. Specialists on the Soviet Union and international communism can be found in dozens of institutes and universities. In Beijing, the largest concentration is at the Institute of the Soviet Union and Eastern Europe within the Chinese Academy of Social Sciences (CASS). It is difficult to characterize the position of the institute as a whole, although its leading economists take a reform position. Other institutes in the CASS system vary in their orientation: at the reform end of the spectrum are philosophers at the Institute of Marxism-Leninism and Mao Zedong Thought, while among the orthodox thinkers are economists at the Institute of World Economies and Politics. Another large grouping of specialists is found at institutes and universities in the provincial centers of Manchuria. Their writings tend to be on the orthodox side. For other concentrations of experts in Shanghai and northwestern China I have not been able to make even preliminary groupings by political orientation. Neither regional nor organizational affiliation is sufficient to analyze the differences in this field.

The terms of debate between orthodox and reform advocates were largely established in 1978. The two sides combined forces in defeating the "Gang of Four" and in blaming the ills of the preceding decade (or two) on them and their associates. They united behind Deng Xiaoping against the heirs to the radical mantle, objecting to Hua Guofeng's attempts to preserve Mao's ideology and policies as dogma. They rallied behind the goals of concentrating on economic growth, relying heavily on the intelligentsia and the development of science and technology, and rewarding workers in conformity with the principle of "to each according to his labor." Both sides favored dismantling many of the structures established in the later years of Mao's life and reverting, to a substantial degree, to the socialist system of the mid-1950s as reflected in the Eighth Party Congress of 1956. In the context of the struggle against radicalism, they even agreed on the slogans, "practice is the sole criterion for testing truth," and "seek truth from practice," which diminished the role of ideology. The "four modernizations" became a rallying cry for the entire

---

[32] "Zuotanhui: Andeluopofu shiqi de Sulian jingji wenti," *Sulian dongou wenti*, no. 4 (1984): 29.

leadership. The Third Plenum in December 1978 established a new course for realizing the "four modernizations" that pointed to a decisive victory over the radicals, but it did not resolve the differences between the orthodox group and the reformers.

The orthodox and reform forces disagree on how to interpret the early years of the PRC before the antirightist campaign of 1957. To what extent was the rapid economic growth of this period sustainable without drastic reforms? Was the balance between centralized control and mass participation correct? Those who look back nostalgically to this era, including many (but not all) trained in the Soviet Union at that time, tend to have a favorable opinion of the Soviet Union. They consider the 1950s a golden age to which China should, in many respects, return. The reformers oppose this view, saying, for instance, that "the fifties' key cannot unlock the eighties' door." This difference of opinion about China's past receded as the new reform program made believers of many and influenced thinking about Soviet reform requirements.

From the beginning of 1980 to the middle of 1981, controversies about the Soviet Union seemed to have receded a good deal from the center of public attention. The premature disclosure in *Wenyi baijia* that most specialists now consider the Soviet Union socialist angered Deng Xiaoping.[33] Concern that this development could frighten capitalist partners led to additional caution about repeating such views in publications available to foreigners. At the same time, Chinese stopped referring to the Soviet Union as revisionist, making it uncertain what of a general nature should be said about that country. (For a time Eastern European countries but not the Soviet Union could be openly recognized as socialist.) Objections were raised first in 1978 against criticizing Soviet income differentials, bureaucratic and managerial authority, and related domestic themes, for fear that they would sustain the Maoist critique of China's emerging reforms. When China's leaders began to worry in 1979 about the democracy movement, there was need to restrict criticisms of the Soviet Union that could be construed as directed against any socialist system. While difficult decisions on how to assess Mao Zedong's role in history remained unresolved in 1980 and early 1981, it was not easy to decide what to say about Stalin and Soviet history. Finally, Soviet aggression in Afghanistan slowed the momentum of efforts to look more positively on that country.

While some academic debates on the Soviet Union were muted in 1980 and 1981, two trends were working in a different direction. First, this was

[33] "Harbin Seminar Examines Soviet Literature, Society," *Wenyi baijia*, no. 2 (1979): 254-56, trans. FBIS, PRC International Affairs, Soviet Union, April 14, 1980, pp. C1-C4.

the very period when articles on the Soviet Union multiplied, many appearing in newly launched *neibu* journals. There was an explosion of information about the Soviet economy and many other aspects of contemporary life. Historical and literary studies also became far more numerous. Translations from Russian were a less controversial source of information than the pointed debates that had preceded. Second, with the impending assessment of Mao looming in the background, questions about Marxist philosophy and leadership remained in the public eye. Humanism and alienation were abstract terms that offered an indirect and therefore safer forum for discussing the nature of socialism. Reformers also approached the history of the Communist Party of the Soviet Union through discussions of Bukharin and Trotsky. Obviously they were criticizing Stalin and, one can surmise, this also provided an approved outlet to redirect criticisms of Mao toward more general problems of socialist political systems and to suggest further reforms toward a more democratic, collective leadership. A long speech at the party school of the Central Committee reviewed the struggle between Stalin and Trotsky, including Trotsky's anti-bureaucratic theory.[34] While the Trotsky theme faded in 1982, Bukharin remained a lively issue.

A faction associated with Trotsky had been labeled counterrevolutionary in the course of the Chinese revolution. To reinterpret Trotsky's status would necessarily raise sensitive historical questions about the rise of the Chinese Communist Party. For this reason, and because China's economic strategy in the 1980s resembles Bukharin's views of the NEP, the two opponents of Stalin have been treated differently.

Interest in Bukharin was mounting in 1980-1982. A translation of Steven Cohen's biography of Bukharin drew attention. Translations of Bukharin's own writings were distributed.[35] Students at some universities read these works and even wrote papers about him. Some equated Bukharin with Liu Shaoqi, China's wronged leader whose course for modernization had been rejected in a political struggle and who died at the hands of his opponents. Each had been criticized wrongly. The hope for reform thinkers was to clear Bukharin and to contribute to a fundamental reevaluation of the history and nature of socialism.

As in other socialist systems, the divergence between reform and orthodox viewpoints centers on the role of the Communist Party and officials in controlling others, especially the intelligentsia. Various terms, such as democracy and law, combatting dogmatism, and reviving the so-

[34] A Chinese informant mentioned this speech, but I have not found any reference to it in Chinese publications.

[35] *Buhalin wenxuan*, Vol. 1 (Beijing: Renminchubanshe, 1981).

cial sciences, refer to the goal of strengthening the intelligentsia vis-à-vis the officials. Both the orthodox and the reform advocates agree on the need to alter the balance from that of Mao's time, but they disagree on the extent of change. The orthodox group stands for something akin to the Soviet system, while the reformers want more far-reaching democratization. To rely on practice rather than theory strengthens the hands of those who can evaluate practice best: the scientists and social scientists. To stress democracy is to keep bureaucrats from implementing their desired policies subjectively, to prevent a personality cult and abuse of power. It also means granting to groups of people the initiative and the incentives to act.

The Orthodox View

Orthodox leaders in Beijing initially were reluctant to endorse the introduction of the responsibility system into agriculture. When the system began in a modified way and on an experimental basis, its phenomenal appeal caught the leadership by surprise. Only after it had spread from below was it fully endorsed above. Resistance became increasingly difficult as reports kept coming in of unprecedented growth rates in agriculture. Some in this camp spent up to two decades regretting that China had gone off half-crazed with wild schemes in the Great Leap Forward and the Cultural Revolution. During these long years, the centralized, planned Soviet system with its granting of prestige and material rewards to specialists stood for rationality against China's chaotic campaigns and struggles. Some supporters of an orthodox position could see no big difference between China's plans for the 1980s and the contemporary Soviet system. Who were the Chinese, latecomers to socialist reforms as they were, to tell the Soviets that there was something wrong with their brand of socialism? Many, it is likely, had wearied of the practice of name-calling; reckless, unsubstantiated charges had given criticisms of Soviet socialism a bad name. Some, maybe a majority, were genuinely impressed with Soviet achievements. Others were conservative on Chinese matters, such as the need to strengthen party control, centralized planning, and ideological restrictions, without showing much support for Soviet socialism. Others who shared the same domestic policy objectives found it advantageous to join in the debate on the Soviet Union. Opinions about Soviet domestic conditions were also aired by those directly concerned with foreign policy. Out of opposition to becoming too cozy with the United States, many sought at least some balance through closer Soviet ties.

The orthodox ideal remains China's First Five-Year Plan when the Soviet model was followed most closely. Leaders of this persuasion criticize economic reform as *ziyouhua*, liberalization that brings a revival of the

capitalist class. Even more vigorously, they object to political and ideological reforms. They have been reassured by the thought that, in the last
resort, the Communist Party and the army remain firmly on the side of
orthodoxy. At times they have been emboldened to push harder—for example, in the fall of 1983, under Chen Yun's leadership, the orthodox
camp argued that even China's economy would be damaged by Western
and capitalist influences and managed to secure Deng Xiaoping's backing
for their calls for action. The propaganda department and the journal
Hongqi vocally present the orthodox viewpoint.

The Reform View

What kind of people become the outspoken reformers in China? The
names that have come to our attention are largely those of Marxist theorists employed in the Chinese Academy of Social Sciences, universities
and institutes, or the mass media. Very few are officials in departments
under the secretariat of the Central Committee. Already at the conference of theorists (*lilun wuxu hui*) led by Hu Yaobang in January and
March 1979, reform spokesmen articulated the principal reform themes
of the Deng Xiaoping era. They favored a full-scale reevaluation of the
Soviet Union, including open discussion of the shortcomings of Stalin
and even Lenin. Although limited by Deng Xiaoping's 1977 statement
that Chinese would never do to Mao as Khrushchev had done to Stalin,
they wanted frank recognition of Mao's errors, including a full-scale
reexamination of the mistakes committed by the Chinese Communist
Party. Moreover, they urged a minimalist approach to Marxist theory,
preferring a streamlined theory consistent with democratic rights and
humanist ideals. This important conference, following immediately after
the Third Plenum with a break for the long New Year's holidays, has not
been openly publicized in China even though it set the tone for most theoretical discussions in the following years. Subsequent restrictions on debate were, in part, a reaction to the far-reaching challenges to orthodoxy
raised at this time. On themes such as scholarly freedom and democratic
participation, such challenges were eventually permitted to be aired for a
time in open publications.

The extended, wide-ranging discussion of the Soviet Union (including
a reexamination of the Nine Commentaries written in the 1960s), de-
Maoization, and Marxist theory exerted a strong influence on officials
and academics as well as helping to invigorate the democratic movement
in 1979. The search for new information and the struggle against the radicals was not limited to reformers. By the summer of 1979, Soviet specialists such as Wang Youping contradicted prevailing views of that country by introducing basic facts about the Soviet system over the past two

decades.[36] From the beginning the Soviet Union figured importantly in the debates between orthodox and reform thinkers.

Reform advocates seek a full historical accounting of the mistakes made in socialist countries. They stand for academic freedom, the pursuit of truth, detailed comparative research, full acquaintance with Western scholarship, and similar scholarly ideals. They seize opportunities to amplify on or reinterpret statements by the party leadership to favor reform objectives. For example, Liao Gailong and Li Honglin followed up Deng Xiaoping's criticisms of insufficient democracy in the Chinese Communist Party in August 1980 with publications that probed deeply into the longstanding overemphasis on centralism and the methods needed for encouraging democracy. Another example can be found in Su Shaozhi's article on academic freedom in February 1985, barely a month after Hu Qili's speech to the Fourth Writer's Congress in favor of greater freedom for intellectuals.[37]

Chinese are understandably much more concerned with the future of their own country than with their writings about the Soviet Union. Orthodox and reform advocates alike may comment favorably or unfavorably about the Soviet Union if they think it can advance their domestic aims. On the whole, the reformers are critical of Soviet practices, but they may praise selectively, for example the NEP years but not the Stalin period, or the Andropov reform proposals but not the Brezhnev policies. So long as reformers perceive Soviet conditions to be at least somewhat better than those in China (e.g. in education, philosophy, policies toward intellectuals), they may choose to write positively about the Soviet Union. Especially if the political situation is tense in China and, as in the anti-spiritual pollution campaign, it is difficult to refer positively to the West, the Soviet Union may suffice to establish the same point. Of course, in those matters where Chinese reforms have gone beyond Soviet ones or China has more freedom, reformers would avoid citing the Soviet Union in favorable terms.

Titles of articles can be deceptive. Writings may appear to support Stalin's thought, as was common in 1979, or Mao's thought, when they contain a strong reform message. For example, in an article published in 1984, entitled "Maintain and Develop Mao Zedong Thought," Su Shaozhi calls for a thorough analysis of how democracy is subverted in a socialist system and warns that without it, there will be no guarantee of healthy development in the future. He cites Khrushchev's handling of Stalin's errors as an example of insufficient analysis of the problems of

[36] "Sulian? Suxiu? ruhe qushe?" *Guangjiaojing*, April 16, 1980, pp. 27-31.
[37] Su Shaozhi, "Xueshu ziyou yu xueshu fanrong," *Wenhuibao*, February 4, 1985, p. 5.

socialism. In addition to the boldness of Su's conclusions, he was one of the first to discuss Khrushchev directly in a publication not restricted to internal circulations.

Khrushchev completely attributed the mistakes and tragedy born in Soviet socialism led by Stalin to the personal character and cult of personality of Stalin. This completely contradicts the basic principles of historical materialism, therefore it cannot provide a rational explanation for the reasons that gave birth to the cult of the individual, and also cannot provide a correct evaluation of Stalin's historical position, even more it cannot find the path to reform, or guarantee that Soviet socialism will follow a healthy path of development.[38]

To Advance Research on Marxism

Back-to-back articles in *Makesizhuyi yanjiu* (Marxist Research, no. 1 [1983]) offer two approaches to advance research on Marxism. The first, by Yu Guangyuan, accepts the need to bring the overall principles of scientific socialism into line with the concrete reality of one's country, to prevent the ideology from becoming revolutionary verbiage or leading the country's revolution to deviate. Writing in 1983, Yu acknowledges that as they approach sixty years since Lenin died, much in the capitalist world has changed, requiring new contents for scientific socialism on the contradictions between the relations and the forces of production. Yu adds that China has its own special characteristics—population size, economic conditions, cultural and historical traditions, historical experiences and lessons—that socialism must grasp in order to achieve Chinese-style socialist modernization. Nevertheless, Yu also warns against a trend in socialist studies toward loosening control over research. He writes, "We cannot agree with the view in certain present-day teaching and research that treats scientific socialism as a separate science from Marxist philosophy and political economy."[39]

The following article, by Su Shaozhi, goes further in specifying how Marxism must change. Su asserts that the revolutionary force of Marxism lies in its continuous absorption of real-life conditions. All [true] adherents are distinguished by their accurate observations of present-day social conditions. In the post-war era, rapid changes have occurred in the proletariat within capitalist countries, in the international communist movement, and in the publication of many drafts of Marx's writings. Su says these should be taken into account for their effects on theory. He calls for the study of the young and the old Marx, Marxism and human-

---

[38] Su Shaozhi, "Jianchi he fazhan Mao Zedong sixiang," *Makesizhuyi yanjiu* (congkan), no. 1 (1984): 23.

[39] Yu Guangyuan, "Jinyibu jiaqiang Makesizhuyi de yanjiu (dai fakanci)," *Makesizhuyi yanjiu* (congkan), no. 1 (1983): 1-6.

ism, the relation of science and ideology in Marxism, and the relations of
Marx and Engels to Lenin. He stresses that the main theoretical need in
China is to build Chinese-style socialism.

Su Shaozhi draws attention to the international attitude that Marxism
is passé or that there is a crisis of Marxism. He notes apathy in China as
well. Although he calls it an error to see Marxism as a historical exhibition piece, he says that these criticisms should not be simply viewed as
lies by class enemies. In the past dogmatism existed, there was a mistaken
tendency to idolize the resolutions of the international communist movement and Soviet experience, the cult of the individual long prevailed, and
leftist errors closed China off. These factors seriously hampered the development of Marxism. It stagnated. It is no wonder that if theory cannot
answer life's questions, theory should meet mass indifference.

The proper way to celebrate the one-hundredth anniversary of Marx's
death, Su suggests, is to develop Marxism creatively in the only way it
can truly be maintained to avoid a crisis or apathy. Publication of additional sources is a step in this direction. Su mentions Lenin's writings
omitted in the Soviet official edition of Lenin's collected works published
in Stalin's time, Lenin's secret diary and testament, memoirs, primary
sources on major events, unorthodox histories. With these materials, Su
urges, we can reexamine and reevaluate many major events. Su himself
singles out the thoughts of late Lenin for their awareness of many shortcomings after the October Revolution, their advocacy of democratization
as well as proletarian dictatorship in Soviet organs, their opposition to
bureaucratism and excessive centralization, and their promotion of the
role of cooperatives. Su argues that on these matters Stalin betrayed
Lenin's thoughts to the point of leading to a serious tragedy. These matters should be studied not only to restore the real face of history, but also
because they relate to the present-day development of Marxism.

In this same article Su Shaozhi makes what may be an indirect criticism
of Lenin—the only one I have found in Chinese communist writings. He
says that Westerners look for contradictions between Lenin and his predecessors, Marx and Engels. They see Lenin overlooking the need for advanced capitalism to build socialism, as deviating from Marx in his stress
on using a vanguard to liberate the proletariat.

Since the 1978 debate on practice as the sole criterion of truth, Chinese
have restored Marxist thought, Su adds, but theorists are not yet up to
the task. He calls for updated Marxist theory to take into account very
sharp, new questions raised by the policies of socialist states and the
conflicts that have divided them. In Su's view, one cannot allow this
recent historical stage full of big events to remain a blank page in Marxist
theory.

Su casts doubt on writings and theories previously spread around the world as general principles. It is necessary now, he concludes, to determine what is, in fact, general, and what corresponds to the specific conditions of Russian social history and cannot be applied everywhere. Su proposes the same test for the theories of Stalin and Mao to determine which should be abandoned. He calls for discarding all theoretical views found to be inconsistent with current conditions and reform needs. He leaves no doubt that the real need in theoretical work is to locate ideas that stand in the way and uproot them as dead wood. This contrasts with the orthodox objective of protecting theories and ideology from challenges viewed as anti-socialist in nature.[40]

In Chinese politics and thought, Su Shaozhi still finds the influence of a certain foreign model [the Soviet Union] that is accepted as the standard for socialism when it actually limits the superiority of socialism from appearing and constricts the creativity of the masses. Consistent with his other attacks on orthodox thinking, Su notes that after Stalin a new situation of diversification exists in the international communist movement, despite the fact that some people dislike the demise of the era of a single center, a single road, and a single model.

Su's article, which I discuss again in Chapter Six, was a forerunner to the December 1984 reform interpretation of Marxism that created an international stir. At that time when reform views were at a peak in Beijing, there was an official announcement that dogmatic repetition of ideas from an earlier age is "naive" and "stupid." The test of experience must be applied to Marxist thought too. Deng Xiaoping's notion of pragmatism had been grafted onto the academic goal of scholarly investigation into the realities of socialist experience. The result was not yet an opening to unfettered scholarship, but it did signify a further relaxation of restrictions.

The Terms of Debate

The terms of debate between orthodox and reform have been continuously reset from 1979 to 1985, although the main standpoints of each camp have remained largely intact. The camps disagree on fundamental matters, but what they actually debate in print at any point in time depends on the policy guidelines from above. Whereas the anti-spiritual pollution campaign emboldened the advocates of the orthodox position such as Deng Liqun at the beginning of 1984, the urban reforms and Hu Qili's speech to the National Writers' Congress started 1985 off on a re-

---

[40] Su Shaozhi, "Lizu dangdai, ba Makesizhuyi tuixiang qianjin," *Makesizhuyi yanjiu* (congkan), no. 1 (1983): 7-34.

TABLE 1.2

Extremes of Orthodoxy and Reform in China
Since the Third Plenum

	Orthodoxy	Reform
Ideology	Marxism-Leninism	Marxism alone; Leninism = Soviet form of Marxism;
	Preserve Mao Zedong Thought; Mao largely correct	Downgrade Mao's thought; Mao largely in error
	Deemphasize themes of humanism and alienation	Humanism and alienation exist under socialism
	Maintain Stalin's view of Marxism	Emphases on early Marx, late Lenin, Eurocommunism, Bukharin
	Spiritual pollution from capitalist world	Commonalities with Western social sciences
Economic System	Centralized planning	Market economy; enterprise autonomy
	Initial opposition to responsibility system	Decollectivization through responsibility system
	Soviet planning; return to model of 1950s	Yugoslavian and Hungarian models; Western economics
Political System	Censorship	Freedom of expression
	Party unity is primary	Democracy is primary
	Party selection of local officials	Democratic elections at county level and below
Foreign Relations	Weight on relations with Soviet Union and Eastern Europe	Weight on open door to the West, Japan
	Slogan "equidistance" to limit capitalist ties	Depiction of Soviet hegemonism as the greater danger
Social Policies	Class struggle still needed	Encourage the rich to join Communist Party
	Reliable party leaders control intellectual organs	Promote intellectuals to official positions with freedom to manage own affairs
	Restrictions on private sector	More freedom to private sector
	Party controls over participation	More democratic participation

form-oriented track. A zigzag course between reform and orthodoxy persisted through 1985.

Contrasting articles on how to interpret the urban reform indicate the terms of debate in 1985.[41] Writing on January 10, Zhang Youyu, legal scholar and member of the advisory board of the Chinese Academy of Social Sciences, insisted that the entire reform comes from the starting point of the constitution and is consistent with its spirit. He added that just because the state had planned too much in the past, this does not mean that China can now do completely without the plan and rely on market regulation. The constitution of an earlier year still applies, and one cannot regard the state as no longer having authority over enterprises. In contrast, in an interview with some Americans, Premier Zhao was asked about the long-term prospects of China's open-door policy. He answered that China will decrease central orders to enterprises and the market will play an even larger role in the life of an enterprise. Noting that the urban reform will be completed in several years, Zhao asserted (without discounting a role for planning) that then China will "completely rely on market regulation" (*wanquan you shichang tiaojie*). His exuberant tone was soon replaced by a cautious approach. The urban reforms ran into increasing difficulty in 1985 as leaders became concerned with spreading corruption as well as inequality.

The Context of Sino-Soviet Relations

We live in a world of two superpowers and two camps. This has been the state of world affairs since the second half of the 1940s, and it is likely to remain so in the foreseeable future. Even though the broad contours of this world order have persisted for several decades, this is not a static order. Many countries in the Third World remain generally nonaligned and thus subject to competitive wooing, and from time to time world attention becomes preoccupied with a country that is, or appears to be, in the process of shifting its alignment. Only one country, China, deserves to be identified as a swing country in this world order. It merits this distinction for three reasons: 1) China has shifted its position from pro-Soviet to anti-Soviet to cooperative with the United States, and in the past few years to a more independent stance with gradually improving Soviet relations; 2) China's shifts have been of major importance for the balance of international forces, perhaps to an extent unequalled by any other readjustments in the world order that had been established by the late

---

[41] "Zhang Youyu tan jingji tizhi gaige tong xianfa de guanxi," *Renmin zhengxie bao*, vol. 1, no. 1, reprinted in *Wenzhai bao*, February 24, 1985, p. 1; "Zhongguo jingji jinhou jiang hui geng hao," *Guangming ribao*, reprinted in *Wenzhai bao*, February 24, 1985, p. 1.

1940s; and 3) China is genuinely linked to each camp—through ideology and revolutionary heritage to the socialist bloc and through commerce and imports of technology to the capitalist bloc. China's future position in this divided world should be a matter of deep concern.

The Chinese break with the Soviet Union was one of three dramatic policy initiatives by Mao Zedong and his close associates in the decade following the socialist transformation. The other two initiatives—the Great Leap Forward and the Great Proletarian Cultural Revolution—have since Mao's death been repudiated as dreadful mistakes. Since the reasoning used to cast doubt on the socialist character of Soviet society was unmistakably associated with the ideological justifications for the Cultural Revolution, one might wonder now if this third initiative also might be reconsidered.

Nobody is fooled about what the stakes are in Chinese discussions about Soviet socialism. The ultimate issue for most statesmen, and many specialists as well, is not what should people think about the Soviet system, nor what Chinese should do internally with the knowledge they gain about socialism. The issue is what will happen to Sino-Soviet relations. As seen in the criticisms of the 1960s and 1970s, these relations have at least four dimensions: strategic, geographical, ideological, and economic. Of these, the strategic and the economic have been the focus of attention in the 1980s. The border problem (or geographical dimension) has turned out to be of little concern.[42]

For over half a century, the overriding interest of China's communist leaders has been power and security in their own country and region. In the 1920s and 1930s, many had been attracted to the communist movement primarily as a means to achieve this end against the imperialists who sought to carve up China and their warlord and comprador accomplices. The Japanese invasion of China was the biggest impetus for party membership; it brought nationalism more deeply into the party's embrace. When the Soviet communist leadership and Stalin advised against a confrontational strategy, as occurred on occasions in the late 1920s, early 1930s, and mid-1940s, China's communist leaders led by Mao rejected this position in favor of direct action. China's willingness to join in the Korean War offers further evidence of its persistent determination to pay almost any price for security on its borders.

Moscow failed to take China's concerns for independence, territorial integrity, and regional influence seriously enough. It sacrificed vigorous

---

[42] Li Huichuan, "Where Does the Crux of the Sino-Soviet Border Talks Lie?" *Renmin ribao*, June 17, 1981, p. 7; trans. FBIS, PRC International Affairs, Soviet Union, June 18, 1981, pp. C1-C7.

action on the Taiwan issue for "peaceful coexistence" with Washington. It failed to support China in its border clash with India and reneged on promised aid with nuclear armaments. Soviet leaders tried to gain a naval foothold on China's coast, contemplating the formation of a joint fleet. Above all, Chinese chafed at Moscow's efforts to control China's foreign policy as part of its leadership of a unified communist bloc.

The Sino-Soviet split brought new circumstances for China to pursue its national and regional goals. Beijing's strategy varied through the 1960s. First it tried to rally other communist countries to its side in the fraternal struggle against Soviet collusion with the United States. With the failure of this strategy and the onset of the Cultural Revolution, China turned inward, saying essentially, "A plague on both your houses." As China began to emerge from the most chaotic and isolationist phase of the Cultural Revolution, its leaders saw signs of a congruence of Soviet and American interests in settling the Vietnam War. Beijing actively intervened in an effort to spoil any settlement. China now was a factor in the superpower relationship. After Washington's announcement in March 1968 of a ceiling on troops in Vietnam and Moscow's invasion of Czechoslovakia, the Chinese strategy changed again. Opposition to the Soviet Union and its threat to China's borders—built up by rhetoric about unequal treaties and Soviet seizure of Chinese territory—became Beijing's primary foreign policy concern. Many of the moderate Chinese leaders did not see the need for the growing confrontation. For a time in the fall of 1969, Zhou Enlai seemed to make headway in finding a negotiated solution to the crisis, but the radicals sabotaged these efforts. At the same time, China was ending its isolation, restoring diplomatic relations with Yugoslavia despite the revisionist label pinned on it, and soon signalling the United States of its interest in better relations. The momentum of this turnabout carried through the 1970s, fueled by the growing perception of Soviet-Vietnamese alliance and of Soviet military buildup along China's borders. In contrast, America's military retrenchment worldwide and especially in East Asia clearly made it the lesser of two evils in Chinese eyes.

Once the post-Mao era arrived and a pragmatic leadership was finally in place, the emotional element in Sino-Soviet relations would inevitably diminish. What would remain in China's quest for regional security? Four issues were clearly in the forefront: the perception of a direct Soviet threat to China; the degree to which Moscow accepted China within a no longer monocentric communist system; the Taiwan issue; and the Vietnamese threat to Beijing's regional aspirations in Southeast Asia. Although security considerations alone would not determine the future of Sino-Soviet relations, they remained paramount.

Despite the continued Soviet military buildup in the Pacific region, China's leaders became less concerned with the direct threat of a Soviet attack. Studies of the Soviet Union increasingly emphasized the super-power rivalry, which China along with other countries sought to defuse. They also stressed the primary Soviet interest in European security. The Soviet military buildup along China's border, including in the Mongolian People's Republic, was identified from 1982 as one of three barriers to "normalization," but as far as one could determine from publications, the issue was diminishing in importance.

The problem of monocentric socialism is a serious barrier to improved party-to-party relations. Chinese leaders demand to have their country treated as an equal; specialists recall past Soviet efforts to exert control; Chinese insist on independence. If accepted as a member of the commu-nist bloc, China could be expected to oppose some Soviet foreign policy actions, as in Afghanistan, and, most vehemently, Vietnam's policies in Southeast Asia. The deep antagonism between China and Vietnam, ex-acerbated by the Soviet naval buildup in Vietnam, may be the biggest stumbling block to better Sino-Soviet relations. It is balanced, to a chang-ing degree, by the Taiwan issue in Sino-American relations.

China's foreign policy is explained by two contradictory theories. For more than a decade, the Chinese have failed to resolve or even to address these contradictions. On the one hand, Chinese spokesmen continue to take for granted the theory of socialism. This holds that the world is di-vided into socialist and capitalist countries and that, sooner or later, the former will defeat the latter. From this point of view, China's recognition that the Soviet Union is socialist means implicitly that the two will be aligned in the struggle against the American-led capitalist bloc. On the other hand, beginning with Mao Zedong, China's leaders have articulated the theory of the three worlds. This theory groups the Soviet Union and the United States together as hegemonists or the "First World," whose interests diverge from those of other developed countries in the "Second World," and the countries of Asia, Africa, and Latin America in the "Third World." China identifies itself as part of the "Third World." Reasserted in 1977 and still, in a less vocal manner, largely accepted in the mid-1980s, the theory of three worlds distances China from each of the superpowers. It remains unclear how a socialist country can be an hege-monist. Some Chinese scholars are troubled by this contradiction, but have not been given an opportunity to try to explain it. This does not, however, prevent writings on other foreign policy questions.

Chinese discuss Sino-Soviet relations within several contexts in the field of international relations. One context is the competition for hegem-ony between the two superpowers: the United States and the Soviet

Union. In Chapter Two we consider year by year how Chinese observers have treated the changing balance of power and the relative threat of the two superpowers. Another concept is China's "open-door" policy toward the world economy. This establishes the setting in which economic relations and scientific exchanges with the Soviet Union can take place. A third context is that of the Pacific region and its emerging role within the world. Again, Chapter Two records some changes in China's perceptions of the region, particularly concerning Vietnam, but it may be useful here to present an overview on this region. A fourth context is that of the socialist bloc and how China sees itself in relation to other countries besides the Soviet Union. Sino-Soviet relations per se from 1976 to 1985 are also examined in Chapter Two.

The Open Door

From the time of the Third Plenum in 1978, China has thrown its doors wider and wider open for trade, foreign investment, study abroad, and the import of science and technology. Numerous Chinese statements indicate that it has sought to gain know-how from the world leaders in modern science and production, and that these are the advanced capitalist countries. This policy has been interpreted as tilting toward the United States and Japan and away from the Soviet Union. The Chinese have argued that there is more to learn from the West and Japan concerning production for the world market than from the Soviet Union; yet they have also expressed increased interest in broadening the "open door." Some Eastern European countries have from the outset been prime participants in this process, while the role of the Soviet Union was growing in the mid-1980s.

Despite widespread support for the "open door," there was also opposition within China. An article published in April 1985 speaks of some comrades whose consciousness is one-sided and of misunderstandings of the "open door." In fact, the article says it is wrong to translate *kaifang* as "open door," as foreigners do, using a term from Chinese history. If it is no more than an "open door," China will not be able to avoid the scars of traditional colonialism. It is not just China that is opening to the outside, the world market is likewise opening to China. To justify China's approach, the article draws a parallel with the Soviet Union in the 1930s, when large-scale imports of equipment and technology from the West were made. This, however, is not the same as China's recent opening. Rather it resembles China's policies of the early 1970s, when foreign economic ties were limited to imports and exports rather narrowly interpreted. China had tightly tied its own hands. China's new policies go much further, allowing Chinese firms operating under state guidance to establish direct links with international markets.

After the doors were opened wider with the creation of many more Special Economic Zones in May 1984 and the announcement of the urban economic reform in October, Li Honglin wrote in *People's Daily* about "Socialism and the Open Door to the Outside." He argues that the "open door" is not just an emergency measure, but is the long-term approach that socialism ought to follow. A socialist country is not in danger of losing its purity by opening the door. To think otherwise is feudal and narrowly nationalistic. Capitalist countries gain from the world market, and socialist ones do too. Self-reliance is necessary for a country of one billion people; yet this does not mean closed self-protection. Self-reliance is actually better served by the "open door," because it permits China to absorb the strong points of others and avoid their weaknesses. One of Li's headings is "socialism ought not to fear capitalism." Of course, there is also the mandatory heading, "In the midst of the open door maintain Marxism."[43]

The Pacific Region

In the first half of 1985 within China's international relations circles interest heightened in the concept of the Pacific region. Spurred by the popularity of articles and conferences on this subject in Japan, Europe, and the United States, Chinese were giving it serious thought. An article by Wu Yikang in *Shijie jingji yu zhengzhi neican* reviews the topic and indicates how Chinese leaders are responding to it.[44] It says that observers in the capitalist countries see the Pacific region emerging as the world political and economic center of the twenty-first century. The article does not disagree with the view that this region will have a growing role, but it finds the idea that the future belongs to the Pacific a non-scientific concept. It explains as follows:

In recent years production has become more and more internationalized. Trade, finances, production, and technology are also bringing countries into closer interdependence. This is producing a great change in the world economy, making it more complex. The basic structure, unlike some decades ago, is the coexistence of the capitalist and socialist economic structures within one world economy, accompanied by the rapid rise of the Third World as an economic force. The direction of change is toward multiplicity. America had used its victory in World War II to gain world hegemony among capitalist countries, but gradually it has been

[43] He Liping, "Guanyu duiwai kaifang zhengce hanyi de yidian tantao," *Shijie jingji yu zhengzhi neican*, no. 4 (1985): 50-51; Li Honglin, "Shehuizhuyi he duiwai kaifang," *Renmin ribao*, October 15, 1984, p. 5.

[44] Wu Yikang, "Qian tan shijie jingji de duojihua qushi—jianping weilai shi 'Taipingyang shidai' de tifa," *Shijie jingji yu zhengzhi neican*, no. 4 (1984): 12-17.

falling from its pinnacle. By the 1970s there were three centers in the capitalist world. From 1955 to 1980 the U.S. share of the capitalist world economy fell from 36 percent to 22 percent, while the European Common Market share rose from 12.6 to 22.4 percent and Japan's share shot up from 2.2 to 10 percent. This led to intensified contradictions in the capitalist world. Meanwhile the socialist economic system was also diversifying. The point has been reached where a single, unified socialist camp already will not reappear. Now to reject the stagnant features of the old model of socialism, each country relies on its own special features to build socialism. This trend will accelerate, while the international influence on each economy will also grow. Finally this period has brought the breakup of the imperialist colonial system and the rise of the Third World, which has fundamentally altered the world balance of forces. A total of 130 countries with two-thirds of the world's land and population have 78 percent of the seats in the United Nations. From 1950 to 1980 their economies grew by 450 percent, with industry climbing 700 percent. The Third World countries have on average grown faster than the developed capitalist countries; they are rich in raw materials, which give them great potential. They are challenging the economic hegemony of the developed countries. Nevertheless, wide inequalities in growth rates characterize the Third World, and the twenty-four Western developed countries with three-fifths of the value of world production make the capitalist economy still superior in the world economy. The COMECON countries have one-fifth of the world totals. These are not three separate economies but one big world economy with many centers and much interpenetration. There also continue to be two economic superpowers seeking hegemony but gradually losing control.

This is the context in which Wu discusses the Pacific region of more than thirty countries, greater than one-half of the world population, one-third of the world land area, one-half of the world income, and eighty percent of grain production, rich in raw materials. He predicts that this region will exceed the average economic growth rate in the world to the year 2000, but, he says, that does not mean one should focus on the region as the new world center. Earlier in this century and especially after 1945, America made the mistake of saying, "The twentieth century is the American century." Before that Europe saw itself as the center of the world. These areas were led astray toward reactionary and hegemonistic policies. In the world today, there is growing diversification; there cannot be a single economic or political center. Moreover, no union of the Pacific region is realizable. From the mid-seventies, Americans have advocated this regional concept because their country's hegemony has been weakening. The Soviet military position in the region has strengthened, but it is encountering growing resistance. The Japanese have expressed hopes for an economic sphere, yet these hopes remain only talk and little has been done to realize them. No regional unity or sphere of influence will emerge. It is wrong to think of the future as the era of the Pacific, Wu concludes.

The Socialist Bloc

To argue that socialism is superior to capitalism is necessarily to commend individual socialist societies as superior to capitalist ones. This is not the same, however, as giving blanket approval for the superiority of all features of socialist societies. In Chinese writings since 1979, at least six types of communist movements or communist-led systems are distinguished. Two are treated sparingly: Eurocommunism was a popular theme primarily in 1980-1981, as the Beijing leadership tried to encourage independent stands from the Soviet Communist Party and a renewal of ties with parties that had tended in the past to shun it following the Soviet lead; and there is virtual silence about the domestic policies of the so-called "little hegemonists" of Vietnam and Cuba, whose foreign policies have been vigorously attacked.

By 1985 the Chinese were moving toward a less negative position, at least in articles for internal circulation, on Cuba. An article on Soviet-Cuban relations and Cuban foreign policy refers to harsh talk of Cuba as an "accomplice" and its policies as "local hegemonism," as having a certain one-sidedness, as not accurately reflecting the reality of Soviet-Cuban relations, and as not advantageous for China's need to set its policies toward Cuba correctly.[45] The article reminds readers of the great tension that existed between Cuba and the Soviet Union from 1959 to 1970, noting even that Castro refused to attend the fiftieth anniversary celebration of the Bolshevik Revolution in 1967. It points to 1965-1970 as a time of improving relations (and a big upturn in the Cuban economy), and finally to 1975 to the present as a period of close military cooperation. By the mid-1970s, the Soviet relationship with the United States had changed, as the Soviets assumed the offensive and used Cuba to fan anti-imperialist enthusiasm and to extend Soviet influence in the Third World. The article equates this Soviet approach with the old imperial policy of using barbarians to control barbarians (yi yi zhi yi).

The Soviets struggling for world hegemony and the Cubans seeking to export anti-imperialist revolution had two different strategies. Each pursued its own needs. It is therefore wrong to see Cuban policies as local

[45] Geng Dianzhong, "Chongxin renshi he pingjie Gu Su guanxi he Guba duiwai zhengce," *Shijie jingji yu zhengzhi neican*, no. 4 (1985): 34-38.

hegemony, the 1985 article concludes. They may, on the surface, exhibit petty-bourgeois thinking and leftist adventurism on some matters where action was taken without concrete analysis of Latin American conditions. But on the whole in Central America, after abandoning the guerrilla-war style of the 1960s, Cuban policy is more positive than negative. The foundation exists for armed struggle by the people themselves against the twin enemies, American imperialism and internal dictatorship. Cuban material assistance, including weapons and advisors, is justified. In contrast, Cuban military intervention in Africa is more negative than positive. Despite some positive influence, the Cubans are acting under the direction of a superpower.

A third type of socialism is something of the past, but remains of relevance because it is the common starting point for all socialist countries. It is the old Soviet model—that of the Stalin period—and figures importantly in the chapters that follow. Chinese spokesmen say that this model persisted in China to 1978 and has left its imprint in ways that still must be uprooted. The Chinese press speaks of combatting leftist thought, breaking down traditional viewpoints, and discarding what were long regarded to be the orthodox standards and prescriptions. At the time of the urban reform of October 1984, the economic system that China was establishing was referred to as fundamentally different from the capitalist model and also greatly different from any kind of rigid socialist model. The press charged that fixed conceptions of socialism, formed under the influence of this old model, had blocked reform, and that some people claimed to be defending the purity of socialism by maintaining the old model.[46] Obviously such statements, which usually omit any reference to the Soviet Union, have the previous Soviet model in mind.

For the most recent periods, Chinese sources frequently adopt a three-fold typology of socialist models. At one extreme is Yugoslavia, which after a short stint of acceptability as a desirable model around 1979 and 1980 has become somewhat suspect. Its deemphasis on central planning and other economic features are now normally described as an extreme model of socialism with elements of anarchy and inefficiency. Yet there are still Chinese authors who praise Yugoslavian socialist self-management as an organized form of democracy and freedom that enables the proletariat to achieve a goal of Marxist theory that is essential for the realization of communism, and to rid themselves gradually of alienation.[47] If the centralized state is allowed to persist for a long time, this argument

[46] "Manhuai xinxin duoqu gaige de quanmian shengli," *Renmin ribao*, October 22, 1984; "Zhongyaode shi xiaohua wenjian jingshen," *Renmin ribao*, October 26, 1984.
[47] Su Shaozhi and Guo Shuqing, "Nansilafu shehuizhuyi zizhi zhidu yu Makesizhuyi lilun de guanxi," *Dangdai guowai shehuizhuyi*, no. 2 (1984): 9-16.

holds, the state can easily turn from being the instrument of the working class to becoming its master and a barrier to its liberation. Yugoslavs have responded to this danger by expanding socialist democracy to the extent possible. Yugoslavia has worker self-management. This is Su Shaozhi's positive analysis of Yugoslavia that stands as an exception to the usual mild criticisms of that country in recent Chinese sources, which, in any case, accept the existence of Yugoslavia as socialist and as representative of one of the three current models of socialism.

The middle ground in the increasingly numerous comparative studies of socialism is occupied by Hungary.[48] It represents the happy median between the inadequately centralized economy of Yugoslavia and the excessively centralized Soviet planned economy. From the early urban economic experiments of 1979 and 1980 to the October 1984 urban reform, China's leaders frequently reaffirmed the need for centralized control over pricing, investment, and many other aspects of management. As concern for tighter central control mounted at the end of 1980 and in 1981, when a policy of retrenchment replaced unrealizable plans for massive investment to stimulate growth, Hungary was deemed to be a suitable model. Roughly at the same time, Yugoslavia's economy was entering a tailspin, and China was emerging from its isolation in the socialist bloc that had permitted close economic ties only with Yugoslavia and Romania (after the Albanian connection had abruptly ended) within Eastern Europe. China's new preference for the Hungarian model—and its refusal to refer to China as a separate socialist model, thus associating China directly with Hungary in the middle category of economic management—signaled also its desire to be accepted into the mainstream of the socialist world.

The Soviet Union figures into the Chinese classification system in two ways. It is the primary example of the old model of socialism past, and it is one of five or more examples (along with Bulgaria, Czechoslovakia, East Germany, Poland, and perhaps Romania) of a still quite centralized form of socialism that has developed in the 1950s-1980s. As later chapters show, lively debates have raged in China about socialism past. These have focused almost exclusively on Soviet history from 1917 to the 1950s; there have been scant comparisons with Chinese or Eastern European historical experiences. On the whole, the positions raised have not been linked to any repudiation of this model of socialism under the circum-

---

[48] Zhou Xincheng and Li Jun, "Shiying woguo jiakuai chengshi tizhi gaige," 15; Ding Zeji et al., *Sulian he dongou guojia nongye jingji tizhi de gaige* (Beijing: Nongye chubanshe, 1982), 11-14. On comparisons of Hungary and China, see "Xiongyali jingji xuejia daibiaotuan tan dui Zhongguo jingji gaige de kanfa," *Shijie jingji yu zhengzhi neican*, no. 1 (1984): 49-52.

stances in which it was applied. Yet flexibility, and an opportunity for creative scholarship, arises from the accepted view that the model became
increasingly outdated and inappropriate, and from the controversial view
that there were socialist alternatives to it. Studies of Soviet history provide the principal arena for reexamining the entire process of the transition to socialism (collectivization), and for developing a centralized
planned economy, just as Soviet studies of China were until 1982 the
arena for a similar reexamination of the significant formative experiences
in the history of socialism.

Chinese interest in the Soviet Union in the post-Stalin era serves two
primary purposes, apart from simply following the course of events in a
neighboring superpower. The first and clearly the major objective is to
understand the process of reform away from the old socialist model. The
scope of this inquiry is wide-ranging, including reforms of education, literature, and government as well as policies toward collective farmers,
workers, and intellectuals. Chinese authors make no secret of their interest in helping their own country's modernization and reforms, keeping
them socialist through borrowing from the Soviet experience. Close scrutiny is being given to the emerging program of reform in the 1980s with
this goal in mind. The second objective in Chinese studies of the post-
Stalin period is to show what can go wrong with reform. There is a consensus on two major failures: in the period 1953-1964, the Soviet
leadership under Khrushchev made repeated errors, contributing to
anti-socialist tendencies; and in the decade of the 1970s under Brezhnev,
the Soviet leadership failed to reform vigorously, leaving their country
socialist but wedded to an outdated economic model that was losing its
effectiveness. Writings about these themes as well as about the development of the original socialist model under Stalin and the introduction of
more lively reforms in the 1980s offer valuable information on Chinese
views of socialism, not only in the Soviet Union but throughout the world
and in China itself.

TWO

CHRONOLOGY: YEAR-BY-YEAR
DEVELOPMENTS

It is no simple matter to characterize Chinese views of the Soviet Union over the transitional decade, 1976-1985. There were repeated changes in the perceptions of some matters, but not of others. Shifting attitudes about socialism at home—both economic reforms and ideological reinterpretations—established new standards for evaluating Soviet practices. Foreign policy considerations, especially the state of Sino-Soviet negotiations, figured importantly in Chinese judgments. The Soviet Union itself experienced more flux than at any time since the 1950s. Moreover, emerging Chinese perceptions were not necessarily simultaneously transmitted in *neibu* and openly circulated publications. The persistence of differing interpretations in the era of "one hundred schools of thought contending" after December 1978 also complicates the identification of a consensus changing over relatively short periods of time, such as from year to year.

The following chapters on separate social classes take a topical approach, only noting changes over the period 1979-1985 where they seem pronounced. Short-term variations on these matters are not as easy to discern as on more volatile foreign policy and ideological themes. In order to obtain a broad picture of how the entire constellation of views of the Soviet Union was changing, it is necessary also to take a chronological approach. Altogether, as summarized in Table 2.1, six sets of background factors are treated in this chapter: 1) China's domestic environment, 2) the Soviet domestic environment, 3) the overall international environment, 4) the Sino-Soviet bilateral environment, 5) China's academic developments, and 6) China's views of Soviet foreign policy. Where these factors have already received considerable world attention, I will treat them again briefly to the extent that they are important for understanding perceptions of Soviet society. In addition, drawing on *neibu* publications, I will add other pieces to the puzzle in search of a comprehensive view of changes over time. Reports on the proceedings of conferences in Soviet studies and Marxist ideology also are utilized in this analysis. This

TABLE 2.1

*Background Factors Shaping Chinese Perceptions
of Soviet Society*

China's domestic environment	*The overall international environment*
1. economic reforms	1. Soviet-third country relations
2. ideological concerns	2. Sino-U.S. and Soviet-U.S. relations
3. leadership changes	3. Sino-Eastern European and Sino-Viet-namese relations
The Soviet internal environment	*The Sino-Soviet bilateral environment*
1. economic reforms	1. direct negotiations
2. ideological concerns	2. visits of delegations
3. leadership changes	3. trade and exchanges
China's academic developments	*China's views of Soviet foreign policy*
1. conferences on the Soviet Union	1. views of Soviet hegemonism
2. trends in Soviet studies	2. comparisons of Soviet and American policies.

chapter draws on all types of Chinese publications covering a wide range of subjects related to the Soviet Union to trace changing views from 1976, the year of Mao Zedong's death, to 1985.

1976

In the decade of the Cultural Revolution Chinese domestic politics took precedence in Sino-Soviet relations. Mao's negative views of the Soviet Union (expressed in the authoritative Nine Commentaries of 1963-1964) and his ideological concerns led the Chinese leadership to resist all overtures from the Brezhnev leadership, which after taking power late in 1964 had set as one of its goals an improvement in relations with China.[1] The Soviet Union became a symbol used to discredit Mao's opponents. In the late sixties, Liu Shaoqi was reviled as "China's Khrushchev." Several years later Lin Biao was branded a traitor for "seeking a Soviet nuclear shield." In 1970-1972 China began the process of normalization with the United States, setting back prospects for improved Sino-Soviet relations. The Soviet Union was described as the more dangerous enemy. In 1973 and 1974 radical campaigns intensified, damaging prospects for further improvements in Sino-U.S. relations and, even more, for a positive re-

[1] *Zhong Su lunzhan wenxian (jiuping ji qita)* (Hong Kong: Wenhua ziliao gongyingshe, 1977); Richard Wich, *Sino-Soviet Crisis Politics: A Study of Political Change and Communications* (Cambridge, Mass.: Harvard University Press, 1980), 17, 27-32; Kenneth G. Lieberthal, *Sino-Soviet Conflict in the 1970s: Its Evolution and Implications for the Strategic Triangle* (Santa Monica, Calif.: Rand Corporation, 1978), 69.

sponse to Soviet overtures. When moderates gained the upper hand for a time, Zhou Enlai's January 1975 report to the National People's Congress, which occurred about the time that Deng Xiaoping was promoted to deputy party chairman, was conciliatory toward the Soviet Union. Zhou said that "Moscow was only 'feinting' to the East while in reality threatening the West. This suggested that China no longer considered the Soviet Union to be a threat. Later in the year, Deng Xiaoping released a Soviet helicopter crew which had been held for more than a year and publicized the act, stating that the crew's profession of innocence was 'credible." [2] At the end of 1975 there appeared to be an opportunity for better relations between Moscow and Beijing.

In 1976 the opportunity for improvement was gone. After Zhou Enlai's death in January, radicals seized the offensive. Articles called for preserving the socialist gains of the Cultural Revolution in the struggle against revisionism and capitalist roaders. In February, Hua Guofeng, who was acceptable to the radicals, was named premier. Deng Xiaoping was soon being portrayed as China's "new Khrushchev" for emphasizing production, centralized industry, foreign technology, and educational and scientific reversals of the Cultural Revolution, while failing to fight

TABLE 2.2

Developments in 1976

January	Zhou Enlai dies; Chinese reject Soviet telegram of condolences
February	Renewal of anti-Soviet campaign in mass media
	Strong Criticisms of Soviet economy around time of 25th Party Congress in Moscow
	Hua Guofeng named premier
April	Tiananmen protest demonstration brutally repressed
	Purge of Deng Xiaoping; anti-Soviet campaign persists
September	Mao Zedong dies; Chinese reject Soviet telegram of condolences
	Soviet polemics against China suspended
October	Brezhnev states Soviet readiness to normalize on basis of peaceful coexistence
	Hua Guofeng named party chairman; Soviet telegram rejected
	"Gang of Four" purged
November	China's Foreign Ministry insists position on Soviet Union cannot change
	China calls for an anti-Soviet united front

[2] C. G. Jacobsen, *Sino-Soviet Relations Since Mao: The Chairman's Legacy* (New York: Praeger, 1981), 85.

against revisionism and to grasp class struggle. From early 1976 the Chinese mass media began the most sustained coverage of the Soviet Union since the Sino-Soviet dispute had erupted sixteen years earlier.[3] More than in previous writings, attacks emphasized what was wrong with Soviet domestic conditions. These were diatribes against the Soviet Union often filled with distortions or misinformation. With little delay they were reprinted in English for foreign audiences. Clearly ideological concerns and leadership changes under Mao's waning sponsorship had brought anti-Soviet polemics to a new low.

After Mao's death on September 9, the radicals struggled for a month to rally people around his so-called final instruction "to act according to the principles laid down." Then the "Gang of Four" was arrested and accused of plotting to seize power and of fabricating Mao's final instruction, and immediately thereafter Hua Guofeng was named party chairman on October 7. A turning point was reached in China that brought encouragement to China's academic specialists and most of its citizens, and to governments throughout the world. The Soviet Union had long awaited Mao's death and eagerly sought to capitalize on it to improve relations with Beijing. Yet despite a Soviet moratorium on critical publications, the sending of official telegrams, and the appearance of a series of articles signaling Moscow's interest, the Hua leadership was quick to reassert the anti-Soviet views of the preceding period. The publication of harsh criticisms of the Soviet Union continued in the final months of 1976.[4]

1977

Hua Guofeng remained in charge throughout 1977, although Deng Xiaoping was able to return to the leadership group in mid-year. Valiant efforts were made under Hua to, on the one hand, criticize the "Gang of Four" for numerous shortcomings and, on the other, proclaim that China was unswervingly following Mao's policies. Ideology remained near the center of attention through the campaign against the "Gang of Four" and the attention given to the publication of the fifth volume of Mao's writings. Chinese leaders recognized that the economy was in serious difficulty, but they blamed the problems on the "sabotage of the Gang of Four" and tried to focus attention on old models such as "self-reliance," "learn from Daqing," and "learn from Dazhai." The effort to boost eco-

---

[3] Card catalogues in Chinese libraries list many volumes published in separate provinces, such as *Sulian shi zen yang tuibian wei shehui diguozhuyi de guojia de?* (Shanghai: Shanghai renminchubanshe, 1976).

[4] *Kitaiskaia Narodnaia Respublika v 1976 godu: politika, ekonomika, ideologiia* (Moscow: Nauka, 1978), 201-203.

TABLE 2.3

Developments in 1977

February	Hua Guofeng proclaims "two whatevers" policy to follow Mao unswervingly
April	Volume 5 of Mao's writings issued; revises Mao's views, 1949-1957, conveying anti-Soviet tone; Hua Guofeng criticizes Moscow for trying to enslave China
May	Chinese delegation visits Yugoslavia Soviet Foreign Ministry protests anti-Soviet campaign
July	Deng Xiaoping returns to earlier posts
August	Eleventh Party Congress; accusations against Soviet leaders Deng calls for "seeking truth from practice" Chinese adopt differentiated approach to socialist countries in Europe
September	Yugoslavian leader Tito visits China Deng calls Sino-Soviet rapprochement hopeless
November	*People's Daily* calls for general struggle against Soviet Union Sixtieth anniversary of October Revolution marked by Chinese criticisms Soviet delegation arrives for border talks

nomic growth, however, brought a number of policy changes; for example, specialists were given more opportunity. This was reflected in the field of Soviet studies by compilations of economic statistics that began to provide accurate information for a select readership.[5]

At the beginning of 1977 the campaign against the Soviet Union continued at full speed. Indeed, the "Gang of Four" was accused of failing to pursue the struggle against Moscow sufficiently, especially of overlooking the need for closer political and military ties to other countries that were opposed to the Soviet Union. China's foreign policy tilted sharply toward the West and Japan. Mao's theory of three worlds (the superpowers, their allies, and the Third World) was reinterpreted to support a vigorous struggle against the Soviet Union. Meanwhile, Hua Guofeng was turning to capitalist countries for massive infusions of capital to achieve a giant leap forward in China's economy. Hopes for economic assistance from the capitalists became a new factor in China's anti-Soviet policy.

Leadership considerations and ideological continuity were other factors in China's intense opposition to Moscow. Insecure in his power, Hua pro-

[5] *Sulian shehui diguozhuyi jingji tongji ziliao* (Beijing: Renminchubanshe, 1977); *Sulian jingji jiben ziliao* (Beijing: Zhongguo caizheng jingji chubanshe, 1978).

claimed the "two whatevers" policy, to follow whatever policies and whatever directives Mao had devised. The concept of the "two whatevers" came to symbolize the Hua leadership's resistance to reform, both of state policies and of ideology. Yet the ideological issue appeared to be waning in comparison to increasing foreign policy concerns. China's growing accommodation with Yugoslavia—the symbol of revisionism at the beginning of the sixties before the Chinese directly branded the Soviet Union with that label—suggested that Beijing could coexist with a country that had a reform-oriented approach to socialism. From the visit of a Chinese delegation to Yugoslavia in the spring, to Tito's official visit to China in the fall, relations with Yugoslavia were rapidly improving. Internal discussions around the time of Tito's visit made it clear that many prominent Chinese recognized not only that Yugoslavia is socialist, but also that all of Eastern Europe is socialist. Such recognition in internal sources preceded by more than one year public information to this effect.

Anti-Soviet attacks increasingly centered on the Soviet threat to world peace. Chinese officials warned the United States and other countries against being too soft on the Soviets. They pointed, above all, to the Soviet military buildup as a destabilizing force in the world.

In 1977, continued criticisms of Soviet revisionism were beginning to conflict with China's own policy reforms. For instance, the growing emphasis on giving priority to economic growth and the new recognition of the importance of education and experts in a socialist society were at odds with mass media critiques of Soviet revisionism. By the time of China's Eleventh Party Congress in August, the "Gang of Four" was being accused of erroneous views on the Soviet Union (e.g. of Soviet literature, and insufficient criticisms of it). Not much was written, however, to clear up the confusion about what actually is Soviet revisionism and how had it been wrongly interpreted. When a Soviet delegation arrived for border talks in November, China's leaders were still in no mood to contemplate serious bilateral steps forward.[6]

1978

The decisive year in China's development after the launching of the Cultural Revolution in the mid-sixties was 1978. A year-long struggle between the forces of Hua Guofeng and those of Deng Xiaoping was won by the latter, although it would take another two years before the former were completely routed. The third plenary session of the Central Com-

[6] *Kitaiskaia Narodnaia Respublika v 1976 godu*, 211; and *Kitaiskaia Narodnaia Respublika v 1977 godu: politika, ekonomika, ideologiia* (Moscow: Nauka, 1979), 144-48.

TABLE 2.4

Developments in 1978

February	Hua Guofeng announces ambitious ten-year economic plan
	Deng Xiaoping publicly cleared of guilt in Tiananmen demonstration
	Soviets rebuffed in call for joint statement on principles of bilateral relations
March	Plan approved for development of science and technology to 1985
	China's new constitution fixes Moscow as first enemy
April	Hua says Soviets take advantage of America's lack of will
May	Hu Qiaomu article calls for payment "to each according to his labor"
	Hu Fuming article says, "Practice is the sole criterion for testing truth"
	Delegation to Yugoslavia and conference on its economy recognize it as socialist
June	Sino-Soviet border talks end without progress
	China says border agreement is a precondition for better Soviet relations
August	Hua Guofeng visits Romania and Yugoslavia; attacks Moscow
	Chinese press begins discussion of East European economic management reforms
September	Beijing declares intent not to renew 30-year-old friendship treaty with Moscow
October	Hu Qiaomu article says, "Observe economic laws, speed up the four modernizations"
	Symposia discuss "criterion of truth," revise Mao's ideas
November	Reversal of verdicts on Tiananmen demonstration; stepped-up rehabilitation of cadres
	People's Daily stresses learning from advanced foreign experience
	"Democracy Wall" posters criticize Mao, including anti-Soviet course and theory of "three worlds"
	Beijing attacks new Soviet-Vietnamese treaty
December	Third Plenum establishes new reform course for "four modernizations"
	Sino-American diplomatic relations announced
	China condemns Vietnamese aggression in Kampuchea

mittee, which met in December, has since become known as the turning point in Chinese socialism. At that time China's leadership approved the reform course that became the hallmark of Deng's modernization program. As the balance was shifting against the theories of continuous revolution and class struggle, the media reduced its diatribes against internal Soviet conditions. A delegation of Marxist theorists, including reform figures such as Su Shaozhi, visited Yugoslavia and reported that it is socialist. The concept of revisionism was quickly losing its earlier meaning; yet for both foreign policy and domestic considerations, time was needed to acknowledge this. When Hua Guofeng visited Romania and Yugoslavia in August, he sharply criticized the Soviet Union for its foreign policy.[7] Whatever possibilities may have existed for amelioration of Sino-Soviet strains were being resisted by at least some of China's leaders. (Domestic problems took priority at that time; it was premature for a new foreign policy line to appear.) Following the Vietnamese invasion of Kampuchea and China's strong condemnation of it, foreign policy differences with the Soviet Union intensified at the end of the year. Under these adverse circumstances, Deng Xiaoping joined in the harsh polemics. The announcements that China would not renew its 30-year-old friendship treaty with the Soviet Union and, a few months later, that China and the United States were establishing full diplomatic relations perpetuated the clear tilt toward the West in China's foreign policy.

Publication in May and then in October of articles expressing new views on economic theory indicated a shift in China's approach to socialism. Much that had previously been condemned as revisionist in the Soviet Union was now becoming part of China's own program for socialism. Hu Qiaomu's articles drew attention to using material incentives to reward workers.[8] The struggle between Hua Guofeng's "two whatevers" status quo approach and Deng Xiaoping's "seeking truth from practice" reform approach was decided by the fall in favor of the latter. In November and December, the new course became ever more prominent both in policies and theoretical debates.

During the second half of 1978, there were intense debates about the Soviet Union as well as about how to treat Mao and the history of Chinese communism. The overall focus was Marxist ideology. Prior to this time only bad news or misinformation was expected about the Soviet Union. Those who knew better concealed the truth out of fear. In 1978 they be-

---

[7] *Kitaiskaia Narodnaia Respublika v 1978 godu: politika, ekonomika, ideologiia* (Moscow: Nauka, 1980), 169-72, 180-81.

[8] Stuart R. Schram, *Ideology and Politics in China Since the Third Plenum, 1978-1984* (London: Contemporary China Institute, School of Oriental and African Studies, Research Notes and Studies No. 6, 1984), 5-6.

gan to come forward. During this period a consensus was emerging between the orthodox and reform forces in opposition to the radicals that
relying on misinformation about the Soviet Union had been a serious
mistake for domestic as well as foreign policy. The orthodox group saw
accurate descriptions of rapid Soviet economic growth, advanced training
of scientists and technicians, and improved living standards as a way to
revive a centralized economic system modeled on that of the First Five-
Year Plan in the 1950s. They found support from officials who had been
stationed at the Moscow embassy, including Ambassador Wang Youping,
in their effort to introduce the facts about the contemporary Soviet economy and society. These officials often had positive things to report. They
wondered how the Soviet Union could still be called revisionist if Yugoslavia was now accepted as socialist. The reformers took the approach that
what had gone wrong in China was in large part a result of following the
Soviet model. Unless that model were carefully reexamined, including
research on Stalin's purges and violation of democratic principles,
Chinese socialism would continue to be endangered by a bureaucratic, to-
talitarian system.[9] The reform group favored dispelling inaccuracies not
only about the economic and educational systems of the Soviet Union,
but also about the most sensitive political issues. They took heart from
the recent emphasis in the Chinese press on Yugoslavia's self-management and market economy.

The reform and orthodox groups agreed on at least three things: 1) the
Soviet Union is much better off than China, 2) the Chinese can learn from
the Soviet experience, and 3) there are no signs that Moscow is contemplating an attack against China. These agreements opened the way to research, to applied studies aimed at borrowing from the Soviets, and to reduced tensions through negotiations. Some in the orthodox camp
probably sought through these debates to reimpose a Soviet-type economic system on China and to dramatically improve state-to-state relations. The latter goal was frustrated almost immediately when China
went to war with Vietnam over Kampuchea, and the former goal slipped
gradually from grasp as China's economic reform movement kept gaining
momentum. But both goals intermittently gained new life as leaders continued to give some emphasis to central planning and projects for Sino-
Soviet normalization resurfaced.

When in the second half of 1978 the academic community became
deeply involved in discussions of Marxist theory, these discussions were
scarcely reflected in publications; as researchers met in uncertainty to debate the fundamental questions of socialism, little was published. There

---

[9] "Sulian? Suxiu? ruhe qushe?" *Guangjiaojing*, April 16, 1980, pp. 27-31.

was no clear line to be followed. These were the circumstances under which research on the Soviet Union resumed. The staff at various institutes met to discuss, among other questions, whether the Soviet Union is socialist. Detailed information about the Soviet Union not available to the public began to circulate. By that time many Chinese researchers had already come to the conclusion that the Soviet Union is a socialist society, but the consequences of that conclusion remained unclear.

1979

During the second half of 1978 and even the beginning of 1979, the basic message of Maoist opposition to Soviet revisionism could still be found in Chinese journals. The Soviet Union is beset by social contradictions.

TABLE 2.5
Developments in 1979

January	Deng arrives in U.S., calls for struggle against Soviet hegemonism
	Conference on theory convenes, then reconvenes in March
February	China attacks Vietnam in response to invasion of Kampuchea
	Wang Ruoshui criticizes Mao and cult of personality
March	Arrest of Wei Jingsheng for poster advocating democracy as the "fifth modernization"
	Deng states the four cardinal principles, limits dissent
April	China fails to renew Soviet friendship treaty, but declares willingness to negotiate improved relations
June	Brezhnev agrees to negotiations, but insists they will not be at the expense of the interests of third countries
July	Meeting of ambassadors discusses Soviet Union; Wang Youping reexamines Soviet socialism
September	Sino-Soviet negotiations open in Moscow; Deng expresses pessimism and Beijing continues criticisms
	Conference in Harbin on contemporary Soviet literature sees Soviet Union as socialist
October	Hua Guofeng arrives in Western Europe, calls for anti-Soviet front
November	Delegations to Hungary praise economic reforms
December	Beijing denounces Soviet military actions in Afghanistan
	Deng Xiaoping angry over premature assertions that Soviet Union is socialist
	Chinese publications have stopped calling Moscow revisionist
	Centenary of Stalin's birthday marked by differing views

Brezhnev has adopted methods even craftier than those of the Khrushchev period. The "three peaces" (peaceful coexistence, peaceful transition, peaceful competition) and "two wholes" (party of the whole people, state of the whole people) are counterrevolutionary and revisionist
ideas. Chinese must wage a struggle in the field of philosophy and other
areas against the capitalist class and revisionists who wield power in the
Soviet Union.[10] Yet this message was steadily receding from view. While
the concept of revisionism continued to be used for a time, analyses of the
social class basis for it had lost the popularity that they had had in 1976.
Already a trend was underway to limit criticisms of domestic developments in the Soviet Union. Sometime in 1979, Chinese sources would
stop referring to the Soviet leadership group as a privileged, ruling class,
a state, monopolistic, bureaucratic class, or even as a class of any kind.
The political system would no longer be termed a "fascist dictatorship"
and the economic system "state monopoly capitalism." The vocabulary
for discussing the Soviet Union was changing.

    Given the sharp denunciations of the Soviet Union at the beginning of
the year in conjunction with China's punitive military incursions into
Vietnam, and at the end of the year in response to the Soviet movement
of troops into Afghanistan, it is perhaps surprising that major improvements occurred in Chinese perceptions and in the climate for negotiations. The first months of the year brought some articles that substantially reexamined the nature of socialism, in addition to further
discussions about Mao and other socialist leaders, including those in Soviet history.[11] Most importantly, the wide-ranging conference on theory
under Hu Yaobang's leadership took up many sensitive issues left unresolved at the Third Plenum. Reformers aired a number of sharp challenges to existing orthodoxy. Clearly the discussions, as well as the big
character posters on "Democracy Wall" and elsewhere and the perceived
outbreak of civil disorder, were seen as threatening the socialist system;
for at the end of March, Deng proclaimed the four cardinal principles that
must be upheld. Adherence to the socialist road was the principle that
could be applied against criticisms that seemed most threatening. Support
of the dictatorship of the proletariat justified limiting democracy, but unlike the 1960s this concept was no longer used as a justification for tearing
the society asunder with class struggle. It was instead, especially from
1982, equated with the old concept of people's democratic dictatorship

---

[10] He Qing and Ze Lin, "Ping Sulian zhexuejie guchui de 'shehuizhuyi bianzhengfa',"
Shehuikexue zhanxian (zhexue), no. 4 (1978): 31-35; Zhang Nianfeng, "Ping Debolin de
zhexue sixiang," *Shehuikexue zhanxian* (zhexue), no. 1 (1979): 54-59.

[11] *Neibu* materials were treated with more secrecy before 1979. I have heard of the 1978
sources, but did not find listings in periodical indexes.

that excluded virtually nobody from the right to participate. Approval of the leadership of the Communist Party was also redefined to permit continued debates of sensitive questions, but the debates were to be controlled and limited to authorized participants who accepted the premise of party leadership. Finally, the principle of Marxism-Leninism-Mao Zedong Thought meant that theory continued to have a role despite the popularity of the slogan, "to seek truth from practice." This last principle served as an impetus for studies of the leading theorists of the Marxist tradition and may have been one factor in the revival of historical studies of the Soviet Union, especially of Soviet ideology in the 1920s.[12]

The preference of Deng and other leaders for more balanced foreign policy ties with the two superpowers may have finally begun to win out over Hua's hostility focused on the Soviet threat. Another factor giving the Chinese increased incentive to act and gain leverage was the deterioration of detente between Moscow and Washington, causing Washington to become more eager for Chinese cooperation.

One of the most powerful stimuli for a new Chinese assessment of the Soviet Union was the depressingly sober view of the Chinese economy and social conditions that prevailed in 1979. The officials and academics who had been targets of the Cultural Revolution looked back to a decade or longer of deterioration in China. At first the search for a socialist model of economic relations centered on Romania and Yugoslavia. In 1977-1978, in internal analyses and in public sources, numerous articles appeared about these countries. Nina Halpern has analyzed the public writings and found them uniformly favorable, with a tendency to gloss over differences between the two countries and the specific features of the reforms.[13] She argues that they were intended to support reforms already adopted in China, not to rethink them. Although the Soviet Union was not yet portrayed as a model for socialist reform, the number of articles on it and translations from Russian publications were increasing rapidly in the second half of the year.[14] From 1979 the Soviet Union became the center of attention in internal publications, displacing Eastern European countries. Chinese leaders sought to have a better understanding of the Soviet system, no longer with the goal of criticizing it, but to find guidance for China's reforms.

Two articles first drew public attention to the sweeping reevaluations

[12] *Quanguo baokan suoyin*, nos. 7 and 8 (1979).

[13] Nina P. Halpern, "Learning from Abroad: Chinese Views of the East European Economic Experience, January 1977-June 1981," *Modern China* 11, no. 1 (January 1985): 87.

[14] Gilbert Rozman, "China's Soviet-Watchers in the 1980s: A New Era in Scholarship," *World Politics* 37, no. 4 (July 1985): 447; *Kitaiskaia Narodnaia Respublika v 1979 godu: politika, ekonomika, ideologiia* (Moscow: Nauka, 1981), 156-60.

underway in discussions of the Soviet system. The first appeared in *Wenyi baijia* in December and reported on the Second National Seminar on Contemporary Soviet Literature.[15] It mentioned that the seminar was warmly supported by the Heilongjiang Provincial CCP Committee, that it brought together 116 delegates from 54 units, and that participants spoke freely regarding the nature of the Soviet socialist system, current developments in Soviet literature, and humanism in literature. On the nature of the Soviet system, four views were proposed: 1) Most participants regard Soviet domestic policy to be basically socialist. Its essence has not changed compared to the Stalin era. It has achieved relatively great development in both its economy and in science and technology and has therefore raised the living standard of the people. Proponents of this view made a distinction between foreign and domestic policies. They were opposed by some participants who argued that foreign policy is a continuation of domestic policy: since the Soviet Union is hegemonist, it is very unlikely that it is a socialist system. 2) Quite a number of participants held that there had been no restoration of capitalism in the Soviet Union. Although socialist, it is an imperfect and rigid socialist society different from the open socialism of Yugoslavia and the moderate socialism of Hungary. 3) A small number of comrades argued that the Soviet Union is now revisionist, as seen in its foreign expansion and its ideology. Although the economy is highly developed, the mental attitude and morality of the people are poor. One cannot rely simply on the system of ownership and various economic factors in judging a social system. Even if capitalists and landlords have not returned to power, there can be revisionism or restoration. 4) Finally, some other comrades asserted that it would be hasty to jump to any conclusion regarding the nature of the Soviet social system. It is first necessary to do more research and master a large number of facts. Literary circles should be joined by economists, sociologists, and others to conduct cooperative research to seek out truth before making a relatively correct judgment.

On contemporary Soviet literature there were two views. One was that development has been great; current policy on literature and art has brought expansion and greater variety in subject matters and styles. The other was that Soviet literature has grown worse; it no longer creates the very exciting and inspiring literature found in the 1920s and 1930s. In evaluating literary works, the participants called for an evaluation of Stalin. They noted that Chinese have considered him too narrowly in terms of the formula worked out in late 1956 of "30 percent errors and 70 per-

[15] "Harbin Seminar Examines Soviet Literature, Society," *Wenyi baijia,* no. 2 (1979): 254-56.

cent achievements." As a sign that new critical views of Stalin would now be entertained, the article reported that Chinese must not categorically criticize all works referring to Stalin's errors as attacking and distorting his image.

At the conference there was a relatively heated discussion on the issue of humanism. One group saw it as having a dual nature and advocated critical inheritance of bourgeois humanism, neither totally negating its progressive side nor totally affirming its backward and even reactionary side. A second view was that humanism is in the final analysis something of the bourgeoisie. Although it has its positive role, it should not be advocated. There were also those who distinguished bourgeois and proletarian humanism, using the criterion of whether it supports or opposes the system of private ownership. Finally, some distinguished between human nature and the bourgeois theory of human nature, calling the latter the core of bourgeois humanism and seeing it as relying on "philanthropy" and moral teachings to change the inhumane social system. This negates class struggle. Some participants said human nature exists, but in a class society it should submit to class nature, or individuals should follow their class interests. Others said that human nature and class nature are not diametrically opposed; the proletarian class nature in fact embodies the best of humanity. Still other participants regarded class nature as a sublimation of human nature. There also were participants who accepted the existence of a common human nature, arguing for example that people from all walks of life in all ages have enjoyed the works of the great writers.

Summarizing the results of the conference, the article referred to "definite breakthroughs on certain issues" and "delightful achievements." It called for future seminars on such themes as Tolstoy and Gorky, humanism, and the Soviet literature of the thaw in the 1950s and 1960s. The article concluded with a call for strengthening Soviet literature societies throughout China and stimulating all places to study Soviet literature in a planned way.

In April 1980, an article in a Hong Kong journal reported on a great debate in China over whether the Soviet Union is socialist or revisionist.[16] It began with a review of the same September conference in Harbin on Soviet literature, stating that the majority of participants regard the Soviet Union from Stalin's time as basically socialist. It then summarized two speeches by important figures in the Chinese leadership—Li Yimang, deputy director of the international liaison department of the CCP, and Wang Youping, chairman of the Sino-Soviet Friendship Association and

---

[16] "Sulian? Suxiu? ruhe qushe?" 27-29.

for a time ambassador to the Soviet Union and then deputy foreign minister. Li's remarks on October 9 indicate that Chinese at that time were already proposing to drop the term "revisionism," while keeping the labels "hegemonism" and "social imperialism."

The report of Li Yimang's speech recounts a long list of Soviet attitudes that the Chinese had opposed and his allegation that the struggle was entirely provoked by the Soviet leadership group. Li asserts that the Chinese case was correct and the criticisms were necessary to maintain Marxism-Leninism; yet in retrospect, on some issues (relying on some facts and theories), the Chinese had been excessive and even wrong. These should be corrected on the basis of seeking truth from practice, with regard to Yugoslavia for example.

Adding that the Soviet Union still has public ownership of the means of production and the surplus value of working class production has not become private, Li nevertheless concludes that one cannot rely on these facts to recognize that the Soviet Union is socialist. Why? A real socialist country could not be hegemonist, and the USSR has become more and more so through the 1970s. Li goes on to link the debate over Soviet socialism to views of Chinese foreign policy, asserting that those who place that country in the camp of socialism say it is wrong to treat Moscow as the principal enemy. In contrast, Li argues that the Soviets are an extreme military threat to China. The Sino-Soviet split is much more than an ideological split; therefore China must continue to oppose Moscow and should not recognize it as socialist. This report alerts us to the fact that already in late 1979 there was a strong force in favor of equidistance between Moscow and Washington, which saw the dropping of the revisionist label for the Soviet Union as a step in this direction.

Immediately following the report on Li Yimang's talk in the Hong Kong journal, there appeared an article on a talk by Wang Youping (apparently delivered in the summer of 1979 to the meeting of ambassadors).[17] Wang begins by asserting that Premier Zhou said that Chinese are in the dark about conditions in the Soviet Union. This was because research on the Soviet Union violated the principle of seeking truth from practice. What was reported was whatever was called for by Chinese domestic needs. Premier Zhou said that research, policy, and propaganda must never be lumped together. For a long time Soviets and Chinese called each other names, often distorting the truth. The Soviets accused China of selling 40-50 billion U.S. dollars of opium a year. The Chinese said the Soviets had twelve million unemployed.

Wang points to several types of errors in past Chinese coverage of the

---

[17] Ibid., 30-31.

Soviet Union. First, he mentions the view that all border areas are concentration camps with millions of prisoners, when in fact Soviet convicts are far fewer than in the past and not all dissidents are arrested. In recent years political and psychological tension has been relaxed. Publications may disagree and are much freer than in the past. The mass media exposes the dark side of society and its problems.

Second, Wang asserts that Chinese views of Soviet social classes have been unclear, especially statements that there was a privileged class consisting of factory managers, collective farm chairmen, and those who made more than a certain amount of money. These views lumped the leaders and some others together in an imprecise category of the privileged and failed to note that the privileges of the leaders were much less than in Stalin's time. Brezhnev lives in a five-room apartment, and the former ambassador to China, who is the first secretary of Leningrad province, lives without children in a two-room apartment. Moreover, wage differences have not risen since before the fifties but have diminished, while the living conditions of the masses have notably improved. Prices did not rise much while wages climbed 60 percent from 1965 to 1977. Housing, transportation, water, electricity, and heating are very cheap. More than half of the population has moved into new housing. Most families own television sets and washing machines. Movies are cheap, parks are free. Wang qualifies his praise with the observation that the standard of living of the masses is much below that of the West, and even of Eastern Europe. The Soviet people are not satisfied. Although goods are available and prices are comparatively stable, high-quality and attractive goods are lacking. The people aspire to better living standards, which is a major reason for internal stability.

Wang's third theme is that although speculators exist, Soviet markets are on the whole controlled free markets. Some of the forms of control are worthy of China's attention.

Fourth, Wang acknowledges contradictions, even sharp ones, among Soviet nationalities. Yet he says that the spread of Russian, the posting of Russian cadres in minority areas, and Russian migration into other republics are not so great. When Wang's group visited minority areas, especially along the Baltic and in Central Asia, people's living conditions were all higher than in the vast area of Russia. We learn here of a high-level delegation (consisting, I believe, of six persons) of Chinese officials, who were guests of the Moscow embassy, and who went on a fact-finding mission to parts of the Soviet Union and returned to report to Deng and other leaders on what they found.

Fifth, Wang Youping turns to the issue of tight control. He says that

Soviet control leads to very little pornography and to tighter control over television than in Eastern Europe.

Wang ends his talk with an appeal for much more research. He points first to economic questions, agreeing with the opinion that Soviet economic strength is well developed. He calls the Soviet Union the second strongest country—militarily it also should not be seen as so awesome. It has many inventions, but they have been applied to industry very slowly. It has many goods, but the quality is quite poor. Its reforms are not deep enough in comparison to Hungary and Yugoslavia. Its economy is now at a crossroads; to reverse the gradual decline in growth rates, more thorough reforms are needed. Wang adds that Soviet economists are in the midst of debating new reforms. Wang brings up the question of COMECON. He says that Chinese are accustomed to talking about Soviet exploitation of Eastern Europe, but instead should say that there is mutual advantage. Of course, Moscow uses this economic exchange to control its strategic environment, but if this is not advantageous to Eastern European countries, how are they able to maintain higher living standards than the Soviet Union? Wang notes that political and military relations are another matter.

Finally Wang explains that in China, researchers in many units and research organs have diverse opinions on what is the nature of the Soviet social order. Rather than rushing to conclusions to end these disagreements, careful study and reasoning is needed. Gradually a united understanding can be achieved. Wang's opinions are, I believe, representative of the growing field of Soviet studies that had come alive as a force in the scholarly world in the second half of 1979. They favor serious scholarship and see many favorable things about Soviet society without hiding its perceived blemishes.

The most challenging reform thrust in the field of socialist theory may have been felt in China in the first months of 1979. At that time theoretical debates were still unresolved. The conservative group was still concerned about the radicals and agreed with reform advocates on many changes that were needed. The democracy movement had not yet been disbanded. Under these circumstances, some reformers could argue that while the Soviet Union was not revisionist, as the radicals had long insisted, it was also not socialist in the true sense of that term. This was their opportunity to raise the question of Stalinism and to echo Western criticisms of totalitarianism. Although these daring ideas circulated in copies of speeches distributed by the Office of Research and Investigation under the Secretariat of the Central Committee and by the Chinese Academy of Social Sciences, they did not win the support of China's leaders, and increasingly in the spring they were prohibited by Deng Xiaoping's insistence on upholding the four cardinal principles.[18]

One of the published articles that presented this reform perspective was a study by Su Shaozhi and Feng Lanrui in the spring of 1979, which asserted that according to classical Marxism, China was not yet a socialist country.[19] Su and Feng may have figured that if the standards for socialism could be set higher, the impetus for reform would be that much greater. Orthodox figures including Hu Qiaomu tried to organize criticism of them for this transgression, but it was not very successful. Nevertheless, the limitations on reform interpretations of socialism were somewhat tightened.

China's leaders were increasingly worried in 1979 about the loss of public order. Rising juvenile crime and youth apathy about communism were but two manifestations of popular discontent. Leaders feared that attacks might be turned against the party's right to hold power. The Maoist critique of a privileged class in the Soviet Union abusing its claim to power might gain new sustenance if reinterpreted by reform critics of insufficient democracy. If the radicals and reformers were to join together on this theme, the orthodox defenders of a centralized socialist system as symbolized by the concept of the dictatorship of the proletariat might not be able to prevail. It was necessary therefore to limit the criticism of the Soviet political system. This became clear in 1979 and was a factor in the decision to stop calling that country "revisionist." Debates about the Soviet system continued to be lively through 1979.

It was important for the voices of reform to get the label of revisionism lifted from the Soviet Union. As long as it remained, many of the reformers' concerns, which had been attacked for two decades as aspects of Soviet revisionism, could not be easily publicized. One such theme—humanism—became the central focus of debate in the 1980s. In an article published in 1980, Ru Xin asks if humanism really is revisionism.[20] He begins by noting that for two decades humanism has been criticized as revisionism. At first this was good, says Ru, because it served to protect the purity of Marxism. But, due to simplistic, one-sided thinking, it became an approval of medieval-like anti-humanism. This means to take man as an instrument, as a toy of the emperor, as a commercial object to be freely bought and sold. Ru says that because capitalists try to seize the banners of humanism, democracy, and freedom it is even more necessary

[18] *Selected Works of Deng Xiaoping (1975-1982)* (Beijing: Foreign Languages Press, 1984): 166-91.

[19] Su Shaozhi and Feng Lanrui, "Wuchanjieji qude zhengquan hou de shehui fazhan jieduan wenti," *Jingji yanjiu*, no. 5 (1979): 14-19.

[20] Ru Xin, "Rendaozhuyi jiushi xiuzhengzhuyi," *Renmin ribao*, August 15, 1980.

to speak clearly of Marxist humanism, democracy, and freedom, and other correct interpretations, and to expose the limitations and emptiness of the capitalist uses of these terms. We must wipe out the hysteria against humanism, Ru appealed.

In the late 1970s there was an old guard in China who sought to set an orthodox, pro-Stalin tone for Soviet studies. Among them was Ge Bao-quan, who originally traveled to Moscow as a reporter in March 1935 and later held a top position in the Friendship Association. Ge worked in China's Moscow embassy in the 1950s and retained a role in the Soviet field as an influential translator of Soviet literature and political analyst. In an article in *Shijie zhishi* in commeration of Stalin's one-hundredth birthday in late 1979, Ge favorably recalls the Stalin he had seen.[21] Ge recounts Comrade Mao's 1939 article, "Stalin is a Friend of China," on the occasion of Stalin's sixtieth birthday, and his congratulatory message that Stalin is a leader and friend to the world's people and the Chinese people at the banquet a decade later in honor of Stalin's seventieth birthday. Ge recaps some of Stalin's outstanding achievements and exclaims about this "great historical personage; we will forever admire and respect the anniversary of Comrade Stalin!" Not a negative word about Stalin is uttered in these reminiscences by Ge Baoquan.

From late 1976 through 1978, debates had swirled through official and even some academic circles in China. It is difficult to learn much about them from bibliographies because there were few journals at the time that were indexed for a wide audience. Only in 1979 was the tightly restricted circulation of papers sufficiently relaxed to permit a rapid proliferation of new journals—some *neibu*, to be sure, but not so sensitive that they could not be listed in bibliographies. The issues that rose to the fore in the journals in 1979 and even for a few years thereafter were in many cases already widely discussed in these early debates after Mao's death and the arrest of the "Gang of Four." Concerning the Soviet Union, discussions centered on the meaning and applicability of revisionism, the reevaluation of the Nine Commentaries and of Khrushchev's treatment of Stalin, and the relevance to China of the post-Stalin process of economic reform.

In 1979, decisions were reached that narrowed the scope for debate in the ensuing years. Deng's insistence in March on adherence to the four cardinal principles was an important dividing line. Of perhaps no less importance was Ye Jianying's National Day speech on October 1, 1979, which showed that China's top leaders, including Deng Xiaoping and Chen Yun, had agreed to fix limits on the negative evaluation of Mao. By extension, criticisms of the fundamental domestic nature of the Soviet

[21] Ge Baoquan, "Huiyi wo suo jiandao de Sidalin," *Shijie zhishi*, no. 24 (1979): 1-3.

TABLE 2.6

Developments in 1980

January   Beijing suspends negotiations with Moscow over Afghan issue
             Deng stresses primacy of party unity over democracy

February   Fifth Plenum rehabilitates Liu Shaoqi, elects Hu Yaobang and Zhao
                Ziyang to Politburo; reform group strengthened
             Beijing announces refusal to join Moscow Olympics
             China gains U.S. most-favored-nation status; boon for trade

April   Gromyko asks Beijing to soften foreign policy
             Beijing rebuffs proposal for renewed negotiations
             Chinese trade delegations report favorably on Soviet economic sys-
                tem
             Sino-Soviet Friendship Association in Beijing sponsors film viewing
                in honor of Lenin's birthday
             Chinese reconsider 1963-1964 Nine Commentaries on Soviet revi-
                sionism
             "Struggle Against Revisionism Street" by Soviet Embassy regains
                former name

May   Deng expresses respect for diversity of communist parties
             Beijing seeks to exploit Eurocommunism

June   Moscow plenum sees China in partnership with imperialism

August   China's leaders oppose cult of personality; Mao's portraits reduced
             Deng calls for more democracy to overcome overcentralization
             Deng criticizes Stalin's disruption of socialist legality
             China approves first "special economic zone" near Hong Kong

September   1978 ten-year economic plan deemed a failure; turn to economic
                readjustment

October   Incident on Soviet border provokes exchange of notes
             Beijing protests U.S.-Taiwan agreement on diplomatic privileges

November   Beijing calls on Spanish communist delegation to oppose Moscow
             Deng says Sino-Soviet relations will not improve in 10-20 years un-
                less Moscow changes its entire foreign policy
             Chinese telegram on anniversary of October Revolution calls for
                five principles in Sino-Soviet relations
             Wang Youping attends anniversary party at Russian embassy
             Liao Gailong's report criticizes Stalin's neglect of democracy

December   Politburo favors Hua Guofeng's resignation; Hu Yaobang chosen to
                be party chairman
             Wang Youping expresses condolences at embassy on Kosygin's
                death
             People's Daily says economic chaos requires centralization
             Deng Xiaoping advocates building a socialist spiritual civilization;
                reasserts four cardinal principles

Union—the character of the Soviet social system, the role of Lenin, and the role of Stalin—were brought under this protective umbrella. Ye signaled the end of references to Soviet revisionism by indicating that he doesn't know what revisionism is and that it would be better not to use that term. In concrete respects, it remained to be worked out how far criticism of the Soviet Union might still go. Rather harsh criticisms were not uncommon in 1980-1981; while the Chinese economic reforms were expanding, the leadership was tightening its grip on ideology.

1980

Until the end of 1980, the reform momentum was mounting appreciably, leaving Hua Guofeng and his allies so isolated that by year end his resignation appeared imminent. Early in the year at the Fifth Plenum, the full rehabilitation of Liu Shaoqi signified a complete repudiation of the Cultural Revolution. Mao Zedong fell further into eclipse. Economic policy shifted too—from rapid development to regularization, which meant a restructuring in favor of light industry over heavy. The responsibility system swept through agriculture. At the end of the year, large budget deficits and the failure of grandiose plans led also to renewed interest in centralization. Uncertainty about the direction of urban reforms heightened interest in the patterns of economic reform in other socialist countries, including the Soviet Union.

After China's reluctant suspension of Sino-Soviet negotiations because of the Afghan situation and the announcement that China would join the boycott of the Moscow Olympic Games, relations between Beijing and Moscow only gradually resumed their course of improvement. The most visible figure on the Chinese side was Wang Youping, the man whose earlier speech had been summarized in April by a Hong Kong paper as supportive of a realistic reassessment of Soviet socialism. Late in the year, in his capacity as deputy foreign minister, Wang attended functions at the Soviet embassy to honor the October Revolution and to express China's condolences on the death of Kosygin.[22] Yet these were minor developments in a year marked mostly by hostile accusations between the two countries. The momentum for improved relations that had been building in China in the second half of 1979 was set back by more than one year following the Soviet move into Afghanistan.

Chinese-American ties expanded in 1980, but not as much as one might have expected given the hostile reaction to Moscow's Afghanistan

[22] *Kitaiskaia Narodnaia Respublika v 1980 godu: politika, ekonomika, ideologiia* (Moscow: Nauka, 1984), 237, 127-31.

policies in Beijing. Beijing continued to draw attention to the Taiwan issue, early in the year identifying its return along with the struggle
against hegemonism as one of the priorities for the eighties. When
Washington worked out a form of diplomatic privileges with Taiwan and
Reagan was elected president with promises of closer ties to Taiwan, the
possibility of closer U.S. ties was diminished. Hopes for the Chinese
economy were shifting from massive foreign investment from Japan and
the West to substantial but careful domestic economic reforms. The
Chinese could not afford even the investments to which they had agreed,
and the American market was not opening up as quickly as Chinese desired.

One of the primary themes in 1980 was China's effort to steer a course
in favor of increased democracy without relinquishing party control.
Much attention centered on internal party life, including criticisms of
abuses of power as well as reevaluations of the rights and responsibilities
of party members. Early in the year Deng stressed the primacy of party
unity over democracy, and at the end of the year he joined advocates of
the concept of a socialist spiritual civilization, with warnings against
those who oppose the four cardinal principles.[23] The danger of going too
far in criticism of Mao and of socialism was a recurrent theme despite the
frequent emphasis on the need for less centralized control and a more
democratic system protected by law.

In February, *Hongqi* carried a sharp attack on Soviet foreign policy
with an emphasis on Afghanistan. It reviews the use of the term "internationalism" under Brezhnev in Czechoslovakia, Africa, Kampuchea,
and Afghanistan, calling it reactionary nationalism, hegemonism, social
imperialism, and big nation chauvinism inherited from Russian tsarism.
The article refrains from calling the Soviet Union revisionist, and only
obliquely refers to the relation of contradictions among nations to class
contradictions, without saying anything more concrete about internal
Soviet conditions. In December *Hongqi* returned to the same topic and
was even more critical of the Soviet Union. The article insists that "the
task of continuously exposing the Soviet leaders for pushing a hegemonistic foreign policy under the signboard of 'internationalism' is now more
important than ever." It continues by criticizing Soviet foreign policy in
all regions, claiming that Moscow just uses the slogan of "opposing imperialism and colonialism" in order to take the place of the old-line imperialists. At the end the article draws the conclusions that "the Soviet
Union has repeatedly proven by its own actions that it is no longer a socialist country but is now a social-imperialist country," and "the Soviet

---

[23] *Selected Works of Deng Xiaoping (1975-1982),* 259-68, 335-55.

leaders have completely betrayed Marxism-Leninism and proletarian internationalism and forsaken the principle of socialism." These conclusions are premised on the observation that "the foreign policy of a socialist country is determined by the nature of socialism and the social
system."[24] This article by Yang Hui and Zhang Xihuang seems to follow
the line of Li Yimang's argument a year earlier, indicating that the split
in thinking about the Soviet Union revealed then was still very much in
evidence.

At the end of 1980, *Xinhua* reporter Wang Chongjie wrote about
"acute contradictions in the Soviet economy." He describes the "mal-
formed economic structure," "the flawed management system," and the
"more conspicuous disastrous results." Regarding agricultural production, he claims that "no significant progress has been made in its output
compared with tsarist Russia of more than 60 years ago." The article goes
on to discuss the much higher growth rate of heavy industry, but regards
the resulting imbalance as abnormal and points also to the downward
trend in the industrial growth rate. Wang expresses bewilderment that
with its gigantic scale and great industrial potential, the Soviet Union
cannot satisfy the people's needs for daily-use manufactured consumer
goods. Wang offers two overall explanations: the heavy burden of the
"all-out efforts to expand armaments" and the failings of the economic
management system.

A *Hongqi* article on the occasion of the 110th anniversary of Lenin's
birth also attacks Soviet attempts to dominate the world, stressing Lenin's objections to similar behavior. It uses the term "Brezhnevism" and
talks of the "new tsars of the Kremlin." Comparing Moscow to Washington, the article states, "Soviet social-imperialism is a budding imperialism more desperate, adventurous and deceptive than the imperialism of
the old school."[25]

In late 1979 and 1980 Soviet studies in China had expanded rapidly.
The overwhelming emphasis was on problems. While the Soviet Union
was treated as socialist, its problems were regarded as severe. Both for-

[24] "Proletarian Internationalism and Soviet Hegemonism," *Hongqi*, no. 4 (1980): 14-18;
Yang Hui and Zhang Xihuang, "Internationalism or Hegemonism," *Hongqi*, no. 23 (1980):
44-48, trans. FBIS, PRC International Affairs, Soviet Union, December 17, 1980, pp. C1-
C5.

[25] Wang Chongjie, "The Acute Contradictions in the Economy of the Soviet Union,"
Xinhua, December 26, 1980, trans. FBIS, PRC International Affairs, Soviet Union, January
2, 1981, pp. C2-C4; Peng Pingshan, "Lenin and the National Liberation Movement: Commemorating the 110th Anniversary of Lenin's Birth," *Hongqi*, no. 8 (1980): 40-44, trans.
FBIS, PRC International Affairs, Soviet Union, May 12, 1980, pp. C3-C8.

eign and domestic policies were in error. Conditions were growing worse and, the reader was told, were unlikely to get much better.

On November 25, Radio Beijing broadcast Deng Xiaoping's answers to questions from an editor of the *Christian Science Monitor*. Deng asserts that the main reason for the split at the end of the fifties was the hegemonic aspirations of the Soviet Union and its attempts to bring China under its control. Failing in this aim, Moscow came out against China. The dispute began primarily with ideological problems, but later went far beyond ideological bounds. Deng adds, "Those people who say that Brezhnev is more moderate have, in my opinion, succumbed to deception. Khrushchev simply wagged his tongue whereas Brezhnev engages in threats of force." Deng points to one million Soviet troops along the Chinese border, to its troops in the Mongolian People's Republic (MPR), to its support for Vietnam's aggression, to Soviet threats to ASEAN and the Asian region and the Pacific Ocean, and finally to its troops in Afghanistan. Deng explains that "all the Soviet Union's deeds in countries neighboring China are directed against China and at the same time constitute a threat to the countries of Asia and the whole world. . . . Its extravagant aim is to establish supremacy over the whole world." Deng injects that he has been asked: Will Sino-Soviet relations change? He answers, only if the Soviet Union changes its global strategy and social imperialist policy will relations improve immediately. The Soviet Union must first prove itself by deeds, by abandoning hegemonism, decreasing its border troops to the level of the Khrushchev era, withdrawing all its troops from Afghanistan, the MPR, Southeast Asia, and other regions.[26] These were the tough preconditions set by Deng Xiaoping on November 15, 1980.

Lending support to Deng's pessimism was a report on July 16 by *Xinhua* that Soviet authorities had obstructed a Chinese delegate from attending the International Weightlifting Federation Congress in Moscow in July. The Soviets had been duly informed but refused to issue a visa.[27] The inability even to cooperate at a sports congress indicates the poor state of Sino-Soviet relations at that time.

Progress was more notable within China in the field of scholarship. The death knell for the old usage of "revisionism" was sounded in the journal *Hongqi* in the first issue of 1980.[28] A few months later a major clue to the

[26] "Deng Xiaoping Interview on Sino-Soviet Relations," *Beijing in Russian to the USSR*, trans. FBIS, PRC International Affairs, Soviet Union, November 28, 1980, p. C1.

[27] "USSR 'Obstructs' PRC delegates' attendance at IWF Congress," *Xinhua*, July 16, 1980, trans. FBIS, PRC International Affairs, Soviet Union, July 17, 1980, p. C1.

[28] "Xiuzhengzhuyi de laiyuan ji qi biaoxian xingshi," *Hongqi*, no. 1, (1980): 42-45.

process of reassessing Soviet "revisionism" was reported in the Hong Kong journal *Ming Pao* on May 21.[29] The article begins with the revelation that newcomers from mainland China have told *Ming Pao* correspondents that CASS (the Chinese Academy of Social Sciences) has held a series of forums to review the Nine Commentaries of the early 1960s. Explaining that these important writings about the Soviet Union and revisionism (which, when they appeared in *People's Daily*, gave a definitive account of China's ideological position in the Sino-Soviet split) were prepared under Kang Sheng, the article states that the commentaries have now been sharply attacked and repudiated; Chinese have agreed that their targets were wrong and many of their viewpoints were lopsided. Criticism of Soviet ideas about peaceful coexistence and peaceful competition was mistaken because, among other reasons, Lenin had advocated them. The Soviet theory of peaceful transition is not wrong, for there is no prospect for violent revolution in developed capitalist countries, and it is not entirely wrong for communist parties to take part in parliamentary elections. China was wrong to advocate exporting revolution. It was wrong to criticize the Soviet Union for restoring collective leadership, strengthening enterprise management, and improving relations with Yugoslavia. The article continues that Soviet hegemonism and expansionism, which should have been criticized, were not. As far as the article reveals, there was no mention at the 1980 (and earlier) meetings of the need to criticize internal shortcomings in the Soviet Union. Above all, the meetings freed Soviet studies of the constraints set by Maoist criticisms of revisionism in the first half of the 1960s. The field could now continue to make foreign policy criticisms, while separately writing about economic reforms with fewer restrictions.

The Hong Kong article summarizes the concluding speech by Yu Guangyuan, vice president of CASS. Yu reports that some comrades praised Khrushchev's secret report at the Twentieth Party Congress for mostly tallying with the facts and for being the first summing-up of the experiences in waging a struggle against deviations from socialism. Khrushchev investigated Stalin's mistakes in later years that had aggravated the contradiction between the Soviet people and party and government leaders and initially summed up the matter. Yu notes that some other comrades believe that in the report Khrushchev repudiated Stalin's mistakes in his later years and advocated collective leadership. He con-

---

[29] "The Chinese Academy of Social Sciences Holds Forum to Criticize Kang Sheng's Role in the Nine Comments on the Soviet Union," (Hong Kong) *Ming Pao* (May 21, 1980): 4, trans. FBIS, People's Republic of China, Hong Kong Communist Press, May 29, 1980, p. U1.

cludes that these viewpoints were above criticism. The report was firmly supported by the Soviet people, which showed that its spirit was accepted in general. But, Yu adds, it was unscientific for Khrushchev to entirely negate Stalin because of his mistakes committed in later years. Khrushchev himself eventually reversed himself. Charging that Khrushchev failed because he was a "low-level theoretical leader who often talked irresponsibly and changed his policies and guiding principles constantly," Yu suggests that Chinese bear this historical lesson in mind and then reveals that Deng Xiaoping and Hu Yaobang are interested in the discussion that the meeting has held. The contents will be relayed to universities and colleges throughout China.

Yu's stress on Stalin's errors came in the midst of a boom in publications about Stalin. In the last month or two of 1979, at the time of the one-hundredth anniversary of Stalin's birth, and in early 1980, many articles discussed Stalin's theories. The way was opened for a deeper investigation into Soviet history of the Stalin era and into the alternatives to Stalin present in the 1920s. Nevertheless, a discussion of such sensitive subjects would have to be carried out with some circumspection.

Writings, especially translations, on the subject of Soviet economic reform, were being sent to press from the summer of 1980. Given Deng Xiaoping's anger the previous winter over the premature revelation that Chinese were accepting the existence of socialism in the Soviet Union and the difficult climate produced by Soviet troop movements into Afghanistan, these writings began cautiously and sometimes apologetically. Justifications were given for why these studies or translations were necessary, for example, that because experiments were underway in many Chinese enterprises and complex reforms were being prepared on a vast scale, a first step should be to investigate carefully practices found elsewhere where some circumstances were similar to those facing economic management in China. Factual observations were placed in the context of negative evaluations of Soviet policies. For instance, the preface to one book noted that the fact one should criticize the past twenty years of Soviet expansionism does not mean one should not study and understand other aspects of the Soviet Union. Likewise, comments on Soviet reforms were prefaced by qualifications, such as that they maintained an over-planned system resistant to an adequate role for market forces. In 1980 some reform themes entered into these explanations that would be less evident a year or so later. For example, the Soviet reforms were depicted as too conservative and inadequate because they left the workers powerless. On the other hand, one also finds in some 1980 and even 1981 writings a strongly pro-Stalin orientation that assumes the Soviet Union deteriorated after his death. One book suggests that in 1952 under Stalin, preparations were well under way for carrying out economic reform, backed by Stalin's theoretical focus on the contradictions of the forces of production and the relations of production under socialism. Due to Stalin's death, the source continues, the economic reform could not be realized.[30]

1981

Until the end of the year 1981 there was little improvement in Sino-Soviet relations. China was preoccupied with shoring up controls at home and resolving questions about Mao Zedong and, more generally, leadership in a socialist system. Although the responsibility system was spreading through the countryside, retrenchment had become the slogan in the urban sector, leading to uncertainty about what reforms should follow and increased emphasis on central control. Negative views of the Soviet Union prevailed; both its aggressive foreign policy and its deteriorating economic conditions were the subject of widely publicized articles. At the same time, the number of publications on the Soviet Union climbed sharply, as it had in 1980, with the founding of many journals and a vast expansion of translations.

In the spring of 1981 the first issue appeared of *Sulian dongou wenti*, the premier journal in Soviet studies over the following years. On the first pages, there stands a statement of the journal's goals by Liu Keming, then the director of the Institute of the Soviet Union and Eastern Europe.[31] Liu explains that the foremost task in China's foreign policy is to combat hegemonism. Research on Soviet and Eastern European problems is therefore of great significance. He adds that one of the greatest changes in the world over the past twenty-some years was the betrayal by the Soviet leadership of Marxism-Leninism and proletarian internationalism, turning the world's first socialist country into a social imperialist country. Under the pretext of socialism, internationalism, and supporting revolution, the Soviet leadership group was intensifying militarism, hegemonism, and expansionism, causing the USSR to become the principal breeding ground for the danger of world war. The journal would strive to expose the true face of Soviet hegemonism, to enable people to perceive clearly its dangerous nature.

Liu Keming goes on to discuss other goals of the new journal. He says

[30] Zhou Xincheng et al., eds., *Sulian jingji gaige gaikuang* (Beijing: Zhongguo renmin daxue, 1981), 1-3; *Sulian he bufen dongou guojia jingji gaige* (Beijing: CASS, Institute of World Economies, 1981), 2.

[31] Liu Keming, "Fakanci," *Sulian dongou wenti*, no. 1 (1981): 1-2.

TABLE 2.7

Developments in 1981

January   *People's Daily* New Year's editorial pessimistic on Chinese econ-
            omy, calls for unity and struggle
            Chinese leaders oppose Polish-inspired calls for independent trade
            unions
            Reagan takes office, advocating closer Taiwan ties
            China pessimistic about Soviet economy; blames militarization

February   Deng tells French visitors of growing Soviet threat

March   Brezhnev at Twenty-Sixth Congress repeats interests in normali-
            zation
            China silent about Moscow's call for confidence-building steps in Far
            East
            Kapitsa visits Beijing; navigation and railroad agreements follow
            Deng criticizes movie, "Bitter Love"; campaign against "bourgeois
            liberalization," for "socialist spiritual civilization"

April   Chinese leaders agree on assessment of Mao

June   Sixth Plenum says Mao's contributions far outweigh mistakes
            Hu Yaobang elected party chairman; Zhao Ziyang becomes premier
            Moscow interprets meeting as whitewash of Mao and no change of
            course
            People's Daily raises anew "unequal treaties," border disputes
            Problems of economic reform delay Twelfth Party Congress

July   Deng opposes laxity and weakness in combatting anti-socialism

September   Moscow proposes negotiations on border problems

November   Chinese sports delegation joins Moscow gymnastics congress

December   *Hongqi* calls Moscow the world's biggest oppressor
            Sino-Soviet trade registers sharp decline in 1981
            Scientific delegations go back and forth, but Beijing silent on pro-
            posal for exchange agreement
            Beijing agrees to talks on border problems, but calls for preparatory
            work

that China needs to study the experiences and lessons of the Soviet Union
from the time of the October Revolution. Lenin opened the road to socialism in Russia. Stalin continued it, leading the country from backwardness to become a strong socialist state, to defeat fascism, and to perform a great service for the progress of humanity. Liu finds both some
problems and many lessons worth studying and applying in the history
of the first socialist country. On domestic issues it is necessary to distinguish right and wrong in the Soviet historical experience. Although
China opposes the hegemonism of the Soviet leadership, it continuously

cherishes friendly and respectful feelings toward the Soviet people and the glorious traditions of the Russian Revolution. Liu adds that it is necessary scientifically to study and sum up the actual experiences of Soviet historical development.

The approach to Soviet studies in Liu's article expresses the leadership's aims for the burgeoning literature on that country. Marxist-Leninist and Mao Zedong Thought must be the guide; the study of actual conditions and theory must be combined, as must contemporary and historical studies; research on separate countries must be joined with comparative study of the Soviet Union and the countries of Eastern Europe. "We must liberate thinking, seek truth from practice, conduct research and investigations, obtain scientific conclusions corresponding to reality through research on problems of the Soviet Union and Eastern Europe, deepen recognition of the important significance of the international struggle against hegemonism, deepen recognition of the extreme importance in our country of supporting the socialist path, supporting the people's democratic dictatorship, supporting the leadership of the party, supporting Marxism-Leninism, Mao Zedong Thought."

This issue of *Sulian dongou wenti* maintains a consistently negative tone. The following articles by Xing Shugang and Xu Kui concentrate on Soviet hegemonism.[32] The negative viewpoint is evident also in the two book reviews presented in the journal.

The first, a review of a 1979 Yugoslavian communist periodical on Soviet orthodox thought in philosophy, finds that Soviet writings are not scientific and are even nonMarxist. The entire review stresses the negative, dogmatic side of Soviet philosophy. A second review of a 1975 Western European book on the political system of communism, translated from the 1978 Japanese edition, repeats the view that the Soviet Union is an anti-democratic, bureaucratic system and a distortion of socialism. It is a bureaucratic monopoly system, not a socialist one. Policies are selected to serve the interest of the party bureaucracy, not the party itself or even less the working class. The review mentions the existence of a privileged stratum, adding that the current leaders, to escape from their own responsibility, blame all the evils on the character of Stalin's personality. Khrushchev tried to transfer blame to the cult of personality to avoid criticism of the bureaucratic system. Under Brezhnev the bureaucratic system has developed further. The West German source is even quoted to the effect that the phenomenon of alienation has deepened in

---

[32] Xing Shugang, "Guanyu Sulian quanqiu kuozhang zhanlue de jige wenti," *Sulian dongou wenti*, no. 1 (1981): 3-9; Xu Kui, "Yici jixu jianchi baquanzhuyi zhengce de daibiao dahui: ping Sugong ershiliu da," *Sulian dongou wenti*, no. 1 (1981): 10-13.

Soviet development. The people have no real democratic freedoms. Exploitation by state bureaucrats has replaced exploitation by private capitalists. The bureaucrats strive to build up the military, while ignoring the people's living conditions.[33]

Sun Chengmu's review of Chinese publications in 1981 on modern and contemporary Russian history leaves no doubt about the emphasis given to foreign aggression. He notes that study of the history of tsarist Russia's aggressive expansion has been an important topic in recent years and then comments on new additions to the field. Later in his review article, Sun asserts that in 1981 there was comparatively great interest among historians of Russia in Russian military feudal imperialism, an epithet used to describe foreign policy in the decades just before the October Revolution.[34]

The Sino-Soviet boundary question reemerged as an issue. In June *People's Daily* published some excerpts from an article by Li Huiquan, one of the negotiators in earlier border talks and the director of the Institute of International Studies, which was soon to appear in *Guoji wenti yanjiu*, refuting "lies" spread by the Soviet side about the Sino-Soviet border talks. The article accuses Moscow of trying to convince the world that China has obstructed resolution of the border question. It asserts that the Chinese government agrees to take the Sino-Russian unequal treaties as the sole basis for solving boundary questions and insists that there is not the slightest trace of territorial claim in China's stand. In contrast, it contends, Moscow demands that boundary decisions be based on "historically formed" and "actually defended" lines, thus seeking to include areas that extend beyond the treaty lines and were annexed by tsarist Russia and the Soviet Union. The article claims that on September 11, 1969, an understanding was reached between the two premiers, Zhou Enlai and Kosygin, which provided a starting point for talks, but afterward the Soviet Union changed its mind and created new obstacles. Zhou and Kosygin agreed that the dispute on principles should not affect the normalization of state relations and that the border talks should be held under nonthreatening circumstances. Moscow, however, denied that any understanding had been reached and insisted that there are no disputed areas on the Sino-Soviet border. The full journal article concludes, "Obviously, the military threats and hegemonistic policy of the Soviet Union

[33] " 'Jinri Sulian zhexue de zhengtong sixiang,' yiwen jianjie," *Sulian dongou wenti*, no. 1 (1981): 52-53; "Sulian guanliao tongzhi de shizhi: 'gongchanzhuyi zhengquan tixi' yishu jianjie," *Sulian dongou wenti*, no. 1 (1981): 56-57.
[34] Sun Chengmu, "Sulian jinxiandaishi," *Zhongguo lishixue nianjian 1982* (Beijing: Renminchubanshe, 1982), 225-28; Li Yuanming, "Historical Roots of Soviet Hegemonism," *Hongqi*, no. 17 (September 1981): 25.

against China are the fundamental obstacles to the settlement of the Sino-Soviet boundary question and the normalization of Sino-Soviet state relations."[35] Despite the overall negative tone, at last the Chinese appeared to be holding out some hope of normalization and suggesting that it depended primarily on Soviet actions in territories along the Chinese border.

Writings on the current Soviet economy remained pessimistic in 1981. On the eve of the Twenty-sixth Congress, Mei Wenbin wrote an article in *People's Daily* under the title, "The Soviet Economy Is in a State of Stagnation." He talks about a "vicious circle of retrogression in recent years" and the negative effects of "frenzied arms expansion and war preparations and its enforcement of hegemonism. . . . The result is an acute shortage of consumer goods, inability to meet market demands and failure to satisfy the people's basic needs." Because economic slowdown is, to a very great extent, the result of militarization of the economy, while external expansion and the pursuit of world hegemony are established Soviet policies, Mei concludes, "We cannot be optimistic about the prospects for Soviet economic development."[36]

Three months later, *People's Daily* carried an article by the economist Lu Nanquan on problems of the Soviet economy that barely mentioned hegemonism. Its focus was inefficient investment in capital construction. Lu reports that the Soviet national income increased by an average of 7.6 percent a year from 1951 to 1979, and that total investment in capital construction rose from thirty percent of the U.S. level in 1950 to overtake the U.S. in the first half of the 1970s. The huge investment helped build a sound industrial base, but overreliance on this method of economic growth, Lu argues, "is beginning to seriously affect economic efficiency." Low efficiency of investment, in his view, is the main cause for the continuous drop in the rate of economic growth.

Later in the year Lu and Zhou Rongkun wrote again about the problems of the Soviet economy. They explain that "in the last 10 years, the overall economic strength of the Soviet Union has been continuously on the increase. Comparing 1980 with 1970, the gross social product increased by 67 percent; the gross industrial output value alone grew by 78 percent. The national income used in consumption and accumulations in-

---

[35] Li Huiquan, "Where Does the Crux of the Sino-Soviet Border Talks Lie?" *Renmin ribao*, June 17, 1981, p. 7, trans. FBIS, PRC International Affairs, Soviet Union, June 18, 1981, pp. C1-C7; and Li Huiquan, "The Crux of the Sino-Soviet Border Question," *China and the World* (Beijing: Beijing Review, Foreign Affairs Series, 1982), 72.

[36] Mei Wenbin, "The Soviet Economy Is in a State of Stagnation," *Renmin ribao*, February 20, 1981, p. 6, trans. FBIS, PRC International Affairs, Soviet Union, March 4, 1981, pp. C1-C3.

creased by 55 percent. Industrial production in over 20 items, such as petroleum, steel, chemical fertilizers, cement, cotton textiles, etc., exceeded
the production of the United States and jumped to the top position in the
world. Since the development of the Soviet economy (mainly during the
years from 1971 to 1975) was relatively rapid, the distance by which it
lags behind American economic strength was being reduced." Lu and
Zhou stress, however, that the gap stopped narrowing; in both 1975 and
1980 Soviet national income and the value of industrial output was 67 and
80 percent, respectively, of American figures. They argue that the Soviet
slowdown resulted from longstanding contradictions in the economy, the
difficulty of converting from extensive to intensive factors to raise productivity as the extensive factors weakened, low investment efficiency,
agricultural difficulties, the heavier burden of armaments, a lopsided economic structure, and defects in the system of economic management.
Due to restrictions of the Soviet system of socialist administration, it is
difficult to effect far-reaching reforms, while the contradictions will continue to grow more serious. Lu and Zhou conclude, "The economic
growth of the Soviet Union in the 1980s will still be at a low level and
slow."[37]

The Chinese yearbook, *Survey of International Affairs 1982*, reviews
developments in 1981 with many negative observations about the Soviet
Union. It asserts that the Soviet Union was in a difficult situation internally and externally. Internationally it was completely isolated. Domestic economic problems were increasing. This was a year when Moscow
continued to carry out an aggressive policy around the world. Chen
Qimao and Liu Guangqing of Shanghai are the authors of this section.
Later in the book, a second section by Lu Nanquan and Gao Zhongyi focuses on the Soviet economy. Its tone is less negative. It begins with the
assertion that the Soviet economy maintained some growth, and in comparison to Western countries, its speed of development was even quite
fast. Some important industrial products such as natural gas, computers,
tractors, and furniture exceeded the annual plan targets. Increases in real
income and wages surpassed the targets. Again in 1981 ten million persons improved their housing conditions. Yet, the authors concede, it was
a difficult year for the Soviet economy, and the vast majority of indicators
were not met. Why were results poor? Lu and Gao point to the direct
cause of a bad harvest, then to the failure of measures to reform the eco-

---

[37] Lu Nanquan, "Principal Problems of the Soviet Economy," *Renmin ribao*, June 11,
1981, p. 11, trans. FBIS, PRC International Affairs, Soviet Union, June 23, 1981, pp. C2-
C5; Lu Nanquan and Zhou Rongkun, "Major Problems Faced by the Soviet Economy,"
Guoji wenti yanjiu, no. 2 (October 1981): 35-43, trans. JPRS 19689 December 18, 1981 CR/
PSm 250, S19, pp. 5-20.

nomic system to yield notable results, and finally to the worsening situations with regard to expanding the labor force and natural resources. They add that the fundamental problem was the further development of long-term contradictions and problems in the Soviet economy. Three are mentioned: 1) bureaucratization of the political system and lack of motivation due to stifled mass participation in the management of production; 2) a backward system of economic management that does not meet the need to transform the existing economic strategy; and 3) the vast burden of military expenditures. The authors predict another difficult year in 1982.[38]

More realistic coverage of the Soviet economy in 1981 corresponds to the changing coverage of Eastern Europe noted by Nina P. Halpern. In her view, the decision in favor of readjustment in the Chinese economy to reduce the large budget deficit, inflation, uncontrollable capital construction, and imports led to increased attention to readjustments in Eastern European economies. After the Chinese government deemphasized urban reform, articles on Romania and Yugoslavia began to express more reservations.[39] New appreciation of the need for central controls over the economy also heightened interest in the Soviet economy.

Along with a reassessment of Mao came a reassessment of Stalin. Indeed, the decision on how to weigh Mao's pros and cons was resolved almost exactly in the manner the Chinese leadership under Mao had decided a quarter-century earlier how to evaluate Stalin. The pros outweighed the cons, the later years were more negative than the earlier ones, some opponents who had offered an alternative vision of socialism had been unjustly persecuted. Articles on Bukharin in 1981 discussed in a favorable tone an alternative to Stalin's approach. In November, *Hongqi* summed up the discussion of Stalin, alleging that leaders in the international communist movement had committed three grievous deviations: the cult of the personality, lifelong tenure, and excessive concentration of power. All of these errors were in contradiction to Lenin's vision of socialism. The civil war in 1918 had necessitated a high degree of centralism, making it impossible for Lenin's vision to be realized. At the same time, Lenin sought to counter a leftist ideological tendency associated with Kautsky and Bauer in the international communist movement, leading him to emphasize unanimity of the leaders and the party as a collective and the need for centralization and discipline. The article contends that Stalin made serious mistakes and explains that it points

---

[38] Shanghai guoji wenti yanjiusuo, ed., *Guoji xingshi nianjian 1982* (Shanghai: Zhongguo dabaikequanshu chubanshe, 1982), 25-33 and 273-85.

[39] Halpern, "Learning from Abroad," 77-109.

them out "to draw lessons from them and eliminate their negative influence upon our party. We do not have the slightest intention of negating the great meritorious achievements and outstanding contributions."[40] The article appeared to be a warning against going too far in criticisms of Stalin, while it was also a further indication that studies of Stalin could continue to discuss his errors as well as his contributions.

From 1979, reform voices in China had been directing attention to mistakes committed by Stalin and his continuing impact on socialist political systems. Some of these articles were brought together in an English-language edition for 1981 put out by the Institute of Marxism-Leninism-Mao Zedong Thought under the Chinese Academy of Social Sciences. The first article, by Yu Guangyuan, insists that Stalin's views of the dictatorship of the proletariat did not lead to a step-by-step transition to enable the workers "to fully exercise their rights as masters of the socialist state." Contrary to Lenin's views, Stalin did not see the dictatorship of the party yielding to the increasing involvement of soviets and other mass organizations in solving important questions. The second article, by Wang Huide, asserts that the purpose of socialist production is to satisfy the material and cultural needs of the people, and he quotes Stalin in support of this end. The following article, by Su Shaozhi, stresses democratic management in Chinese enterprises, including worker assessment, supervision, and election of leading personnel.

In another article in this book, Su criticizes Stalin for "the erroneous theory of class struggle becoming increasingly sharp, which resulted in the magnification of the struggle for eliminating counter-revolutionaries in the Soviet Union in the late thirties." Su contrasts the correct criticism of Stalin in 1956 for intensifying the class struggle in the Soviet Union to the accusation in the Ninth Commentary which appeared in *People's Daily* in 1964, that Stalin one-sidedly stressed the internal homogeneity of socialist society and refused to recognize class struggle. Then Chinese leaders carried Stalin's mistake of magnifying class struggle further.

Another article by Yu Guangyuan reports a speech he gave on August 6, 1979 to what is called "a study class of the 'socialism' section of political economy." In it, Yu calls for comparative study of the forms of organization of the socialist economy adopted by various countries, starting from the Soviet model and leading to increasing differences beginning in Yugoslavia of the 1950s and including some countries such as Hungary in the 1960s, that adopted economic forms quite unlike that of the Soviet

[40] Yin Chengshan, "How Should Deviations on the Question of Leaders in the International Communist Movement Be Understood and What Is Their Negative Impact on Our Party?" *Hongqi*, no. 22 (November 16, 1981): 32-34, trans. FBIS, PRC National Affairs, December 4, 1981, pp. K22-K24.

Union.[41] It is clear that as early as the summer of 1979 the concept of three models of socialism—Yugoslavian, Hungarian, and Soviet—already was under discussion, and consideration was being given to comparative study. The fact that this speech could be published in April 1981 indicates that the three-fold division and the plan for comparative study were no longer as controversial.

The reform forces kept up their struggle for more democracy: Liao Gailong gave a report in October 1981 recalling Mao's remark in his 1960 reading notes on a Soviet political economy textbook that the Soviet constitution gave workers various rights, but "no right to supervise the state, the economy, culture and education, whereas these were the most fundamental rights of the people. . . . Without democracy, he argues, the productive forces cannot develop, and you will move toward the 'dead end of Soviet-style socialism.' "[42]

In 1980-1982 there were many translations of reform socialist views. Reform writings of the Soviet 1920s, the "Prague Spring," and Eurocommunism all appeared. If direct advocacy in print of similar reform ideas was uncommon, translations could fill the gap and add to the information that would sustain a reform perspective.

The trend in 1981 was, however, toward tightened control over intellectual and artistic criticisms of socialism. The slogan of "socialist spiritual civilization" was widely cited toward this end, and the movie "Bitter Love" was singled out as an example of a deviation from the four cardinal principles, and of the dangers of "bourgeois liberalization." Renewed interest in centralization made Chinese more aware of similarities with the Soviet Union and increased their interest in Soviet experiences, especially with economic reforms.

In late 1980 and early 1981, the Chinese Communist Party felt threatened by shifting political tides inside China and uncertain prospects for economic growth. Democratization was producing some unpleasant byproducts. At universities, students who were running for office won applause when they announced that they are not members of the Commu-

---

[41] Yu Guangyuan, "On the Question of Exercise of Proletarian Dictatorship 'By the Party' and then 'By an Organization Embracing the Whole Proletariat'—Study Notes," 21-23; Wang Huide, "Some Questions About the Purpose of Socialist Production," 10; Su Shaozhi, "Some Questions in China's Socialist Economic Construction," 19; Su Shaozhi, "Tentative Views on the Class Situation and Class Struggle in China at the Present Stage," 33-38; Yu Guangyuan, "Some Theoretical Questions Concerning the Socialist Economy," 20; in *Selected Writings on Studies of Marxism* (Beijing: Institute of Marxism-Leninism-Mao Zedong Thought, Chinese Academy of Social Sciences, 1981).

[42] Stuart R. Schram, "Economics in Command? Ideology and Policy Since the Third Plenum, 1978-84," *The China Quarterly* 99 (September 1984): 427-28.

nist Party, while polls showed that a majority of the students do not
believe in Marxism. Many party leaders felt a need to reassert control.

The reevaluation of Mao in 1981 was part of a strategy to provide answers—or at least clear guidelines—to resolve an unsettled situation. As
part of the decision, it was agreed not to criticize Chinese foreign policy
under Mao. This also closed the door to any effort to reduce Soviet blame
for the Sino-Soviet split. In fact, the resolution praised Mao's "just struggle" against Moscow, but reinterpreted it as a struggle against "big nation
chauvinism," not revisionism. Harsh negative assessments of Soviet domestic conditions, which had gradually been declining since 1978, remained common in 1981 before essentially disappearing in 1982. Sharp
criticisms of Soviet foreign policy would not begin to slacken until 1982.

Cycles of open debate and intensified censorship have marked the years
since the Third Plenum in 1978. In mid-1979, early 1981, and late 1983,
there were new restrictions placed on publications, while in early 1979,
early 1983, early 1985, and certain other times, a greater degree of openness prevailed. In 1979, repression of the democracy movement led to renewed reticence in political discussions, but perhaps the most decisive
clampdown occurred in connection with the criticism of Bai Hua in 1981
for his movie script, "Bitter Love." Rumors quickly spread that groups
had been named to check all publications over the previous two years in
order to identify those who were disloyal. Thoughts went back to the recurrent antirightist movements in the first three decades of the PRC.
Journals, including university bulletins, became less lively; they turned
to less controversial topics. While the *neibu* journals would become increasingly lively, the journals available to foreigners have still not fully
recovered from this blow. With their emphasis on translations from Russian, the *neibu* publications of 1980-1981 had become a powerful force for
factual coverage of the Soviet Union. Gradually a discrepancy between
open and *neibu* writings on the Soviet Union was developing as the open
materials were slower to turn from the negative assessments of 1980-
1981.

1982

In the last months of 1981 and early 1982, Deng Xiaoping and the
Chinese leadership decided to respond to Soviet overtures with some
small steps of encouragement. Many factors apparently intersected to
produce this turnabout: new eagerness to establish a more independent
foreign policy; increased disillusionment with the United States and its
capitalist allies, especially in response to Reagan administration views on
Taiwan and the transfer of advanced technology; sharpened perceptions

Table 2.8
Developments in 1982

January
Soviets agree to expand transshipments by railroad between China and Europe

Beijing proposes expansion of trade in 1982

Chinese arrange for guests of Soviet embassy to visit enterprises, institutes

Liaowang article describes growing ties with Western European communist parties

February
Chinese sportsmen join in biathlon in Moscow

Chinese economics group begins two-month visit to USSR

March
Brezhnev recognizes China as socialist; calls for talks without preconditions

Kapitsa visits China again

May
CASS conference held on Soviet economy

Soviets report on widened study in PRC of Soviet literature, science, economy

June
Soviet sportsmen join in Beijing track-and-field meet

August
Sino-American communiqué on Taiwan arms sale

Liberation Army Daily issues self-criticism for denying importance of education and science in socialist spiritual civilization

Conference held on the history of the international communist movement

Yu Hongliang visits the Soviet Union

September
Hu Yaobang calls for independent foreign policy

Twelfth Party Congress dubs Moscow as Number One enemy, Washington Number Two

Hu says Beijing will judge Moscow by deeds not words; possibility of normalization exists

Sino-Soviet negotiations announced for October

Zhao Ziyang identifies "three obstacles" to normalization of relations

China's National Association for Soviet and East European Studies secretly established

November
Brezhnev dies; Andropov succeeds him

Chinese issue optimistic message

December
Chinese are quick to note Andropov's reform agenda

of the relevance of Soviet and Eastern European reform experiences to China; changing expectations of the leadership that would likely replace Brezhnev; and the consolidation of power by Deng Xiaoping. Visits to the Soviet embassy in Beijing by influential Soviet sinologists and foreign ministry officials M. S. Kapitsa and S. L. Tikhvinsky and their success in arranging meetings and learning of China's interest in better relations encouraged the Soviet leadership. In early March 1982, Soviet spokesmen were already predicting normalization with China. Vladimir A. Krivtsov made that prediction in an interview with a Japanese correspondent. He also contrasted Deng's inclination toward imperialism (a close Sino-U.S. relationship) and rightist socioeconomic policies with the views of Ye Jianying, Chen Yun, Hua Guofeng, and China's military leaders. Krivtsov referred to Deng Xiaoping's "arbitrary anti-Sovietism." In March, Brezhnev was sufficiently encouraged to issue his important Tashkent speech, recognizing China as socialist and calling for talks without preconditions. By May, Soviets were additionally emboldened to write optimistically in *Pravda* under the authoritative byline of Aleksandrov and for Kapitsa, using the pseudonym Ukraintsev, to report on the many positive steps over the past half-year in Sino-Soviet relations.[43]

Various Chinese delegations to the Soviet Union wrote reports that helped shape impressions of that country. At first these were informal delegations attached to the Chinese embassy in Moscow. Eastern European capitals had to suffice in some cases; for example, Yu Guangyuan went as a guest of the Chinese embassy in Budapest. A group from the International Liaison Department under the Central Committee, which remained the foremost center of Soviet-watching until the Institute of the Soviet Union and Eastern Europe was detached from it at the end of 1980, went to Moscow in the last months of 1978. In late 1981, a delegation went from the Central Committee's party school. These fact-finding missions of roughly two months each drew some positive conclusions—conditions in the contemporary Soviet economy are better than were earlier thought, China can learn much from the Soviet experience, there is no danger of a Soviet attack on China—and some negative ones about the immediate problems in the USSR faced by an aging leadership slow to reform.

One of the most publicized delegations consisted of three economists who, also in the capacity of guests of the Chinese embassy, studied the

[43] Gilbert Rozman, "Moscow's China-Watchers in the Post-Mao Era: The Response to a Changing China," *The China Quarterly* 94 (June 1983): 216; Hajime Suzuki, "Soviet Academician Discusses Relations with PRC," *Sankei shimbun*, March 6, 1982, p. 5, trans. FBIS, USSR Annex, March 12, 1982, pp. 1-4.

Soviet economic management system from February to April 1982. This was a critical period for improving relations, producing the first signals by Brezhnev that Moscow accepts the PRC as socialist and is optimistic that negotiations leading to normalization would soon begin. Within China intense debates were underway, in which the Soviet Union and Eastern European countries figured importantly, on the proper balance between central planning and market forces. What the group of Liu Guoguang, Liu Suinian, and Zheng Li (at least two of whom had been Soviet-trained in the 1950s) reported on the Soviet economic system in a book on their trip, *Sulian jingji guanli tizhi kaocha ciliao*, figured into these debates.[44] Liu Suinian predictably represented the views of his own Institute of Economics under the Planning Commission and argued for strengthening centralized planning. In contrast, Liu Guoguang, the director of the Economics Institute under the Chinese Academy of Social Sciences, appeared to seek further relaxation in the controls of centralized plans. The fact that his openly stated views seemed to oppose the position in support of strengthening central planning adopted by Hu Yaobang at the Twelfth Party Congress, which had just taken place, put Liu Guoguang in a difficult position for a time. The stance of Liu Suinian, which apparently reflected Chen Yun's position, disagreed with Liu Guoguang's emphasis on market forces.

The group's 300-page coauthored book offers a factual account of twenty-seven meetings with Soviet economists and responsible personnel in production units as well as translations of documents. It also contains the group's report, reviewing Soviet management reforms from 1957, analyzing the current situation (central-local relations, state, enterprise, and worker authority in making economic decisions, etc.). By the time it appeared in 1983, there was already a substantial literature in Chinese on the problems and prospects of reform in the Soviet economic management system.

Shortly after the economics delegation's return from Moscow, the Chinese Academy of Social Sciences sponsored a large conference on the Soviet economy. Whereas in 1977-1979 economists (and over 100 delegations) had most prominently discussed the Yugoslavian system, and from late 1979 through 1981 Hungary had become the apparent focus of discussion, the spring 1982 conference left little doubt that by this time the Soviet economic management system had at last attracted the most attention. The overall judgment on the Soviet planning system was mixed; many positive things were said, and the system was seen by many

---

[44] Liu Guoguang, Liu Suinian, Zheng Li, eds., *Sulian jingji guanli tizhi kaocha ziliao* (Beijing: Zhongguo shehuikexue chubanshe, 1983).

as superior to the inadequately centralized Yugoslavian system and, because of the large size of the Soviet Union and other factors, perhaps at least as relevant to China's needs as Hungary's planning system. The decision by China's leaders in 1982 to tighten central planning in industry while continuing the reform process was, on the whole, supported by the debate at this conference.

In this year, views of Soviet domestic conditions had mellowed to the point that in place of criticisms of the Soviet economic crisis, one found mixed discussions of economic difficulties and inefficiencies. On the whole, the Soviet economic system was perceived as having worked well until recently and as having provided a basis from which improvements could be made. In comparison to two or three years earlier, Chinese were less critical of bureaucratism and centralization. On foreign policy, Chinese were able to acknowledge that the projects imported from the Soviet Union in the 1950s and the experts trained by the Soviets had been a success, and even that the Soviet system had once worked well in China. The forces of centralization associated with Chen Yun did not favor reimposing the Soviet economic model, but they opposed harsh criticisms of its centralized character. Reform-oriented critics increasingly had to resort to euphemisms to keep alive negative views of the Soviet centralized, planned economy, referring for instance to socialist tradition (*quantong*) or transplanted (*yizhiguolai*) socialism.[45]

During the first half of the year Chinese publications available to foreigners also showed some change in tone. On January 30, *People's Daily* carried an article called "Signs of Crisis as the Soviet Economy Enters a New Year," which quoted Western newspapers on Soviet failures to achieve the planned rate of economic growth. Because of heavy expenditures for military purposes, new problems of energy production, and a shortage of manpower, the Soviet economy will continue to be in crisis, the article concludes. A week later *Xinhua* analyzed the Soviet global strategy for 1982. It asserted that the Soviet harvest shortfall of 1981, together with the protracted war in Afghanistan and the Polish crisis, has more or less shackled the feet of the Soviet giant in pressing ahead with its expansion abroad. . . . Looking at the crystal ball, one may say that there probably won't be another Afghanistan for some time to come. With these observations, the article indicated that Soviet aggression is not as serious a threat as argued earlier. Furthermore, the article pointed out that "Moscow will continue to focus its attention on the West." Although these comments were qualified by the comment that the Kremlin

[45] Yu Guangyuan, "Fazhan jingji kexue genghaode wei shehuizhuyi xiandaihua jianshe fuwu," *Jingji yanjiu*, no. 10 (1981): 8.

bosses have not "been driven into utter passivity or inaction" and that no one would vouch that the Kremlin "would hold itself back for the good of the world when there is an opportunity to fish in troubled waters," the critical tone was much softened from articles not many months earlier.[46]

On May 15, Zhao Ziyang referred to Sino-Soviet relations in an interview with a delegation of Japanese reporters. Noting first that the two countries are sharply divided on principles and that China opposes Soviet hegemonism and policies of foreign expansion, Zhao added that his country consistently advocates the maintenance and development of normal state relations on the basis of the five principles of peaceful coexistence, and China has repeatedly urged negotiations to resolve problems that exist in the relations between the two countries. Zhao said that Chinese have noted Brezhnev's recent speech in Tashkent concerning improving Sino-Soviet relations. "What we emphasize is the actual behavior of the Soviet Union in Sino-Soviet relations and international affairs."[47]

China's shift away from a one-sided anti-Soviet foreign policy may have been best confirmed in an article signed by Mu Youlin, the international editor of People's Daily, on August 9. (The article appeared at about the same time that Yu Hongliang, the Director of the Department of Soviet and East European Affairs and Kapitsa's counterpart, visited the Soviet Union.) In boldface the text begins, "It is said that in China opposing hegemonism is used as a synonym for opposing the Soviet Union. What do you think?" Mu replies, "We oppose anyone seeking hegemonism anywhere . . . as the Soviet Union is on the offensive and the United States is on the defensive in their contention, the major threat to world peace comes from the Soviet Union. . . . China's focus on opposing Soviet hegemonism does not mean that it does not oppose the hegemonism of the United States. China's foreign policy is a principled and independent one." The article goes on to say, if the United States is less offensive than before, it is because it has been weakened.[48] From 1982, as the Reagan military buildup continued, the perception seemed to be growing that the United States was regaining strength while the Soviet Union was mired in Afghanistan and rather isolated, thus the reasons for siding with the United States were disappearing.

As late as February 25, 1982, an article appeared in a Shanghai univer-

[46] "Signs of Crisis as the Soviet Economy Enters a New Year," Renmin ribao January 30, 1982, p. 6, trans. FBIS, PRC International Affairs, Soviet Union, February 2, 1982, pp. C1-C2. "News Analysis: Whither Soviet Global Strategy?" Xinhua in English, February 6, 1982, reprinted in FBIS, PRC International Affairs, Soviet Union, February 8, 1982, C1-C2.

[47] Zhao Ziyang, "Jianli he fazhan Zhong Ri changqi wendingde youhao hezuo," Renmin ribao, March 15, 1982, p 1.

[48] Mu Youlin, "Opposing Hegemonism," Beijing Review, no. 25 (August 9, 1982): 3.

sity journal that seems to have been opposed to "normalization" of relations with Moscow. Written by Zhang Yueming, it begins, "Independence is a spirit of Mao Zedong Thought." Zhang criticizes the early relationship of the Comintern and the communist parties in various countries as "the leader and the led." He argues that from the late 1920s and early 1930s, there emerged a tendency "to make Marxism a dogma and to make the resolutions of the Comintern and the experience of the Soviet Union sacred." Stalin "demanded that the parties in various countries copy mechanically the experiences of the Soviet revolution." The Cominterm's appointed personnel became " 'imperial envoys' who could 'command everything.' " Mao led China out of this situation and through the revolutionary movement gave meaning to independence.

In the civil war, the Chinese revolution was victorious despite the orders of the Soviet leadership to stop the fighting. Zhang argues that although Stalin's approach, as in the treatment of Yugoslavia from 1948, was marked by great-nation chauvinism, Chinese leaders "defended the principle of independence and the Soviet Union did not interfere excessively in our affairs." However, under Khrushchev and Brezhnev, Soviet "great-nation chauvinism swelled malignantly until it developed into social imperialism." Moscow tried to tighten its grip on the socialist camp and demanded obedience from China. Yet the Chinese would not yield. Zhang concludes, "The matter is very clear: if we do not carry out a tit-for-tat struggle against social imperialism but let it be as overbearing as it wishes, the Chinese nation will again fall under the control of a different nation and the international communist movement will suffer ever greater damage."[49] Such concerns must have continued, because in August there was a conference on the international communist movement. It may not be coincidental that it preceded by only one month the public announcement that Beijing and Moscow would begin negotiations in October.

As one might expect, with the decision to negotiate in earnest with the Soviets came an effort to coordinate and reassess Chinese research on the Soviet Union. From September 21 to 28 in Shanghai occurred the opening meeting of the Chinese Association of Soviet and East European Studies (Zhongguo Sulian dongou xuehui). Over 320 persons representing more than 130 organizations gathered together. Liu Keming gave the opening speech. Qian Junrui was chosen as president. An article announcing the meeting for internal audiences (until 1985 the existence of the association was not communicated publicly) referred to the establish-

[49] Zhang Yueming, "Independence and Internationalism," *Huadong shifan daxue xuebao*, no. 1 (February 25, 1982): 1-4, trans. JPRS, Party and State, pp. 1-8.

ment of this association as a major event (*yijian dashi*). The meeting divided into four groups, to discuss: 1) reform of the Soviet economic system, especially in the mid-1960s; 2) the Soviet political system, including the historical influence of the Soviet model, reform of the system, and the political situation; 3) reforms of Eastern European economic systems; and 4) Soviet foreign policies in the 1980s. On the last subject, the group of discussants identified as the determinants the developing international situation, the changing ratio of economic forces in the East and West, the evolving political situation inside the Soviet Union, and especially the leadership succession.[50] These groups reexamined the discussions of the Soviet Union held in China over the previous several years, including the results of many conferences. Although few, if any, unified conclusions were reached, the new association and its review of the field were a stimulus to further research.

After the agreement on negotiations was reached, Soviet foreign policy did not look as ominous. The final issue of *Sulian dongou wenti* in 1982 opened with two articles on Soviet foreign policy, which clearly contrasted with the articles in the opening issue of the journal in 1981. The first article by Zhang Jinglin sought to answer some questions about the present anti-hegemonist struggle.[51] It did not refer to the Soviet Union in the title and opened by lumping the two superpowers together as global hegemonists, each aiming in its foreign policy to seize world hegemony and each responsible for world tension and the danger of a new world war. The article asserted that there is a great historical current on each continent to oppose both Soviet and American hegemonism, and that China conducts a principled, independent foreign policy. Zhang refers to the five principles recently restated by Hu Yaobang at the Twelfth Party Congress to support the idea of an independent foreign policy. He explains that his article is in the spirit of studying Comrade Hu's report on foreign policy.

Reviewing the balance between Washington and Moscow, Zhang recognizes that from the end of the war to the late sixties or early seventies, America had the stronger force. The Soviet military caught up as its economic base was also narrowing the American lead. Westerners refer to the Soviet Union as "an economic beggar and a military giant." Zhang says this is an exaggeration, but it has a kernel of reason. The Soviet national income and value of industrial production by 1975 were 75 and 80 percent of the U.S. figures and remained at these levels in 1980. On a per capita basis, however, the Soviet Union was farther behind. Because So-

[50] "Zhongguo Sulian dongou xuehui chengli dahui ji shoujie nianhui zaihu zhaokai," *Sulian dongou wenti*, no. 1 (1983): 78.

[51] Zhang Jinglin, "Shilun yu dangqian fanba douzheng youguande jige renshi wenti," *Sulian dongou wenti*, no. 6 (1982): 1-5, 49.

viet leaders want both butter and guns, Zhang adds, its economy has
fallen into difficult times. Zhang describes Washington in the immediate
post-war period as on the attack, trying to expand its war gains, while
Moscow was defensive in protecting its own gains. Then, he adds, the rise
of national liberation movements put America more on the defensive; it
became more conservative in its attacks and gave Moscow opportunities
to go on the attack despite its defensive posture. Through the sixties this
situation prevailed, but soon after it was reversed: Moscow became an offensive power and Washington retreated in defense of its prior gains.
Zhang argues that America began its fall when it lost the Korean War and
was seriously wounded in Vietnam, plunging the country into crisis.
Moscow did not let the opportunity go by to take advantage of Washington's retrenchment and to seize the offensive. Both countries still plotted
to gain a monopoly position in world hegemony, Zhang adds, but they
were each becoming overextended in protecting their gains and eventually had to become defensive.

At the end of the seventies and the beginning of the eighties, adds
Zhang, already a little change in the balance was visible. In the mid-seventies, Soviet economic development began to stagnate, and Moscow no
longer was narrowing the gap with America. Entering the eighties, the
Soviet economic situation further deteriorated, while it faced larger-scale
military competition from America. Limits on resources and on personnel tied Moscow's hands. The Soviet decline was underway. Although
the results of recent expansion had widened Moscow's sphere of power,
its economic problems could not be overcome. It is bogged down in Afghanistan the way Washington was in Vietnam. Zhang notes too the importance of the rising aspirations of the Soviet people for an improved
material life.

The United States cannot escape the inevitable fate of the overall collapse of the capitalist imperial system, says Zhang, but under Reagan its
foreign spirit has risen. There is some truth to the view of Western public
opinion that the residue of the Vietnam War and Watergate has passed.
Soviet internal and external troubles have inspired America to act, taking
advantage of its economic and technological superiority. Moscow can use
its highly centralized economic and political system to match Washington, but it must take into account internal and external economic and political consequences. From Angola to Afghanistan, the Soviet Union was
on the attack, but America, despite its defensive posture, was also attacking. Zhang cites the case of Camp David negotiations with Egypt and Israel and the Soviet-Egyptian split as an example of America on the offensive. In the eighties, on balance, the Soviets are still on the attack and
America on the defense, but after the Twenty-sixth Congress, Moscow's

foreign behavior has been much constricted to focus on internal economic problems and to maintain political stability. Zhang mentions the Polish problem and the Israeli invasion of Lebanon as examples of Moscow under restraint. He finds Moscow interested in disarmament and in a summit meeting with Washington. Unlike Carter, Zhang concludes, Reagan is taking the offensive more.

This late-1982 article continues with a discussion of the danger inherent in the hegemonism of the two superpowers. These two countries create instability in the world. If there is a world war, they will provoke it. They are both the most dangerous enemies; neither is better than the other. War is always provoked by aggression. The aggressor is more dangerous than the defender, but the difference is not absolute. China must resolutely oppose hegemonism no matter what the source. It is necessary to assist nations that want independence or national liberation, and people seeking revolution—these three great historical currents. Only in this way can world peace be preserved.

Zhang's article keeps returning to the question, which of the two countries is the more dangerous enemy? The answer he gives is that both countries are very dangerous enemies. In many areas of the world, especially the Third World where America has assumed the colonialist mantle, America is more dangerous. It is understandable that countries would seek Soviet aid. But the Soviet Union is a twin (also one of the two countries in the "First World," according to Chinese theory) and turns out to be the secondary enemy in these regions. As for China, the Soviet Union still pursues hegemonistic aims, threatening China's security on four sides; and America still supports the Taiwan situation, infringing on China's sovereignty. This is Zhang's evenhanded conclusion.

Chinese policy, he continues, correctly supports the "Second World," especially Western Europe, against Soviet hegemonism, but this is complex because the Europeans seek to combine detente and defense to soften Soviet expansion. (Eastern Europe and Japan are other developed areas regarded as part of the "Second World.") A single-centered capitalist bloc in the early seventies was replaced by three centers—the United States, Western Europe, and Japan. America has not yet completely lost its leading position; since Reagan took office he has tried to restore it and has threatened Washington's allies. However, the "Second World" countries demand more right to speak out. Zhang predicts ever more divergence with American foreign policy. A new tendency is emerging of the "Second World" and the "Third World" (the less-developed countries) uniting against hegemonism, but colonialist elements persist in the "Second World," as seen in the military struggle between Britain (seen as the aggressor) and Argentina in the "Third World." Zhang sees the "Second World" in favor of a stronger China in order to oppose Soviet hegemonism, yet worried about a truly strong China and limited by American relations with China. This leads to a mixture of unity and struggle in relations with China.

A second article in the same journal is entitled, "Seizing Western Europe Is the Focus of the Soviet Global Strategy." The article explains why economically, politically, and militarily Moscow is primarily interested in Europe. It concludes, however, that in the eighties there is not much possibility that the Soviets can obtain an advantage there.[52] By implication, the threat against China seems to be lessened by this preoccupation with the West.

The *Survey of International Affairs 1983* did not single Soviet foreign policy out for criticism, as was true a year earlier. In one section after another, the Soviet Union is treated with the United States, neither receiving much praise. A separate chapter on the continued depression in Soviet agriculture is preceded by a chapter on the American economic crisis of 1982. For both countries Chinese authors point to policy changes (e.g. the new Soviet food program), and assess the chances of these changes leading to an economic turnaround. Lu Nanquan and Gao Zhongyi note that Andropov is completely serious about resolving the agricultural question, advocating increased autonomy of collective and state farms and examining the experiences of brother states. They describe policies to expand various contract systems, to widen the use of material incentives, and to improve management. Nevertheless, they conclude with a wait-and-see attitude about the effectiveness of the Andropov reforms.[53]

At the time of Andropov's succession, China's leaders sought to reassert their interest in improved relations. On November 15, 1982, *People's Daily* carried an article on the departure of the foreign minister, Huang Hua, to Moscow for Brezhnev's funeral. The principal message was one of Chinese goodwill. These are two great countries with a long common border and with traditionally deep ties of friendship. Better relations are in the interest of both sides and of peace in Asia and the world. The article says that Brezhnev's death is a great loss to the Soviet state and people. To support the claim of China's sincere desire for better relations and gradual normalization, the article expresses the hope that Andropov and the Soviet leadership would devote new effort to this pursuit and says

[52] Yang Jiarong, Jiang Yuelian, Li Xinghan, "Zhengduo Xiou shi Sulian quanqiu zhanlue de zhongdian," *Sulian dongou wenti*, no. 6 (1982): 6-11.

[53] Shanghai guoji wenti yanjiusuo, ed., *Guoji xingshi nianjian 1983* (Shanghai: Zhongguo dabaikequanshu chubanshe, 1983), 7-11, 23-52, 226-46.

that the Chinese people sincerely welcome the increasing development of Soviet economic construction, the continuing improvement in the material and cultural life of the Soviet people, and the further strengthening of the unity of the Soviet multi-nation state.[54]

The case for 1982 being the decisive year in the improvement of Sino-Soviet relations rests not only on the repeated Soviet assertions of recognition of Chinese socialism and optimism about future relations, on the agreement to begin bilateral negotiations, and on the dramatic change in tone in views on the Soviet Union expressed in Chinese publications. Another factor is the reaction in China to developments in Moscow. Andropov's major reform-oriented speech in December attracted great attention among Chinese leaders and scholars. Andropov managed to echo many of China's reform themes with regard to both economic and phil-

TABLE 2.9

Developments in 1983

January   Failure of Sino-American textile negotiations

February   Schultz visits Beijing; Chinese stress divergence in views
            Alexander Bovin visits Beijing

March   Second round of Sino-Soviet negotiations in Moscow; Beijing issues
                statement calling for Vietnam's departure from Kampuchea
            Conference marks one-hundredth anniversary of Marx's death:
                Zhou Yang reports on humanism and alienation in a socialist so-
                ciety
            Soviet-American arms talks break down

May   Soviet chess players compete in China
            U.S. reclassifies China as friendly but nonaligned; permits more
                technology transfer

September   Deputy Foreign Minister Kapitsa officially visits Beijing; agreement
                to double trade, increase exchange students from 10 to 100

October   Third round of Sino-Soviet negotiations in Beijing
            Tourist groups begin to go back and forth from China and USSR;
                agreement to reopen trade at border points
            Drive against spiritual pollution begins at Second Plenum

December   Textile dispute with U.S. settled
            Wu Xueqian states that Sino-Soviet talks are stagnant; Soviets re-
                fuse to discuss "three obstacles"

[54] "Zhong Su heping youhao fuhe liangguo renmin he shijie heping liyi," *Renmin ribao*, November 15, 1982, p 1.

osophical issues. Informal discussions of Andropov's ideas soon occurred
at each of China's major social science institutes.

1983

The international situation was unusually tense in 1983. Soviet-American relations degenerated as Moscow abandoned the negotiations on strategic weapons in Europe, and Washington was angered by the shooting-
down of a civilian airplane over Soviet airspace. Sino-American relations
also ran into many difficulties, on textile trade where China objected to
American quotas, on Washington's granting political asylum to a
Chinese tennis player, and on the Taiwan issue over American weapons
sales. Even so, the serious strain over America's Taiwan policy had lessened in comparison to the problems of the first part of the Reagan administration. Sino-Soviet relations did not experience smooth sailing either.
The two rounds of bilateral negotiations did not produce any breakthroughs, while Chinese articles continued to report critically on Soviet
foreign policies and economic difficulties. Nevertheless, there was gradual improvement in both relations and Chinese perceptions, especially in
the second half of the year.

In April 1983, when Sino-Soviet negotiations were underway, Hu
Yaobang made it clear why China is justified in distancing itself from the
United States and branding that country's behavior hegemonistic. In a
statement to a Swedish communist delegation, he asserted, "The United
States instituted a 'Taiwan Relations Act,' persisted in its arms sale to Taiwan, connived in the enticement and coercion of Chinese athletes and
students in collusion with Taiwan agents, and even granted 'political asylum.' These are all acts of interfering in China's internal affairs, injuring
China's sovereignty and hurting the Chinese people's feelings, which are
hegemonistic behaviors." In the same interview, Hu was critical of Soviet
hegemonism.

From time to time, beginning in the first half of 1982, Chinese articles
restated the principles set forth by Hu Yaobang for developing relations
with communist parties. In July 1982, an article in *Banyuetan* suggested
how to interpret these principles in support of independence, equality,
mutual respect, and noninterference in internal affairs. This may have
been a timely message, as Beijing and Moscow were approaching an
agreement on negotiations. In January 1983, an article in Hongqi pointed
out, "The Chinese and Italian Communist Parties have unanimously
agreed not to say anything about who was correct and who was wrong in
past debates." It noted that in the past, the Chinese Communist Party was

"controlled by some party which proclaimed itself a father party," and the article insisted that this situation would not recur, while adding that the Chinese "are ready to establish and improve close friendly relations in all fields with communist parties and other working-class parties who are willing to establish friendly relations with our party."[55]

An article in *Sulian dongou wenti* reports on a conference in Beijing convened by the Association of Soviet and East European Studies (an organization that was referred to in *neibu* sources only) on problems of the theory and practice of building a spiritual civilization in the Soviet Union and Eastern Europe.[56] More than forty papers by fifty Chinese participants were heard at the six-day conference in August 1983. About two-thirds of the article treats the Soviet Union, followed by short sections on Romania, Czechoslovakia, and the German Democratic Republic. As far as the Soviet Union is concerned, the article indicates that after the Soviets introduced the idea that it already had a developed socialist society, theoretical circles made the theory of building a spiritual civilization an important part of the theory of developed socialism. Nevertheless, Soviet scholars have diverse explanations of "civilization," among them the view that it includes waging a struggle against the thought of the capitalist class and its influence. They agree that the core of the socialist spiritual civilization is Marxist-Leninist ideology. The necessary condition for the development of such a civilization is correctly to recognize a communist worldview and concretely and systematically to carry on thought education.

From the early 1970s Soviets talked about the "socialist way of life" and its improvement as a major goal of socialist development. The article explains that in the sixties, and especially from the seventies, Western capitalist thinkers loudly propagated the theory of the "quality of life," confusing the real difference between this and the way of life in order to spread the capitalist class "consumer mentality" and the "mass consumption society." The Soviet response was to propose the "socialist way of life" and to point to its principal differences with the capitalist way of life, by this means to resist the corrupting influence of the capitalist way

[55] "Hu Meets Swedish Group, Criticizes U.S., USSR," Beijing *Xinhua*, April 7, 1983, trans. FBIS, PRC International Affairs, General, April 8, 1983, p. A1; "How to Interpret the Four Principles Governing Relations Between One Party and Another," *Banyuetan*, no. 14 (July 25, 1982): 50-51, trans. FBIS, PRC International Affairs, General, August 10, 1982, pp. A1-A2; and Li Ji and Guo Qingshi, "Uphold the Marxist Principle in Developing Our Party's Relations with Communist Parties of Various Countries," *Hongqi*, no. 2 (January 16, 1983): 10-14, trans. FBIS, PRC International Affairs, General, February 24, 1983, pp. A1-A7.

[56] "Sulian dongou guojia jingshen wenming jianshe de lilun yu shijian wenti taolunhui jiyao," *Sulian dongou wenti*, no. 6 (1983): 13-16.

of life. The Soviets point to five features of the socialist way of life: 1) there is no class opposition, 2) there are friendly and equal relations in the community of various nationalities, 3) there is a self-conscious attitude toward work and a collectivist spirit, 4) living standards continuously rise and the quality of life improves, and 5) there is social optimism and a high level of humanism. The main path to achieving these ends has been to increase education, science, and culture among the people, to emphasize scientific research and expansion in the ranks of scientists and technical specialists, to increase libraries and other mass cultural facilities, to provide all-around education in primary and middle schools including political education, labor education, and moral education, and to emphasize Marxist-Leninist training in higher education.

The Chinese conference participants recognize that the Soviets have a systematic theory and in practice have made quite a few achievements, but note that it is not enough to look at political and economic aspects; one must also examine a country's culture, education, and ideology. It is not enough to look at domestic policy; one must also look at foreign policy. The conference stressed three serious Soviet problems: hegemonism, severe shortcomings in the bureaucratized political and economic system that are the major obstacles to economic progress, and theory racing ahead of reality. The consciousness and spirit of the people are not as described by Soviet scholars. The country is not as developed as stated. Social problems are serious, including political apathy among youths. The article concludes with a list of current social problems in the Soviet Union including corruption and theft, criminal behavior, alcoholism, rising divorce rates, and increasing numbers of religious believers.

In the middle of 1983, China's concern with anti-socialist dangers appeared to be growing. In 1979 and 1980, after the Maoist view of class struggle had been overturned, some theorists argued that class struggle had ceased and all class enemies were gone. But in 1981 and 1982 articles began to add the qualification that individuals can become enemies and there are some new-born enemies regardless of their class background. The middle of 1983 saw an upsurge in arrests of so-called new-born reactionaries (xinsheng fangemin) accused of spying for the Guomindang, and a new secret police organ was set up. The spiritual pollution campaign was the culmination of this trend.

Early in 1983, the voices of the reform group were particularly audible. In the second half of 1982, as Stuart R. Schram observes, two orthodox publications had been obliged to issue a self-criticism or even to submit to a purge of the editorial board.[57] Controversial articles increased in num-

[57] Schram, *Ideology and Politics in China Since the Third Plenum, 1978-1984*, 38-57.

ber (e.g. on the originally orthodox theme of "spiritual civilization").
The reform trend in ideology culminated at the March conference com-
memorating the centenary of Marx's death. As Schram points out, Su
Shaozhi's paper (discussed in Chapter One) called for research on the errors of Stalin and Mao (lumping the two leaders together) and other
problems of socialism. Hu Yaobang in March attacked those who accused
China's leaders of betraying Mao's revolutionary heritage, and Zhou
Yang wrote approvingly in *People's Daily* about the use of the terms "alienation" and "humanism." Shortly afterwards, at the conference on
Marxism, Zhou's ideas were presented and discussed along with replies
sent to *People's Daily*. Schram finds that only at the end of May did *People's Daily* stop its frequent appeals for moving boldly forward with reform.

For the remainder of the year, the tide against reform was swelling.
Deng Liqun, Chen Yun, Wang Zhen, and Hu Qiaomu, at least in the final
stages of the 1983-1984 movement, raised the specter of spiritual pollution. They objected to people who claim that China is not yet socialist or
who find alienation present in Chinese socialism. With Deng Xiaoping's
support, the Second Plenum in October focused attention on the perceived anti-spiritual threat from the right. It may not be coincidental that
important strides toward normalization in Sino-Soviet discussions occurred against the background of this campaign against reformers in the
field of theory and persons contaminated by Western pollution, nor that
the dying-down of the campaign in the late winter and its abrupt end in
the early spring coincided with a short-term deterioration in Sino-Soviet
relations. With the campaign in full progress late in 1983, Soviet specialists did not remain silent. At a November conference of Russian-language teachers in Chongqing, there was a call to join in the struggle
against spiritual pollution.[58]

A Chinese group investigating sea transport and ports spent three
weeks in November 1983 travelling in the Soviet Union. They came away
with a positive overall impression, as reported in an article in *Shijie jingji
yu zhengzhi neican* in mid-1984. Above all, they commented on recent
major reforms in the organization of work. A new contract system had
been spreading based on increased autonomy and responsibility for individual work brigades. Large bonuses could be earned for quality work,
safety, and conservation of energy. If the work was performed slowly,
there would be no bonus at all. The article describes great effects on
worker motivation, seen in reduced labor turnover and increased effi-

---

[58] "Zhongguo eyu jiaoxue yanjiuhui diyici xueshu taolunhui longzhong zhaokai," *Eguo
eyu jiaoxue*, no. 1 (1984): 1-3.

ciency. Without failing to point out the excessive controls in the Soviet economy, the article stresses recent improvements. It concludes by explaining that China and the Soviet Union have similar conditions although the market figures more heavily in China, and that there is not a little that China can borrow from the Soviet reform experience.[59]

It would be an error to overlook the role of personal relationships in the resumption of Sino-Soviet contacts. Old acquaintances renewed their ties after long years of involuntary separation. Such meetings could not avoid a degree of emotion. The Arkhipov visit to China at the end of 1984 was a high point in this regard, bringing together economic planners and even high officials (including Chen Yun) who had worked together a quarter of a century earlier. In 1983 there were other reunions of note involving intellectuals and officials. When Alexander Bovin, the political observer for *Izvestiia* and a television foreign affairs analyst, came to Beijing, he met Chinese counterparts in the international relations field. For instance, he saw Huan Xiang, the veteran foreign affairs expert, whom he had known earlier. Huan had also known Andropov, and Bovin may have carried a message from or to the top Soviet leader. Personal contacts may have played a role also in M. S. Kapitsa's visit in September, which signaled an upswing in Sino-Soviet relations. Kapitsa was described at the time as having "attended many important talks between Chinese and Soviet leaders. He came to China as a guest of the Soviet ambassador in Beijing in 1980, 1981 and 1982, then was promoted to be deputy-foreign minister in charge of Far Eastern and Southeast Asian Affairs."[60] More than any other Soviet official, he is identified with the effort to work out a solution to Sino-Soviet problems.

Two articles published on the last days of the year show the mostly positive mood toward the Soviet Union at that time. Wang Wenxiu's review of the 1983 Soviet economy in *Jingji ribao* (a paper fully on the orthodox side in the spiritual pollution campaign underway at that time) gives substantial credit to Soviet reform measures for raising the growth rate of industrial production and fulfilling major economic targets. Wang notes: 1) the strengthening of weak sectors (fuel and power, metallurgy, capital construction, and transportation); 2) the promotion of politically mature, professionally competent people to handle organizational work in place of "incompetent, feckless, and irresponsible" leaders who resisted new things; 3) the tightening of state discipline, planning discipline, labor discipline, and technological discipline coupled with prefer-

[59] Ma Guofeng, "Sulian haiyun he shangkou de guanli tizhi," *Shijie jingji yu zhengzhi neican*, no. 7 (1984): 24-26.

[60] "Kapitsa Arrives in Beijing, Talks to Xinhua," *Xinhua* in English, reprinted in FBIS, PRC International Affairs, Soviet Union, September 8, 1983, p. C1.

ential wages, bonuses, vacations, and housing to workers who performed well; 4) the encouragement of science and technology through planning and material incentives; and 5) the organization of agricultural and industrial combination bodies at all levels, along with the spread of collective contracts and the increase of farm purchase prices. Wang also notes the plan to begin pilot schemes of expanded self-management on January 1, 1984. Nowhere in his article does he even hint that the Soviet Union was not well along the way to overcoming its past economic problems. The problems themselves are summarized with the introductory observation that "from 1979 to 1982, the growth rate of industrial production in the Soviet Union stayed at a level under 4 percent, while industrial output has increased over 4 percent this year."

On the previous day another orthodox-leaning newspaper, *Guangming ribao*, contained an article by Liang Shufen on a 16-day tour of the Soviet Union in November by a travel group from the Chinese People's Association for Friendship with Foreign Countries and the Sino-Soviet Friendship Association. Liang notes by way of explanation that at the recently concluded Twelfth Party Congress Hu Yaobang said, "The Chinese people have a lasting and long friendship with the Soviet people and whatever the state of diplomatic relations between the two countries we must all work hard to maintain and develop this friendship." The Chinese group of fourteen people, including scholars of Russian and Soviet affairs, musicians, photographers, and representatives of a translators' group and of the peoples' communes, "were very well treated and received courteous receptions." The group laid wreaths at Lenin's tomb in Red Square, at tombs of the unknown soldiers of World War II in the four cities visited, and at the Monument to the 26 Commissars in Baku. It met with many dignitaries at the republic level, including those in the Supreme Soviet, and with a minister for higher education.[61] At the central level, this first group to be organized by the friendship associations met with Kapitsa.

Contrast these articles to a December 30 review of the Soviet economy issued by *Xinhua* News Service and written by its correspondent Wang Chongjie. It begins with the statement that under the new leader, Yuri Andropov, the Soviet economy has had some improvement and stopped its years-long slide in the growth rate of production; however, the ills that afflict the economy have not yet been cured and the arms race bur-

[61] Wang Wenxiu, "The 1983 Soviet Economy," *Jingji ribao*, December 31, 1984, p. 4, trans. JPRS, PRC International Affairs, Soviet Union, January 13, 1984, pp. C2-C3; and Liang Shufen, "Traveling in the Soviet Union for 16 Days," *Guangming ribao*, December 30, 1984, p. 4, trans. JPRS, PRC International Affairs, Soviet Union, January 13, 1984, p. C3.

den, "which will inevitably affect the living standard of the average Soviet," has become heavier. The 1983 results are placed in a dim light with the assertion that, according to official statistics, "national income this year increased 3.1 percent, below the planned 3.3 percent." Wang's prediction is not very optimistic. Noting the military burden, he says, "It is hard, indeed, for the Soviet Union to attain a balanced economic development and keep the present growth rate in the new year." The article credits the Soviet Union with some economic progress, but considers it "only a beginning."

For a third view, intermediate between the above extremes but closer to *Xinhua* on the Soviet economic performance in 1983, we can turn to Yang Futian, writing in *Liaowang* in February 1984. Yang says that "although the Soviet Union failed to reach the scheduled target, the growth rate increased considerably as compared with the preceding year." Later Yang adds that there was no "conspicuous improvement in market supplies" and that queues still exist. Yang attributes cases of failure to fulfill the plans to excessive state control, an outdated management system, and excessive expenditures on national defense. The article then discusses Andropov's reforms in various areas. Its pessimistic conclusion is that "people have not yet seen a proposal which can essentially resolve problems. Even those measures adopted have not been carried out so smoothly."[62]

In January 1984, the Shanghai Institute for International Studies completed its annual review of the previous year. A 25-page English language synopsis by Li Dai highlights the main themes. First Li notes the intensified U.S.-Soviet confrontation that made 1983 more turbulent than prior years. Then he comments that the "U.S. has strengthened its military presence in an attempt to revive its hegemony" in the Middle East, North Africa, Central America, and Northeast Asia. Its leaders put regional conflicts into the framework of the confrontation with Moscow, leading numerous countries to object.

While blaming both superpowers and contending that they remain in a stalemate, Li's first paragraph focuses most criticism on Washington. On page 2, he elaborates, "Washington was apparently more on the offensive, whereas Moscow was in a passive position." Li finds that "Sino-US relations advanced amid twists and turns." "The first half of 1983 saw numerous cases of [sic] US violating the two parties' agreements, impair-

---

[62] Wang Chongjie, "Year-ender: Progress and Dilemma of the Soviet Economy," Beijing *Xinhua* in English, December 30, 1983, reprinted in JPRS, PRC International Affairs, Soviet Union, January 3, 1984, pp. C2-C4; Yang Futian, "Commentary on World Economy," Beijing *Liaowang*, no. 6 (February 6, 1984): 37-38, trans. JPRS, CPS84-028, Soviet Union, pp. 1-4.

ing the two countries' relations and hurting the Chinese people's feelings,
which aroused strong resentment from the Chinese people. The Chinese
government time and again lodged protests with the US government.
. . ." Li notes that later in the year relations improved, and there was
agreement on an exchange of visits by leaders of the two countries. Then,
he adds, the Taiwan issue flaired in November with "two serious cases of
US infringement upon Chinese sovereignty," both U.S. Senate actions
that even went so far as to mention "Republic of China, Taiwan." Li interprets this as flagrantly advocating "two Chinas."

Li assesses Sino-Soviet relations in a more favorable light. He mentions the two rounds of consultations on normalizing, noting that "relations between the two countries were improved somewhat. There was
some increase in trade and exchange of personnel between the two countries." At the end Li adds that Moscow has refused to remove the three
obstacles to normalization, "so the consultations have not made substantial progress. . . . Only when the three obstacles are removed, can Sino-
USSR relations achieve real normalization."[63]

We can contrast this year-end summary to Zhao Ziyang's June speech
to the first session of the sixth National People's Congress. Zhao said that
"to improve Sino-Soviet relations, the first step to be taken is for the Soviet side to remove the real threat to China's security. This is a major issue that cannot be evaded. We are waiting for the Soviet side to prove its
good faith by deeds." Similar statements had been made in March when
the second round of negotiations was held, and at other times in the first
half of the year, but the tone was improving in the second half of the year.
In August, a Chinese newsletter reported that the Soviet economic situation had taken a favorable turn, while *Xinhua* described the warm welcome given in Kiev to China's women's volleyball team.[64]

Above all, by the end of 1983 there was an upbeat mood about the reform orientation of Andropov's policies. In specialized publications and
popular articles as well, commentaries emphasized the gains in theory
and practice over the year. They varied, however, in whether they
stressed how substantial the gains or how difficult the remaining problems were. An example of the latter conclusion can be found in the year-
end review in *People's Daily*. The text begins with the statement, "This
year, there has been a preliminary turn for the better in the relatively

[63] Li Dai, "International Situation in 1983: Retrospect," (English version of *Guoji xingshi nianjian 1984*) (Shanghai: Shanghai Institute for International Studies, 1984), 1-25.
[64] "Soviet Economic Situation Takes a Favorable Turn," *Shijie jingji daobao*, August 8, 1983, p. 6, trans. FBIS, PRC International Affairs, Soviet Union, August 30, 1983, p. C2; Wang Chongjie, "PRC Volleyball Team Scores Victory in Kiev," *Xinhua* in Chinese, trans. FBIS, PRC International Affairs, Soviet Union, August 24, 1983, p. C1.

stagnant Soviet economic situation which has existed for a long time." It ends with cautious observations, such as "it is not so easy to make any major changes in the system," and "it is inevitable that there will be hidden worries in the prospects for its economic development."[65]

Chinese interest in improving relations could be clearly detected in a radio broadcast by Liu Keming, then the director of the Institute of the Soviet Union and Eastern Europe under the Chinese Academy of Social Sciences, on the occasion of the sixty-sixth anniversary of the October Revolution. Liu offered warm congratulations on behalf of his institute, spoke of Chinese gratitude for bringing Marxism-Leninism to them, and stressed that China is also building socialism guided by the basic principles of Marxism-Leninism. He reminded his "dear Soviet comrades" that "the Chinese and Soviet peoples have been linked by bonds of strong friendship." He added that "the Chinese people profoundly value friendship with the Soviet people" and "wholeheartedly wish to overcome all obstacles in relations between our two countries, and are prepared to really improve these relations and effect their normalization." Liu seemed to apologize for his institute's previous misinformation about the Soviet Union, saying, "We will work more and better in order that our lectures include the development and strengthening of friendship between the peoples of China and the Soviet Union."[66]

1984

The year 1984 opened in China with the forces of ideological orthodoxy flailing away at spiritual pollution from the capitalist world. Hundreds of articles appeared in Chinese journals in opposition to recent Chinese interpretations of Marx that had suggested that his concepts of humanism (*rendaozhuyi*) and alienation (*yihua*) are applicable to China. These reinterpretations of Marx were attacked as a dangerous manifestation of spiritual pollution from the outside. For several years debates had raged in China about how to interpret communist ideology from Marx to Engels to Plekhanov to Lenin to Bukharin and to Stalin. Now with the apparent support of the party leadership at the Second Plenum of the Twelfth Party Congress in October 1983, it appeared that an orthodox position would succeed in quelling further debate. But as 1984 proceeded, views on ideology and the history of socialism became more reformist

[65] Zhou Xiangguang, "Year-End Review: The Soviet Economic Situation in the Past Year," *Renmin ribao*, December 24, 1983, p. 7, trans. FBIS, PRC International Affairs, Soviet Union, December 28, 1983, pp. C1-C3.

[66] "PRC USSR Institute Director Marks GOSR," FBIS, November 6, 1983, trans. FBIS, PRC International Affairs, Soviet Union, November 14, 1983, p. C1.

TABLE 2.10

Developments in 1984

January	Huan Xiang article sees Moscow as Number One enemy; soon after Chinese stop referring to Moscow as Number One enemy Spiritual pollution drive narrows to a debate Zhao Ziyang visits U.S. *Guoji wenti yanjiu* sees U.S. taking the offensive in superpower relations
February	Andropov dies; Vice-Premier Wan Li attends funeral
March	Fourth round of Sino-Soviet talks; Soviet position hardens Gromyko-Qian Qichen talk raises hopes for Sino-Soviet ties
April	In Japan Zhao says Moscow is biggest security threat; Moscow angered Spiritual pollution drive ends; *People's Daily* attacks left deviations Ronald Reagan visits China; Chinese delete anti-Soviet remarks from television broadcast Vietnam times border fighting to hamper Sino-Soviet talks; *People's Daily* carries protest to Hanoi next to photo of Reagan with Deng
May	Arkhipov's visit postponed; sign of worse Sino-Soviet relations Chinese remain optimistic that "normalization" continues Special economic zones extended to 14 more cities
June	Peasant entrepreneurial rights broadened Chernenko critical of China in meetings with Southeast Asian ambassadors Beijing conference held on Soviet foreign policy in Lenin's time
August	*People's Daily* article blames Moscow for isolating itself; Gromyko protests Chinese reassure Moscow of absence of alliance with U.S.
September	Sino-British agreement on future of Hong Kong United Nations meeting of foreign ministers leads to upturn in Sino-Soviet relations
October	Urban reform gives enterprises more independence Chinese leadership criticizes leftist orientation of Chinese army Deng justifies low military spending, sees too much spending as a cause of Soviet economic paralysis Deng equates U.S. in Taiwan to Soviets in Vietnam Deng reaffirms invitation to Arkhipov
November	Vietnam again times border fighting to affect Sino-Soviet relations; Chinese response is low-key
December	*People's Daily* article opposes dogmatic Marxism Arkhipov's visit shows warmth in Sino-Soviet relations; plans for substantial increase in trade Hu Qili speech at Writers' Congress favors intellectual freedom

rather than more conservative. The year 1984 ended in just the opposite way it began—with a crescendo of voices saluting ideological flexibility and freedom. The Third Plenum in October proclaimed massive urban reform to be China's most pressing need. A December 7 article in *People's Daily* stated that the writings of Marx and Lenin should not be taken as binding statements for the present, but require updating as conditions change—and Hu Qili's speech in late December to the National Congress of Writers emphatically called for freedom for intellectuals and the removal of lingering leftist controls and tendencies.

The Chernenko succession in February 1984 was greeted with some caution in China. Wei Zhe's article in the March 10 issue of *Banyuetan* notes in the first sentence that Chernenko is in his seventies, and Andropov had been 68, which "shows that the Soviet Union is faced with a 'serious and long-standing problem'—in this country, successors to the leader, generation after generation, are of more and more advanced age when they assume office." The article goes on to note Andropov's initial successes in domestic economic construction and in improving relations with China to a certain extent, but it adds that "quite a lot of problems in the Soviet economy remain" and in negotiations "so far no substantial progress has been made regarding the elimination of the 'three great obstacles.' ' It concludes with a remark about Gorbachev's standing next to Chernenko in the new leadership.[67]

Within weeks of this article, the first assessments of Chernenko's leadership were appearing. *Liaowang's* Tang Xiuzhe published two favorable articles on his domestic policies. Each praised Andropov's economic reform activity, even going so far as to talk of "some rather remarkable achievements" and measures that "had won the support of the masses," and then indicated that Chernenko is continuing the revitalization of the economy started by Andropov. The second article, appearing on April 23, however, ended on a negative note concerning Sino-Soviet relations, indicating that some disappointment must have occurred. "Over the past 2 months or so since Chernenko came to power, no important breakthrough has been achieved in foreign affairs. Some major issues are still at an impasse."[68]

Reporting on the situation in early 1984, the high-ranking veteran spe-

[67] Wei Zhe, "From Andropov to Chernenko," *Banyuetan*, no. 5 (March 10, 1984): 53-55, trans. JPRS, PRC International Affairs, Soviet Union, April 10, 1984, C1-C2.

[68] Tang Xiuzhe, "Soviet Attempt at Economic Reform," Beijing *Liaowang*, no. 13 (March 26, 1984): 26-27, trans. JPRS, PRC International Affairs, Soviet Union, May 4, 1984, pp. C1-C3; Tang Xiuzhe, "Chernenko Elected Chairman of the Presidium of the USSR Supreme Soviet," Beijing *Liaowang*, no. 17 (April 23, 1984): 6, trans. JPRS, PRC International Affairs, Soviet Union, May 22, 1984, pp. C1-C2.

cialist on socialist-bloc relations, Wu Xiuquan, expresses sober views of the prospects for both Sino-American and Sino-Soviet relations.[69] Rather than referring to Moscow as the greater danger, he seems to be assigning blame quite equally. He asserts that both Moscow and Washington are to blame for the dangerous intensification of the superpower competition. Wu characterizes China's foreign policy as independent, in favor of disarmament agreements between the superpowers, against hegemonism, for equality of the big powers and smaller and weaker countries, for peaceful coexistence and mutual respect. China would not subordinate itself to any country or alliance. Wu summarizes the five-year history of diplomatic relations with the United States as a twisting course that was far from approaching the level it ought to have reached. Taiwan is the main barrier. Wu predicts that if this question is not resolved, the base of relations between the two countries would be weak and could worsen. Most recently, Wu adds, some progress was made when Premier Zhao Ziyang met with President Reagan in January in the United States. As for Soviet relations, he says that China wants improvements. It seeks normalization, but first must resolve the main barriers threatening China's security: Soviet troop withdrawals on the border, in Mongolia, and in Afghanistan, and withdrawal of support for Vietnam in Kampuchea. Some improvements have occurred, but Moscow has been using the excuse of not causing harm to any third country to avoid discussing the three principal barriers. There has been no decisive advance, and none can be expected in the short term. If these barriers are removed, Wu believes that a long-term path of improvement looms ahead.

On August 4, 1984, in a radio program beamed in Russian, China's leaders may have given one of their clearest signals that a new, independent, and essentially equidistant foreign policy had been formulated.[70] Reviewing the first six months of 1984, the broadcast comments on the "striking diplomatic activity by China." Along with meetings in Beijing with heads of state and top world leaders, the program notes three events that drew general attention: the presence of Vice-Premier Wan Li at Andropov's funeral, the fourth round of Sino-Soviet consultations, and the talks on Hong Kong between China and Britain. It asserts that bilateral relations with Washington had further developed, bringing concrete results, then adds that although China and the U.S. have similar or common views on the Afghan and Kampuchean issues, their positions differ on Korea, the Middle East, Central America, southern Africa, and espe-

[69] Wu Xiuquan, "Guanyu shijie zhanlue xingshi de jige wenti," *Sulian dongou wenti*, no. 3 (1984): 1-3.

[70] "Beijing Russian on PRC-U.S., PRC-Soviet Ties," trans. FBIS, PRC International Affairs, Soviet Union, August 7, 1984, pp. C1-C3.

cially Taiwan. The negative focus was reinforced by the strong assertion, "The leaders of China require the United States to abandon the four so-called unsinkable aircraft carriers—Taiwan, South Korea, Israel, and the Republic of South Africa."

If Moscow still had suspicions that the U.S. and China were teaming up, the next sentences should have helped. "China's principled position indicates the unreality of the efforts of certain Americans to establish a U.S.-Chinese strategic relationship. China will under no circumstances permit the United States to play the China card in the struggle against its rival." Then, to indicate agreement with a Soviet official's suspicion that China's leaders were not pleased with Reagan's anti-Sovietism, the program adds, "Zagladin, first deputy chief of the International Department of the CPSU Central Committee, while appearing one day on television, said of Sino-U.S. relations: The United States is always trying to play the China card against the Soviet Union. During his visit to China, Reagan made anti-Sovietism the main subject of his public address. This may not have been entirely to the liking of his Chinese hosts."

The program remarks that the Soviet Union has been wrong to reproach China for "so-called cooperation with imperialism." It asserts that China "sincerely desires normalization of relations with the Soviet Union" and, despite the last-minute postponement of Arkhipov's visit, China is striving to normalize relations. It is not doing so to play the Soviet card in the strategic triangle, as apparently some Soviets contended. Rather, China is acting on principle, and if the United States persists with its Taiwan position, the article warns, "Sino-U.S. relations will invariably regress." It equates this problem with the U.S. to the obstacles in Sino-Soviet relations, which hold up normalization. The radio talk insists that China's foreign policy is not equidistance, as some call it, but then says little more than that China will not indiscriminately accuse both the U.S. and the Soviet Union for the sake of equidistance without examining who is guilty of what. Then it equates Soviet guilt in Afghanistan with U.S. guilt in Grenada. It concludes by referring to China's "stepped-up independence and self-sufficiency diplomacy activities in the first half of the year." All of this seems to indicate a new foreign policy in 1984, approaching equidistance even if not blessed by that term. Chinese rejected Soviet attempts to blame Beijing for insufficient progress, contending that it is no more than an excuse for Moscow's own slowdown in seeking normalization for Moscow to blame China for cozying up to the United States. The fact is, the talk concludes, Sino-American ties are developing but are unlikely to develop very far and are, in any case, in no way inconsistent with normalization of Soviet relations.

A day before this broadcast, Wang Chongjie of *Xinhua* reported posi-

tively on Soviet economic experiments. "Productivity has risen mark-
edly," and "the production team's accounting and contractual systems
have developed in depth."[71] Wang notes that his positive views are based
on recent Soviet press items and reports on visits to enterprises (presumably by Chinese).

What makes this positive mood interesting is that less than a month
earlier, *Beijing Review* published a speech by Wang Jinqing of the Research Center for International Issues on growing strains in Sino-Soviet
relations. Wang says that the problems "are, in essence, a struggle between control and anti-control." The Soviets try to control China, which
resists. Wang adds, "Recently they have become even more stubborn
about it [refusing to budge on the three major obstacles]. In a matter of
days, Chernenko twice attacked China publicly, and some Soviet officials
published articles under assumed names calling into question the independent policy followed by China and some East European countries."
Wang says that Chinese sincerely hope for improved relations, but
"judging from the foregoing analyses, the improvement of Sino-Soviet
relations will be long and slow, despite the progress already made by both
sides in expanding economic, cultural, educational and sports exchanges,
and visits between non-governmental organizations."[72]

It should be clear that neither Beijing nor Moscow was satisfied in mid-
1984 with the progress being made toward normalization. Yet improvements were taking place at a quite rapid rate. The volume of trade in 1984
was to be 1.2 billion, 60 percent more than in 1983. The two sides agreed
to send seventy students each to the other country in the 1984-1985 academic year. Contacts in science, sports, health, culture, and other
spheres were increasing day by day. Exchange visits between friendship
associations were restored.[73] With all of these gains, what further was expected from normalization that caused such disappointment and accusations in mid-1984? This question was not answered very clearly.

Beijing Review published an interview with the head of the International Liaison Department of the Central Committee on the occasion of
the thirty-fifth anniversary of the PRC. It came just at the time of the
foreign ministers' meeting in New York, which gave new momentum to
Sino-Soviet relations. The article reiterates the four principles for developing relations with other communist parties: independence, complete

---

[71] Wang Chongjie, "Experiment in Expanding Enterprises' Decisionmaking Power Yields
Initial Results in the Soviet Union," Beijing *Xinhua*, August 3, 1984, reprinted in FBIS,
PRC International Affairs, Soviet Union, August 7, 1984, p. C3.

[72] Wang Jinqing, "Why the Sino-Soviet Strains," *Beijing Review*, no. 28 (July 9,
1984): 31-32.

[73] "Zhong Su heping youhao fuhe liangguo renmin he shijie heping liyi," 1.

equality, mutual respect, and noninterference in each other's internal affairs. This means that the CCP recognizes no guiding center or model in
the international communist movement. The article notes that "in the
past few years, our Party has actively tried to resume and advance its
once-suspended relations with other communist parties." If other parties
with differing views "seek common ground while reserving differences,
and gradually iron out differences through friendly consultations and
mutual forbearance . . . there will be no difficulties on the part of our
Party in establishing, restoring and developing friendly relations with
communist parties of various countries." Although it was not clear which
communist parties might be included in this statement, one could con-
strue this as a signal to the Soviet Union that more than state-to-state
normalization could be expected. Nevertheless, the official went on to say
that "party-to-party and state-to-state relations are different in nature
and belong to separate categories." Presumably the first would have to be
resolved before the latter was possible in the case of the Soviet Union,
while for other parties in general, the article indicated, it is normal to
have contact. Only the four principles need to be accepted for such relations to develop.[74]

The improvement in Beijing's relations with Moscow in 1984 did not
come in one steady line of progress. Although initial developments were
positive, including an announcement that Arkhipov would visit China in
May (an obvious effort to balance to some degree Reagan's visit in April),
a setback occurred before Arkhipov was to set off. Moscow was offended
that the Chinese were leaning too far on the American side. Increasing
signs of Sino-American military cooperation, Zhao Ziyang's statement in
a meeting with Japanese Prime Minister Nakasone that the Soviet Union
is the main threat to security in the Asian-Pacific region, the closeness
with the United States indicated during President Reagan's visit to China
in April, and other developments disappointed Soviet expectations that
had been built up in previous Sino-Soviet discussions. Moscow showed
its displeasure in small ways—Chernenko's failure to meet Wan Li at Andropov's funeral, an apparent retreat on certain issues at the fourth round
of bilateral talks in March, intensified anti-Chinese propaganda in the Soviet media, renewed pressure on Eastern European countries not to go too
far in the lead in their China ties, and negative comments by Chernenko
about China when meeting with Indochinese ambassadors in June—and
in May in the highly visible signal of postponing Arkhipov's visit. Some
of the strain between the two countries that developed in the spring of

[74] "Foreign Contacts of the Communist Party," *Beijing Review*, no. 42 (October 15,
1984): 19-20.

1984 can also be attributed to Vietnam's timing of military actions on the Chinese border to exacerbate tensions with China that Moscow then interpreted as forcing a choice between its ally, Vietnam, and its negotiating partner, China.

Sometimes, it is said, things have to get worse before they can get better. That seems to have been the case with Sino-Soviet relations in the summer of 1984. The low point in the strained relations was signaled by an article by Yu Sui in *People's Daily* on August 28, which charged the Chernenko leadership with worsening Soviet foreign relations throughout the world.[75] Yu opens by noting that more than six months have passed since the change in top Soviet leaders, and that over this period international opinion holds that Moscow has become more inflexible, "heavy-handed," arbitrary. It has hardened its foreign policy. Yu adds that these comments are not groundless. As for Sino-Soviet relations, Yu accuses the Soviet leaders of only wanting "to ease the tension a little to improve economic and trade relations," and of using the excuse of " 'refraining from harming the interests of a third country' in refusing to remove the three obstacles that have hindered a radical improvement in Sino-Soviet relations." He says that "since last March the monthly volume of anti-Chinese materials published by Soviet central press and TASS has doubled compared with last year. These materials not only attack China's foreign policies of maintaining independence and keeping the initiative in its own hands, but also have attacked our country's domestic policies of socialist construction. Soviet supreme leader Chernenko personally attacked China by name on 11 and 24 June in order to defend Vietnam's aggressive actions." Yu continues with comments on Soviet leaders who are frustrated with Reagan, venting their anger on China and on leaders who "lack vitality," trying to appear self-confident to hide their weakness and buy time. Whether these views are correct will be determined, he concludes, by the next actions of the Soviet leaders. In other words, the next step is up to them.

According to one informant, Gromyko interpreted this article as a one-sided attack and further evidence that China was not "equidistant" and "independent," but was aligning with Washington. He apparently signaled his concern to China's leaders, who did not take long to signal back their further interest in negotiations. Whatever may have been Gromyko's personal role, it seems likely that the Politburo in Moscow reached an important decision in September 1984 to improve relations simultaneously with China and the United States. If in the late summer of 1982

[75] Yu Sui, "Soviet Foreign Policy for the Past Half Year," *Renmin ribao*, August 28, 1984, p. 7, trans. FBIS, PRC International Affairs, Soviet Union, August 28, 1984, pp. C1-C2.

it was Beijing that at last acceded to Soviet urgings to open negotiations, exactly two years later it was Moscow's turn to yield after a period of recalcitrance.

Scarcely three weeks after Yu's article was published, at the United Nations in New York, Wu Xueqian and Gromyko held the first meeting between the foreign ministers of these two countries in many years. They talked for six hours over two days, and Beijing *Xinhua* said the talks were "helpful to the enhancement of mutual understanding between the two countries."[76] In contrast to the previous meetings between deputy foreign ministers, which the Soviets had insisted could only discuss bilateral issues, the two foreign ministers exchanged views on the international situation. Shortly afterward the Arkhipov visit was rescheduled. Another turning point had been reached. The fifth round of negotiations brought some progress toward normalization. By the end of October, Deng Xiaoping was talking about extending the "open-door" policy to the Soviet Union.[77] Finally 1984 ended on a warm note when Arkhipov's visit at last took place. In welcoming a leading figure in the organization of Soviet financial assistance during the 1950s, Chinese leaders expressed their gratitude for past aid and their eagerness for expanded economic ties. In turn, by visiting the Shenzhen special economic zone next to Hong Kong, Arkhipov signaled Soviet interest in China's bold economic reforms.[78] It was reported to me that Arkhipov had said that he was moved by what he saw at Shenzhen. Criticisms of China's economic reforms became more restrained in the Soviet press.

The warmth of Soviet hospitality toward visiting Chinese groups was fully expressed in a *People's Daily* article of June 23, 1984, on the occasion of a musical and artistic group's visit to Moscow.[79] The article interpreted the enthusiasm of the audience as a reflection of the friendly feelings of the Soviet people for the Chinese people. Spectators crowded around after the performances, shaking hands in congratulations and requesting autographs to remember the occasion. Some came from far away. Some even were excited to the point of tears. The article says that the people of both countries look forward to normalization. It invokes memories that bind the two peoples.

Positive feedback from Moscow and its allies came at various times

[76] "Second Gromyko Meeting," Beijing *Xinhua* in English, September 22, 1984, reprinted in FBIS, PRC International Affairs, General, September 24, 1984, p A3.

[77] Deng Xiaoping, *Jianshe you Zhongguo tese de shehuizhuyi* (Beijing: Renminchubanshe, 1984), 66.

[78] Rozman, "China's Soviet-Watchers in the 1980s," 436.

[79] "Renmin de qingyi: ji Zhongguo yinyue yishutuan zai Sulian fangwen yanchu," *Renmin ribao*, June 23, 1984, p. 6.

over the year and encouraged the Chinese to expect improved relations. Grounds for Chinese optimism can be found in a January 1984 interview with a visiting Hungarian group, which indicated the group's approval of China's economic reform advance.[80] Later in the year, Soviet economists would also privately inform the Chinese that they regarded China's reforms as largely successful. Soviet publications criticized China's economic reforms less and less, for the most part expressing continued doubts indirectly through citations of Western criticisms.

A November 1984 article by Zhou Xincheng and Li Jun explains the relevance of China's economic reforms to studies of the Soviet Union. They comment that after the Third Plenum, work in theoretical economics broke out of the chains of extreme-left thinking. It was liberated in all areas, from the systematic grasp of actual materials to deep theoretical analysis, from one-country research to different models of comparative research. Now, five years later; they assert, the starting points in studies of economic reforms in the Soviet Union and Eastern Europe are the needs of China's reform of the economic system.

What are the lessons of the experiences of these countries that can be borrowed? Zhou and Li note that not long after the Third Plenum, China's economic circles raised questions about which model is most appropriate for China's economic reform. This exerted a positive influence on research on the economic reforms of the Soviet Union and Eastern Europe. Especially when Yugoslavia's reforms were introduced, people realized that there can be different models of the economic management system under socialism, each supporting the nationalization of materials of production and "to each according to his work." At first, Zhou and Li continue, Chinese emphasized Yugoslavia and Romania in their studies. Then there was great approval for Yugoslavia's experience and methods. Later, some comrades also approved the methods and experience of the Soviet reforms, considering that China ought to restore the economic system of the First Five-Year Plan period. After the flourishing of comparative research, the majority perceived Yugoslavia as excessively fragmented and the Soviet Union as excessively centralized, and neither as appropriate for China. Attention gradually concentrated on Hungary's reforms. Its combination of planning and marketing, centralization and dispersal, overall control and decontrol over details offered a very good starting point for Chinese economic theorists. Of course, China's concrete conditions must be the starting point for China's reform; it cannot simply copy a foreign model. Nevertheless, there is no doubt, say Zhou

[80] "Xiongyali jingji xuejia daibiaotuan tan dui Zhongguo jingji gaige de kanfa," *Shijie jingji yu zhengzhi neican*, no. 1 (1984): 49-52.

and Li, that study of the differing reform models of the Soviet Union and Eastern Europe is advantageous for borrowing, setting the direction of China's economic reforms.

Zhou and Li go into more detail about the borrowing process. They say that economists who study theory, material conditions, planning, experiments, training of personnel, etc. in the Soviet Union and Eastern Europe have made suggestions, of which very many have already been adopted by the Central Committee and separate ministries in China. Especially in 1983, when the State Council decided on a planning system, prices, taxes, wages, etc., concrete practices in these other socialist countries were discussed in detail and borrowed. Five years of research brought valuable materials and suggestions, contributing to China's reforms. Writing in late 1984, Zhou and Li observe, that new conditions have developed because of the reform of the urban economic system in China. Even higher demands are being placed on research about the Soviet Union and Eastern Europe. Over the past five years, because China lacked practical experience and for other reasons, China's urban economic reform steps came too slowly and did not do a good job of overcoming the fundamental shortcomings of the original system. Continued tight controls over enterprises blocked the advance of forces of production. Now it is necessary to get rid of everything that does not correspond to the needs of developing the forces of production while operating under the preconditions of strengthened public ownership of the means of production and "to each according to his work." Success in urban reform depends on research, increasing study of the world economy, especially not overlooking the Soviet Union and Eastern Europe. In the past, Chinese research was within the historical framework of Soviet and Eastern European economic reforms over 20-30 years. This approach is too limited. A longer and more comparative perspective is needed on the necessary trends of the development of the economic system. Zhou and Li call for linking economic reforms to history and comparing socialist and other economic systems for their strengths and weaknesses as well as their rules of development.

Conferences and seminars on the Soviet Union had become commonplace in 1984. Before this time they were mostly exceptional events, often important for setting a new course in thinking or bringing together diverse viewpoints on a disputatious issue. For example, in 1983, after China's responsibility system had been widely embraced as fully consistent with socialism, Soviet specialists were brought together in Wuxi to discuss the merits of agricultural collectivization under Stalin. In 1984 the range of conference topics had become more diverse: the Stalin socialist model, Lenin's thoughts on art, Sukhomlinsky's ideas for educa-

tional reform, and Soviet cultural construction 1917-1924 were among
the topics. Interest in applying the lessons of Soviet history remained
high among Chinese concerns in 1984. Scholarship was advancing
quickly after the effects of the spiritual pollution campaign were overcome. Research plans ranged into new subjects, including Soviet political
history from the time of Stalin; new periods, such as the 1950s; and new
comparative interests, including comparisons of socialist and nonsocialist
countries and of China and other socialist countries.

In July, as China's urban economic reform policies were in the final
stage of preparation, a seminar was held at the Party School of the Central
Committee in Beijing. It centered on the reforms of the economic management system in the Soviet Union and Eastern Europe. Twenty-two
topics were covered altogether; while each of the other seven countries
was examined as a single topic, or in the case of Hungary and Yugoslavia
as two topics each, twelve topics focused on the Soviet Union. The separate topics for the USSR included reforms of: the planning, price, credit,
wage, industrial management, agricultural management, and foreign
trade management systems. The final session treated comparisons of reforms throughout the region.[81]

Even in the summer doldrums of uncertain progress toward normalization, there were optimistic articles about the benefits of improved Sino-
Soviet relations. Hu Yanfen published an article in August reflecting back
on Sino-Soviet trade and looking ahead to new developments. She praises
the results of the 1950s, noting four gains for China: low-interest loans,
the construction of enterprises, mutually-operated joint companies, and
the training of students and personnel assisted by Soviet advisors. She
sees the Soviets benefiting in areas in which they were weak: agriculture,
light industry including textiles, and raw materials such as minerals, for
example. They also received interest payments. Both sides were hurt by
the loss of these benefits in the 1960s.

Hu contends that in the 1980s, the Chinese and Soviet economies are
of a mutually complementary character. She disagrees with some Western economists who argue that the two economies are scarcely compatible. China needs to renovate firms built with Soviet aid in the 1950s. It
needs machinery and technology where the Soviet Union is ahead of
China. It also needs wood. In turn, China can provide foodstuffs, textiles
and other light industrial goods, and minerals. Hu concludes that a very
large reserve exists for increased bilateral trade, although both countries
lack Western technology and need the competitiveness of the world mar-

[81] Zhou Xincheng and Li Jun, "Shiying woguo jiakuai chengshi tizhi gaige," 15-19; [Back
cover], *Sulian dongou wenti*, no. 2 (1984): 97.

ket. Hu suggests that if gradual normalization occurs in the 1980s, there may even be mutual enterprises and cooperative mining ventures set up.[82]

In late 1984, a high tide of reform swept across China. The orthodox group had retreated following the complete repudiation of the spiritual pollution campaign in the spring. The October plenum of the Central Committee approved a far-reaching urban reform program. This approval did not stop at economic reforms. China's leaders had decided that urban reform is much more difficult than rural reform, explaining that cities are not just economic centers but also cultural and political centers. This phraseology signaled that more than just the economy was involved. The early December article in *People's Daily* against dogmatism in ideology was seen by many as opening the way to greater freedom for scholars. By year's end, Hu Qili's speech to the Fourth Writers' Congress for the first time gave approval to freedom of expression in the arts. Reforms of intellectual activities were being actively discussed—some reflected in ambitious new plans for Soviet studies, such as those presented at the September 1984 conference organized by the journal *Shijie jingji yu zhengzhi neican*.[83]

1985

After the announcement of the urban economic reform in October 1984, articles on relevant economic matters rose even more prominently to the fore. The bibliography in the journal *Shijie jingji yu zhengzhi neican* of the major *neibu* publications for January-February 1985 (including as well many articles that appeared late in 1984) shows the keen interest centered on the economy.[84] The ten articles on the Soviet Union include studies of trade in technology with advanced capitalist countries, enterprises set up abroad by the Soviet Union, and Soviet trade with developing countries. There are also studies of the Soviet economic experiments, the theory and model of reforms of the economic system and the wage management system in the Soviet Union and Eastern Europe, an article on environmental protection, and two articles on Soviet agriculture—its specialization of production and its personal auxiliary activities, such as personal plots. Even more than over the past five years, the Soviet economy was at the center of attention.

[82] Hu Yanfen, "Su Zhong maoyi de huigu he zhanwang," *Shijie jingji yu zhengzhi neican*, no. 8 (1984): 16-19.

[83] Shu Yan, "Ba dui Sulian dongou wenti de yanjiu xiangqian tuijin yibu," 1-4.

[84] "Shijie jingji yu zhengzhi bufen neibu ziliao mulu suoyin (1985, 1-2 yue)," *Shijie jingji yu zhengzhi neican*, no. 5, (1985): 64-65.

TABLE 2.11

Developments in 1985

January	Optimistic mood following Arkhipov visit persists, but Chinese and Soviets exchange polemics over Afghanistan, Vietnam
March	Gorbachev succeeds Chernenko; Chinese refer to "Comrade Gorbachev"; Vice-Premier Li Peng meets with the Soviet leader
	Chinese call for improved relations, including political ties, with the Soviet Union
April	Sino-Soviet negotiations fail to make a breakthrough, but end with Gromyko's expressions of hope
	Gorbachev refers to the PRC as one of the socialist countries
June	Favorable Chinese press coverage of visits by Chinese delegations to the USSR
July	Vice-Premier Yao Yilin visits the USSR, signs long-term trade expansion pact
September	Foreign Ministers Wu Xueqian and Shevardnadze meet at the United Nations
October	Sino-Soviet negotiations meet for a seventh round; optimism of the previous winter has diminished
December	Chinese distance themselves from Kapitsa's overoptimism on Sino-Soviet relations
	Sino-Soviet trade rises sixty percent in 1985
	Li Peng and Arkhipov named chairmen of new Sino-Soviet Commission on Economic, Trade, Scientific and Technological Cooperation

The May issue of the same journal carries an article by Zhou Xincheng and Wang Degen with its own analysis of Soviet agriculture.[85] While details on the article appear in Chapter Three, here, I think, it is important to note the overall tone. The main thrusts are the positive accomplishments over the most recent thirty years and the favorable results of unified central planning. Zhou and Wang argue at the outset that the speed of agricultural development has been comparatively fast (a three-percent average, which few countries around the world can match), and the appearance of agriculture has undergone a relatively big change, despite the continued backwardness and tight supplies of some goods. Per capita consumption is 3,443 calories, which is 22 percent above the normal level and exceeds that of Western countries. Thus the problem is quality, not quan-

[85] Zhou Xincheng and Wang Degen, "Sulian nongye zhong jige zhide tantao de wenti," *Shijie jingji yu zhengzhi neican*, no. 5 (1985): 28-33.

tity, and differs from the situation in undeveloped countries. Zhou and Wang add that it is groundless to attribute agricultural backwardness to the unified planned economy. One must not reject the basic principles because of shortcomings in concrete operations.

The Gorbachev era had barely begun when Chinese articles began to accentuate his commitment to reform of the entire economic management system. In March and again on April 23, at his first two major speeches, Chinese observe, Gorbachev stressed the urgency of reform. They quote approvingly from his realistic assessments of the severity of the problems facing his country and of his insistence that nothing short of overall structural reform will suffice. In an article in the popular journal *Liaowang*, Wang Chongjie recalls that at the December 1984 all-union conference on ideological work, Gorbachev had declared that one of the reasons why the Soviet economy had worsened in the late 1970s and early 1980s was the failure to discover in time the need for reform of some aspects of the relations of production. That realization of the need for deep and thorough recognition of the existing situation and ideological reform at the level of adjusting the relations of production is a promising basis for change, in Chinese eyes.

Chinese pay close attention to the economic experiment of 1984, which was widened in 1985, with its focus on enterprise autonomy and increasing material incentives. They write too about the broadened incentives resulting from economic accountability practices and the collective brigade system in the villages. Wang notes that the highly centralized Soviet planning system demonstrated its superiority in concentrating resources to realize the main goals, but since the 1950s it has become less and less suitable for economic development needs. Wang's view of the reform process is that over twenty-some years it has been continuous and has led to very great improvement in planning work and the level of technology. Yet it has not allowed for sufficient autonomy and market regulation; many longstanding contradictions have not been resolved. The Soviet Union, he concludes, is a country with very great economic reserves, and there is little doubt that an earnest reform of the management system will advance the intensification of the entire economy and raise the standard of living of the people. Gorbachev has the right goals, and this article makes an upbeat prediction of the likely results.

Assessing the first three months of Gorbachev's tenure, another *Liaowang* reporter, Tang Xiushan, comments favorably on his initial efforts to express his own personality. From the time Gorbachev assumed office he has devoted his main energy to producing an economic upturn. His favorite expression has been, "We need less talk and more action." The article reviews the main initiatives during these months. Some of them (e.g. the effort to develop economic and trade relations with capitalist countries), clearly parallel China's reforms. Mention is also made of Gorbachev's expression of hope for a serious improvement in Soviet relations with China.[86]

The Chinese assessment of Gorbachev for internal distribution was also favorable. The May 1985 issue of the important journal *Shijie jingji yu zhengzhi neican* provides a profile of the new Soviet leader.[87] First, it appraises his fifteen years in local leadership positions, indicating that he rose rapidly because of his leadership talents. The impression is of a hardworking, able organizer who rose on the basis of merit to a position on the Central Committee at age 40. Second, having become known as an agricultural specialist, he served from 1978 in the difficult job of party secretary for agriculture. Although this was not a good period for agricultural production, the journal praises his talents in this area, noting the favorable results he obtained in agriculture for ten years as a local leader and arguing that from 1978 Soviet agriculture began a gradual recovery, even if the value of output was still declining somewhat. Gorbachev is given special credit for the reforms in agriculture, notably in 1983, and for the quite good results obtained that year. Under him, the article reports, there was a big change in Soviet agricultural conditions.

Third, the Chinese coverage draws favorable attention to continuities in Soviet leadership. Gorbachev was praised by both Brezhnev and Andropov. The author, Zhao Lianhong, finds it noteworthy that both Andropov and Gorbachev were from the same area (*tongxiang*). Their personal and work relations were both very close. Gorbachev was Andropov's main advisor. He was given wide responsibility over overall economic policy as well as party work and foreign affairs. He performed his job energetically, often acting in Andropov's name. Under Chernenko, Gorbachev was the number-two leader with major responsibilities, including work on drafting the new program of the Communist Party and meetings with foreign leaders. Fourth, Zhao speaks of the positive reaction of Soviet public opinion. In and out of the party, people wanted a young, energetic leader. Age represents a favorable element for him.

Fifth, the strongest praise centers on Gorbachev's advocacy of economic reform. He is referred to as a reformer (*gaigepai*, a term used only after Andropov took office) and a man of action (*wushipai*) and is quoted as seeking deep reform of the entire structure of economic and social re-

---

[86] Tang Xiushan, "Geerbaqiaofu jiuren sange yue," *Liaowang*, no. 25 (1985): 36-37.

[87] Zhao Lianhong, "Sugong zhongyang xinren zongshuji Geerbaqiaofu," *Shijie jingji yu zhengzhi neican*, no. 5 (1985): 61-63.

lations. He sees the fundamental problem in the mutual ties between the forces of production and the relations of production. Specifically, he is associated with the reforms in livestock-raising away from the one-sided pursuit of large-scale herding; the development of collective contracts and autonomous small brigades in farming; the encouragement of personal auxiliary farming; and the 1984 experiments in five types of enterprises and territories.

Finally, the article turns to Gorbachev's foreign policy. It notes that he has publicly said very little on relations with China, but adds that right after assuming office he called for a great improvement and observed that it is entirely possible if both sides are willing. The Chinese report that when Gorbachev met Li Peng on March 14, he called for continuing talks, raising the level in the leadership at which the conversations take place, reducing differences, and achieving advances over a broader arena. The article adds that his trips to Canada and England left a deep impression on people. He showed that he is skilled in the use of language, self-confident, and able to appear flexible without departing from known Soviet positions.

Commentaries in the Chinese mass media unrelated to Soviet reform policies tended to be factual and sympathetic. For instance, a feature article on the Volga River as the main artery in the Soviet river transport network praised the continuous attention given to developing the world's longest river system and described recent improvements in it.[88] Articles on Soviet-American relations and negotiations strove for impartiality. There was little sign in writings on most subjects of the hostility that had been expressed toward Moscow only a year or two earlier.

The upbeat mood in Chinese coverage of meetings between delegations of Chinese and Soviets continued in June 1985. Reporting on an official delegation from the National People's Congress Standing Commission (Quanguo ren da changweihui), which on June 15 issued a report on its March visit to the Soviet Union, *People's Daily* announced that the trip had been successful. It advanced mutual understanding and friendship and had a positive influence on the development of relations between the two countries.[89] In their conversations, old comrades recalled friendly times together in the 1950s. We feel, the article continues, that the traditional friendship between the peoples of the two countries is very deeply rooted. The legislatures (*guoyi*) of the two countries planned to

---

[88] Mu Yizhi, "Buerjiahe: Sulian hangdao de zhugan," *Liaowang*, no. 21 (1985): 36-37.

[89] "Sulian renmin dui Zhongguo renmin huaiyou youhao ganqing," *Renmin ribao*, June 16, 1985, p. 4.

send more delegations, including groups of specialists for investigations and understanding.

On June 22, 1985, *People's Daily* reported on a visit to the Soviet Union by a tourist group of activists from the China Friendship Association and the Sino-Soviet Friendship Association.[90] The report is highly complimentary, recalling first the widespread commemoration of the fortieth anniversary of the victory against fascism that the group encountered and then the completely new look of high-rise apartments one after another amidst the beautiful park-like atmosphere of Soviet cities. The group was deeply impressed by the achievements the Soviet people have obtained since the war in the construction of socialism. But the most unforgettable sensation, the article reports, was the friendly feelings of the Soviet people toward the Chinese people. It was like a cord that tied together the visit from beginning to end. Participating in meetings were sinologists, translators of Chinese literature, old soldiers, and old specialists who served in China during the war period or the time of construction. They all retain heart-felt memories of the times they spent together with Chinese comrades. From a second-grader studying Chinese to an old man moved to ask to embrace the group's head one more time, the group's experiences are touchingly recounted. What could be more valuable than friendship among peoples! Saying this, the article concludes with the wish that friendship between peoples of the two countries will continuously develop.

On June 29, 1985, in *Zhongguo qingnian bao*, a Chinese citizen who was working in Moscow talked about today's Soviet youth.[91] His headings convey the positive tone of the article: "enthusiastic love for work," "concern for politics," "leisure-time life." The first section describes the hundreds of thousands of Soviet youths who willingly contribute their labor to society over the summer in Siberia, the Far East, and elsewhere and make a very great contribution to socialist construction. Many construction brigades give part or all of their labor to a peace fund or for the cause of social welfare, the article explains. Soviet youths in general are comparatively interested in politics: 85 percent often watch political movies, while more than 90 percent voluntarily contribute part of their income to help poor countries. Youths frequently join in various political activities, such as those to celebrate forty years since the victory over fascism. In the final section the reader is told that youths mainly use their leisure for reading books, sports, travel, viewing plays and movies, or listening to music or ballet. Even in the subways or in line to make a pur-

[90] Ding Yiwei, "Fang Su yinxiang," *Renmin ribao*, June 22, 1985, p. 7.
[91] Sheng Shiliang, "Jinri Sulian qingnian," *Zhongguo qingnian bao*, June 29, 1985, p. 3.

chase, Soviet youths do not put down their reading matter. But there is a portion who often get drunk. Youth follow fashions. The Komsomol does not excessively limit their seeking after fashions, but it emphasizes their upbringing with a correct worldview, good morals, and a reduced consumer psychology. It demands that young people continue the three great traditions of revolutionary, soldier, and worker. The article ends with this statement, suggesting that Soviet youths remain firmly in the socialist tradition.

In April 1985 an article appeared on one of the most threatening topics concerning Soviet foreign policy—its buildup in Southeast Asia.[92] The article draws together the most recent materials by Japanese, American, and other military specialists to analyze the directions and strategic plans of the Soviet Union in the South China Sea or Cam Ranh (Jinlan) Bay. The analysis traces the success of Soviet strategy from 1975 in gaining use of the bay and making it an indispensable part of its southern strategy. What are Soviet goals? The article mentions three: 1) to struggle with America for hegemonism at sea, 2) to surround China; and 3) to move south into Southeast Asia and the Pacific Ocean. Discussing the last two, the article asserts that the Soviet Union sees Vietnam, the Kampuchean puppet, and Laos as "fortress countries" opposed to China, and plans through military and economic assistance gradually to bring them into the framework encircling China that is formed by the Soviet Union, Mongolia, Afghanistan, and India. For this end, it wants to maintain for a long time the existing situation on the Sino-Vietnamese border and foment long-term tension (*buhe*) between Vietnam and China. Through aid to this region, the Soviets seek to draw countries closer to their country. In the future, if there is a clash between China and the Soviet Union, the Soviet Union can then open a front on China's south, creating the advantageous situation of a two-sided attack on China. Today, we are told, the Soviets are also using divisions inside ASEAN to try to split the alliance and to interfere with Indonesian relations with China.

The final part of the article examines Soviet-Vietnamese relations. It points to the vast Soviet expenditures on aid, but claims that they are not to strengthen Vietnam but to help Moscow control it. Moscow seeks to exploit the situation in Kampuchea, to make Vietnam more dependent in order to give Moscow a long-term occupation of Cam Ranh Bay, and to make the three countries of Indochina the equivalent of Cuba under Soviet control. But cooperation between a big and a little hegemonist lacks a deep foundation, and if one adds to this Vietnam's historical national-

[92] Guan Jian, "Sulian zai Jinlanwan de junshi dongxiang ji qi zhanlue yitu," *Shijie jingji yu zhengzhi neican*, no. 4 (1985): 43-44, 49.

ism and resistance to subjection, in the long run the contradictions in the relation will widen. The Soviet southern strategy is definitely not an easy matter, the article concludes.

This article on the Soviet naval buildup in Vietnam was not an isolated publication. A few months earlier the same influential journal carried an article on Soviet strategy in East Asia.[93] It begins by saying that the Soviet strategy in East Asia is an important wing of its global strategy. The basic aim is to place China and Japan under Soviet influence and to drive American power to the other shore of the Pacific. From the mid-sixties to the mid-seventies, Moscow planned to isolate and control China, applying political, economic, and military pressure, even to the point of provoking border clashes and causing bilateral relations to worsen to the extreme. At that time the Soviet Union carried out detente with America and tried to attract Japan, pursuing its anti-China policy. From the mid-seventies to the beginning of the eighties, Moscow opposed the development of American-Chinese-Japanese relations, especially continuing to expand its Far East naval forces. The third stage began in 1981 after Reagan's inauguration and continues to the present. The Soviet-American opposition is the major contradiction, and Moscow is intensifying the struggle to change the situation in the Far East. It has not reduced its threat against China.

Of what does the Soviet Far Eastern strategy consist? Economically, Moscow seeks a way out of its slowdown in economic growth through creating a foreign security zone in East Asia and drawing into its plans for speeding the development of Siberia its two great East Asian trading partners, China and Japan. Militarily, the Soviet Far Eastern naval zone is of ever more strategic significance for Soviet naval hegemony. The foreign elements: 1) Reagan's policy is maintaining stronger forces against the Soviet Union; 2) although Sino-Soviet relations have not yet been normalized, the two sides are talking and the Chinese are adopting the line of centering on building their economy and are striving hard to improve Sino-Soviet relations in order to ensure a peaceful foreign policy; 3) Sino-American relations are developing, but the Taiwan question is still not resolved; 4) Japan is actively joining the American global strategy, developing its relations with China, and increasing its "political role;" 5) American, Japanese, and South Korean triangular relations are drawing progressively closer. The main Soviet strategic calculations are: 1) to build a triangular structure of peaceful coexistence among the Soviet Union, China, and Japan and to prevent the formation of a triangle among

[93] Liu Jiangyong, "Sulian de dongya zhanlue ji woguo de duice," *Shijie jingji yu zhengzhi neican*, no. 2 (1985): 35-39.

America, China, and Japan; and 2) to strengthen Soviet-Vietnam-Mongolian relations and to prod North Korea to join in opposition to the American-Japanese-South Korean alliance.

In March 1982, Brezhnev's Tashkent speech sought talks with China without any preconditions and improved relations, and called for policies to strengthen trust with Japan. This was a new strategy in the effort to disrupt the disadvantageous situation toward the Soviet Union of the development of American-Chinese-Japanese relations. With its assertion to Japan in October 1983 that it would be advantageous for the relaxation of Asian tensions to form a peaceful coexistence triangle among the Soviet Union, China, and Japan, Moscow was making a long-term calculation of a fundamental change in the East Asian strategic situation.

When Chernenko took office, his first acts were to maintain Sino-Soviet talks, to avoid a deterioration in relations, to skirt the "three obstacles," and to break the stalemate by turning first to economic and cultural relations. He reasoned that if economic relations do not advance, political relations cannot advance. But soon afterwards the Soviet attitude toward China again hardened. The main expression of this came after Reagan visited China, when the Soviets suddenly postponed the visit of Arkhipov. Then, on June 11, Chernenko for the first time criticized China for taking actions antagonistic to Vietnam. It is said that the Soviets, in opposition to the improvement in Chinese-American ties, intended to control China by intensifying the Sino-Vietnamese confrontation.

These Soviet actions, the article maintains, reveal the deep contradictions present in the Soviet Far Eastern strategy. Following the intensification of the Soviet-American struggle in the Pacific region, Moscow on the one hand wants to improve relations with China, and on the other wants to continue to increase its military strength, to strengthen the strategic gains it has already obtained in Vietnam and Afghanistan. But the latter without doubt can pose a threat to China, and the former can cause Vietnamese resentment and lead to contradictions between Vietnam and the Soviet Union; therefore the two are very difficult to carry out together.

It appears that Chernenko regarded as the immediate task the strengthening of relations with Vietnam, Mongolia, and other Asian allies, and treated normalization of Sino-Soviet relations as a long-term objective of secondary priority. Proof of this was the parting statement in the spring of 1984 of the foreign ministers of the three countries, testifying to a unanimous position on Kampuchea and Afghanistan while indicating that improvement in relations with China ought to be carried out without harming the interests of third countries. The Chinese article then cites *Mainichi Shimbun*, saying that after Chernenko took office, Soviet troops in Afghanistan rose rapidly from about 160,000 in February to 200,000 by October, and cites another Japanese source as stating that Soviet aid to Vietnam rose from 2.5 to 6 million American dollars per day after 1980, making it comparable to the total figure for Cuba. Vietnam has already become the most important Soviet foothold in the Third World and Asia. What these circumstances show is that after Chernenko took office, the possibility of Soviet concessions on the "three obstacles" narrowed, permitting Moscow only to be able to make expressions on the questions of reducing troops stationed on the Sino-Soviet border. This resulted in a definite limitation in Chernenko's authority to improve relations with China.

The contradictory nature of the Soviet Far Eastern strategy brings foreign relations losses to Moscow, says the article. Continuous military buildup in the Far East, the support of Vietnam's invasion of Kampuchea, the long-term occupation of Afghanistan, and the buildup in Cam Ranh Bay especially pose a threat to China and Japan and almost the entire Pacific region. The article construes these Soviet offensive actions as actually constituting assistance to Washington for seizing other parts of this region. The result of these Soviet policies is paradoxically to put the Soviet Union militarily in a more reactive and serious situation in the Pacific region.

How should China respond? The 1985 article argues that its policies should change in accord with the stages of the Soviet military strategy. They must not lose their flexibility. China must on the basis of maintaining its anti-hegemonist position promote conversations and deepen mutual understanding with the Soviet Union. Apart from widening economic and trade relations and cultural exchanges, the two countries can regularly bring together their international affairs specialists to exchange views and make sure that the current Soviet leaders and their successors all understand that China's sincerity to improve Sino-Soviet relations is important.

If America can further strengthen its relations with Japan and China, the Soviet position resulting from its contradictory East Asian strategy will become more reactive. Therefore, it is important not to wipe out the possibility for future Soviet leaders to adjust their strategy in international relations as a whole and in East Asia. Moreover, as the relative strength of the two superpowers tends to decline, the development of healthy Sino-Japanese relations is extremely significant. If, into the twenty-first century, Sino-Japanese relations can respect the five principles of peaceful coexistence and the four principles of Sino-Japanese relations, and if economically the strength of the two countries increases even more, not only can this become an enormous force for controlling the outbreak of a Soviet-American war, but it can give rise to a positive influence for Soviet-American detente. The article ends with a discussion of the possibility of a relatively stable new situation of relations among America, the Soviet Union, China, and Japan in the Pacific region.

Shortly after this critical treatment of Chernenko appeared in print, the Soviet leader was dead. The repeated message in the article to impress China's concerns and sincerity upon the successors of the current leadership suggests that they were not expecting much from Chernenko but were looking ahead to Gorbachev to speed the process of normalization.

Of all the obstacles to Sino-Soviet relations, the differing relationship of each country to Vietnam was apparently the most serious. Yet in 1985, the significance of this problem may have been lessening. On July 1, *People's Daily* reported that leaders of the Soviet Union and Vietnam had signed a joint communiqué in Moscow on June 29.[94] It called for increased Soviet foreign aid. The brief Chinese article concluded that the two sides also recognized that normalization of relations by the Soviet Union and Vietnam with the People's Republic of China will correspond to the goal of strengthening peace in Asia and international security.

By mid-1985, the Chinese position on the three barriers to negotiations had shifted to make it easier for Moscow to seek a compromise solution. The Chinese were no longer calling for Soviet action on all three problems simultaneously. They also were indicating that they did not expect that any obstacle would be removed at once. What mattered was that the Soviets show a willingness to solve one of the obstacles, that they take a constructive attitude. Of the three problem areas, the Chinese were increasingly indicating that their primary concern is Southeast Asia. The crucial issues are Vietnam's military presence in Kampuchea and the Soviet military presence in Cam Ranh Bay.

Sino-Soviet relations were advancing on two distinct tracks. They were progressing rapidly on the state-to-state track of economic, scientific, and cultural exchanges, while the Chinese were awaiting Soviet action on one of the "three obstacles" before proceeding with the track of strategic cooperation and party-to-party relations. By the end of 1985, five friendship association delegations had visited from each country, seven rounds of biannual negotiations between deputy foreign ministers had been held, and economic ties had been expanded and were accompanied by increasingly high-level contacts. Prospects in these areas were improving; yet the Chinese were still waiting for Soviet action in the strategic area. They were waiting for the new Gorbachev administration to decide whether it

[94] "Sulian jueding zengjia dui Yue yuanzhu," *Renmin ribao* (haiwai ban), July 1, 1985, p. 6.

could reduce its military presence in Asia and establish a spirit of cooperation with an independent, socialist China.

Heartened by the Chinese response, Soviet leaders accentuated the
positive. Kapitsa and then Gorbachev at the Twenty-seventh Congress in
early 1986 expressed satisfaction with the improvement in relations.
Chinese spokesmen sought to distance their country somewhat from this
optimism. While Moscow had urged Beijing to sign a nonaggression pact,
the latter had refused in recognition that this would have given the sem-
blance of great progress without the substance of Soviet concessions on
any of the three obstacles. Moreover, Beijing had resisted Moscow's call
for a special relationship based on the common socialist character of the
two countries. Moscow was trying to avoid being treated along with other
countries in accord with the five principles. Beijing resisted, clinging to
an independent course, and sought to maintain some pressure on Moscow
to make strategic concessions.

Conclusion

From 1978 to 1985 a debate raged in China over how to interpret domestic
and foreign policy in the Soviet Union. Chinese domestic considerations
prevailed. Maoist criticisms of the USSR could not be maintained for they
aroused radical thinking inside China. Reformist critiques had to be suppressed or toned down, for they threatened centralized control by China's
communist leadership. The Yugoslavian model by 1981 came to be
viewed as too market-oriented and a danger to central control. Poland's
Solidarity movement was seen as a danger too, capable of inciting labor
unions and others to demand a transfer of power from the central leadership. Eurocommunism had the drawback of being associated with some
reinterpretations of key Marxist concepts (such as alienation) that draw
attention to the privileges and powers of leaders. The principal alternatives to the Soviet Union in the socialist world could not be easily embraced for long by the Chinese. Rather than judging the Soviet Union inferior to some alternative model of socialism, the Chinese accepted it as
socialist on its own terms. Criticisms continued, but were restricted by
this context.

A progression can be seen in Chinese thinking about the Soviet Union.
In 1978, the first big question that Chinese sought to answer was: *What
is socialism?* In the process of answering this, they dropped many older
criticisms of the Soviet Union. In 1978 the Chinese also sought to move
decisively away from their policy of self-reliance. Since they could not
easily open up to the West and the Soviet Union simultaneously, they
chose to "lean to one side." Economic priorities, the hostile relationship

with Vietnam, and the difficulties of repairing deeply damaged Soviet relations quickly all probably figured into the decision. Beginning secretly
in 1977, and continuing more publicly in the second half of 1979, Chinese
debated: *Is the Soviet Union revisionist?* This was the second big question that affected Sino-Soviet relations. Reformers and the remnants of
the radicals both had a stake in answering that the Soviet Union is less
than fully socialist, the former in order to encourage more liberal policies
than had been adopted in the Soviet Union. Nevertheless, the reform
group had to be of two minds because of past abuse of the ideal of socialism, and they must have welcomed the decision to stop using the term
"revisionism" or any other pejorative term for the Soviet domestic system. The Chinese were not fully satisfied with the fruits of leaning to the
American side following their unsuccessful war with Vietnam and moved
later in 1979 to bolster Soviet ties, but this process was interrupted by the
Soviet entry into Afghanistan. Later, in 1980 and 1981, relations with
Washington were not proceeding smoothly; the impetus grew for some
balance through Soviet ties.

Finally, in 1982, leaders faced their third big question: *Should China
actively pursue normalization?* All of the factors came together to
bring a real turnabout in Sino-Soviet relations. China had been moving
toward greater party control and centralization at home. The Chinese
were looking to the Soviet Union and Hungary for lessons to apply in industrial reform. Soviet foreign policy was perceived as more defensive
than it had been. Finally, the emerging Andropov leadership was eager to
improve relations.

In late 1983 and through early 1984, a fourth big question arose:
*Should Chinese foreign policy become equidistant between the United
States and the Soviet Union?* Again domestic controls were being tightened, U.S. relations were cool, and favorable signs were coming from the
Andropov reform program in the Soviet Union. Beijing saw the U.S. as
increasingly on the offensive in the world, justifying its own partial move
toward equidistance. Yet the debate was resolved with the decision not to
use the term "equidistance."

Without any Soviet concessions on the "three obstacles" to normalization, China's leaders first in the second half of 1984, and then again in
the second half of 1985, faced a persistent problem: *How much normalization should China agree to without progress on strategic issues?* In the
fall of 1984, China acquiesced to substantial state-to-state improvements—in trade, in exchange visits, and in a friendlier atmosphere.
China extended the open-door policy to the Soviet Union, but without
concluding that normalization had been achieved. After the honeymoon
phase of Gorbachev's accession began to fade, the Chinese were faced

again a year later with the question of what further steps toward normalization should be approved: *What is required to realize full normalization—to extend normalization from state-to-state to party-to-party relations?* With the Soviet Union in the midst of a reorientation of its foreign policy under a new general secretary and a new foreign minister, it was appropriate for China's leaders to await further Soviet initiatives that some expected to come in 1986.

These stages in improving bilateral relations were mirrored in changing scholarship on Soviet society. The first phase, in 1978, was mainly treated in writings on Marxist ideological themes. After that, the Soviet Union figured directly in all of the stages in the debate. In 1978-1979, writings in literature and the arts were the focus of discussions of revisionism; Chinese recognized the existence of a common socialist culture. In 1980-1982, the background for discussions of normalization was the growing literature on Soviet economic reform. In 1983-1984, foreign policy itself became a subject, albeit mainly in *neibu* publications, for direct examination.

After a rapid buildup of scholarship from 1979 to 1982, Chinese sources were making detailed examinations of Soviet history and contemporary conditions. Background factors, especially China's domestic environment, encouraged sympathetic but sometimes critical study of the development of Soviet society. A combination of background factors, including the increasingly reform-oriented Soviet internal environment and the improving Sino-Soviet bilateral environment, led to generally favorable perceptions in the years 1983-1985. At the same time, the intense struggle between orthodox and reform views within China made Soviet studies a lively arena for contending interpretations of socialism.

Soviets have also kept track of Chinese views on their country. O. B. Rakhmanin, the most powerful official in the China field, kept a count for at least a decade of so-called "anti-Soviet" statements in three leading official Chinese publications. His tallies are not inconsistent with my observations. As seen in Table 2.12, criticisms of the Soviet Union mounted sharply in the mid-1970s, especially during the radicals' campaign of 1976, and then again in 1980 in response to the Afghanistan fighting. (The figure for 1979, which I did not find, should also have been high because of the coverage of Vietnam.) Sharp drops in criticism occurred first in 1977 after Mao's death and the fall of the "Gang of Four," and then in 1981. Undoubtedly the number of severe criticisms continued to decline after 1981. In fact, there was probably no longer any point in keeping this kind of tally by 1982 or 1983 since the tone of Chinese writings had become decidedly less negative. Whereas for most of the 1970s a crude count of anti-Soviet statements may provide a useful account of Chinese views, for the period beginning in 1978 it is increasingly important to examine the contents of Chinese writings on specific subjects. A new era has dawned in Chinese scholarship. In order to understand Chinese perceptions accurately, it has become necessary to look closely at a substantial academic literature.

TABLE 2.12

Rakhmanin's Count of Anti-Soviet Statements in
People's Daily, Guangming ribao, *and* Hongqi[a]

1972	430	1975	1800	1979	—[b]
1973	900	1976	3700	1980	3400[c]
1974	1500	1977	2700	1981	2500
		1978	2500		

[a] *Kitaiskaia Narodnaia Respublika v-1974 godu: politika, ekonomika, ideologiia* (Moscow: Nauka, 1977), 162; *Kitaiskaia Narodnaia Respublika v-1976 godu: politika, ekonomika, ideologiia* (Moscow: Nauka, 1978), 203; *Kitaiskaia Narodnaia Respublika v-1977 godu: politika, ekonomika, ideologiia* (Moscow: Nauka, 1979), 147; *Kitaiskaia Narodnaia Respublika v-1978 godu: politika, ekonomika, ideologiia* (Moscow: Nauka, 1980), 171; O. B. Borisov, "Nekotorye aspekty politiki Kitaia,"*Kommunist*, no. 6 (1981), reprinted in *Opasnyi kurs* 11 (Moscow: Politizdat, 1981), 23.

[b] A count of "anti-Soviet propaganda" in *People's Daily* finds about 400 examples during the period August, September, and the first ten days of October, 1979. *Kitaiskaia Narodnaia Respublika v-1979 godu: Politika, ekonomika, ideologiia* (Moscow: Nauka, 1981), 159.

[c] *People's Daily* alone.

THREE

PEASANTS AND THE AGRICULTURAL
SYSTEM

For a time in the 1960s and 1970s, China, more than any other country, captured the imagination of foreign observers as a country in which peasants took fate into their own hands. Maoism stood for revolution by and for the peasants. To a vocal minority of foreign observers responding to the rhetoric of the Cultural Revolution, Chinese communism even represented the brightest hope for the majority of people in the world—the struggling peasants of the less-developed countries. At the core of these optimistic assertions was a widely perceived contrast between the revolution from above in the Soviet Union, which dragged peasants against their will into collective farms and kept them in conditions of forced production with little in return, and the revolution from below in China, in which the masses gave their enthusiastic support for each turn of the revolutionary wheel from land reform, to collectivization, to communization, and then to the mass upheavals of the Cultural Revolution. Criticisms in China of Soviet mistreatment of peasants supported these sympathetic assessments of the Chinese approach.

In 1979 and the early 1980s, there was an abrupt turnaround in China's rural policies. It was acknowledged that the reality of poverty and despair made a mockery of past rhetoric. Under the leadership of Deng Xiaoping, that which had been denounced for almost two decades now became the ideal. At the same time as a new understanding developed for China's rural transition to socialism, a different interpretation was required for the history of rural development in the Soviet Union. The old Maoist critique failed to distinguish between the new policies being successfully implemented in China and the long-vilified Soviet practices. A new literature on Soviet rural society was born. Before considering what came under Deng's leadership, it will be useful to reexamine the Maoist views that preceded it.

THE MAOIST CRITIQUE OF SOVIET RURAL LIFE

Public criticism of the Soviet model of socialism began in China shortly after Khrushchev's de-Stalinization speech of February 14, 1956. In

April, the Chinese Communist Party echoed Khrushchev's criticism of a communist leadership cut off from the masses.

The personnel of the Party and the state, beset by bureaucratism from many sides, face the great danger of using the machinery of state to take arbitrary action, alienating themselves from the masses and collective leadership, resorting to commandism, and violating Party and state democracy.[1]

Also in April, Mao Zedong's speech, "On the Ten Major Relationships," criticized the Soviet Union for "lopsided stress on heavy industry to the neglect of agriculture and light industry." Mao added that the Soviets had made "grave mistakes" in their treatment of peasants and in policies that "squeeze the peasants very hard." Their methods of accumulation "had seriously dampened the peasants' enthusiasm for production. You want the hen to lay more eggs and yet you don't feed it, you want the horse to run fast and yet you don't let it graze. What kind of logic is this?"[2]

Mao's first lengthy assessment of Soviet socialism came in critiques of the Soviet publication *Political Economy: A Textbook* and Stalin's *Economic Problems of Socialism in the USSR*. Although not published until 1967, these critiques, which were written in 1958-1960, show the development of Mao's thinking at a time when the Great Leap Forward was unfolding in China and Sino-Soviet relations were reaching a crisis.

Mao's criticisms of Stalin's approach toward peasants dwell on three main themes. First, the masses were not given sufficient opportunities to participate. Stalin's view that collectivization is carried out by the government expropriating land and parcelling it out is a rightist deviation that substitutes the leaders for the masses. He is wrong to depict history as something that planners rather than the masses create, to see the creative activity of the masses as just "one important factor." Mao adds that the Soviet state controlled the peasantry "very, very tightly, inflexibly" and that "mistrust of the peasants is the basic viewpoint of the third letter," which is included in Stalin's book.[3]

Second, Mao considers Stalin's theory of socialist development to be incorrect. The idea that socialist industrialization is the precondition for agricultural collectivization is not only wrong, Mao asserts, but it contributed to delays in agricultural collectivization even where industry was

[1] "On Historical Experience Concerning the Dictatorship of the Proletariat," *Hsinhua* (Xinhua), no. 4 (April 5, 1956): 54-59.

[2] Mao Zedong, "On the Ten Major Relationships," *Peking Review*, no. 20 (January 1, 1977): 1.

[3] Mao Tsetung, *A Critique of Soviet Economics* (New York: Monthly Review Press, 1977), 44, 79, 130, and 134.

advanced, as in certain Eastern European countries. Stalin failed to observe growing contradictions between advancing forces of production and stagnant relations of production, which should have led to steps beyond agricultural collectivization. Instead of moving forward from collectives to ownership by the whole people, Stalin referred to the "fully consolidated" collective farm system, indicating he had no interest in further transformation. Mao also criticized the Soviet Union for unbalanced development, walking on one leg—heavy industry—but not on the other—light industry and agriculture—and he concluded that this imbalance ends up hurting heavy industry too.[4]

Finally, Mao accuses Stalin of erring in his analysis of rural social classes and the closely related issues of equality and incentives. Stalin's unsatisfactory assertion that following collectivization, middle peasants became the principal figures in the villages, Mao says, is bound to make former poor peasants feel as if they had been "put in the shade." It opens the way for the middle peasants to assume leadership. Stalin failed to consider that a private-owner point of view persisted in the upper middle and prosperous peasants. He too optimistically concluded that the broad mass of the peasantry would not waiver again. Moreover, he overlooked the danger of the continued presence of private property and subsidiary occupations. As a result, Stalin underestimated the need for changing the consciousness of peasants, of attending to ideological change as well as mechanization and material incentives. Stalin did not consider how to advance the worker-peasant alliance, what contradictions operate at each stage, and how they may be resolved.[5]

On July 14, 1964, in the authoritative Ninth Commentary published in *People's Daily*, Mao made public his critical outlook on Soviet society. The language was stronger than in the then-unpublished notes on Stalin's writings, and the criticisms were updated to attack Khrushchev's leadership directly. Now Mao condemned the Soviet system as a dictatorship over the mass of peasants. He argued that the collective farms had fallen under the control of functionaries and their gangs who steal and speculate at will, freely squandering public money and fleecing the farmers. These farms had virtually become private property, and the broad mass of farmers are among the groups "seething with discontent against the oppression and exploitation practiced by the privileged stratum."[6]

This revisionist outcome is linked to mistaken Soviet theories of de-

[4] Ibid., 48, 54-59, 77, 97, and 129.

[5] Ibid., 45-47, 55, 70.

[6] "On Khrushchev's Phoney Communism and Its Historical Lessons for the World," in William E. Griffith, *Sino-Soviet Relations, 1964-1965* (Cambridge: The M.I.T. Press, 1967), 323-24, 330, 340.

velopment. Stalin, Mao said, prematurely declared that there were "no longer antagonistic classes in the Soviet Union and that it was free of class conflicts." Failing to recognize that spontaneous capitalist tendencies persist and that the soil for the growth of new rich peasants still exists, the Soviets did not rely on the masses in order to wage a struggle against the forces of capitalism. Khrushchev compounded this error by pushing through policies that hastened the growth of the forces of capitalism. He attacked the system of socialist agricultural planning, describing it as "bureaucratic" and "unnecessary."[7]

Some 11 to 12 years later, after the interval of the Cultural Revolution and the intermittent publication of scathing diatribes against Soviet "revisionism," a wave of new writings hostile to Soviet society swept across China. These materials, which appeared from 1975 to early 1978 and which represent the final stage in the Chinese interpretations of Soviet society along Maoist lines, elaborate on the timing of the deterioration of Soviet agriculture and rural life. For example, one 1978 book notes that "Russia was historically known as the 'granary of Europe.' During the socialist period, the Soviet Union not only had sufficient grain for home consumption and a large reserve build-up, but was also one of the world's important grain exporters. It was only after the restoration of capitalism in the country that agricultural production started on its downward trend. In the eleven years when Khrushchev was in power, Soviet farming was already in a mess. Since Brezhnev took over, it has worsened." In other words, it was only after Stalin's death that "the original Soviet collective and state farms degenerated."[8]

Attempts at "economic reform" only made matters worse, argued the Chinese. The March 1965 program especially, adopted by the Central Committee under the slogan of using "economic stimuli," totally uprooted the original socialist system of economic management in favor of the profit motive and the capitalist path.[9] In December 1968, new land-use regulations permitted the free transfer and rental of village lands, and additional decisions in November 1969 approved of a changeover to a rich peasant economy.[10] Agricultural decline appears in this literature as the inevitable result of regression from socialism to capitalism. We read that "agricultural has continued to decline so much that Brezhnev is now reel-

[7] Ibid., 317, 321-22, 327.

[8] Wei Chi, *The Soviet Union Under the New Tsars* (Beijing: Foreign Languages Press, 1978), 23 and 25.

[9] Kan, *jintian de Sulian: zibenzhuyi quanmian fubi* (Shanghai: Shanghai renminchubanshe, 1975), 22.

[10] Xia Changan, *Sulian jingji de tuibian* (Hong Kong: Xianggang Chaoyang chubanshe, 1977), 12-13.

ing under the impact of the blow. Official Soviet statistics reveal that since Brezhnev assumed power in 1964, grain production has dropped sharply seven times [to 1976]. During the Ninth Five-year Plan period (1971-1975), it showed a substantial decrease in four of the five years, and 1975 saw the poorest harvest in ten years and the biggest slump in twenty years."[11] The conclusion is unmistakable: the more recent the period in the Soviet Union, the worse the state of Soviet agriculture.

Capitalism, to China's critics of the Soviet Union, means "mercilessly fleecing" the rural masses, grabbing much of the produce through a high procurement rate, exploiting the peasants through accelerating the scissors movement of prices between industrial and agricultural products, and plundering the peasantry through a high turnover tax. Land reclamation, especially in Kazakhstan, was a response to the increasing crisis in grain production. Despite claims of rejuvenation through this means, the facts show, say the Chinese, that grave damage resulted. The results were dust storms, water erosion, land turning alkaline, and shrinking arable land. "This is a capitalist system of management, namely, draining the pond to catch all the fish."[12] Chinese also noted that military expenditure eats up more than one-third of the Soviet budgetary outlay, leading to little progress in farm improvement for lack of funds.[13]

These condemnations of Soviet agriculture are accompanied by criticisms of exploitative social class relations. The Soviet "agricultural laborer is forced to work intensively at the hardest jobs, his hours are the longest, his pay the lowest. On the basis of official statistics . . . almost 30 percent of the rural population are earning less than enough for maintaining the subsistence level prescribed by the Soviet revisionists."[14] The Soviets violate the socialist principle "to each according to his work." Through "legal" and illegal means, collective farm leaders "greedily squeeze the blood and sweat out of the collective farm members, thus exacerbating polarization in the countryside." "The salaries of those usurping farm leadership are several times, a dozen times or even 20-30 times those of ordinary farm members. Moreover, they have all kinds of additional remuneration and bonuses . . . they obtain illegally large amounts of income by embezzling, stealing, speculation and extortion."[15]

---

[11] Wei Chi, *The Soviet Union Under the New Tsars*, 22.

[12] "The Brezhnev Renegade Clique Damages Soviet Agriculture," *Social Imperialism: The Soviet Union Today* (reprints from *Peking Review*) (Berkeley: Yenan Books, 1977), 108-112.

[13] Wei Chi, *The Soviet Union Under the New Tsars*, 28-29.

[14] Ibid., 27-28.

[15] "Soviet Collective Farms Degenerate," *Social Imperialism: The Soviet Union Today*, 106.

Chinese point to a fundamental problem in the distribution of power. Using the excuse that agricultural officials lacked education, the Khrushchev leadership had removed most of the original collective farm party secretaries and chairmen of worker and peasant origin and had appointed to replace them its own faithful agents (i.e. representatives of revisionism). "The Soviet press . . . acknowledged that many collective farm chairmen dictate everything and act like petty tyrants." "The collective farm members are denied all power. . . . They [farm chairmen] often have protectors in higher organizations and no one can touch them. . . . The farm chairman . . . takes all power into his own hands. . . . The farm authorities can usually make regulations as they wish to punish farm members." These new village capitalist elements monopolize all power in labor remuneration and bonuses and use administrative and economic means to mete out punishments. The living standards of most peasants get poorer and poorer. In turn, most peasants have completely lost their motivation to work. This has led to a mass exodus, particularly of young people, from the farm. Farm workers "resort to slowdowns, absenteeism, and leaving the land." Instead of solving these problems, Soviet leaders try to shift the blame. They dismiss their ministers of agriculture, treating them as scapegoats. They blame the weather, and they even blame "the Soviet farmers for their 'lack of necessary love' for the soil, but [are] unable to explain why. All their excuses have turned out to be mere humbug."[16]

In short, the Maoist critique, which endured for nearly two decades into 1978, noted continuous deterioration of Soviet agriculture and rural life due to: 1) exploitation by Soviet officials accompanied by insufficient incentives for the farmers; and 2) concentration of power in the hands of a few with insufficient participation by the majority. In one of the rare footnotes one encounters in Chinese sources of this period, the Soviet journal *Literaturnaia gazeta* is cited for its revelation that at meetings of collective farmers, fewer and fewer people were speaking; the numbers in one farm fell from 2.9 percent in 1965 to 0.4 percent in 1976, and over ninety percent of these remarks came from capitalist elements who were transmitting orders. The Soviet rural masses no longer had a say in the running of their collective farms.

According to the Chinese, the most recent Soviet information showed only continued deterioration in the Soviet countryside. By 1976, rural citizens were in desperate straits. Citing the journal *Nedelia*, Chinese noted that in Kalinin oblast', many villages were only supplied bread once

[16] Wei Chi, *The Soviet Union Under the New Tsars*, 26-28; "Soviet Collective Farms Degenerate," 105-106; and *Kan, jintian de Sulian*, 21, 32.

or twice a week. In that same year, rationing of meat had begun along
with meatless days. Black market prices for foodstuffs had climbed to
alarming levels.[17] These were the messages conveyed to the Chinese people as recently as 1978.

THE LEGACY OF RUSSIA'S PAST

In the new scholarship, which began to appear in 1979, different explanations are offered for the problems of Soviet rural life. One factor that
is noted is the historical development of the country. Prior to the October
Revolution, Russia's peasantry was backward. This is the unequivocal
message in those Chinese writings which treat the historical origins of the
Soviet system. Not many do. It suffices merely to take for granted the
backwardness of rural Russia without examining the degree of backwardness or the distinctiveness of Russian rural society.

Chinese are largely content to reassert critiques of serfdom articulated
by Russian revolutionaries. A 1980 article in memory of the 190th anniversary of the publication of Radishchev's *Journey from St. Petersburg to
Moscow* repeats the viewpoint that serfdom held the Russian people back,
but that the people wanted to live, thus revolution was inevitable.[18] Three
years later, an article on the Pugachev rebellion of 1773-1775 stressed the
historical achievement of this intense class struggle as an inspiration for
opposing feudal oppression, serf exploitation, and the entire feudal serf
system.[19] Occasional articles also assess the reigns of individual rulers.
For example, a 1980 article observes that Catherine II expanded and
strengthened the serf system. Having abandoned the deceitful pose of
"enlightened monarch" after the Pugachev uprising, she tightened control over the peasants (e.g. through a centralizing administrative reform
in the 1770s). While Russia's national market and handicrafts developed
rapidly, Russia remained extremely backward in comparison to England,
reflecting the limits imposed by the serf system on the forces of production. In other words, Chinese conclude, only the struggle against serfdom
held out hope for significant improvement in rural life.[20]

Chinese authors recognize four peasant rebellions in Russian history:

[17] Xia Changan, *Sulian jingji de tuibian*, 19 and 128-29.
[18] Song Changzhong, "Tao fa Eguo zhuanzhi nongnu zhidu de xiwen: jinian Lajishefu
'Cong Bidebao dao Mosike luxingji' chuban 190 zhounian," *Jilin daxue shehuikexue xuebao*, no. 5 (1980).
[19] Xu Yunxia and Han Chengwen, "Pujiaqiaofu qiyi," *Henan shida xuebao* (shehuikexue
ban), no. 1 (1983): 110-14.
[20] Liu Zuxi, "Yekatelinna ershi he shahuang Eguo," *Beijing daxue xuebao* (zhexue shehuikexue ban), no. 1 (1980): 61-73.

those of 1606-1607, 1667-1671, 1707-1708, and 1773-1775. In each instance, spontaneous explosions could not lead to big changes because of banditry and disorganization. Peasants needed worker leadership to emerge victorious, but there was no working class to fill this role. One Chinese writer describes the peasant nature as two-sided: on the one hand, the peasant is a worker opposed to feudal oppression, and on the other, he is a small proprietor influenced by a backward mode of production to be conservative. With this short-sighted vision, the Russian peasant embraced the slogan of the "good tsar"—a persistent illusion that contrasted the peasant's direct and nearby enemy, namely the landlord, to the distant tsar above all classes. Under these circumstances, peasant rebellions generated pretenders who claimed that they were the true tsar opposed to a usurper. In comparison to Chinese peasants, Russian serfs were directly dependent on their feudal lords. In turn, Russians were not as much anti-monarch in their violent struggles, although, the Chinese add, the peasants of their country also were heavily influenced by the illusion of a "deified emperor."[21]

Chinese views of Russian economic history and rebellions are deeply rooted in Lenin's and Stalin's writings and the historiography of the late Stalin years. One exception is an article by Wu Dakun that applies the Asiatic Mode of Production theory to Russian history.[22] Published at the beginning of 1980, this article represents a line of critical analysis that was permitted for only a short time. Although a lively debate on the Asiatic Mode of Production persisted through 1981, references to its applicability to the Soviet Union were not repeated. For example, an article that reviews a conference on this subject in Tianjin on April 21-27, 1981 discusses wide differences of opinion, but neglects to mention any implications for Russian history.[23] The mood of uncertainty about the nature of Soviet society and of searching for deep-rooted historical explanations of distorted development did not last for many months after Wu's article was written in late 1979.

Wu Dakun, on the one hand, accepts the Stalinist view that Soviet dis-

[21] Liang Jun and Shao Yun, " 'Huangquanzhuyi' yu Eguo nongmin zhanzheng," *Beijing daxue xuebao* (zhexue shehuikexue ban), no. 2 (1980): 73-85.

[22] Wu Dakun, "Guanyu Yaxiya shengchan fangshi yanjiu de jige wenti," *Xueshu yanjiu*, no. 1 (1980): 11-17; Wu's views can also be found in "The Asiatic Mode of Production in History as Viewed by Political Economy in Its Broad Sense," *Selected Writings on Studies of Marxism*, nos. 1-20 (Beijing: Institute of Marxism-Leninism-Mao Zedong Thought, Chinese Academy of Social Sciences, 1981), no. 19, pp. 1-25. For a later view dismissing the need to consider the AMP, see Song Min, " 'Makesi yu dongfangxue ji chita' yiwen shangque," *Shehuikexue zhanxian*, no. 1 (1984): 138-43.

[23] Dong Zhi, " 'Yaxiya shengchan fangshi' yu shijieshi yanjiu," *Shijie lishi*, no. 4 (1981): 75-78.

cussants of the Asiatic Mode in the 1920s and 1930s committed serious
political errors and became part of the Trotsky faction, and on the other,
claims that it was a mistake to stop discussion of this concept introduced
by Marx for fear that others would accuse one of being in Trotsky's faction. He notes that additional material by Marx on this subject was later
discovered and that Western scholars have recently studied the Asiatic
Mode further. Wu calls for a reexamination in China without fear of differences of opinion. As opposed to the Stalinist five-stage model of history, he suggests that there may be six stages and, consistent with Marx's
thought, history may be multilinear. Wu repeats a view that Russian society was half an Asiatic Mode of Production, while China was completely
so. Then he adds that now, scholarly circles throughout the world are debating the character of Soviet society. Theoretically, how can one account
for social imperialism there, as revealed in the 1968 invasion of Czechoslovakia? Wu dismisses the explanation that the Soviets have restored
capitalism, because they have no private capitalist class and their society
is very different from that of the United States. Then he considers the
view that Russia and China are both bureaucratic, collectivist societies
and agrees that today's Russia developed out of yesterday's Russia; because it was half an Asiatic society, the tradition of bureaucratism was
very strong. Wu observes that just as Marx explained the absolutist
Asiatic state as a product of state ownership of land, and its ability to force
all workers to serve it, one can explain the transition of society in the
same way. He hastens to add that the same reasoning does not apply to
China, but stems from misleading impressions at the time of Lin Biao and
the "Gang of Four."[24]

Serfdom appears in Chinese writings as a major barrier to capitalism at
several stages. Prior to 1861, the existence of serfdom meant that peasants lacked any motivation to develop their production. The cruel circumstances of serf existence resulted in very low labor productivity. After
1861, when the aristocratic revolution gave way to the period of populism, the legacy of serfdom and the hostility of the peasants to remnants
of serfdom and to capitalism (as well as the insufficient maturity of capitalism and of the worker movement) gave rise to anarchist movements.
Although progressive in their opposition to tsarism, these movements
mistakenly saw the peasantry as the real base of socialism and sought to
create a new order by breaking down everything, including the state.[25]

After 1861, Chinese contend, capitalism developed quite rapidly over-

[24] Wu Dakun, "Guanyu Yaxiya shengchan fangshi yanjiu de jige wenti," 11-15.

[25] Xiao Busheng, "Luelun Lajishefu sixiang de geming xingzhi," *Lanzhou daxue xuebao*
(shehuikexue ban), no. 4 (1983): 102-109; and Peng Shuzhi and Guan Jingxu, "Bakuning
yu Eguo mincuizhuyi yundong," *Shixue yuekan*, no. 2 (1983): 79-83.

all in Russia, but more gradually in the villages of that country. One 1981 article asserts that by the early 1890s, there were more than three and one-half million agricultural laborers in Russia; by the beginning of the twentieth century, rich peasants had developed to the point that they comprised 20 percent of the peasant population and held over 40 percent of the cultivated land; and later, following the Stolypin reforms, class differentiation expanded much further. Nevertheless, Russia's land problem—too little land for most of the rural population—continued to operate as a brake on overall capitalist development. For instance, large landlord ownership continued on a vast scale as reflected in the large holdings of 30,000 big owners, while masses of poor peasants lacked enough of their own land to farm; they rented from the owners, using only their primitive tools to eke out a living. The traditional *mir* persisted, maintained especially during the centuries of serfdom by those peasants who were not enserfed. It helped keep peasants in their own separate, closed worlds.[26]

In one modern world history textbook, which was originally published at the beginning of the 1970s, then was revised in 1980 and was still being reissued in 1984, two pages are devoted to Stolypin's "reactionary control," including his agrarian policies.[27] The text argues that Stolypin's program was first to pacify and then to reform. By pacification was meant "counterrevolutionary white terror," leading to the deaths from 1907 to 1910 of thousands of revolutionaries. Stolypin's land policies met the interests of representatives of the landlords and capitalists—mostly the reactionary Octobrists who when elected to the Third Duma in 1907 held 46 percent of the seats. Stolypin's land law forced peasants to leave the village, reassigning land for the private use of peasants and to permit free buying and selling. Rich peasants forcibly occupied the best land and relied on government loans to seize lands of the poor peasants arbitrarily, then hired bankrupt peasants and ruthlessly exploited them. In this way, apart from the landlords, the tsarist government also cultivated village capitalists—rich peasants—to become a new class pillar in support of its reactionary control. Because the Stolypin reform did not interfere with large-scale landlord ownership, it did not eliminate the very deep roots of the democratic revolution. At the same time, because it extended the rich peasant economy, on top of the original contradiction between peasants and landlords it added the contradiction between poor and rich peasants, thus intensifying and making more complex class conflict within the vil-

[26] Fan Daren, "Lun Sha E zhunshi fengjian diguozhuyi," *Beijing daxue xuebao* (zhexue shehuikexue ban), no. 5 (1981): 77-87, and Liang Jun and Shao Yun, " 'Huangquanzhuyi' yu Eguo nongmin zhanzheng," 82.

[27] Lin Judai et al., *Shijie jindaishi* (Shanghai: Shanghai renminchubanshe, 1984), 590-92.

lage. Instead of realizing the goal of building a stable social order, the Stolypin reform sparked more peasant violence.

These occasional articles on the rural society of Russia before 1917
break little new ground and cite almost no secondary literature of the
post-Stalin era. For writers on post-1917 Russia it suffices to draw the
conclusion that the rural population remained backward. Russia lacked
mature conditions in the countryside for socialism. When the crisis of
World War I arose, it made clear to the peasants that the provisional government could not resolve the land problem. Lenin seized the opportunity to offer them land, thereby winning rural support for the Bolsheviks. Although the peasants played a positive role in the revolutionary
struggle, Chinese conclude, they were of questionable reliability in the
transition to socialism.

War Communism and the NEP

In late 1917 and the first months of 1918, peasants seized the lands of the
landlords. Chinese write little about this seizure, but invariably refer to
it approvingly as part of the revolutionary process. Russian peasants
turned against the exploiters, both redistributing their property and suppressing their resistance to the revolution. By March 1918, the main task
had begun to shift from suppression to management, to the restoration
and development of the rural economy. Yet this new goal proved elusive
for several years.

Chinese historians and economists diverge in their explanations for
this failure. Some still repeat the long-accepted explanation that the deterioration of rural production was an unavoidable result of imperialist
armed intervention, which fueled continued struggle by the exploiting
classes. Violent resistance by rich peasants and capitalists forced a change
in policy. The Soviet leadership did not, as Western critics charge, follow
a zigzag course and violate objective economic laws by politically destroy-
ing the alliance of workers and peasants and economically provoking a
sharp deterioration. War Communism was a temporary measure necessitated by war. If Lenin would have been free to follow the strategy set
forth in his early 1918 article, "The Present Task of the Soviet Authorities," there would have been a gradual transition to socialism instead.[28]
These Chinese insist that War Communism did not constitute Lenin's
theory for building socialism.[29]

[28] Luo Gengmo, "Zhongdu 'Suweiai zhengquan de dangqian renwu': jinian Liening
danchen yibaiyishi zhounian," *Hongqi*, no. 8 (1980): 22-27.

[29] My interviews and meetings with more than sixty Chinese specialists on the Soviet

The defenders of War Communism point to the system of expropriation of surplus grain as an essential emergency wartime measure to enable the Red Army to continue fighting, to keep workers from completely dispersing or starving to death, and to prevent industry from closing down altogether. Of course, it could not lead to increased rural production, but rather than being the cause of economic deterioration, they insist, it maintained the most important productive force—the workers and their industries. Peasants made a great sacrifice, but not they alone; the whole people had to pay a great price. "The workers relying on the system of collecting surplus grain from the peasants' lands obtained grain, from the working class state the peasants obtained all the land, managing to avoid the oppressive exactions of the protective force of the landlords and rich peasants. Clearly the advantages the peasants obtained from the revolutionary war could be greater than those of the working class. Therefore in the years of the civil war, the working peasants of many regions willingly sent their grain to the starving workers and to help the soldiers at war."[30] Excesses, such as requisitioning grain that the peasants themselves needed, were understandable, given the heavy burden that the war imposed and the lack of experience. The overall approach, including the prohibition on free trade, was correct, some Chinese authors argue.

Even some defenders of War Communism recognize that at the end of 1920 and 1921 it had outlived its usefulness. It was being fed by an illusion that a continuation of these policies could smash capitalist economic relations and build communist ones in their place. Supposedly, the continuation of grain requisitioning would enable Russia to distribute according to need without reliance on money, markets, and merchants. This illusion led to a 55 percent increase in the collection of surplus grain in 1920/1921 over the most difficult war year of 1919/1920. Although this was a serious error, the defenders insist, it should not be allowed to obscure the great contribution of War Communism to saving the world's first Soviet Socialist Republic.[31]

By 1921, according to defenders of War Communism, peasants were very dissatisfied and the worker-peasant alliance was badly shaken. They acknowledge that some Chinese historians do not consider this reaction an inevitable result of the war, but instead share the foreign assessment

---

Union add to the information I obtained from published sources. I cite these conversations only where they fill in a gap in the written sources.

[30] Xie Youshi, " 'Zhanshi gongchanzhuyi' shi yizhong gonglao," *Shijiie lishi*, no. 1 (1981): 27; and Zhou Huizhen, "Lun Suweiai Eguo xiang shehuizhuyi guodu de lishi jingyan," *Zhengzhou daxue xuebao* (shehuikexue ban), no. 2 (1980): 1.

[31] Xie Youshi, " 'Zhanshi gongchanzhui' shi yizhong gonglao," 27-29.

of War Communism as, on the whole, an erroneous line based on premature pursuit of communism. For instance, Duan Binglin writes about the serious negative influences on Russian economic development of War Communism.[32] He notes that in the first half of 1919, workers received one-half of their grain consumption from the state and then had to turn to speculators to buy more at nine times the state price. The black market filled the gap. Duan adds, in a small peasant economy, it is impossible and disadvantageous to prohibit free trade. Soviet peasants, according to Duan, sharply curtailed their sown acreage and concealed additional acreage because of their dissatisfaction.

Chinese have debated the significance of Lenin's admission in the spring of 1921 that an error was made in the policies of War Communism. One response has been that all leaders make mistakes, but what sets Lenin apart is the brilliant example he offers of "seeking truth from facts" by admitting his mistakes and charting a new course.[33] Another interpretation is that Lenin's admission has been exaggerated. His self-criticism for seeking to make a "direct transition to communist production and distribution" was based on a definition of communism, consistent with that used previously by others, which is inclusive of the socialist stage of development. Lenin had never tried to achieve a "natural economy" without money exchange or to realize "to each according to one's need." He had instead tried to move directly to socialism by confiscating small and middle-sized enterprises, prohibiting private commerce, and giving the state a monopoly in the exchange of products between the city and the countryside. In the early twenties, Lenin was warning not against communism but against proceeding without caution with these socialist measures. If his meaning had been correctly interpreted by Soviet and Chinese scholars alike, later policy errors of the same type might have been averted. Although Lenin set Russia on the correct course by late 1921, his warnings would later go unheeded.[34]

Critics of War Communism in the countryside attribute its failures in economic policy to the "spirit of the time"—errors in thought that created a mood that anything could be accomplished by the new regime. This is referred to as the "sickness" of being too much in a hurry. Although both Marx and Lenin had made it clear prior to the October Revolution that the transition should be gradual, the rush to communism from 1918 violated the principles they had set down. War Communism was a fail-

[32] Duan Binglin, "Xin jingji zhengce yu Sulian jingji de huifu he fazhan," *Beijing shifan daxue xuebao*, no. 3 (1980): 56-57.

[33] Ibid., 57.

[34] Luo Gengmo, "Liening guanyu shiyue geming hou sizhong jiaohuan guanxi de fenxi," *Zhongguo shehuikexue*, no. 1 (1980): 37-43.

ure, not of Marxism-Leninism's first stage of socialist development, but
of exceeding that stage through an "egalitarian transition to a socialism
of poverty."[35] In the rural areas, class differentiation increased because of
the black market, while many state farms and collective farms formed as
part of the militarized and excessively centralized organization of the period. Great harm to the economy and to mass support for the government
resulted.

Wen Yi identifies four stages in War Communism: 1) the summer of
1918 to January 11, 1919; 2) the remainder of 1919; 3) the beginning of
1920 to the summer of 1920; and 4) the summer of 1920 to the summer
of 1921. From period to period, requisitioning, distribution in kind, and
other forms of interference in the economy intensified. Peasant dissatisfaction with the government also mounted.[36] Eventually, in early 1921,
some peasants recently inducted into the army joined in the Kronstadt
uprising, demanding free trade. Conditions grew increasingly serious,
and finally Soviet leaders decided to rebuild the alliance of workers and
peasants by giving the latter industrial goods and improving their living
conditions.[37]

Reconsideration of the New Economic Policy of the 1920s began even
before the Third Plenum in December 1978. At the Eleventh Party Congress in 1977, Hua Guofeng accused the "Gang of Four" of distorting scientific socialism and Soviet history under the pretext of fighting revisionism. One article in early 1978 applauded Lenin's appeal in 1921 to the
principle of "to each according to his work" and his attack on egalitarian
thought.[38] This was followed shortly by an article that claimed the "Gang
of Four" had distorted the transition from War Communism to the NEP
and had attributed to Trotsky Lenin's view that the primary task is economic construction in order to attack as anti-Leninist those who advocated the "four modernizations." In fact, the author points out, Lenin
recognized that politics must follow economic construction. In a small
peasant country, only on the basis of trust between the masses and the
vanguard of the revolution can peasants be led along the path to socialism. Rather than consigning the NEP to Trotsky's erroneous position, as

[35] Feng Lanrui, "SuE cong zhanshi gongchanzhuyi de xin jingji zhengce," *Xueshu
yuekan*, no. 8 (1982): 20-31.
[36] Chen Huijun, "Shilun SuE xin jingji zhengce chuqi de tuique," *Shijie lishi*, no. 1
(1982): 8-10; and Wen Yi, " 'Zhanshi gongchanzhuyi' zhengce he 'zhanshi gongchanzhuyi' sixiang," *Shixue jikan*, no. 2 (1983): 57-63.
[37] Shen Yongxing and Qin Xiaoying, "Suweiai Eguo cong zhanshi gongchanzhuyi xiang
xin jingji zhengce de zhuanbian," *Shijie lishi*, no. 5 (1979): 10.
[38] Wang Shouhai, "Liening, Sidalin lingdao shiqi Sulian guanche 'ge jin suo neng, an lao
fenpei' yuanze de yixie qingkuang," *Shehuikexue zhanxian*, no. 1 (1978): 111-13.

the "Gang of Four" had done, the transitional view of early 1978 approved the economic priority in the Soviet Union at the beginning of the 1920s.[39]

A year later, an article by Su Shaozhi and Feng Lanrui described the NEP in much more positive terms. It said that Lenin recognized that the transition to socialism is much more difficult in a country where peasants predominate than in a capitalist, developed country. Classes, including capitalists, must persist for a long time, and the transition to socialism will require more time because of the low development of the forces of production, the extremely low cultural level of the people, and the predominance of small-scale producers. This article created a stir in China because it suggested that China was not yet socialist in Marx's and Lenin's classical sense. Su and Feng argued that China had surpassed the level of the Soviet Union in 1918, when Lenin had declared that his country was not yet socialist, but was still in the transition to socialism. They contended that China still had some capitalism and even remnants of feudalism, that small producers still had a considerable position, and the force and psychology of their customs was still widespread.[40] Although this reform viewpoint was soon criticized for suggesting that China is not yet socialist, it was one of many appeals to the NEP as a model for new policies in China.

A voluminous literature has been produced by the debate in China over the NEP. On the whole, differences of opinion are not broached directly, but there are exceptions (especially in *neibu* journals). For example, an article that appeared in 1984 mentioned that many differences of opinion still exist about state capitalism in the Soviet Union. At one extreme are many persons who, in the tradition of Stalin, see it as occupying only a very small place in Soviet history, exerting little influence on the society or economy. Some deny it existed in 1918, or consider it no more than a post-war salvation policy, or contend that Lenin himself had decided to abandon it in 1923 or even as early as October 1921. The article disagrees with these views, insisting that Lenin consistently advocated it and that it had a long-term, wide-reaching existence as the main economic form of the 1920s. According to this view, confusion resulted from Lenin's early death before he had had time to provide an overall appraisal of state capitalism and from Stalin's inaccurate assessment of it at the Fourteenth Party Congress in December 1925. The article argues that state capitalism

[39] Wu Shuqing, "Ershi niandai Sulian zhigonghui wenti zhenglun he 'sirenbang' de daoguishu," *Beijing shifan daxue xuebao*, no. 2 (1978): 2-8.
[40] Su Shaozhi and Feng Lanrui, "Wuchanjieji qude zhengquan hou de shehui fazhan jieduan wenti," *Jingji yanjiu*, no. 5 (1979): 17-18.

should be conceived as a fundamental economic element for the entire history of the transition from capitalism to socialism.[41]

Two contrasting lines of reasoning are used to argue the importance of the New Economic Policy: the appeal to Lenin's authority and the seeking of truth from practice based on the actual results of the policy. Many authors find in Lenin's late writings a correct program for constructing a socialist economy. For example, one writer refers to Lenin's last five articles as precious instructions based on a scientific overview of the Russian revolutionary experience, and as setting forth a long-term strategy of socialist development. There Lenin resolved the question of what should be the basic class relations for socialist construction. He pointed to the peasantry as the dependable ally of the proletariat and to the worker-peasant alliance as the highest principle of proletarian dictatorship. Lenin called for economic relations through the market system and increasing the supply of goods to the masses. The article attributes to the leftist opposition the erroneous view that middle peasants are an unreliable ally.[42]

Studies of the Soviet economy point to the great successes of the NEP period. Not only did agricultural production recover rapidly, peasants regained hope and motivation. NEP policies strengthened the worker-peasant alliance. Some development of capitalism was unavoidable; however, it posed no threat to socialism in the Soviet Union. Adequate economic means, including taxation, were available to enable agriculture to serve the development of the national economy without leading to the restoration of capitalism. The historian Wen Yi also praises the NEP policies of renting out land and hiring labor for enabling the Soviets to make good use of hidden labor power.[43]

Chinese leaders have decided that the New Economic Policy legitimizes today's socialist model in China. In turn, specialists write approvingly of this policy's historical effects. They also draw attention to recent articles elsewhere in the socialist world that appear to rejuvenate this model. For example, they have reported on the Bulgarian decision in the early 1980s to call that country's extensive reforms a new economic policy.[44] More-

[41] Chen Huijun, "Sulian guojia zibenzhuyi wenti chutan," *Shijieshi yanjiu dongtai*, no. 8 (1984): 24-26.

[42] [Author unknown], "Shilun xin jingji zhengce yu ershi niandai Sulian dangnei douzheng," *Sulian lishi*, no. 1 (1984): 47-53.

[43] Zhou Huizhen, "Lun Suweiai Eguo xiang shehuizhuyi guodu de lishi jingyan," 5-7; Lin Shuiyuan, "Liening Sidalin shiqi Sulian shehuizhuyi gongyouzhi de jianli ji qi jingyan jiaoxun," *Shijie jingji*, no. 8 (1981); and Wen Yi, "Sulian ershi niandai de tudi zudian he guyong laodong wenti," *Shijie lishi*, no. 1 (1984): 43.

[44] "Baojialiya de xin jingji zhengce," *Shijie jingji yu zhengzhi neican*, no. 2 (1984): 57; Liu Keming and Cao Ying, "Baojialiya de xin jingji zhengce zhidu," *Sulian dongou wenti*, no. 4 (1984): 1-7.

over, it was only three months after the publication date of an article in
the Soviet journal *Problems of History* when a Chinese article by Wen Yi
responded that the Soviet article "recognizes that the New Economic Policy 'model' still has life force."[45]

It was inevitable that Chinese reexamination of the NEP would require
a new decision about Bukharin, the Soviet leader who is best known for
seeking to continue the NEP and to develop a theoretical grounding for it
in opposition to Stalin. Perhaps the boldest stroke in China's reevaluation
of the history of Marxism-Leninism in the Soviet Union is the partial rehabilitation of Bukharin from 1980. Chinese theorists have translated
many of his writings and, more importantly, have translated recent publications on Bukharin by Marxists and non-Marxists around the world.
On the whole, Chinese articles about Bukharin are positive, although the
subject remains sensitive and circuitous routes to publication may be required. The message that comes across is that War Communism was a
temporary, emergency approach with little value as a model, while the
NEP is the correct path to socialism. Understanding this, Bukharin was
the true heir of Lenin. He expanded Lenin's views of socialism after talking a great deal with Lenin about how to lead a largely peasant country
down the path of socialism. Bukharin wrote what Lenin told him, in contrast to Stalin, who went against Lenin's mature ideas. Bukharin understood the need for patience. He realized that the state cannot use force or
exploitation against the peasants to achieve socialism. It should preserve
an economic balance—between production and consumption, between
industry and agriculture. He did not see the village as a colony, but as a
market. Bukharin respected the peasant market and believed that rich
peasants can be trusted. Even though capitalists will be present, they can
be dealt with through economic means. Rural capitalists pose no threat;
there is no need for violence or suppression. This is the point of view in
various writings about Bukharin, including a 1984 article about Bukharin's thoughts on building a socialist economy.[46] When Lenin fell ill,
the NEP fell into trouble. After Lenin died, the NEP soon was abolished.
Stalin's opposing views prevailed against Bukharin.

Some writers take a more critical view of the NEP. They place it in essentially the same category as War Communism: NEP was a necessity
because of emergency conditions, but its negative consequences soon demanded a change in course. Lu Shoucai takes this position in a 1980 article, which argues that a grain-supply crisis was threatening production

[45] Wen Yi, "Su 'Lishi wenti' fabiao wenzhang, renwei xin jingji zhengce 'moshi' reng you
shengming li," *Shijieshi yanjiu dongtai*, no. 7 (1984): 37-38.
[46] Zheng Yifan, "Lun Buhalin shehuizhuyi jingji jianshe sixiang," *Shijie lishi*, no. 4
(1984): 11-24.

plans by 1925. Despite the success of the NEP in raising peasant motivation and forging a new base for the worker-peasant alliance, the market
system, dominated by new merchants, could not meet the growing needs
of the economy.[47] Other writers refer more directly to class enemies in
the countryside who were taking advantage of the peasantry, and indicate
that these enemies had to be disarmed.[48]

The historian Xie Youshi depicts the 1920s as a time of intensifying
class conflict. The poor peasant economy provided fertile soil for the
spread of capitalism and the growth of the capitalist class. The free trade
permitted in the NEP, combined with the renting of land and the hiring
of labor, led to village polarization as rich peasants cornered entire village
markets. Although the proliferation of private markets contributed to a
lively national market, the results were serious waste and intense class
struggle in the villages. Xie argues that the Communist Party of the Soviet Union had failed to exercise sufficient oversight. It had underestimated the extent of village differentiation and exploitation. Eventually,
however, under Lenin's direction, the ineffectual supervision of 1921-
1923 was recognized, and the erroneous direction began to be corrected
with encouragement for cooperatives. In 1924, the Soviet Union established an inspection commission for private trade. Citing more than
twenty Soviet publications of the 1950s and 1960s and a few from the
early 1980s to support his arguments, Xie appears to be presenting the
Soviet point of view about why the NEP had to be abandoned.[49]

COLLECTIVIZATION AND ITS AFTERMATH

On October 25-31, 1983, a conference in Shanghai brought together fifty
participants from more than twenty research and teaching organizations
as well as eleven auditors to discuss Soviet collectivization. This was the
Second Symposium on the Contemporary History of the Soviet Union,
the purpose of which was to examine in detail various directions of study
in order to deepen overall research. The report on it in the *neibu* journal
of the Shanghai Teacher's Institute, the host organization, begins by reviewing the debate on the reasons for the overall collectivization of agri-

---

[47] Lu Shoucai, "Sulian liangshi caigou zhengce de yanbian ji qi chubu fenxi," *Shijie jingji*,
no. 12 (1980): 60.

[48] Li Shuzhi, "Suweiai Eguo xin jingji zhengce shiqi yunxu duozhong jingji chengfen
bingcun de keguan yiju," *Xuexi yu sikao*, no. 3 (1983): 69-74.

[49] Xie Youshi, "Lun guomin jingji huifu shiqi Suweiai Eguo jingji lingyu nei de jieji
douzheng," *Shixue jikan*, no. 2 (1983): 64-70.

culture, which it refers to as an important socialist reform movement.[50] The review mentions four points of view. First, some said that collectivization in the second half of 1929 was an historical necessity for Soviet economic development. They reasoned that an economy of owners producing on a small scale with backward technology, low productivity, and weak commercialization could not meet the needs of building socialism. In the aftermath of land reform, production capabilities were increasing slowly. It was an objective necessity for economic development to reform this small peasant economy. Furthermore, the reform of agriculture into socialism could be achieved because of the Marxist-Leninist theoretical base and the hold that the proletarian class dictatorship had on the economic arteries of the country. These were the general conditions that required collectivization.

Conference participants also claimed that there were special conditions in the Soviet Union at the end of the 1920s that made collectivization necessary. The worsening of the international situation—imperialist encirclement and the approaching war—compelled the only country with socialism to achieve high-speed industrialization. In turn, national industrialization and the development of industry, with heavy industry at the center, required large supplies of grain and capital from agriculture. Heavy industry was too backward to supply simultaneously industry itself, agricultural communications and transport, national defense, and other needs. Collectivization, to a very large extent, resolved the life-and-death question of developing in the Soviet Union an independent heavy industrial system. In the conference summary, this point of view is credited to some (*you xie*) of the participants.

The three other views on the preconditions of collectivization are each attributed to a few (*you de*) of the participants. As distinct from the first view, which argues that collectivization was a national necessity, the second sees it as the people's will. The peasant masses of the Soviet Union started the collective farms themselves; action proceeded from the bottom up. Proponents of this view claim that evidence from some villages and areas shows that the establishment of machine-tractor stations corresponded to the mutual requests of production organizations and production managers.

The third view suggests that the needs of industrial development were themselves responsible for collectivization. Guided by the thought that agriculture should meet the needs of industrial development, the Soviet leaders acted. The economy had already been restored, large-scale

[50] Wei Shaobo, "Sulian xiandaishi dierci taolunhui zongshu," *Shanghai shifan xueyuan xuebao* (shehuikexue ban), no. 1 (1984): 118-22.

planned construction had begun, a network of village cooperative associations had been gradually established, and the state had no choice if it were not to simply watch its economic plans be ruined but to collectivize in order to obtain sufficient grain and other materials.

Only briefly is the fourth point of view mentioned. Unlike the others, it argues that collectivization was unjustified. Political factors, including the needs of the inner-party struggle, account for it. Theoretical errors are also responsible; Stalin betrayed Lenin's thought on collectivization in his pursuit of the idea of "one big, two public"—a slogan often mentioned in Chinese criticisms of Stalin, which refers to his policies to make the scale of production units larger (the bigger, the better) and the form of ownership more public (the more public, the better).

The review article on the conference next discusses the course of collectivization in two stages: 1928-1929, when Stalin prepared public opinion, and 1930-1933, the high tide and what followed. The article mentions the complete divestiture of rich peasants, the coercive methods, the one-sided pursuit of speed, the groundless pursuit of "one big, two public," the severe attacks on middle peasants in the course of driving out the rich peasants, and the generally excessive conduct. It is clearly critical of these mistakes, but then adds approvingly that in 1933 the focus changed to increasing the rate of commercialized grain from the collective farms.

Why did these mistakes occur in the course of collectivization? The article summarizes conference views about the lack of foresight among Soviet leaders. In 1925 when the economic recovery was nearing completion, theory was not ready. The rush to large-scale industrial investment produced contradictions. The costs of industrial products rose, as did the demand for agricultural products. Unprepared for this problem, Soviet policies failed. Stalin's crackdown on rich peasants in 1928 both responded to this earlier failure and led to collectivization. Without siding with Stalin or Bukharin, the article reviews the debate over peasants and collectivization in the 1920s and adds that evaluations differ about the pros and cons of collectivization in 1929-1930. Some participants distinguished the mistakes of November 1929 to March 1930 from the more correct policies that followed the resumption of collectivization in the fall of 1930, suggesting that the mistakes were largely corrected after careful thought was given to the problem. In other words, collectivization itself was not the problem. Conference participants separated the short-term errors of the all-out collectivization of 1929-1930 from the correct long-term course of collectivization.

The article ends by comparing the overall attitudes of participants toward Stalin's all-out collectivization. It notes first that many (*xuduo*) comrades believe that Stalin's all-out collectivization ought to be approved. The basic direction followed Lenin's views on reforming small-scale production and the system of individual peasant ownership. Collectivization advanced socialist reforms and showed that peasants must travel the socialist road. Along with mechanization, it was one of the two preconditions for agricultural development. Advocates of this view added that as the only socialist country, the Soviet Union had no experience from which to borrow. Through collectivization it rid itself altogether of the shackles of the feudal village system, of the small peasant (*xiaonong* or small-scale proprietor with weak market ties) economy. They also applaud the elimination of the rich peasant class and the end to class differentiation, claiming that the result was a strengthening in the organization of the worker-peasant alliance and in Soviet authority. The approval from this large group of Chinese specialists extends further. It attributes to collectivization an advance in the reform of agricultural technology; an increase in productivity per farm worker; improvements in the material and cultural life of the peasantry; and provision of capital, grain, raw materials, labor power, and a commercial market for industrialization. In short, this group alleges that collectivization created the material conditions for socialist industrialization.

The 1984 article mentions that not a few (*bushao*) comrades, while basically approving Stalin's collectivization, consider its organizational form and methods to have been a serious error. They condemn its hasty class struggle, its confiscation of property in one sweep, and Stalin's methods that disobeyed Lenin's thought. In addition, a few (*you de*) comrades pointed out that there were many shortcomings in the collective farm system, such as a monolithic property structure, rigid planning, a democratic management system not in good health, an imperfect organization of labor and remuneration, and a long-term tendency for high accumulation from the collective farms. Stalin's system could not successfully resolve the mutual relations of the state, the collective, and the individual and give the peasant a positive interest in production.

Finally, the conference report mentions participants who believed that collectivization in 1929-1930 exceeded the stage of development of production, thus violating objective economic rules. Mechanization, including the supply of tractors, was relatively backward. Moreover, the cultural level of village cadres and the consciousness of the peasantry were exceeded. As a result, scientific management was unrealizable, as was the planned economic superiority of the new system that was to heighten the peasants' resolve to follow the socialist road. Middle peasants in conditions of a largely natural economy were unprepared for collectivization. The negative reactions of this very large group caused great damage to production, resulting in slow development or even stagnation for a long time. Agriculture remained the weak link in the economy. Some comrades asserted that peasants—under the burden of high taxes and low purchase prices—lacked material interest in their work. They were controlled to the point of paralysis. Overcentralization of planned management caused bureaucratism and the need to follow the leadership blindly. Some Chinese specialists made these criticisms in the face of the overall approval at the fall 1983 conference of Soviet collectivization in 1929-1930.[51]

Other articles also place some harsh criticisms of Stalin's collectivization within an inconclusive overview of the achievements and losses from this transformation of the Soviet village. For example, a review of the inner-party struggle in the 1920s contrasts Stalin's full-scale attack on capitalism and decision to make 1929 a year of great change to Lenin's original prediction that it would take a few decades or generations before socialism would be complete. It suggests that Bukharin was correct in wanting to continue the NEP. His ideas better corresponded to Soviet reality. At that time, collective farms were not healthy for the development of agriculture. Nevertheless, the article ends inconclusively with a reference to the gains and losses of Stalin's model.[52]

Back-to-back articles on the system of collective farms appeared in 1984 in the *neibu* journal *Soviet History*. The first article, by Wu Renzhang, begins with the statement that collectivization occurred not because peasant conditions for it were mature but for other reasons, including the international environment, the need for rapid socialist industrialization, and Stalin's theory of "one big, two public." The new system ended exploitation in the village and corresponded to the overall Soviet socialist development. Wu suggests that it also corresponded to the interests of the broad mass of peasants. Noting that the means used to destroy the rich peasants were excessively heavy-handed and that the enlarged scope of the movement led to the loss of a very large part of the rich and middle peasantry, Wu nevertheless adds that they did not harm the masses or 85 percent of the rural population, including the middle peasantry in general. This explains why there was no uprising despite some violent reactions. Later, learning from their mistakes, Soviet leaders gave rich peasants and their children a way out of their status. They continuously improved the collective farm system in the 1930s, which

[51] Ibid., 22.

[52] [Author unknown], "Shilun xin jingji zhengce yu ershi niandai Sulian dangnei douzheng," 53-54.

was a major reason the system still had life. Wu identifies five improvements: 1) agricultural mechanization; 2) advances in the organization of labor, including the creation of stable production teams; 3) rejection of egalitarianism, which in 1931 had been rampant—by 1933 the highest incomes were four times the lowest and, after stabilizing, these inequalities exerted some positive stimulus on work effort; 4) acceptance of personal plots and livestock; and 5) restoration of market trade. Comparing rural conditions in 1937 and 1932, Wu finds certain successes. Agricultural production had gradually improved, as had peasant living standards. Even the tendency of "one big, two public" had to a certain extent been corrected. The Soviet Union had established the first socialist collective farm system.

The next section of Wu's article identifies six main shortcomings in the collective farm system of the 1930s: 1) excessive state control largely resulted in a lack of development of self-administration; 2) numerous orders were sent down from the center to the collectives; 3) within the rural areas, power was concentrated to a great extent in the hands of the upper party organs; 4) the state took a vast surplus production with little or no compensation to the peasants; 5) the distribution of payment for work had not eliminated elements of egalitarianism; and 6) the scale of each farm unit was very large. These shortcomings had serious consequences. Individuals had little interest in the results of their own production or in its further development. In turn, agriculture developed slowly. These negative consequences were partly a result of historical conditions. The Soviet Union had as its historical duty to rapidly increase industrial production, and to mobilize people and goods to protect the only socialist country and to prepare for the approaching war. Wu adds, however, that mistakes also played a role. The collectivization movement came from the top down. The system it created had a forced character. And Stalin's theoretical errors, especially his one-sided emphasis on a great leap in the production of large-scale units, had a big influence.[53]

In the second article in *Soviet History*, Xie Youshi argues that despite great results from the socialist reform of collectivization, there were problems in the distribution system that developed in the 1930s. After 1935, there was no great reform in this system for more than thirty years, during which time the system had a great influence on other socialist countries. Xie notes two errors in distribution. First, the split among the state, the collective farm, and the farmers themselves was incorrect. Too little was left for the farmers, who therefore lost interest in

[53] Wu Renzhang, "Lun sanshi niandai Sulian de jiti nongzhuang zhi," *Sulian lishi*, no. 2 (1984): 53-62.

the collective sector. Second, the cadres on the collective farms received an excessive reward, very much greater than the incomes of the farm members. This unjust distribution contributed to bureaucratism and commandism on the part of the cadres. Together these features of the remuneration system were a major factor in the continued backwardness of agriculture.[54]

Occasional Chinese articles have been more forthright in their criticisms of collectivization in the Soviet Union. A striking example is Liu Zhi's discussion of Stalin's model for the Soviet path to socialism, which offers many sharp criticisms without any attempt to balance them with favorable assertions. Liu cites as a major reason for collectivization the imbalance that resulted from the program to boost heavy industrial production in the preceding years. Heightened demand for agricultural goods without any plan for supplying more industrial goods to the peasants led to the grain crisis of late 1927 and early 1928. Having failed to prepare for this dilemma, Stalin turned to collectivization as the solution. Liu condemns agricultural collectivization for relying completely on administrative means. Under the supervision of worker detachments, collectivization was forcibly carried out. Liu also resorts to no euphemisms in describing the great famine that followed, which had not been seen before. He observes that a few million persons died of repression and then an equal number died from the famine. While the state secured a vast increase in grain from collectivization, the effects on agricultural production were severely destructive. the number of livestock declined sharply, and over the long term, grain production failed to grow.

Liu refers to collectivization as the nationalization of the peasantry. The nationally operated machine-tractor stations, which held all the big pieces of equipment, served the state's interests and transferred large revenues to the state. State personnel, operating according to national plans, decided questions pertaining to the rural economy. The chairmen of collective farms and technicians were sent by the state and paid by it. They were a separate group of outsiders who controlled the peasants, who could not freely leave the farm and move to the city. Liu concludes that the notion of "collective property" was an empty term in the absence of self-administration.

Liu Zhi also discusses the sensitive subject of political purges. He notes that even before the great purges of 1935-1938, Stalin had issued orders to look inside work units, including collective farms, for enemies. Almost all who were arrested and even killed were said to be opposed to indus-

---

[54] Xie Youshi, "Sidalin shiqi Sulian jiti nongzhuang fenpei zhidu cunzai de jige wenti, " *Sulian lishi*, no. 2 (1984): 63-69.

trialization and collectivization. Liu leaves no doubt that force had become the dominant policy in rural areas.[55]

In the fall of 1984, a conference was held at the Institute of the Soviet
Union and Eastern Europe on problems of the economic system of the
Stalin period. (There was also a 1984 conference in Lanzhou on the political and economic system of the Stalin period.) Although I have not seen
a report about it, conversations with participants indicate that the prevailing view was that, on the one hand, there is no question that the Soviet system was socialist, and on the other hand, some methods exceeded
the existing level of the forces of production. This assessment of excesses
differs from what Chinese regard as the current Soviet view on the economic history of the Stalin period. Yet the view of many Chinese is on
the whole positive, even if it is not as positive as that of the Soviets. As
the historian Mei Wenbin explained to me, many Chinese approve Stalin's approach because it was the only way possible given the historic circumstances of the time. History proved Stalin right. It is wrong to criticize him from the perspective of another time, such as China in the 1980s,
because one must not depart from the historical conditions of the Soviet
Union in the 1920s and 1930s. Mei added that one must approve Stalin's
methods because they did not allow the overturned classes to reappear.

Mei also asked the question: Were these the most effective methods?
His answer was that it is not easy to say that they were. There could have
been even better results for socialism. The most important measure of
success is economic development. While the results for heavy industry
were great, other sectors remained backward, as did the living conditions
of the people. Later it would be difficult to alleviate the dissatisfaction of
the peasants. He added that collectivization was too coercive and too
rapid, although the direction of change was correct. Mei calculated that
most Chinese now agree that agricultural errors were committed under
Stalin. Even part of the necessary produce, as well as the surplus production, was taken from the peasants. This was exploitation of the peasantry.
When asked about Western sources, Mei commented that they are one-
sided, assuming for example that collectivization is not desirable at all,
even if such sources include some objective materials. He added that, on
the whole, Chinese rely on Soviet materials and do not study Western
views very much.

In a review article on Chinese historiography of the Soviet Union in
1982, one learns that Li Zhongjie proposed three subjective reasons why
Soviet agriculture from the October Revolution to the early fifties de-

---

[55] Liu Zhi, " 'Yiguo shehuizhuyi' yu Sidalin moshi—Sulian shehuizhuyi daolu yanjiu
zhier," *Sulian lishi wenti*, no. 1 (1984):13-15.

veloped slowly. First, the scope of attack in dealing with the middle and rich peasant problem was excessive, causing inappropriately tense class relations and having a big influence on the motivation to produce. Second, collectivization came too quickly, which was disadvantageous for maintaining stable forces of production in the transitional period. Third, because of one-sided consciousness and insufficient experience, certain economic policies were inappropriate, such as excessive reliance on administrative coercion, neglect of the market economy, incorrect handling of state relations with the peasants, excessive extraction, and a distribution system for the peasants that was not intimately linked to conditions for the development of production.[56]

It is possible to detect in Chinese writings on Soviet rural history to the 1940s many of the most important critical themes in the study of socialism. Chinese authors describe insufficient participation in decision-making, inadequate material incentives, a lack of prosperity, and policies based on ignorance. The problems of reliance on coercion rather than persuasion began in the first months after the October Revolution. An article by the historian Xu Tianxin indicates that peasants were small owners and long had been affected by the political and economic influence of the capitalist class; there were policies of the state of the proletariat dictatorship that were not understood. The party should not have used force to impose its views and methods on the peasants, but should have led peasants gradually to recognize the correctness of its policies. It sometimes failed in this task; instead it aroused dissatisfaction. the decision to close the constitutional convention, where the Bolsheviks were in the minority, Xu describes as a blow to the peasantry. The Social Revolutionary Party still enjoyed a superior position among the peasantry, who had "very big illusions" and saw the convention as a democratic organization. Its closing led peasants to lose trust in the Bolsheviks. The state's demands for large grain supplies, leaving little to dispose of on the market, were another reflection of coercion from above. Xu says that the peasants saw this as the same as Tsarist expropriation.[57]

Collective farms and their precursors in the joint tillage arrangements advocated in 1918-1920 had negative effects on incentives. Egalitarian distribution meant that everyone ate from a "big pot." "The impairment of the peasants' personal incentives and private trade interests was bound to throw cold water on their enthusiasm." "The peasants' 'individualism' was not to be feared by socialism," but in fact it was, thus sapping eco-

[56] Chen Qineng and Yu Pei, "Sulian jinxiandaishi," *Zhongguo lishixue nianjian 1983* (Beijing: Renminchubanshe, 1983), 248.

[57] Xu Tianxin, "Ping SuE chuqi de nongmin zhengce," *Shijie lishi*, no. 3 (1983): 58-64 and 72.

nomic initiative. Collective farming "organizations often provided a shelter for lazy bones, parasites, loafers and pilferers."[58] The dearth of incentives in the early years is sometimes related to harsh policies toward the middle peasants that drove them into the enemy camp. Chinese suggest instead that the "industrious peasant" should have been the central figure.[59] In the absence of encouragement for industriousness, agricultural prosperity could not be achieved.

Finally, Chinese writers find various ways to comment on the ignorance that guided rural policies. They discuss the zigzag course of policies in the early years. They write that "much attention needed to be given to canvassing the peasants' opinions and to studying the social effects of various forms of organization," but indicate that this was not done. And they contend that Lenin's correct views, after he realized the consequences of War Communism, were distorted by the view that prevailed from the late 1920s that Lenin had called for total collectivization.[60] These are forms of ignorance in the guise of theory that Chinese find in Soviet history.

COMPARISON WITH THE CHINESE EXPERIENCE

Wang Dingyuan is one of the few Chinese authors to treat Chinese and Soviet rural organization together in a single study.[61] Writing early in 1983, he begins by proclaiming China's responsibility system a success. Yet, he adds, whenever there is something new, not all people are able immediately to recognize it. A minority of Chinese call the new system a retreat or see it as a necessary step backward to be eliminated as soon as peasants become richer. Wang suggests that history is the best teacher. The development of the socialist cooperative system in China has been a zigzag, but the same is true in many other socialist countries.

Wang traces the history of collectivization beginning with the Soviet Union. Why was the process speeded up despite Lenin's estimation that it would take longer? The country was an isolated island encircled by capitalists. The international situation was worsening, and the shadow of war was drawing nearer. The Soviet Union had to rely on its own accumulation of capital to industrialize and build its defenses. There was no way for the state to exchange enough commercial goods with peasants;

[58] Yang Chengxun and Yu Dazhang, "From Joint Tillage of the Land to Cooperatives— The Shift in Lenin's Strategic Thinking," *Social Sciences in China*, no. 3 (1984): 35-37.

[59] Xu Tianxin, "Ping SuE chuqi de nongmin zhengce," 63; and Yang Chengxun and Yu Dazhang, "From Joint Tillage," 29.

[60] Yang Chengxun and Yu Dazhang, "From Joint Tillage," 34 and 45-47.

[61] Wang Dingyuan, "Shehuizhuyi nongye hezuo zhi fazhan de 'zhi' zixing," *Shehuikexue*, no. 11 (1983): 20-25.

the only recourse was a pricing scissors to concentrate a portion of the peasant surplus without compensation in the state's hands. A highly centralized, unified system of public ownership for the rural economy was Stalin's response. Wang faults the Soviet leader for overlooking Lenin's plan to make the cooperative system the principal form. Stalin proceeded at too early a date to reject the historical role of agricultural cooperatives in favor of the very different collective farm system, which he made the only form of bringing socialism to the village. He demanded that co-ops immediately be transformed into the higher form. Whereas Lenin approved socialist agricultural cooperatives, Stalin rejected them. He completely rejected their individual management and dispersed labor, requiring that payment be solely according to work within a large organization. The collective farm became the standard of socialist agriculture in many socialist countries, including China.

Wang acknowledges that the collective farm system had some historical achievements in reforming the small-scale peasant economy, strengthening socialist public ownership, and building state power. But he also finds serious negative elements in the system: the lack of autonomy by the collectives, the excessive dependence on administrative methods, the overly centralized management, the suppression of the worker's sense of being the master, and the damage to the producer's motivation by the distribution system that enabled all to eat from a "big iron bowl." Under the collective farm system, agriculture became the weak link in the building of socialism.

To put a stop to agricultural backwardness and to improve worker incentives, the Soviet Union and other socialist countries that had copied its agricultural system experimented with improvements and reforms. At the end of the 1970s, Wang says, the responsibility system that emerged in China was one of the most resolute and comprehensive steps in this wave of reform. It differs greatly from Soviet collective farms and China's people's communes because it divides the team economy into a collective and a household-contracted economy. Under the guidance of the state plan, households enjoy autonomy, with land and equipment allotted for their use. There is diversity of cooperative farms based on voluntary participation. This reform overcomes the excessive centralization of management and egalitarianism. It both bolsters the strong points of the small peasant economy and continues the positive results of collectivization. In many respects, the Chinese responsibility system seems to restore the first stage of Lenin's cooperative system; therefore, if one traces the development of cooperative farms from Lenin to Stalin to China in the 1980s, one sees a zigzag course. Wang adds that this new system only seems to be a restoration or a retreat. In fact, in comparison to the Soviet system in the 1920s, China's system is on a higher foundation—the deep feelings of the peasantry toward the party, the long history of the cooperative movement, the strengthened presence of socialist elements, and the material and technological foundation count among the differences. Wang also stresses that the new Chinese system is socialist and differs sharply from capitalist agriculture, where private owners are the main factor.

Wang explains what had gone wrong in the Soviet Union. There was no predecessor to follow. The Soviets had little experience and imagined too simply and optimistically that they could very quickly eliminate private owners and achieve "pure socialism" in the organization of production and distribution with agriculture similar to industry. The Soviets treated the peasants like a part of the working class, striking out against the peasants' interests, violating objective econimic laws, and encountering peasant resistance. Stalin failed to follow Lenin's cooperative system not primarily because of his personal character, but because of the limitations of historical conditions. There was no way to satisfy the needs of socialist industrialization due to the increase in peasant self-reliance and the drop in agricultural products available for state purchase. If one adds to this the speculative transactions and the appearance of polarization, then it is clear that contradictions with socialism had arisen. Facing this new situation, not a few (bushao) party members considered the time for preserving the cooperative system based on individual, small-scale producers to be past. The collectivized farm system was established in the psychological state when there was fear of peasants getting richer. It was done out of consideration of the "public interest," but without very good linkage of the private individual's interest to it.

In the 1950s, Mao criticized Stalin for not trusting the peasants, not selling them tractors, and leaving them in great poverty. Mao insisted that China would not follow that route. Yet, Wang declares, history shows that to learn from the experience of others requires a process of digestion, even to the point of having to pay a certain "tuition." Because of the development of leftist erroneous thought in economics work, Chinese transformed recently established agricultural cooperatives into people's communes and then for twenty years, to December 1978, sometimes overestimated the level of peasant social consciousness and sometimes doubted the peasantry's socialist motivation. Now, Wang admonishes, Chinese must recognize that peasants are, after all, peasants, having a dual nature, unlike workers. Today they love the party and socialism. They demand public ownership and payment according to work. This is their socialist and their leading side. Neverthless, it is unavoidable that yesterday's private owners have lingering thoughts associated with old forms of production, regarding dispersed household management and labor, that serve to give them very great motivation.

Wang concludes with the observation that in a backward economy the most advanced class—the working class and its vanguard, the communist party—can pass over the capitalist stage, but economic and cultural backwardness demand that development of the forces of production and learning from "capitalist advanced, useful things" be given priority too. This leads, as a general rule, to a zigzag course of development.

REFORM OF STALIN'S MODEL

Whatever the merits of collectivization and Soviet rural policies in the 1930s and the war years of the 1940s, Chinese find less to recommend these policies after World War II, when the Soviet economy suffered from a serious disequilibrium. There was an imbalance between industry and agriculture. Although in the late twenties, collectivization had been intended to overcome this very imbalance, the problem had been greatly compounded.[62] In the post-war era, imperialist encirclement had ended and the Soviet people now had considerable experience with socialism. In other words, there were no excuses for not reforming the agricultural system to correspond to the actual level of development of production. Even many of those who contend that collectivization was necessary see Soviet rural organization of the late 1940s and early 1950s as a negative factor.

The historian Wu Renzhang insists that not only was the Soviet position rigid at this time, there was even an exacerbation of the features of the collective farm system that failed to correspond to real economic needs. He mentions five examples: 1) the scale of the collective units grew larger and larger; 2) stricter limits were placed on personal farming, including private plots; 3) restrictions were more fully enforced to deny collective farmers personal possession of equipment and materials used for production, and Stalin added theoretical justifications for this; 4) a more negative attitude emerged on commodity production and the commercialization of agricultural production; and 5) more property was raised to the status of national property.[63] Increasingly, collective farms blocked the development of production in the Soviet Union, but Stalin insisted that they were needed.

Liu Zhi adds that Stalin's theory claimed that only his approach was socialism. He tried to control popular consciousness, to incubate the view

[62] Yao Hai, "1929 nian Sulian jingji zhengce de zhuanbian," *Shijieshi yanjiu dongtai*, no. 11 (1984) 1-5.
[63] Wu Renzhang, "Lun sanshi niandai Sulian de jiti nongzhuang zhi," 60-62.

that only his policies conformed to the "laws" of socialist development. He forced his model on others, making the international communist movement an instrument of the Soviet Communist Party. After World War II, despite changing conditions, this inertia of thought persisted. Even today, Liu contends, one cannot say that it has been completely eliminated.[64] Blindly following Stalin's model, other communist parties damaged their own economies.

An article by Li Renfeng leaves no doubt that social class analysis was at fault in Soviet collectivization. The mistake was to treat peasants as capitalists. Rich peasants are, in fact, both exploiters and productive workers. They are a complex group. The coercion used against them and extended to the middle peasants had serious consequences. Li argues that Marxist-Leninist theory establishes that this approach to social classes in the countryside was incorrect.[65]

By the early 1950s conditions of exploitation and egalitarianism in the Soviet countryside created an urgent need for reform. The combined effect of very low collective incomes and very high tax—even tribute—to the state from the collective sector eliminated motivation to participate in that sector. The peasants were so poor that they had no surplus—even a part of their necessary production was removed through high prices on necessary purchases and minuscule payments for agricultural goods. The only interest of most of the rural population was in their auxiliary plots. These criticisms were reported to me by a participant in the fall 1984 conference on problems of the economic system of the Stalin period.

In 1982, a book appeared that compares Soviet and Eastern European rural reforms away from the Stalin model. Entitled *Reform of the Agricultural Economic System of the Soviet Union and Eastern Europe*, this book begins with an explanation of the reasons for the reforms. It notes that in these countries, agriculture was long backward and in disequilibrium with industry. The masses were dissatisfied by the early 1950s because of a shortage of agricultural products and marketed consumer goods. Later the book elaborates on the three great shortcomings of this centralized Soviet planning system, which was based on orders from above. First, it reduced labor motivation; denied the authority they should have had to manage and plan, farm laborers lost interest, which seriously impeded the development of production. Second, the system failed to take into account the thousands of differences in and the ever-changing nature of natural conditions from one area to another; central-

---

[64] Liu Zhi, " 'Yiguo shehuizhuyi' yu Sidalin moshi," 16-18.

[65] Li Renfeng, "Sulian nongye jitihua de jingyan jiaoxun," *Jingji yanjiu cankao ziliao*, March 9, 1981, pp. 32-49.

ized planning under the guiding thought of the time meant blind leadership. Third, concern was often given only to the interests of the state, not to those of the collective and individual.[66] Under these circumstances, grain production did not exceed the highest level reached before collectivization.

To improve this situation, it was necessary to reform existing policies and the guiding thought for developing agriculture, which, in turn, would lead to reform of the agricultural economic system. Yugoslavia acted first in 1951. By 1953 the agricultural situation in the Soviet Union had begun to be linked to political questions, forcing emergency measures there to develop production; however, the entire agricultural system of production, distribution, and exchange relations remained under highly centralized state management. Comprehensive control did not permit rural units to arrange their own affairs. They could not respond to time and place differences in area, soil, weather, and natural conditions. The system hindered creativity. It created dependency on the state, which monopolized the movement of most agricultural goods through the machine-tractor stations (MTS). Under this coercive exchange, peasants lost interest and hope in production. "Not only like industry and other sectors did the state manage very rigidly (*guan de hen si*), moreover unlike industry, the state gorged to the point of great distress (*wa de hen ku*)."[67]

A great transformation in the Soviet agricultural economic system began in 1953. From this time Soviets established the direction of broadening the self-administration of economic units. In 1958, the MTS were abolished. The purchase system was completely reformed. Conditions for commercial exchange were created. Chinese economists conclude that the reform steps of the mid-fifties were quite large. But, they add, from 1958 through the first part of the sixties the process of relaxing state controls stopped.[68] A promising beginning had not been carried forward.

In one respect, Soviet rural policies took a step backward from the late 1950s. Under the impact of a theory of property that equates state ownership with ownership by the whole people, the Soviet Union advanced the theory of the merging of collective and state ownership. In other words, collective ownership—a transitional form—was to be abolished in order to extend the higher, more developed, more mature system of state ownership. From 1954 to 1970, more than 24,000 collective farms were converted into more than 7,000 new state farms. These conversions oc-

[66] Ding Zeji et, al., *Sulian he dongou guojia nongye jingji tizhi de gaige* (Beijing: Nongye chubanshe, 1982), 2-3 and 41-42.

[67] Ibid., 2-3.

[68] Ibid., 4-5.

curred within entire regions in a short period through administrative orders and campaign methods. The results were poor. Centralized state management was strengthened. Collectives lost their distinctiveness and flexibility in using natural resources. The new capital investments were used unproductively, without eliminating the long-term backwardness of these areas.[69] Ownership theory and policies worked against increases in self-administration in the Soviet countryside.

From the reforms, beginning in the mid-fifties, emerged three types of planning systems. Although the reforms in the Soviet Union and Eastern Europe all expanded enterprise-planning authority, used commercial and commodity relations and prices, and strengthened economic incentives, there were great differences among the reforms. From one model arose many. In general, there were three types: the Soviet model remained highly centralized, the Hungarian model combined central planning and commercial relations, and the Yugoslavian model relied on planning through self-administration. Nonetheless, even the Soviets recognized that the old methods were "bureaucratism, which stifled initiative." Comparing the three approaches, Chinese specialists emphasize that the Soviet reforms kept administrative means as the main form of management of the economy. They kept relying primarily on orders from above. Material incentives were given only a very limited function. In reforms of its agricultural planning system, the Soviet Union completely rejected market regulation of the economy.[70]

Following the resumption of a reform program, Soviet agriculture developed quite rapidly from the mid-1960s. From 1965 to 1980, the total value of agricultural production rose 50 percent, or 2.7 percent per year: intensification, including an increase in investment, was a factor.[71]

Back-to-back articles by Liu Keming and Jiang Changbin in the December 1983 issue of *Sulian dongou wenti* explained why Soviet agriculture remained backward under Brezhnev.[72] Liu, the former director of the Institute of the Soviet Union and Eastern Europe under CASS, discounts the explanations given by Brezhnev in 1982 and identifies the real reasons for backwardness as the policies and theory of the Soviet leadership. In particular, he singles out three mistakes. First, he points to the overestimation by Soviet leaders of the level of economic development in their

[69] Ibid., 21-23.

[70] Ibid., 42-43 and 52-54.

[71] Shi Jundi, "1979-1982 nian de Sulian nongye," Zhongguo Sulian jingji yanjiuhui, *Sulian jingji 1982* (Beijing: Renminchubanshe, 1984), 54-58.

[72] Liu Keming, "Sulian nongye luohou de yuanyin ji qi fazhan qianjing," *Sulian dongou wenti*, no. 6 (1983): 25-33; Jiang Changbin, "Zai tan Sulian nongye changqi luohou de genben yuanyin," *Sulian dongou wenti*, no. 6 (1983): 33-38.

country. They hastily pursued the specialization and intensification of agriculture, based on large-scale units and state supplies. Despite Brezhnev's criticism of Khrushchev for subjectivism in overlooking the objective laws of the economy, Brezhnev was also guilty of this adventurous rushing ahead, of blind pursuit through administrative means of an advanced goal, without taking actual local conditions into account. For instance, large-scale livestock units (industrial methods applied to agriculture) replaced smaller ones, which led to a drop in the production of livestock products. When the results were poor, as in the 1975 harvest, Soviet leaders not only failed to understand the correct reasons, they redoubled their hasty programs for specialization and intensification. Given the limited development of industrial services and the low level of rural economic development, these programs could not meet with great success. Much money was wasted, as huge investments brought a low return. At the same time, greater limitations were placed on personal auxiliary farming. The social result was accelerated flight of peasants from the village. Leaders wrongly blamed local cadres. They criticized departmentalism and localism, without addressing the principal problems.

Second, Liu sees a continuation of unequal relations between agriculture and industry. Despite periodic increases in the purchase prices for agricultural products, the prices for industrial goods needed in agriculture also rose repeatedly. The vast funds invested in agriculture through various means were transferred to the many specialized industrial organs. In the end, agriculture remained subordinate. Leaders gave primary attention to heavy industry and national defense. The contradiction between the proclaimed priority of agriculture and the reality damaged morale. Reliance on industry to expand agriculture turned out to be an empty hope. Unequal prices, in effect unequal relations based on longstanding thinking that downgraded the importance of agriculture, remained decisive.

Third, Liu Keming argues that the system of agricultural management maintained excessive control. Although over more than twenty years there were quite a few changes, administrative means (described as commandism and campaign methods) prevailed instead of democratic ones. Reforms in 1965 provided for some autonomy of collective and state farms, but the effect was short-lived. As the prices for industrial inputs to agriculture rose, hundreds of organizations, each with its own plan and indicators, exerted some control over the individual farms. This colossal, multi-departmental operation revived the old forms of control, leaving essentially no autonomy to the agricultural production units; excessive centralization led to mistakes such as the reduction of idle land in the 1970s far below the amounts that should have been left fallow.

Liu also mentions the responses of the farming population to this system of centralized management. They were only concerned about receiving their wages, without developing a responsible attitude toward the land and the end result of their labor. Wages rose precipitously after 1965: by 100-130 percent in fifteen years. This improved the lives of rural producers and temporarily increased their motivation. Nevertheless, negative results gradually appeared. With labor productivity and the value of overall production lagging way behind, rural producers found that their income was disassociated from the end results of production. They were time servers. Liu cites articles in the Soviet press that give examples of how quality of work was sacrificed.

A solution to at least some of the Soviet agricultural problems was long at hand. Liu comments that intermittently for over twenty years Soviets talked about experiments with the brigade-contract system in agriculture. At the beginning of the eighties, this form was reported to be superior, but still it was not widespread. Why? Liu blames the attitudes of collective and state farm leaders. They were used to commands and traditional ways of running their units. More importantly, they were concerned about threats to their own power as managers. Egalitarian sentiments also interfered with the adoption of brigade contracts. There was fear that some farmers and state farm workers would receive too much money. Liu concludes that the failure to adopt this measure for greater autonomy kept wages divorced from production.

Jiang Changbin is no less negative about the shortcomings of Soviet agricultural policy under Brezhnev. He argues that the Soviet development strategy, while less exploitative than under Stalin's model in the 1930s-1950s, remains the most important barrier to agricultural development. In Jiang's opinion, the primary reason for this continues to be unequal prices. Purchase prices for agricultural products are still far too low, and rural real income remains far below that of industrial workers. Jiang explains that four price increases for agricultural products from 1976 to 1983 had each followed by one year the crisis of a poor harvest. Each time the increases were made reluctantly and kept too low. The Stalin policy of price differentials has not been replaced. Although acknowledging gains in rural income from the collective or state sector, Jiang notes that private income has fallen since 1965 from 36.5 to 25.3 percent of the income of the collective farmer. In addition, because seventy percent of rural housing is private, as opposed to state-provided urban housing, real rural incomes are not as high as they seem. Jiang adds that neglect of rural services, such as transportation and storage, also contributes to agricultural backwardness. The only long-term solution is to change the development strategy of the Soviet Union, ending the exploitation of peasants, developing the service sector, and abandoning a one-sided approach to development.

These views about the absence of far-reaching reforms under Brezhnev leave little hope that anything but drastic reforms of the managerial system can end the backwardness of Soviet agriculture. Fundamental changes are needed in the theory and policies of the Soviet leadership.

The public journals *World Economies* and *World Agriculture* carry frequent articles on Soviet rural conditions. Their evaluations have also been largely negative. Early in 1979, Wang Degen looked back at Soviet agricultural mechanization. He notes tremendous increases in the production of farm machinery; for example, while in 1940 the Soviet Union built 31,600 tractors, by 1978 it produced 576,000 tractors a year—first in the world. Wang adds, however, that in the management and utilization of the machinery, there are serious problems. The quality is poor. The machines do not perform efficiently. Their average lifespan is short. They break down often. They are out of service for long periods and are costly to repair. Service personnel are not well-trained; many with training migrate to the city. Recent measures have not succeeded in redressing the rural-urban gaps, which leave villagers with low incomes, poor living conditions, poor working conditions and cultural opportunities, and insufficient spiritual motivation. In 1979, when China's leaders were still debating their options for agricultural reform, Wang seems to have been saying that heavy investment in mechanization has been tried and found wanting in the Soviet Union.

Later in 1979, Ge Linsheng described the low return on investment in Soviet agriculture as not only a serious economic problem but also a political problem. He writes about the blind leadership of agriculture. One example was Khrushchev's wasteful virgin lands developments, which caused great damage because of the failure to take natural conditions adequately into account. After Khrushchev's fall from power, the tendency of blind leadership was still evident, as in the blind pursuit of larger-scale units, especially in the management of livestock. Ge mentions the dispersed investments and drawn-out operations that could not yield a timely return. He refers to great waste because of poor quality equipment. Finally he comments on the absence of an effective scientific management system for agricultural modernization and services. Throughout the article Ge gives the impression that what was lacking was competent leadership.[73]

[73] Wang Degen, "Sulian nongye jijie shengchan he shiyong zhong cunzai de zhuyao wenti," *Shijie jingji*, no. 2 (1979): 47-52; Ge Linsheng, "Sulian nongye touci xiaoguo weishenme xiajiang," *Shijie jingji*, no. 9 (1979): 32-37.

At the end of 1980 Lu Shoucai wrote about the changes in Soviet food purchase policies.[74] After presenting an historical overview of Soviet policies from 1917 to the present, which shows shortcomings in each period in providing material incentives, Lu suggests that three problems are apparent. First, there is the problem of the relationship of planning regulation and market regulation. He argues that grain is a commodity, but that completely free trade would be a mistake. Planning is necessary to guarantee proportional developmnent and to meet the basic living needs of the masses and the needs of socialist construction. The failures of the NEP's completely free trade, when market prices rose continuously and supplies became extremely tight, shows that Stalin drew the correct lesson that both planning and market regulation are needed. Lu takes an orthodox position in his criticism of the NEP, as in his assertion that while the Civil War was continuing, the majority of peasants could accept the emergency measures of grain requisitioning in order to preserve newly allotted lands from the repression of white guard elements, landlords, and rich peasants. He argues that in 1920, after the war was over, the peasants expressed their violent dissatisfaction, which class enemies then took advantage of to incite the Kronstadt counterrevolutionary uprising and other violent incidents. The state then realized it needed to rely on commercial means of exchange. Lu adds that regretfully Stalin did not resolve the problem of the balance between planning and the market. Too little grain was permitted to be marketed; the market could not exercise its function because of high delivery quotas at low prices.

The second problem identified by Lu concerns stabilizing the peasant's grain burden. Both Khrushchev and Brezhnev had to address this problem after they came to power. Lu says that Khrushchev failed. He deceived the peasants with his public pronouncements of long-term purchase plans when he, in fact, did not give them high prices and kept increasing the purchases above the planned levels. Brezhnev promised higher prices for above-quota deliveries, but then raised the quotas and also failed to motivate the peasants.

The third problem is how to apply price laws to agriculture correctly. Lu argues that from 1933, when the Soviet Union established the compulsory delivery system, there were objective conditions for low grain prices because of the ominous world environment and the necessity to accumulate capital for industrialization from within the USSR. Yet the irrational balance of prices among economic sectors persisted for a quarter of a century. The result was an average growth rate in agriculture of 1.5 percent. From 1957, when the system was abolished, over the next 21 years, the average growth rate rose to 3.5 percent. Acknowledging that

---

[74] Lu Shoucai, "Sulian liangshi caigou zhengce de yanbian ji qi chubu fenxi," 59-65.

the development of agricultural science and technology and other policies were factors, Lu nevertheless concludes that increases of farmer income were an important reason. This shows the function of prices—the necessity for satisfactory purchase prices and terms of exchange. Lu's article appeared after China had substantially raised its own purchase prices for grain.

As China's responsibility system was taking firm hold in 1981, a new wave of articles examined Soviet personal auxiliary farming. One by Li Renfeng reviews the history of the personal or private sector.[75] Li stresses its importance in the two decades after collectivization was completed, despite the small amount of land permitted, for the production of vegetables, livestock, and livestock products, and for the income of rural households. Especially in the first post-war years, when the Soviets faced a difficult transition, this sector developed rapidly. Yet on the whole, Li finds that excessive controls and taxes slowed the development of the personal sector in the more than two decades from the time of collectivization to 1953.

In the decade of Khrushchev's power, there were three sudden changes in policies toward the personal economy. Khrushchev criticized Stalin for violating the principle of material incentives and from 1954 to 1958 adopted measures to stimulate this sector. The result was very rapid development of the personal auxiliary economy. In contrast, in 1958 he publicly advocated abolishing this economy and followed with measures to restrict it, provoking violent dissatisfaction among the vast masses. Then, from 1961, after great damage had been done to livestock production, he made a complete turnabout and again promoted the personal sector. Yet because the people had become distrustful and bad harvests followed, livestock were slaughtered, and at the time of Khrushchev's downfall, the personal sector was continuing to decline.

Learning the lesson of Khrushchev's failure, Brezhnev started by giving great attention to the development of personal auxiliary farming; however, from the late 1960s, he overemphasized livestock specialization and blindly combined units to achieve large-scale production. This damaged the personal economy and livestock production in general. Li notes that from 1967 to 1977, personal cows and milk dropped by 22 percent; the value of this portion of agriculture slipped from 33 percent in 1961-1965 to 28 percent in 1971-1975. This led to supply problems and, Li adds, created favorable conditions for speculators. Of late, Soviets are thinking of all kinds of ways to correct these mistakes. They are investing

[75] Li Renfeng, "Sulian geren fuye jingji de fazhan bianhua," *Shijie nongye*, no. 8 (1981): 26-32.

a lot of effort into encouraging the development of the personal auxiliary economy. Li concludes that with these new policies, this economy can have relatively great development in the near future.

Almost simultaneously with Li's article appeared a *neibu* study by Huang Lifu on the same topic.[76] Huang mentions that there already have been *neibu* articles introducing and analyzing the Soviet personal auxiliary development, and he will not repeat their coverage. Instead he is drawing on the most recent Soviet publications to discuss new directions of development. Huang states that in 1980, about one-quarter of state farmers did not have a pig, more than half had no sheep, and 64 percent lacked poultry. The long-term decline in the relative weight of the personal sector had led to this low point, where farm households only receive one-quarter of their income from the personal economy. Many economists had emphasized the negative role of this economy, calling it a barrier to overcoming the remnants of the private system in the consciousness of the peasantry and a possible source of a capitalist metamorphosis. But of late, says Huang, complete rejection of the personal economy is extremely rare. Officials and economists alike stress the importance of expanding this economy. Areas throughout the country are now working hard to create a social atmosphere conducive to the personal sector. Economists are proclaiming its socialist nature. Soviet periodicals are introducing the experiences of Eastern European countries, especially Hungary. Moreover, the Soviets are planning to follow a new path, bringing village production and personal production together in a better combination. Above all, Huang's article stresses the ideas of Soviet economists as the wave of the future that will bring major changes in favor of personal auxiliary farming.

Two years later, when more of the Soviet rural reforms were in place and there was much discussion in the Soviet press of additional reforms, Chinese tended to be more cautious in their predictions. By 1983 they could look back to four consecutive bad harvests in the Soviet Union. Under Andropov, the Soviets had also decided to stress the difficulties of reform. Moreover, China's own responsibility system had led to more drastic reforms than earlier anticipated, establishing new standards by which to judge Moscow's policies. In the journal *World Economies*, Guo Zhuanling writes that Soviet agriculture is an acute political problem. It was one reason for Khrushchev's fall, and in the 1980s it has caused a rise in mass dissatisfaction and unstable elements. Later in 1983, writing in the same journal, Zhou Xincheng comments approvingly on the recent

---

[76] Huang Lifu, "Sulian xian jieduan geren fuye fazhan de yixie dongxiang," *Guowai shehuikexue qingbao*, no. 9 (1981): 1-6.

spread of a collective contract system in Soviet agriculture. He identifies such basic principles of this new system as support of the principle of voluntary organization without interference from administrative orders; creation of units of an appropriate scale; self-management for contract brigades; and assurance within these units of distribution of rewards according to work performed. Zhou's optimism is tempered, however, by the remark that whether the collective contract-brigade system realizes the anticipated results depends not only on the organization work in expanding this system, but also on work with other links in the economy.[77]

THE POST-BREZHNEV ERA

While Brezhnev's program to increase rural income met with some success in reducing migration from the villages, it failed to motivate the rural population to work more diligently. Farmers reasoned that no matter what effort they put into the collective sector, their reward would scarcely change. This atmosphere began to change in 1982. On April 3, 1984, a discussion on Soviet economic problems in the Andropov period was held at the editorial bureau of *Sulian dongou wenti*. One of the participants, Chen Yiqu, contrasted the old approach to agriculture, to the new one that developed in 1982-1983. Before, Moscow stressed high investment, rapid mechanization, increased chemicals, and increased irrigation. Then, without abandoning these inputs, attention was also given to adjusting the relations of production and the management system. In a mere fifteen months, a great deal had been accomplished; joint agricultural-industrial producer associations were set up throughout the country, new work organizations and criteria for remuneration were adopted. Chen traces these changes initially to the May 1982 resolution of the Central Committee, but claims they were difficult to introduce in 1982. Only after Andropov took office were there special conferences, new laws, and concrete measures to bring about these changes.

Chen emphasizes collective contracts as the major development in this reform process. Whereas previously the basis for calculating how much was owed to the state was determined every year, the new system brought calculations based on the level of the previous five years. Collective contracts were based on smaller brigade units on which to determine rewards. From March to October over 150,000 brigades formed, covering more than one-sixth of all farm land. Under this influence, Chen concludes, agricultural output rose five percent in 1983. The results were still

[77] Guo Zhuanling, "Sulian nongye liannian qianshou suo zaocheng de yingxiang," *Shijie jingji*, no. 2 (1983): 70-75; Zhou Xincheng, "Sulian nongye zhong de jiti chengbao zhi," *Shijie jingji*, no. 8 (1983): 68-71.

far from adequate, but in only one year it is not possible to fundamentally change a backward situation.

Li Renfeng's comments at the same symposium identify a major breakthrough in learning from the experience of other socialist countries. Having long seen itself as big brother (*lao da ge*) with no need to learn from the experience of its little brothers, the Soviet Union changed its view under Andropov, now recognizing that the socialist world is comprised of diverse experiences and has been created by the peoples of many countries. Li says that nowhere is it clearer than in agriculture that each country can make its contribution to socialism. At last under Andropov, Soviet officials recognized that it is very important to analyze the agricultural experiences of other COMECON countries.[78]

In the same issue of *Sulian dongou wenti* that carries the symposium discussion, there is an article by Tang Zhuchang on reform of the economic management system in the Andropov period. Tang writes about the expansion and improvement of the contract system at the level of brigades and households. He observes that some regions have begun to use household contracts on collective farms. Livestock, land, and certain forms of capital such as machinery and fertilizer are distributed in return for a promise to sell a certain amount of production. These contracts simplify management, reduce the need for personnel, and increase productivity, say the Soviet reports. Many Soviet papers, according to Tang, now say these new forms of organization permit the use of economic reserves. They are getting rid of the view that diversity of form is merely a relic from an old time and are coming to the conclusion that the modern stage of developmewnt requires a multi-formational economy, including individual enterprises to a certain degree.[79]

Wang Shuzhong and Sui Qiyan published back-to-back articles in the November 1984 issue of *World Economies*, each comparing the Soviet and American economies. Wang looks ahead to the end of the century and finds the gap likely to be narrowing. He differentiates one stage, from 1945 to 1975, when the Soviet Union grew rapidly at 8.1 percent per year while the United States grew at only 5.3 percent, from a second stage, to 1983, when the lower Soviet rate of about 4 percent exceeded the U.S. figure of roughly 2 percent. Both countries in the 1980s are at their low post-war economic growth level, and both were struggling in 1983-1984 against some serious barriers in an effort to improve their results. The Soviet economy in the mid-eighties is about two-thirds that of the United

[78] "Zuotanhui: Andeluopofu shiqi de Sulian jingji wenti," *Sulian dongou wenti*, no. 4 (1984): 25-26, 28-29.

[79] Tang Zhuchang, "Andeluopofu shiqi de Sulian jingji tizhi gaige," *Sulian dongou wenti*, no. 4 (1984): 19-22.

States, while militarily the two are about even, concludes Wang. If the Soviet economy can return to its earlier path and the U.S. economy, as many expect, enters an economic crisis in the 1980s and early 1990s, the gap will again be narrowing.

Sui also describes a catch-up process in the post-war era. He finds grain production in 1950 at 58 percent of the U.S. level, while in 1983 it was at 90 percent. Meat production did not come as close to the U.S. figure, but it rose from 40 percent to 63.6 percent in 1982. Sui notes that although the Soviet Union is the second largest agricultural producer in the world, the gap in animal products is still large, especially if measured in per capita terms. A much greater gap exists in productivity of agricultural workers. Sui explains that there are poor natural conditions in the Soviet Union and agricultural science is behind. It will not be easy to catch up. Yet he extrapolates the gains in the past, suggesting a tendency to narrow the gap and noting that some Soviet crops have already pulled ahead of the American output totals.[80]

Comparison with the Hungarian Experience

Late in 1983 a Chinese article compared Hungarian and Soviet agriculture policies, drawing on discussions in Russian-language publications by Soviet economists. The article contrasts Hungarian successes after its 1968 reform to recent Soviet problems and says that without doubt Soviets are extremely interested in this contrast. For a long time Soviet scholars closed their eyes to Hungarian and other Eastern European agricultural theory and practice and did not correctly report on it; even less did they talk of borrowing and applying these experiences. The current discussion represents a great change. Soviet economists now explain that the main reasons for Hungary's success are not national conditions or increased investments, but policies concerning the management system, such as the small size of the farm units. The article ends inconclusively with a call for watching the attitude and determination of the leading Soviet economic organs to see if these ideas are put into practice.[81] The clear implication is that a good example exists for the Soviets to study and apply, and that there are reformers in the academic community who are aware of what needs to be done. It is up to Soviet leaders to listen to their experts and to borrow from other socialist countries whose reforms are compatible with a socialist system.

[80] Wang Shuzhong, "Dui ben shiji mo yiqian Mei Su jingji shili ji qi yingxiang de guji," *Shijie jingji*, no. 11 (1984): 27-33; and Sui Qiyan, "Su Mei nongye bijiao fenxi," *Shijie jingji*, no. 11 (1984): 34-38.

[81] Zou Yongjiu, "Xiongyali he Sulian nongye zhengce de bijiao," *Shijie jingji daobao*, October 31, 1983, p. 11.

CONCLUSION

Chinese publications recognize that agriculture is one of the Soviet Union's most glaring weaknesses. They point to shortcomings in policies under Stalin, Khrushchev, and Brezhnev. Whereas they debate whether the serious problems of the late Stalin years were, on the whole, justified by the needs of World War II and of the rapid establishment of a heavy industrial sector, they do not hesitate to blame Khrushchev's bungling of reforms for the problems of the early sixties. Soviet agricultural difficulties of the 1970s and early 1980s are attributed, above all, to ideological barriers to reform and to the tendency not to make fundamental changes in the economic management system.

Article after article in Chinese journals during the first half of the 1980s examined the latest Soviet pronouncements concerning agricultural reform. These writings agree that serious difficulties exist although, in comparison to Western writings, they speak rather positively about what had been accomplished over the previous quarter-century before the end of the 1970s. Chinese emphasize that the Soviets are actively engaged in a reform process that, in great measure, resembles the situation faced in Eastern European countries and in China itself. Solutions consistent with the socialist system can be found by learning from the experiences of other socialist countries; they are based on state ownership of the land, and payment of "to each according to his work." Contracts to small groups of agricultural workers or individual households, which reward them for greater efforts and orient their production toward the market, are part of the solution to Soviet agricultural problems.

The Soviet system is socialist and continues to have the potential to be superior to capitalist farming systems despite natural conditions that Chinese recognize as disadvantageous. Andropov and, already in the first year of his tenure, Gorbachev have recognized the need for sweeping rural reforms. They are more pragmatic than their predecessors and are more committed to obtaining increased growth rates. Optimism was increasing in Chinese publications from 1982 to 1985 about the prospects for successful reform of Soviet agriculture, but there was also recognition that the problems were serious and could not be resolved by half-measures.

With the obvious success of their own responsibility system, Chinese developed a standard by which to judge—implicitly more often than explicitly—Soviet agricultural reorganization. As they grew more confident of their own successes in 1982 and 1983, they could be more critical of the gap between Soviet problems and reforms. At this very time the Soviets, in adopting the food program reforms of May 1982 and with Andropov's broadening of these reforms in 1983, were becoming more self-critical. Approval of Andropov's reform agenda (along with reports of a better Soviet harvest in 1983) shifted the balance in China toward greater optimism. Many, however, retained a wait-and-see attitude, expressing uncertainty, even under Gorbachev's more vigorous leadership, about whether far-reaching rural reforms could be put into effect quickly against the opposition of bureaucratic lethargy and continued ideological barriers.

The line between reform and orthodoxy shifted with the success of China's responsibility system. Writings on Soviet agriculture from the 1950s to the 1980s largely reflect the reform position. The principal arenas for debate about alternatives were further back in history, especially the periods of collectivization and War Communism. On these subjects, sharp disagreements emerged. The reformers express criticisms of how collectivization had taken place in the Soviet Union, seizing this opportunity to attack various shortcomings of Stalin's leadership and apparently even advocating Bukharin's alternative strategy for the rural economy. They accuse communist leaders of coercive policies against the interests of critical groups of rural residents, particularly the middle peasants, but also the rich peasants, whose cooperation could have been obtained. Leaders violated the principle of voluntary participation. Chinese also find that material incentives in Soviet collective farms were inadequate. Hard work was not sufficiently rewarded. These problems, which appeared already in War Communism, returned with collectivization and would continue to plague Soviet agriculture to the 1980s.

Comparisons with Soviet Views of China

Striking parallels can be found in the perceptions each country expresses about what went wrong in the other country. A similar chronology appears in each country's publications; there are at least five stages of rural development that they share in common. 1) The transition to socialism was plagued by rural backwardness. Although Chinese writers do not stress this theme as much as Soviets do, they note the impact of serfdom, the complex nature of class conflict at the time of Stolypin's reforms, and the absence of mature conditions for socialism in the countryside. 2) Shortly after the victory of the revolutionary movement, serious mistakes disrupted the alliance of workers and peasants. Chinese are more critical of War Communism's effects on Soviet peasants than are Soviets of the excessive centralization and equalization during land reform, yet both point to the harmful consequences for middle and rich peasants and for the development of a market economy. These mistakes are somewhat excused by Chinese who point to the civil war and imperialist threats to the Bolsheviks, and by Soviets who note the severe population-to-land ratio in China. 3) The most positive assessments are given by Chinese to the moderate policies of NEP and by Soviets to China's brief interlude before collectivization. This stage created relatively favorable material incentives and market opportunities. On the whole, peasants were satisfied, while interference by the central government was limited. One can also find opposing orthodox views in each country's publications, which point to the danger of increasing class conflict in the countryside and contend that the policies of the time could not be long maintained. 4) Both sides argue that collectivization was necessary, but that it was mishandled and its consequences were, in many respects, negative. Stalin and Mao acted hastily. Theoretical errors guided their actions. There was insufficient support from the middle peasants, and the cultural level of the peasantry as a whole was too backward for the timing of this transformation. Many Chinese specialists give Soviets (and Stalin) higher marks for collectivization, justifying the need for acting quickly and asserting that Soviet leaders learned from their mistakes. Nonetheless, the two sides agree on the serious, negative, long-term consequences of agricultural collectives in the other country: rigid, centralized planning in large-scale units with little democratic participation in decision-making; the absence of material incentives, as incomes scarcely reflected work effort in the collective sector and the state drained the agricultural surplus through administrative means, exploiting the peasants; widespread rural poverty and slow development of agriculture. Although Soviets describe the dissatisfaction of rural Chinese in much greater detail, each side points to a situation, thirty years after the revolution, of mass peasant discontent and rampant rural mismanagement. 5) While welcoming the reform process that followed Stalin's and Mao's deaths, neither side credits the other with doing a satisfactory job. The Chinese are much more positive about Soviet reforms than the Soviets were, at least to 1983, about the post-Mao reforms, but the Chinese also insist that the major rural problems have not been overcome. Soviet theory continues to err in what it regards as acceptable in a socialist society. Centralization remains excessive. The farming population continues to have little incentive to work hard. Ignorance is reflected in the lack of interest shown in reforms of socialist agriculture taking place in other countries.

The orthodox-reform split in the two countries is remarkably similar. For all five of the above stages of development, differences of opinion are notable in the literature published in each country. For most periods, the orthodox viewpoint is more approving of what occurred in the other country. It is reluctant to acknowledge the negative implications of historical backwardness (feudalism), to criticize Lenin's or Stalin's policies or

China's policies at a time when it was clearly following the Soviet model, or to judge collectivization severely. The reform viewpoint sees more alternatives in history, and proposes more fundamental changes to bring rural policies in line with some implied, but as yet unattained, model of socialism. In both countries, the orthodox viewpoint retains a large voice in assessments of rural conditions in the other country (especially the need for collectivization); yet the reform side has vocally expressed its differing views.

Above all, the difference between the interpretations of socialism emanating from the Soviet Union and China is the difference between Soviet hostility and Chinese sympathy. Whereas Soviet sources find nothing good to write about Mao or the policies of essentially his final two decades, Chinese sources are largely positive toward Stalin and even to his rural policies. Soviet orthodoxy condemns China's responsibility system, while Chinese orthodoxy supports, on the whole, the centralized Soviet system and the reforms of the Brezhnev era. The tone of Soviet coverage in the early 1980s was negative, intimating a wish that China's rural reforms would fail. Nevertheless, there could be heard a muffled reform voice that could be construed as hoping for Chinese successes as a means of prodding Soviet rural reforms.

On the Chinese side, the tone has become largely supportive. By 1982, and even more so in 1983, the sentiment favored the reform steps being proposed in the USSR. Chinese find similarities in the rural histories of the two countries and write based on the assumption that convergence within socialism will take place even if each country develops socialism consistent with its own internal characteristics. If some of the gloomier Chinese forecasts suggest doubts that Moscow can move vigorously toward reform, the implication may not be that the two countries will drift further apart, but that China's economic reforms may also be curtailed due to the absence of political reforms, and the two countries will still wind up on parallel tracks. The prevailing tone among the doubters is that socialist pragmatism will prevail in the Soviet Union; the current reforms are moving in the right direction and more will follow.

In 1984-1985 the Soviet side was groping to make the switch from hostility to sympathy with China's agricultural policies. There was still no unequivocal statement in favor of the responsibility system as a socialist form of organization, but the gap had narrowed between the two countries.

FOUR

WORKERS AND THE INDUSTRIAL
SYSTEM

Workers in China never fit the Marxist image of the modern proletariat. Their numbers remained small relative to others, and they failed to lead the way in the revolutionary struggle to 1949. In Maoist ideology, although referred to as the leading class (*lingdao jieji*), they often found themselves grouped with peasants as part of the masses rather than being singled out as a separate and cohesive class with a distinct historic role. As early as 1958-1960, Mao began to criticize Soviet policies toward workers, and at the same time to popularize a different image of China's proletariat. His extensive notes, written in 1960, on a Soviet text on political economy form the basis of criticisms of the Soviet industrial system over the next two decades.

After the Third Plenum in 1978, Chinese officials increasingly repudiated the previous policies toward Chinese workers and, at the same time, previous evaluations of Soviet workers. Studies of workers and industrial reforms in other socialist countries carried added weight because, unlike the rural responsibility system, urban reforms came piecemeal over many years and did not become part of a comprehensive program until October 1984. Specialists published numerous articles and translations about Soviet conditions with the justification that China could learn from them. In the process, a new image emerged of the Soviet system that in most respects contrasts with the Maoist attacks on Soviet treatment of workers.

THE MAOIST CRITIQUE OF SOVIET WORKERS AND FACTORIES

In his writings of 1958-1960, Mao quarrels with Soviet neglect of the superstructure or politics. In 1958 Mao wrote, "Stalin's book from first to last says nothing about the superstructure. It is not concerned with people; it considers things, not people."[1] Mao claims, "It is not enough to assert that the development of large industry is the foundation for the so-

---

[1] Mao Tsetung, *A Critique of Soviet Economics* (New York: Monthly Review Press, 1977), 129.

cialist transformation of the economy," and he criticizes the fact that "this textbook [Stalin's *Economic Problems of Socialism in the U.S.S.R.*] addresses itself only to material preconditions and seldom engages the question of the superstructure."[2]

The issue of balance also figures in Mao's objections to Soviet opposition to projects of small—and medium—scale. He insists that concurrent promotion of enterprises of varying scale is the best approach. In response to the statement, "We must fight against 'crash programs' and work in a well-balanced way according to predetermined schedules," Mao finds, "This utter repudiation of crash programs and accelerated work is too absolute. . . . In nature there are gentle breezes and light rains and there are high winds and violent rains. Use of crash programs appears and disappears, wavelike. . . . If one wants to overtake the advanced, one cannot help having crash programs." Wavelike patterns characterize the development of socialist economies, not the perfectly linear pattern alleged in the Soviet text.[3]

This early critique of the Soviet system touches also on problems of ownership and control. Mao claims that "in the Soviet Union the period of coexistence between the two types of ownership [by the state and by the collective] has lasted too long." The system has become "less and less adaptable to the development of the productive forces." It is necessary to transform ownership by the collectives into ownership by the state.[4] Mao also faults the Soviet text for failing to discuss "labor's greatest right under socialism"—the "right to run the state, the various enterprises, education, and culture." He wonders why "single leadership" is needed and suggests that leaders must work to earn the trust of the masses by setting aside their pretensions. Only in this way will the workers look on the factory as their own and not be reluctant to observe labor discipline. Mao finds much omitted on the subject of "human relations in the course of labor, e.g. concerning the leadership's adopting egalitarian attitudes . . . worker participation in management and management participation in productive labor." Finally Mao faults the text's treatment of trade unions for overemphasizing welfare without pointing out that "the primary task of the unions is to develop production" and discussing "ways to strengthen political education."[5]

A separate subject in Mao's 1960 commentary on a Soviet text is the distribution system under socialism. First he casts doubt on the continued need in socialist society for "distribution according to labor" and com-

[2] Ibid., 51.
[3] Ibid., 53, 90-91, 87, 80.
[4] Ibid., 53-54.
[5] Ibid., 61, 86, 67-68, 73.

modity production. Then he adds that "'distribution according to need' has to be brought about gradually," but suggests that there will be problems because this transition will cause "vested interest groups" who benefit from higher pay according to more work to become uncomfortable. Returning repeatedly to this subject, Mao finds that the Soviet text "makes an absolute out of concern for individual material interest . . . [which] is bound to entail the danger of increasing individualism." "To treat distribution of consumer goods as a determining motive force is the erroneous view of distribution as determinative." Mao calls this a "distortion of Marx's correct view and a serious theoretical error."[6] Adding that in many places, the Soviet text "speaks only of individual consumption and not of social consumption, such as public welfare, culture, health, etc.," Mao argues that this view is one-sided. "If a socialist society does not undertake collective efforts, what kind of socialism is there in the end? Some say that socialism is more concerned with material incentives than capitalism. Such talk is simply outrageous." "Even if the importance of material incentive is recognized, it is never the sole principle. There is always another principle, namely, spiritual inspiration from political ideology." Mao also criticizes the text for saying that "socialism is fundamentally superior to capitalism because wages steadily rise."[7]

The Ninth Commentary of 1964, which along with the other commentaries is widely attributed to Mao, develops some of the same concepts in a more pointed way. It says that in order to emancipate itself, the proletariat must abolish the differences between ownership by the whole people and collective ownership, and between mental and manual laborers. In other words, the goals of communism must be considered soon if the proletariat is to be able to resist capitalist tendencies. It warns also of influences that constantly breed political degenerates in the ranks of the working class as well as in the party and government organizations. Part of the blame Mao attributes to Stalin, who "departed from Marxist-Leninist dialectics in his understanding of the laws of class struggle in socialist society," [and] "prematurely declared after agriculture was basically collectivized that there were 'no longer antagonistic classes' in the Soviet Union and that it was 'free of class conflicts.' " Although Mao adds that Stalin remained a great Marxist-Leninist, he faults Stalin for failing "to rely upon the working class and the masses in the struggle against the forces of capitalism." After Stalin, Mao continues, Soviet factories fell into the clutches of capitalists who exploit the workers. Khrushchev "has widened, and not narrowed, the gap between the incomes of a small mi-

[6] Ibid., 54, 62, 79.
[7] Ibid., 69-70, 83, 86.

nority and those of the workers, peasants and ordinary intellectuals."[8] This rhetoric suggests that Soviet workers were now no better off than their counterparts in the capitalist world.

A decade later, the invectives against the Soviet Union were rolling off the presses. Attacks against falling growth rates gave the Chinese one more theme to accentuate. A 1975 Shanghai book on the complete restoration of capitalism in the Soviet Union wastes no space on its first page in condemning the severe crisis that had already befallen the "Soviet revisionist" economy. The Soviet economy was steadily weakening, various contradictions were further intensifying. Light industry and consumer goods industry could not meet their planned increases, while the armaments industry was continuously expanding. "Guns were driving out butter." Vast sums of capital were being spent, but efficiency was very low and waste was alarmingly high. The Soviets themselves acknowledged that roughly half of consumer goods did not meet quality standards. The economic situation was continuously worsening. Anarchic conditions in industry, as a result of the restoration of capitalism, had plunged the economy into crisis.[9]

In the last gasp of this harsh Maoist perspective in the two years after Mao Zedong's death, citations from both Lenin and Western sources became more frequent. On the sixtieth anniversary of Lenin's *Imperialism Is the Highest Stage of Capitalism*, Chinese were asked to reread this book in order to understand the essence and laws of development of social imperialism, to help them "oppose imperialism, oppose hegemonism, oppose the struggle of contemporary revisionism."[10] In a July 1977 book published in Hong Kong, a section called "Militarization of the National Economy" begins with Lenin's assertion, "Contemporary militarism is the result of capitalism." The book adds, "After the Soviet Union completely restored capitalism, transformed into a social imperialist country, it engaged in an intense struggle with American imperialism in various regions around the world. Therefore, it had to madly expand military armaments, to speed up its firepower production, resulting in the militarization of the national economy."[11]

[8] William E. Griffith, *Sino-Soviet Relations, 1964-1965* (Cambridge, M.I.T. Press, 1967), 320, 317, 321, 327.

[9] *Kan, jintian de Sulian: zibenzhuyi quanmian fubi* (Shanghai: Shanghai renminchubanshe, 1975), 1-2, 8, 11.

[10] Shen Xueshan, "Fanba fanxiu de ruili sixiang wuqi: chongdu *Diguozhuyi shi zibenzhuyi de zuigao jieduan* de yidian tihui," *Nanjing daxue xuebao* (zhexue shehuikexue ban), no. 2 (1977): 116.

[11] Xia Changan, *Sulian jingji de tuibian* (Hong Kong: Xianggang Chaoyang chubanshe, 1977), 98.

Articles translated in *Peking Review* in 1975 and 1976 also excoriate the economic results of the Ninth Five-Year Plan for 1971-1975. Ridiculing the fact that "it took five years to accomplish the tasks set for four years," one article claims that the result

reveals the extremely decadent nature of Soviet state monopoly capitalism and completely explodes the lie of "high-speed" development and the "welfare plan" trumpeted by Brezhnev and company at the 24th congress. . . . The production of consumer goods was astonishingly low. . . . The people's standards of living are low. According to reports in the Soviet press, one-quarter of the total population are now living below the level "guaranteeing the lowest standard of material life." Retail prices of major foodstuffs and other goods have been constantly rising and exorbitant taxes and miscellaneous levies are continually on the increase. . . . The Soviet Union's all-out drive for arms expansion and war preparation inevitably reduces the people's consumption, sacrifices agriculture and light industry and brings about a serious lopsided development of the national economy . . . To seek profits, accounts are often falsified and embezzlement and theft as well as extravagance and waste are rampant within the enterprises, while new technology is not being fully utilized. In particular, the labouring people who are unwilling to sweat for the bureaucratic-monopoly capitalists, resist or fight back by work stoppages, slow-downs and other forms of struggle. All this has caused complete failure to the state plan."[12]

From 1975 to 1977, Chinese writings added many details about the degeneration of the Soviet factory system. They trace the history of this decline to resolutions of the mid-fifties that strengthened the hand of managers at the expense of workers, and to Khrushchev's call at the Twentieth Party Congress for "giving workers a personal material incentive." They were followed by Khrushchev's emphasis five years later at the Twenty-second Congress on "the enhancement of the forms of material incentives" and in 1963 by two articles in *Pravda* by "Liberman, an economist in the pay of the Soviet revisionists, who proposed that profit be taken as the final yardstick in judging the efficiency of an enterprise," and in 1965 by a "'new economic system' with profit at the core." In 1965, enterprise directors were given vast powers, among them the right to recruit and dismiss personnel. Additional labor law provisions set forth in 1970 strengthened the hand of management in annulling labor contracts. By the mid-seventies, a second stage in the "new economic system" had been reached. Thousands of huge combines, known as produc-

[12] Hsiao Lou, "Five Years of Continual Backsliding: From the Soviet revisionists' 24th Congress to Their 25th Congress," *Social Imperialism: The Soviet Union Today* (reprints from *Peking Review*) (Berkeley: Yenan Books, 1977), 87-89.

tion and production-scientific associations, were being formed, copied "from the blueprints of capitalist-imperialist monopoly organizations."[13]

Chinese critics attribute "harsh oppression and exploitation of workers" to the power granted to enterprise leaders under the "new economic system." First, the workers were deprived of the right to participate in running the enterprise. Second, no consideration was given to objections by workers or employees to layoffs or punishment for such varied reasons as incompatibility with the position they held, inadequate qualifications, feeble health, or temporary disability. Third, managers could choose among wage systems, work out the methods of reward and the sum of bonuses and even withhold or reduce the bonuses. "The relationship between the directors or managers and the workers is one between the oppressors and the oppressed, between employers and wage-slaves."[14]

One focus of Chinese anger was the "Shchekino experience," which became a model for permitting managers to lay off superfluous workers and to use the money left in the wage fund as they see fit. Under the pretext of applying "the notorious 'Shchekino experience,'" managers in the Russian Republic had dismissed 70,000 workers by July 1, 1973. "A quarter of the industrial workers in the Armenian Soviet Socialist Republic were fired in 1974." "Thousands of workers lost their jobs and became destitute."[15]

Under Soviet conditions of the 1960s and 1970s, what did "to each according to his labor" mean? The Chinese answer was that while paying lip service to this principle, "Soviet revisionism is actually practicing the principle of distribution to each according to his capital and power." "Material incentives" are the means used to force the workers to produce greater surplus value. "The result of pushing 'material incentives' is increasingly serious exploitation of the workers. At the Aksaisk Plastics Plant, for instance, to get one ruble as a bonus, a worker is required to create an additional surplus value of 16 rubles and 60 kopeks for the bureaucrat-monopoly bourgeoisie. . . . Bonus is another form the bourgeois privileged stratum uses to pocket for itself the fruits of the workers' labour. . . . Obviously watered-down government figures show that in 1969 in Soviet industrial firms a worker's bonus was only 4 percent of the wage, whereas for managerial personnel it could constitute more than 40

[13] Wei Chi, *The Soviet Union Under the New Tsars* (Beijing: Foreign Languages Press, 1978), 31-32, 46-47.

[14] "Fictitious Ownership by Whole People in Soviet Union," *Social Imperialism: The Soviet Union Today*, 96; and Wei Chi, *The Soviet Union Under the New Tsars*, 47, 42, 33.

[15] "Fictitious Ownership by Whole People in Soviet Union," 96-97; Wei Chi, *The Soviet Union Under the New Tsars*, 48-49.

percent of the salary, and even double or triple the salary in some cases."[16] Chinese reported Soviet statistics showing that industrial profit equals more than twice the total wage bill. They equate this with capitalist exploitation of the workers, even arguing that this rate of exploitation of more than 200 percent is "double the rate in tsarist Russian industry at the beginning of the 20th century."[17]

The litany of charges against the Soviet system includes political oppression, mass poverty, widespread safety violations, and unemployment.

In the Soviet Union today, the workers have no guarantee of employment and those in jobs are constantly under the threat of dismissal. When employed, they are oppressed politically, exploited economically and personally humiliated. The managers of enterprises, using the power in their hands, work out regulations and rules which fleece and persecute the workers. They often unscrupulously abuse, interrogate and detain workers. The Soviet revisionist authorities are known to have thrown workers who dared to resist into "labour camps" and committed some of them to "mental hospitals." They have even installed "floodlighting," "supervisory posts," "people's censors," "comrades' courts," and so on to spy on and persecute the workers. . . . The workers in the lowest wage brackets who account for more than half of all workers, can seldom make ends meet, and their conditions are appalling. Even worse off are the 40 million retired employees and workers who must live on pensions. Many who are already old and failing in health have to look for new jobs.

In order to extract maximum surplus value from the workers, the bureaucrat-monopoly capitalists force them to labour under harsh conditions without the least labour safety precautions. . . . [They] show them the factory gate when they are disabled, ill, or otherwise lose their capacity to work.

The revival of the capitalist system of wage labour in the Soviet Union has led to the migration of large numbers of workers. . . . The workers are driven from pillar to post like slaves, subjected to the bitterness of unemployment.[18]

In response to these harsh conditions, workers are defiant and ready to struggle for their rights. "The cruel oppression and exploitation by the Soviet revisionist rulers have aroused ever stronger resentment and resistance on the part of the Soviet workers, who struggle against them by slowdowns, absenteeism, strikes, protest meetings and demonstrations."[19]

As late as 1977-1978, this was the negative image presented to the Chinese people about workers in the Soviet Union. When China's poli-

[16] "Fictitious Ownership by Whole People in Soviet Union," 97-98.
[17] Wei Chi, The Soviet Union Under the New Tsars, 34.
[18] Ibid., 49-50.
[19] Ibid., 51.

cies toward workers changed abruptly in 1977 and 1978, this image served a counterproductive purpose. Shortly there appeared a new literature on Soviet workers with a very different message.

THE LEGACY OF RUSSIA'S PAST

In December 1982 an article by Zhu Qing was published, reviewing recent developments in studies of Russian history. Of the four sections into which the article is divided, only one focuses on domestic developments. It is entitled, "Evaluations of Peter I and Catherine II." The other sections, "Tsarist Russia's Strategy of Foreign Expansion," "Was Tsarist Russia an Imperialist Country or a Semicolonial Country?" and "Sino-Russian Relations," examine issues that appear to have been, for the most part, already familiar to Chinese readers. Nevertheless, the novelty of the newly developing field of Russian history can be surmised from the introductory sentence of the article. "In recent years, studies by domestic scholars of the history of Tsarist Russia have achieved many new results, and there has even been progress in divergent and strange aspects that nobody has cared to inquire about in the past."[20]

Zhu begins his section on Peter I with the assertion that China's historians have always held varying opinions on the evaluation of Peter, especially of his reforms. He then reviews the "present positive evaluations of Peter's reform achievements by some scholars." Zhu neglects to mention any differing opinions, although he acknowledges the "pronounced military coloration" of the reforms.

Praise for Peter I centers on his major role in ending Russia's backwardness and building the material foundation for the development of capitalism. Zhu observes that Mark and Engels had recognized this contribution by Peter. Chinese scholars now consider him "a link between past and future," "a man of great talent and broad vision," a leader who "accelerated Russia's development." Peter "vigorously fostered country fair trades, and cut canals, all of which fairly rapidly promoted the formation of markets throughout Russia. Spurring the growth of Russia's capitalist elements, Peter's reforms obviously played a role in the development of the working class."[21]

Zhu notes that Chinese opinions of Catherine II have been changing. "Our country's traditional view holds that she was a personage who should be thoroughly evaluated as negative and that her life was an evil, reactionary one. But in recent years, there have been some scholars who

[20] Zhu Qing, "Jinnianlai guonei Eguoshi yanjiu gaishu," *Sixiang zhanxian*, no. 6 (December 1982): 91-94, 90.

[21] Ibid., 92-93.

think that this was a personage worthy of a fresh evaluation. They maintain that in the period of her rule there also appeared some distinctly new elements." Zhu explains that in her early period she made the utmost effort to take an enlightened and reform attitude; on the foundation of the ruthless exploitation of the serfs, she led Russia to "a very big development of the productive forces." She was progressive because she gave "precedence to the interests of the rising bourgeoisie" and encouraged "the development of capitalist relations." Clearly she too helped bring about the emergence of a working class. Nevertheless, Zhu spares no words in condemning her in the field of foreign policy as "completely reactionary" and "a wildly arrogant hegemonist."[22]

Typical of Chinese review articles, Zhu's review mentions no authors or titles. One of the studies he may have had in mind was a 1982 article by Zhao Keyi on the history of Russia's handicraft industry. Zhao refers to the birth of handicraft industries in the time of Peter I and to "the most flourishing period of comparatively rapid development of domestic handicraft industries" in the second half of the eighteenth century. He points to sectors such as metalworking, textiles, and shipbuilding, where there were many factories, and to the Urals as a regional leader. Nevertheless, Zhao's main point is that the relations of production between laborers and their bosses or owners remained feudal in nature. He contrasts the personal dependency of the Russian system in which labor was recruited through administrative measures, such as assignment of state peasants, purchase of peasants, or conscription, to the impersonal capitalist labor market already present in the West. While Russian factories were essentially the same in their division of labor, production technology, and organization, they were fundamentally different in their relations of production. The feudal serf system had been extended to the factory; workers often owed a part or most of their wage to their owner, and the owner could directly interfere in their lives. Zhao adds that a debate has been taking place in Russia in which some historians claim that the eighteenth-century system was capitalist in character. He totally rejects this attempt to exaggerate Russian development, insisting that Lenin had recognized its feudal character.

In the first half of the nineteenth century, labor relations based on personal dependency operated as a brake on Russian capitalist development, according to Zhao. Weakened by such relations, the working class developed slowly. After the 1830s, the system was in crisis in the face of increasing competition from peasant capitalism and the rising need to apply modern machinery. Bankruptcies were common, and workers, who were

---

[22] Ibid., 93.

doubly exploited, were continuously rising up to demand equal treatment and rewards with freely hired labor. While recognizing a gradual trend over more than 100 years toward the use of hired labor, Zhao concludes that Russia was unable to pass beyond the stage of sprouts of capitalism.[23]

In 1983, Zhao took another look at seventeenth- and eighteenth-century capitalism in Russia. In support of Stalin's views of Russian history, he argues that sprouts of capitalism and a national market formed with Moscow at the center. Merchants broke out of the narrow boundaries of local markets. They accumulated capital on a large scale, but from the beginning were closely linked to feudal authorities—assured of monopolies and controlled at the same time. Lacking the means to seize power, the rising merchant class sought protection instead. They became part of the ruling group, winning the right to considerable self-administration in the cities and supporting the tsarist government's foreign expansion. Although there were contradictions, the mutual interests of the merchants and aristocracy became closely intertwined. This was a distinctive feature of Russian development.[24]

How capitalist was Russia before 1917? How distinctive was its form of capitalism? A 1981 article by Fan Daren attempts to answer these questions. He begins by insisting that among Chinese historians there is no difference of opinion about the conclusion that a peculiarity of Russian imperialism is that it was military feudal imperialism. This in no way means they are denigrating the extent of capitalism. According to Fan, after the 1861 reforms, Russian capitalism developed comparatively rapidly. The speed of industrial development even surpassed that of some Western capitalist countries, for example in coal production and railroad mileage. In 1913, the development of industrial capitalism already placed Russia in the middle level of developed countries, fifth behind America, Germany, England, and France, although on a per capita basis Russia remained among the most backward European countries. Following changes in the economic foundation, especially the revolutionary blow of 1905-1907, the tsarist absolutist system gradually changed in the direction of making the capitalist class the masters.[25]

While recognizing the ascendancy of capitalism, Fan finds some unusual features in Russia. He singles out four. First, industrial production was relatively concentrated. By the early twentieth century, there were a

[23] Zhao Keyi, "Luelun Eguo de lingyou shougong gongchang," Shixue yuekan, no. 4 (1982): 62-67.

[24] Zhao Keyi, "Shiqi zhi shiba shiji Eguo shangren de diwei yu zuoyong," Henan shida xuebao (shehuikexue ban), no. 4 (1983): 77-85.

[25] Fan Daren, "Lun ShaE junshi fengjian diguozhuyi," Beijing daxue xuebao (zhexue shehuikexue ban), no. 5 (1981): 77-83.

number of monopolies, such as that of the Nobel family in oil. Second, feudal-style relations persisted, which was atypical of an imperialist nation. Enterprise owners often had a dual role as large landowners. They continued to rely heavily on feudal forms of exploitation, keeping workers in a position of personal dependency. In turn, many workers kept ties to the land and to agriculture. Third, the state itself held some of the economic arteries. Fan notes that one book referred to it as the world's largest landowner, largest capitalist, largest railroad builder, and largest enterprise director. The state sold all alcoholic beverages and it controlled national finances. In World War I, Fan adds, the state's controls were further strengthened. Such state power was made more significant by the narrow scope of the domestic market. Fourth, because of the tsarist state's desperate need for capitalist cooperation to repress the revolutionary movement and hold on to its power, it tolerated the most barbaric measures, including interest rates two or three times those of Western capital. The big capitalists, in turn, sought the violent support of the state in squeezing the workers and suppressing their resistance. All of these conditions in one way or another reflect the continued deep feudal imprint on Russia's industrial system. As Mei Wenbin writes, the level of industrial development in Russia was about 50-100 years behind the developed capitalist countries; economically and technologically, Russia was still quite backward.[26] A review article in the 1982 *Yearbook of Chinese Historical Studies* places Fan Daren's article in the perspective of two other articles on Russian military feudal imperialism. It finds Fan in agreement with Yan Zhong that feudal relations persisted into the monopoly stage of capitalism in Russia. Yan argued that the militarized character arose from this.[27]

Although few Chinese studies of the Russian workers' movement have appeared in recent years, newly issued histories of the world do not fail to give lengthy coverage to this subject. The exceptional article on the period tends to focus on political leaders such as Lenin, Plekhanov, or Bakunin rather than on the workers themselves. In 1983, one article on the occasion of the hundredth anniversary of the founding of the Workers' Liberation Society discussed the history of the workers' movement from 1883-1901. It praised the role of the society: in translating and propagating the writings of Marx and Engels; in spearheading the struggle against the misguided ideas of populism that capitalism and the development of a proletariat could be avoided in Russia; in exchanging experiences with

[26] Ibid., 80-86; Mei Wenbin, "Sulian xiang shehuizhuyi guodu de ruogan wenti," *Shijie jingji*, no. 9 (1981): 13.

[27] Sun Chengmu, "Sulian jinxiandaishi," *Zhongguo lishixue nianjian 1982* (Beijing: Renminchubanshe, 1982), 225-28.

other European revolutionary movements and thus educating Russian workers; and finally, in combatting anarchism, opportunism, and revisionism. The article takes exception to an unduly negative Soviet evaluation of this movement in 1938. The Soviet source erred in leaving out some of the contributions of the movement and exaggerating its shortcomings. Specifically, the Soviets were too critical of the populist early views of the society, failing to see these as understandable transitional views held by people who were breaking with the populist movement. Also, the Soviets were too critical of Plekhanov, the society's leader, for not noting that the proletariat should lead the peasants and for assigning too great a role in the revolution to the capitalist class. They were guilty of transposing Plekhanov's errors of 1905 to an earlier period. Chinese who "seek truth from facts" can determine that the Workers' Liberation Society did not commit serious errors.[28] It made an important contribution to the development of the workers' movement.

In the world history books designed for study at institutions of higher education almost all the suggested references are to Lenin's works. A few Soviet histories of the 1950s may also be cited. For the most part, Chinese history texts repeat Lenin's views of the developing revolutionary situation. They present a history of the Bolshevik Party and its struggles with its enemies during the revolutionary movement. Above all, they seek to answer the question: Why was socialist revolution successful in Russia?

One part of the answer is the size and structure of the working class in Russia. Between 1865 and 1890, the number of large factory and railway workers doubled to 1.4 million. By 1905, the figure was 3 million, one-third of whom worked in factories with at least 1,000 workers. And in 1917, according to a 1984 world history text, the total proletariat actually numbered sixteen million, including 3.5 million factory workers, 3.3 million in transport and construction, 4.5 million in handicrafts, and 4.5 million in commerce. Not only are Chinese impressed with these raw numbers, they also stress the concentration of the work force in units of over 500 workers each in such sectors as textiles, metals, mining, and the railroads. Size and concentration made it easier to organize Russian workers.

In Chinese histories, much more emphasis is given to another part of the answer to the question of why socialism won in Russia first. Each book repeats the familiar story of Russia entering the stage of monopoly capitalism at the beginning of the twentieth century with feudal-serf

[28] Gao Fang and Gao Jingzeng, "Eguo laodong jiefangshe de lishi gongji: jinian laodong jiefangshe chengli yibai zhounian," *Henan shifan daxue bao* (shehuikexue ban), no. 4 (1983): 57-63.

remnants still greatly in evidence, especially in the landowning system and in the political leadership of the tsarist autocracy; the aristocracy remained the ruling class even as the capitalist class was gaining control of the economy. The tsarist government needed capitalist development to support and advance its coercive government and hegemonism, while the weak capitalist class depended on the tsarist government to control its workers, to meet the competition of foreign capitalists, and to expand its raw material supplies and its markets. The term used to describe this combination is the "military-feudal character of Russian imperialism." For the workers, this brought the most barbaric and cruel forms of oppression. A Chinese text describes the whole country as a "military camp" and a "warlord, bureaucratic, police autocracy."[29] Not only were people deprived of all political rights and minorities subjected to Russification and repression, the Russian system was doubly exploitative: tsarist and capitalist forms of exploitation were combined. World War I worsened the conditions of the workers, increasing further their already high level of revolutionary spirit.[30]

Of course, the third factor that is stressed in Chinese histories dealing with the Russian Revolution is the role of theory and of Lenin. Lenin developed the theory and forged the links to the workers' movement. In opposition to the Mensheviks, Lenin understood that workers must take the lead in a socialist revolution based on force.[31] He understood that peasants are natural allies of the workers. Chinese continue to glorify Lenin's role in the revolutionary struggle, while writing little about the workers themselves.

WAR COMMUNISM AND THE NEP

In 1984, a section of a review article by Chen Zhihua offers an overview of Chinese studies of the contemporary (post-1917) Soviet Union since the formation of the People's Republic in 1949. Chen notes that at the beginning there was keen interest in the history of the first socialist country. That was met through translations, especially three volumes of the *History of the Soviet Union* edited by Pankratova that were published in 1951-1954. These books not only developed the study of Russian history, they taught Marxist historical theory and research methods to Chinese historians. Chen acknowledges that the first nontranslated articles during

---

[29] Dongbei shifan daxue, ed., *Shijie xiandaishi* (Shenyang: Liaoning renminchubanshe, 1984), 9-10; Lin Judai, Chen Zongwu, and Ai Zhouchang, eds., *Shijie jindaishi* (Shanghai: Shanghai renminchubanshe, 1982), 564-66.

[30] Dongbei shifan daxue, ed., *Shijie xiandaishi*, 8.

[31] Lin Judai et al., *Shijie jindaishi*, 580.

the next few years did not exhibit much creativity, but he considers them to have made a good beginning in this field. He is more critical of the state of the field from the late fifties to the mid-sixties. Under the influence of the leftist leading thought, very many areas were closed to research and the others were treated simplistically to correspond to party and state domestic and foreign policies. The scope of research grew ever narrower; one-sided subjectivity increased daily. Historians of the Soviet Union feared committing a mistake and being criticized. When it came to the ten years of disorder, this tendency worsened; the sprouts of research were on the verge of withering away. After the "Gang of Four" was smashed in 1976, especially following the Third Plenum in 1978, the field at last experienced unprecedented development.

According to Chen, the first area to be emphasized by researchers was the transitional (1917-1937) economic history of the Soviet Union. This was not accidental. As the attention of the whole country turned to socialist modernization, it was necessary to draw from the experiences and lessons of the world's developed countries, especially its first socialist country. China needed to borrow. Chen observes that in the past, everything about War Communism was simply approved because it enabled Soviet Russia to get through the Civil War; it saved the new Soviet government. In recent years, however, there has been a division of opinion. One group approves of War Communism as an emergency measure in response to the war, while others see it as a serious error and a defeat in the attempt to make a direct transition to communism. Some researchers divide it into two stages: 1918-1919, when it corresponded to wartime needs, and 1920 to early 1921, when it was aimed at a "direct transition." Chen concludes that both those who see War Communism as an error and those who praise its accomplishments agree on one point: it broke down traditional thinking.[32]

The 1982 *Yearbook of Chinese Historical Studies* indicates that in 1981, lively debates were in progress over the period 1917-1921 and the NEP years. Unlike most review articles, this one lists the relevant articles and indicates where they stand in the debates. Noting the existence of sharp differences in the evaluation of War Communism, it identifies the historian Xie Youshi, who wrote, "'War Communism' is a Kind of Contribution," with the view that no other policy could have worked. This policy saved the world's first Soviet Socialist Republic and received the support of the mass of workers and peasants. In an article in the same is-

[32] Chen Zhihua, "Sulian xiandaishi yanjiu de xin jumian ye yi xingcheng," in "Huigu sanshi nianlai de chengjiu kaishi shijieshi yanjiu de xin jumian," *Shijie zhishi*, no. 5 (1984): 5.

sue of *World History*, Rong Xin called War Communism a serious error:
it exceeded the objective social conditions of the time; it forcibly nation-
alized small and medium-size enterprises, abolished commerce and took
other measures that were too constraining, and through grain requisitioning violated the interests of the peasants, especially the middle peasants, damaging the worker-peasant alliance. The review by Sun
Chengmu adds that various other opinions completely reject the policy of
War Communism. Jiang Yihua considers it "pure agricultural socialism,"
"emotional socialism," "a theory of the omnipotence of political power
formed under the longstanding control of Russian absolutism, as well as
sentiments of a religious nature" that had penetrated into the minds of
proletarian revolutionaries. Writing about the Kronstadt rebellion, Du
Like says the Bolshevik Party in War Communism chose completely mistaken means. In a wave of enthusiasm, some leaders of the party tried to
apply communist principles to production and distribution in a small-
peasant country. In 1981, Xie Youshi published another article in answer
to Jiang Yihua, arguing that War Communism was a wartime response
that had nothing in common with "peasant socialism" or "emotional socialism."[33]

Of course, workers were among the many groups that suffered from
the conditions of War Communism. Although some of the economic
measures of War Communism were taken to save workers from starva-
tion and to prevent industry from closing completely, the impact of the
crisis on workers was severe. The number of workers dropped below half
of the prewar level as many of the leading workers died in the Civil War
and vast numbers left for the villages to obtain enough grain to survive.
The crisis also weakened the class nature of the remaining workers.
Chinese articles point to the mass dissatisfaction of workers and to their
weakened motivation under conditions of egalitarian distribution in kind.
To rebuild the working class required a sharp and abrupt turn in policy,
which came at the beginning of the 1920s with the NEP.[34]

The 1984 overview by Chen Zhihua observes that in recent years research on the NEP has grown continuously deeper. Chen states that very
many researchers are dissatisfied with arguing the necessity of the transition to NEP from the overall situation or general theory and have progressively differentiated agriculture, industry, commerce, and other

[33] Sun Chengmu "Sulian jinxiandaishi," 228-29.
[34] Zhou Huizhen, "Lun Suweiai Eguo xiang shehuizhuyi guodu de lishi jingyan: jinian
Liening danchen yibaiyishi zhounian," *Zhengzhou daxue xuebao* (shehuikexue ban), no. 2
(1980): 1-10, Feng Lanrui, "SuE cong zhanshi gongchanzhuyi dao xin jingji zhengce," *Xueshu yuekan*, no. 8 (1982): 29-32; and Wen Yi, " 'Zhanshi gongchanzhuyi' zhengce he
'zhanshi gongchanzhuyi' sixiang," *Shixue jikan*, no. 2 (1983): 57-63.

areas in order to study the concrete circumstances of the NEP. Agricultural studies have examined land relations, hired labor, and cooperatives; industrial studies treat the concession system to foreigners, the leasing of enterprises, and the management system; studies of commerce include such topics as policies toward privately operated commerce and the character and functions of "nepmen."

Other specialized research discusses the worker-peasant alliance, the commercial economy, state capitalism, and the inner-party struggle. Some researchers contrast the NEP and the economic policies of the thirties. There is also specialized research on the historiography of the period. Chen concludes that we can say without exaggeration that in recent years a relatively high scholarly level has been reached in research on the NEP.[35]

Sun Chengmu's review of publications that appeared in 1981 adds more detail and cites the sources in question. He notes an article by Li Shufan that recognizes that the NEP was a policy selected for the period of transition from capitalism to socialism in Soviet Russia. It enabled the country to get through a serious economic and political crisis and to strengthen the alliance of workers and peasants. Sun sees Duan Binglin's 1981 article as recognizing the necessity for the change from requisitioning to a grain tax as a means for bringing about a clear improvement in agriculture, but Dun added that Trotsky elements in the party used this situation to arbitrarily raise prices in order to accumulate capital for industry through the exploitation of the peasantry. This led to the scissors problem in agricultural and industrial production, which in turn induced peasants to develop their own handicrafts to satisfy their own needs. When industry stagnated, the party and government responded with resolutions to lower the prices of industrial goods in order to aid the peasantry and restore the economy. Han Anjun's article is credited with recognizing the effectiveness of important industrial policies, such as the electrification plan, the tractor reform, and the worker wage-equivalency policy.

Sun Chengmu's review article singles out the concessions policy in the NEP as a topic of interest to Chinese historians in 1981. He mentions three articles. The first, written in 1980 by Wen Yi, saw this policy as a compromise with foreign capitalists that only involved about 1 percent or, at its peak, 3 percent of industrial production, but that opened a window. An article by Xie Youshi contrasted with Wen's, contending that Lenin's aim in the concessions was to use the contradictions among the imperialists to strengthen socialism and that this policy was a form of struggle.

---

[35] Chen Zhihua, "Sulian xiandaishi yanjiu de xin jumian ye yi xingcheng," 5-6.

In the process, the Soviet government paid a high price: "Some of the contracts even had a very great servile character." In addition, Sun mentions an article by Li Xiuyun on the concessions policy in the Far Eastern region, which regarded it as a success in transferring technology, conserving national capital, resolving unemployment problems, training technical cadres, and developing the region. This policy took advantage of the contradictions of imperialism to realize a comparatively long period of peaceful construction.[36]

A year later, Chen Qineng and Yu Pei prepared the review article in *The Yearbook of Chinese Historiography*. On War Communism, they recognize that two different opinions could be found: 1) Feng Lanrui's view that it violated the fundamental theory of Marxism and could not bring socialism, the first stage of communism, but instead was a transition to egalitarian and poverty-ridden socialism; only in 1921 did Soviet Russia shift from a direct attack on capitalism to the development of commercial relations in order to achieve a transition to socialism; and 2) Zhang Peiyi's view that War Communism had a two-fold nature, as wartime measures to concentrate human and material resources and as plans to use these measures to make a direct transition into socialism—the latter resulting in serious consequences in the form of popular dissatisfaction and fallen productivity. More in support of War Communism were the views of Ye Shuzong and Wang Side, who accuse others of departing from historical analysis when they reject the historical role of War Communism and see it as the cause of later calamities. Ye and Wang argue that only in 1920-1921 was the mistake made of unnecessarily continuing the emergency wartime measures with the aim of restoring and building the economy and making the transition to socialism. In the fall of 1921, Lenin, through deeper analysis of War Communism, recognized this error and corrected it. Ye and Wang contend that one should not contrast the early and late analysis of Lenin since these were just two stages in the consciousness process as his thoughts deepened. This is an obvious warning to those who focus on late Lenin in an effort to justify reform policies in China.

Chen and Yu point out that in 1982, there were quite a few articles on the essence and significance of the NEP.[37] Chen Huijun writes about the twists, complexities, and complications of building socialism. Zhao Changfeng also sees the NEP as a policy of retreat in order to turn danger into order. Wen Zhimin elaborates cryptically on many reasons for the

---

[36] Sun Chengmu, "Sulian jinxiandaishi," 230-31.

[37] Chen Qineng and Yu Pei, "Sulian jinxiandaishi," *Zhongguo lishixue nianjian 1983* (Beijing: Renminchubanshe, 1983), 246-47.

retreat: the peasant problem, revolutionary order, leftist thought, education and training of personnel, strengthening the party and state authority. Hu Shangzhi sees the NEP from the angle of the worker-peasant alliance. No mention is made of sharp disagreements in scholarship. Instead the reader gets the impression of multi-faceted studies serving to deepen Chinese understanding.

Chen Huijun's full article explains the retreat from War Communism to the NEP in favor of state capitalism and, to a certain degree, the restoration and development of private capitalism. He finds two distortions long present in explanations of this retreat (tuique): either to regard it as a reversal (daotui) or to consider it an advance. These are the two extremes, each of which avoids explaining the need for retreat through concrete historical analysis. Only on the surface did it seem to be a reversal, although many in Soviet and Chinese historical circles have subscribed to this view. According to Chen, the NEP returned the Soviet Union to the right track for moving forward to socialism.[38] Only by developing commercial production and exchange, using capitalism, could socialism be realized.

Many Chinese studies argue that the NEP posed no threat to the proletariat's superior political and economic position. As Li Shuzhi writes, "Coexistence is not peaceful coexistence." The state held the land, the big factories, the railroads, water transport, foreign trade, and other important economic arteries. Socialist economic elements grew day by day. The working class and the administrators gained experience, which, although it did not signify the building of socialist society, was necessary and sufficient for it. The working class in various ways controlled the activity of nonsocialist elements and limited their interference and negative influence on the development of the socialist economy. They could not become a political force. Given the limited development of the material foundation, managerial ability, and cultural level, it was necessary to use the skills of capitalists in the service of socialism. Having gained power, the working class's main interest was to increase production: only in this way could a foundation be established for socialism and the contradictions between the superstructure and the economic base be resolved.[39]

There is also another viewpoint that accentuates the threat posed by the capitalist class in the early and mid-twenties. Xie Youshi presents this view that the struggle and contradictions between socialist and capitalist development were substantial. Because of the NEP policies of foreign in-

[38] Chen Huijun, "Shilun SuE xin jingji zhengce chuqi de tuique, *Shijie lishi*, no. 1 (1982): 13-14.
[39] Li Shuzhi, "Suweiai Eguo xin jingji zhengce shiqi yunxu duozhong jingji chengfen bingcun de keguan yiju," *Xuexi yu sikao*, no. 3 (1983): 69-74.

vestment and domestic relaxation of controls on private enterprises, capitalist elements developed to a considerable degree. The most lively
sphere of their activity was commercial exchange. Although private commerce enlivened the domestic market, it led to great waste and to the
emergence of the "nepmen": According to Xie, in 1924 these "nepmen"
numbered 1.5 percent of the population, but received 5 percent of the national income. "In the cities, industrial and commercial capitalists not
only violated state labor laws, acted cruelly and exploitatively toward the
workers in their enterprises, they even stole and concealed taxes, illegally
purchased state materials, deceitfully obtained bank loans, stole state
loans to their enterprises, opened underground factories, engaged in
large-scale speculation and smuggling, took away markets from state enterprises, illegally purchased grain and agricultural auxiliary products,
inflated prices, as well as conspiring with and corrupting Soviet cadres and
others in criminal activity, directly threatening the development of the
socialist economy and the direct ties of state-operated enterprises and the
peasant economy." Because of this, Xie concludes, the Soviet government
began to intensify the regulation, inspection, and limitation of private
capital.

Expanding the socialist economic camp and reducing the capitalist one
ensured the restoration of the national eonomy, says Xie, but class struggle in the economy did not stop; in the first years of the NEP, the development of capitalism in Soviet Russia was faster than expected, expanding to a loathsome degree. From 1921 to 1923, controls were so
ineffective that capitalism could grow spontaneously. This was anarchic
development. Only in 1924 did the state establish a committee to regulate
merchants and the Central Statistical Agency begin to take the first steps
toward control. Xie sums up the dangerous consequences of the activities
of the "nepmen": they "severely damaged socialist accumulation, poisoned the socialist atmosphere, corrupted people's thought, directly
threatened socialist construction." In his opinion, class struggle was the
dominant theme of the NEP economy.[40] His views appear to represent
the orthodox opposition to the rural reforms in China that resemble those
of the NEP.

As early as 1978 in the campaign against the "Gang of Four," Soviet
labor unions in the 1920s became a topic for scrutiny. Wu Shuqing wrote
that the "Gang of Four" had used the Soviet trade union debate in the
twenties to vilify Deng Xiaoping and attack Hua Guofeng. They had distorted history to claim that Trotsky had played on sentiments of the So-

---

[40] Xie Youshi, "Lun guomin jingji huifu shiqi Suweiai Eguo jingji lingyu nei de jieji
douzheng," *Shixue jikan*, no. 2 (1983): 64-71.

viet people to restore the national economy, speaking only about organizing production while remaining silent on the class struggle and the proletarian dictatorship, and to insist that Lenin had criticized an emphasis on production and stressed the political point of view. In this way, the "Gang of Four" opposed the "four modernizations." In fact, Wu continues, Lenin was concerned about how to change the past command methods demanded by the military situation to a different approach to unions that would appeal to the workers to restore and develop production, respect labor discipline, and increase labor productivity. It was Trotsky, Wu adds, who opposed persuasion and the expansion of democracy and an election system in the unions. He favored "nationalization of the unions," militarization of the workers' labor. Lenin advocated giving priority to socialist construction. Writing in 1978, before Bukharin became a subject of debate, the author identifies Bukharin with Trotsky, saying his calls for "moderation" and taking economics first were also incorrect and would have led to the collapse of the proletarian dictatorship. Only Lenin understood what unions should be under socialism; unlike Trotsky he would keep them separate from the state and not rely on orders in dealing with them.[41]

INDUSTRIALIZATION IN THE STALIN ERA

Review articles normally accessible to foreigners have much less to say about industrialization and collectivization than about War Communism and the NEP. The 1984 review of thirty-five years of accomplishments in research on world history manages to discuss industrialization and collectivization for only eight lines, in the midst of over one hundred on the previous decade of Soviet history. It mentions that the majority of researchers have shifted from the starting point of assuming the achievement of building Soviet socialism to investigating the shortcomings and mistakes of the guiding thought and policies of the party and government in this historical process in order to draw overall conclusions on the lessons of this experience. The paragraph concludes that conditions were not sufficiently ripe for overall collectivization, its methods bore a certain administrative character, and therefore the results were not ideal. These problems, the reader is told, were related to some mistakes by Stalin in theory and practice.[42]

The 1982 historical yearbook omits the 1930s altogether, while the 1983 yearbook discusses them only in relation to personnel policies and

[41] Wu Shuqing, "Ershi niandai Sulian zhigonghui wenti zhenglun he 'sirenbang' de daoguishu," *Beijing shifan daxue xuebao*, no. 2 (1978): 2-8.

[42] Chen Zhihua, "Sulian xiandaishi yanjiu de xin jumian ye yi xingcheng," 6.

the long-term explanations of agricultural stagnation to the 1950s.[43] A brief study note in 1980 by Zhang Xiang indicates much livelier interest in Stalin's economic theory. On many points Zhang refers to criticisms of Stalin expressed by his comrades. Some comrades consider Stalin's description of the fundamental economic laws of socialism too vague and incomplete; he did not say a word about the principles of enterprise management, and he failed to emphasize how one arouses worker motivation. Stalin also did not adequately examine the differences between collective ownership and ownership by the whole people. Stalin's approach did not enable enterprises to become relatively independent units of commercial production with their own material incentives. He did not clearly point out the relations and distinctions between the aims of society's production and the aims of the enterprise's production. And he did not make a detailed analysis of society's needs and the individual's needs.

Not a few comrades, Zhang adds, believe that Stalin did not cast off the influence of a natural economy. He half-accepted and half-rejected the law of value, allowing it to operate to a certain extent in regulating the flow of consumer goods, but not in production. Some comrades say that Stalin considered the means of production not to be commerce; only the means of livelihood were to be part of commercial exchange. Zhang mentions that some comrades see Stalin as stressing relations of production without correctly discussing their preconditions. This neglect of the forces of production was one-sided; it was a huge mistake. Among the forces of production he emphasized labor power and work equipment, completely neglecting the objects of labor. Stalin completely denied competition in a socialist system, although he approved of socialist emulation. He disparaged industrialization, beginning with light industry, as following the capitalist road. Stalin's interpretation of "from each according to his work" took an unscientific approach to determining the amount and quality of work invested by people. Finally, when Stalin declared in 1936 that the Soviet Union had established socialism, he did so too early and on the basis of too low a standard. The Soviet Union was economically still behind the advanced capitalist countries, it had not completely wiped out poverty, and the standard of living was still not well-off.[44]

In 1983-1984, a pair of articles in *Xuexi yu tansuo* examined Stalin's methods of industrialization. They both agreed that in theory and in historical experience, heavy industry develops faster than light industry. The first article credits Stalin with grasping this point, but accuses him of

---

[43] Sun Chengmu, "Sulian jinxiandaishi," 225-32; Chen Qineng and Yu Pei, "Sulian jinxiandaishi," 247-48.

[44] Zhang Xiang, "Guanyu Sidalin jingji lilun zhong ruogan wenti de taolun zongshu," *Shehuikexue*, no. 4 (1980): 157.

being unscientific only in believing that capitalist industrialization begins
with light industry. The second article qualifies this criticism by noting
that textiles were often the starting point for the major capitalists. Not
long after textile production began to grow, the rate of heavy industrial
growth overtook it. Given this fact, it is incorrect to reject Stalin's view.
The author remarks, "Of late many theoretical economics articles in criticizing Stalin's one-sided preference for the development of heavy industry do not pay attention to the correctness of Stalin's industrial theory—
a minority of articles completely reject it." The author follows this defense of Stalin with mention of at least three shortcomings of Stalin's
theory of industrialization. First, Stalin neglected the past state of a country; for example, was it correct in China to stress heavy industry when in
"old China" light industry had been less backward? Second, Stalin erred
in making the experience of the Soviet Union the single model for all socialist countries rather than distinguishing what is general and what is
particular to individual countries. Third, Stalin committed the serious error as early as 1926 of seeing industrialization only as the growth of
heavy industry.[45]

At the Eleventh Party Congress in 1977, Hua Guofeng accused the
"Gang of Four" of distorting Marxist philosophy. Under the pretext of
fighting revisionism, they had distorted the history of the proletarian dictatorship in the Soviet Union. In early 1978, Wang Shouhai published an
article to explain the principle of "from each according to his abilities, to
each according to his needs" in the time of Lenin's and Stalin's leadership. He argues that in 1921, Lenin saw the need to discard all egalitarian
thought. Attacking Trotsky's plans for equalization and entrusting power
to Stalin, Lenin supported bonuses and other rewards to labor. Wang argues that Lenin's views completely reject the "Gang of Four's" efforts to
separate distribution from labor. Wang also accuses the "Gang of Four"
of publicly opposing Chairman Mao's evaluation of Stalin as 30 percent
in error, 70 percent correct, saying they even wanted to criticize Stalin as
a "revisionist."

In Wang's view, Stalin was correct to oppose egalitarianism in the
1930s wage reform, but erred in inappropriately widening the differences
and granting one group high wages. Unlike Trotsky, Bukharin, Tomsky,
and other "opportunists," Stalin recognized that there are differences in
skills and sectors, and that task rates as well as time rates of remuneration
are socialist. The opportunists in the left tide of 1930-1931 advocated "so-

[45] Ji Shuiyong and Xi Yanyang, "Guanyu Sidalin de gongyehua fangfa wenti," *Xuexi yu
tansuo*, no. 2 (1984); and Fan Lichang, "Ye tan Sidalin de gongyehua fangfa ji youguan
luanshu," *Xuexi yu tansuo*, no. 2 (1984): 12-15.

cialization" of the wage and communes where members consumed in complete equality. In contrast, Stalin in June 1931 realized the need for more inequality; nevertheless, because the Soviet Union was the first socialist country, there was no experience from which to borrow. Stalin widened wage differences too much. The highest wages were ten, twenty, or even thirty times the lowest, and bonuses or other devices further widened the differences. Wang adds that after the October Revolution, it was, of course, necessary to attract capitalist specialists with high wages, but by the late thirties there was a considerable cadre of intelligentsia from worker and peasant background. Such differentials not only were unnecessary, they also led to corruption and were one factor in producing a new capitalist class. The analogy to the "Gang of Four," this 1978 article concludes, shows that the abuse of position by officials and the accumulation of unlimited wealth leads to the revival of capitalism.[46] At that time, the "Gang of Four" was being portrayed as a rightist threat in China, while wider wage differentials were being advocated. Wang's analysis toed a narrow line.

As late as 1980, articles continued to refute charges publicized in the time of the "Gang of Four" against the Stalinist approach to workers and work incentives. These charges had branded the Stakhanovite movement of the mid-1930s as "widening the jurisdiction of the capitalist," "casting off proletarian politics," or "raising a worker aristocracy." In contrast, Wang Shouhai vigorously concludes that this movement was a great boon to the Soviet Union, without departing from the principle of "to each according to his work." Zhou Shangwen adds that in order to wipe out the lingering position of the extreme leftist line in China, it is very instructive to assess the Stakhanovite movement accurately. He proceeds to do so in an article highly positive about the movement.

Zhou observes that in the 1920s and 1930s, Soviet workers often increased production in order to greet a holiday. As early as 1919, Moscow workers began the practice of "Communist Saturdays," voluntarily donating a day's labor. This represented the first stage of socialist competition and spread throughout the country, helping socialism survive at a time when there was nothing available to give out as a bonus. A decade later, as part of the First Five-Year Plan, a new stage of socialist competition was needed in the form of "shock work," with the goal of fulfilling the plan. The Stakhanovite movement from 1935 continued and developed these traditions. Realizing the necessity for improved technology to

---

[46] Wang Shouhai, "Liening, Sidalin lingdao shiqi Sulian guanche 'ge jin suo neng, an lao fenpei' yuanze de yixie qingkuang," *Shehuikexue zhanxian* (jingjixue), no. 1 (1978): 111-20.

meet the goals of industrialization, Stalin had coined the slogan, "Technology decides everything." Then, when the principal bottleneck was skilled personnel to use the new equipment, in 1935 Stalin added a second element to the slogan: "Cadres decide everything." The Stakhanovite movement combined socialist competition to outperform other units and workers, especially by beating the existing record for output in one day, with the skilled utilization of new technology to increase labor productivity. Within a span of months, records were doubled, quintupled, or even raised by a factor of ten. This set a new standard for other workers to emulate. Zhou praises the movement for enlivening the worker's creative spirit, raising his consciousness and his skills, and demanding an attitude of serving the people.

Zhou credits Stalin with realizing that to eliminate the differences between manual and mental labor requires raising the cultural and skill levels of workers to the level of engineering and technical personnel. The Stakhanovite movement did that for many. It identified and brought into leadership posts people of worker background, deeply familiar with workers and better able to accelerate socialist conditions on the basis of objective conditions. This movement greatly raised productivity and the use of modern technology. Moreover, Zhou argues, it followed the socialist principle of the more you work, the more you receive, as opposed to the capitalist system of exploitation. If some workers get rich first, that is in keeping with the socialist principle. Recognizing that in the course of the movement some localities and ministries overlooked the more numerous shock workers and working masses, and that some units falsified appearances, Zhou concludes that the criticisms of these mistakes made in 1937 helped advance the Stakhanovite movement along the correct course.[47]

Two years later, another article on the Stakhanovite movement was equally positive and insistent that this approach is not capitalism. In capitalist societies, according to Tong Baochang, workers sell themselves to the exploiting classes, while after the October Revolution they worked for their own class, for creating a rich socialist nation. This produces a fundamental change in the worker's viewpoint, increasing his motivation and creativity. The Stakhanovite movement was born in this new attitude toward work. It was made possible by the growing participation of workers in socialist competition and the recent introduction of new technology. At the start of the Second Five-Year Plan, technology was becoming more plentiful, but skilled cadres were scarce. Tong makes clear that the

[47] Wang Shouhai, "Sulian sanshi niandai de Sidahannuofu yundong," *Shehuikexue zhanxian*, no. 1 (1980): 82-89; Zhou Shangwen, "Chongping Sidahannuofu yundong," *Shanghai shifan daxue xuebao*, no. 2 (1980): 22-27.

success of the plan ahead of schedule was due to rising labor productivity, which in turn resulted from the Stakhanovite movement. The movement carried over to World War II and the post-war reconstruction; so its importance extends beyond one plan. It even extended to China and other people's democracies, spurring their economic recovery and development. Tong adds that at the beginning of the 1930s, wage egalitarianism caused severe losses in the Soviet Union. Only after task rates of remuneration were favored in the wage reform from 1931, when the principle of "to each according to his labor" was more fully applied, could the Stakhanovite movement flourish and raise the qualifications of the workers at the same time that it spurred the economy forward.[48] The lesson for China seems obvious.

A 1983 article discusses the Soviet trade union model and its impact on Eastern Europe, as well as the reforms in response to its shortcomings. The article identifies a common process of establishment and development of this model, adding that to a very great degree it deviated from Lenin's thought, which he had explained after the October Revolution. Lenin wanted the working class to become masters with their unions representing them and supporting their interests. The unions were to be a "school of communism," where the workers learn to take control. Under Stalin, despite continued citation of Lenin's theory of unions, in application and gradually in actual spirit practice deviated from thought. Stalin emphasized that the party rely on the unions to transmit its will to the workers. He said that under conditions of economic socialism, contradictions between social organizations diminished and disappeared. He did not talk about contradictions between the individual, the collective, and the state. Although he talked of opposing bureaucratism, he did not talk about the activities of unions to support this.

In Stalin's time, the principle of a "school of communism" merely meant to educate the worker to respect discipline and to strive to advance communist thought and moral education. The principle of "mass participation in management" was interpreted narrowly to encourage some suggestions for production, but not to include genuine participation in state management or even in the great affairs of enterprises. Overlooking the true meaning of socialist democracy, Stalin overemphasized centralized, unified control by the party and state over industrial and political life. From the thirties to the early fifties, three features of trade union activity stood out: the organization of socialist labor competition; the operation of social insurance and other welfare and employment-related

[48] Tong Baochang, "Shilun Sulian Sidahannuofu yundong," *Shixue jikan*, no. 3 (1982): 54-60.

benefits; and the enhancement of political thought education and cultural and technical education. The work style of unions was to take commands from above. The author adds, "Here one needs still to point out, the thirties was a time of the expansion of the movement to purge counterrevolutionaries, trade union organs also were repeatedly purged." Not a few union leaders were branded criminals, as "other class elements" or "enemy elements," and purged. After this, in the Soviet Union there never again emerged much discussion of the position or functions of unions. Union work became increasingly predictable and lifeless.[49]

No topic has been the subject of as many studies by China's Soviet specialists as the economic management system. Chinese writers examine the history of this system in order to explain why it was in need of thoroughgoing reform by the 1950s. In 1982, three economists, Jin Hui, Lu Nanquan, and Zhang Kangqin, jointly edited a book on the Soviet management system. Their historical observations review the factors that shaped the formation and development of Stalin's economic system. The system began to take shape in the early twenties, and in the thirties it was basically established. Despite later reforms, they observe, the basic features of what the West calls the "command economy" have not changed to the 1980s.[50]

Some Chinese contend that both Soviet and Western scholarship is one-sided, while their own views are in-between. The Soviets say almost nothing about Stalin's individual role in establishing the planning system, insisting that Stalin, along with others, applied Lenin's way. Westerners exaggerate Stalin's personal role and his errors, arguing that he completely rejected Lenin's way. Chinese specialists take the middle ground, stressing conditions other than the individual role of Stalin. Yet Chinese publications reveal a range of views that appear to cover the entire spectrum. The 1982 book approaches the Western extreme in its sharp criticisms of Stalin. The authors point to Stalin's political report to the Fifteenth Party Congress in 1927 in which he claimed that capitalist nations are planning, but their plans are not binding, while socialist plans are compulsory. With this sort of plan, the direction of the future development of the economy on a national scale can be decided. This reliance on central commands was related to Stalin's rejection of commercial production in favor of a natural economy. Two factors led to this kind of thinking: the state of consciousness at that time and historical conditions.

The three economists trace the state of consciousness to War Com-

[49] Lu Wen, "Guanyu dongou guojia de gonghui gaige: shilun shehuizhuyi tiaojian xia gonghui gongzuo de lishi jingyan," *Sulian dongou wenti*, no. 6 (1983): 19.

[50] Jin Hui, Lu Nanquan, and Zhang Kangqin, eds., *Lun Sulian jingji: guanli tizhi yu zhuyao zhengce* (Shenyang: Liaoning renminchubanshe, 1982), 3-5.

munism, when military conditions led to concentrating all human and material resources in the fight against the enemy, eliminating commerce and currency.[51] After the NEP was declared, many Soviets considered it a necessary but temporary retreat, a compromise with capitalism that would not endure. Elsewhere Chinese have written that from the viewpoint of theory, the NEP was not seen as necessary; therefore the way was open to a full-scale attack on "capitalism" several years later. They add that the centralized character of the political system was a negative influence on the continuation of the NEP.[52] The volume by Jin, Lu, and Zhang describes the theorists as waiting for the development of production and the switchover from private to collective farms in order to widen the scope of planning and eliminate trade and currency relations. Part of the problem was that theorists confused these relations with capitalism. They assumed that in conditions of socialism, public replaces private ownership, and the commercial economy along with the laws of value become exhibition items in the museum of human history. The state could do without them in exchanging goods among producing units. To the theorists, a socialist economy means planned, direct control of the natural economy. Another theoretical influence was that right after the October Revolution, Lenin and others had erred in preparing immediately to substitute direct distribution of goods for commercial exchange. Although several years' experience had shown the folly of this approach, and Lenin had recognized their mistake and launched the NEP, theorists did not grasp that this reversal was more than a temporary retreat.

Apart from the theoretical problem, there were historical conditions that led to Stalin's economic system. The 1982 book explains that there was no precedent for the development of communism, and the conditions of Soviet Russia, a backward country with only an intermediate level of capitalism, did not correspond to those expected by Marx and Engels following the revolution. Their ideas could not resolve problems of planning and management. Lenin died before he had time to give a complete answer. The responsibility fell on Stalin's shoulders.

Summarizing economic management in the period of Stalin's leadership, the 1982 book finds it excessively centralized with little local authority, and with even less authority at the enterprise level. Very few enterprises were under local management; in 1936 the value of their production was just 11 percent of the industrial total, while 89 percent

[51] Ibid., 5-7.

[52] Pang Chuan, "Sulian dongou guojia zai jihua gongzuo fangmian de yixie gaige he bianhua," *Sulian dongou wenti yicong*, no. 3 (1982): 19; Jin Hui, "Shilun zhengzhi tizhi he jingji tizhi de guanxi: jiantan Sulian zhengzhi tizhi dui jingji gaige de yingxiang," *Sulian dongou wenti*, no. 4 (1984): 9.

was issued by central enterprises. The local figure rose to nearly one-third by 1950, but financial management and construction capital were much more centralized. Localities could not take conditions in their own areas into account to change plans sent down by the state. This severely limited their incentives. Bureaucratism and commandism stifled the motivation of localities and enterprises, unfavorably influencing the economic development of production.[53]

Chapter Two of the 1982 book traces the history of the industrial management system, pointing to the excessive reliance on administrative orders and bureaucratism in War Communism and then to the improvements in the labor remuneration system and other reforms that led to economic recovery by 1926. After reviewing the successive reforms during the Stalin period, the authors note three basic features: 1) state administrative organs directly controlled all enterprise activities; 2) administrative measures took over, leaving only a narrow scope for market and currency relations; and 3) economic authority and economic responsibility were separated despite appearances of economic accountability for the enterprise. The authors explain that historical conditions of the late 1920s and early 1930s prompted the Soviets to industrialize in the shortest time, concentrating personnel, material resources, and financial resources on heavy industry. The only socialist country in a European environment of rising fascism, the Soviet Union needed to protect itself and had no choice but to rely on administrative means and a unified, centralized management system.

The authors add that some officials had been accustomed to coercive measures from War Communism and that a "leftist faction" with Trotsky in the lead had advocated suppressing the market. Although Bukharin had said the NEP should continue and warned that centralization would interfere with the motivation of localities and enterprises and give rise to bureaucratism, he also said that economically backward Russia required a very long transitional period. The Chinese authors note that the party leadership with Stalin at its head had these opponents purged and then followed Stalin's conception of a highly centralized economic model. When the international situation became more tense later in the 1930s, World War II erupted in the 1940s, and post-war recovery took place, these conditions all further increased the need for a concentrated effort to develop heavy industry and the military industry. The Soviet centralized management system suited these needs. It enabled the Soviet Union in a very short time to rise from a backward country and become the second strongest country in the world, to defeat German fascism. For these rea-

[53] Jin Hui et al., *Lun Sulian jingji*, 9-11.

sons people gained the wrong impression that this system of management was superior, that it was the model that the Soviets needed to maintain, and that other socialist countries all should copy as the common
path.[54] In addition, theorists contrasted this model's features to the market system, making it seem as if the alternatives to the status quo were
unacceptable.

The 1982 book on the Soviet economy evaluates the pros and cons of
the management system in the Stalin period. First it reports the extraordinary rates of industrial growth, averaging 17.1 percent per year from
1929 to 1940, while none of the leading capitalist countries in their period
of industrialization had exceeded 10 percent. The authors assert that at
that time the speed of economic development was the prime question in
the economic competition between socialism and capitalism. A second
positive result was the rapid change in the structure of the Soviet economy, favoring heavy industry and especially machinery. Third, the
highly centralized, unified management system played a big role in spurring the development of the backward regions of Siberia and the Far East,
where raw materials were abundant.

On the negative side, the system in the Stalin period spawned massive
bureaucratism, commandism, and blind direction as the scale of industrial
production and the number of enterprises and ministries proliferated.
Second, the effectiveness of the micro-economy declined as waste
mounted, and technological progress was slow. Quantity was pursued at
all cost, while quality was overlooked. Firms sought to hide their production capabilities while maximizing their capital inputs. New technology
on goods could interfere with the immediate needs of plan fulfillment; so
it could not easily be introduced. Third, the system overlooked the material interests of enterprise collectives and individual workers. As a result, few cared about the results of economic operations. Fourth, cutting
down ties among ministries was harmful to the overall development of
the local economy. Departmentalism reduced cooperation and led to
much duplication and inefficient use of equipment and transport. This
was a very wasteful approach, conclude the three authors.[55] While elements of the system played a positive role in initial industrialization and
the wartime period, their negative consequences were fully evident.

The 1982 book on the Soviet economy mentions in only a few places
the problems of living conditions. It notes that because of the continually
falling percentage of the industrial total in light industries, from 60.5 percent in 1928 to 31.2 percent in 1950-1951, the people's living conditions

[54] Ibid., 55-67.
[55] Ibid., 67-70, 91-92, 156-57, 288-92.

for a long time could not rapidly improve. It also comments on the declining percentage of capital for housing from private sources, from 54 percent of urban residential construction in 1918-1928 to 20 to 25 percent in the 1930s. After the war, because the state gave priority to investment to restore the damaged economy, there was no way to find the needed capital for housing; the role of private funding rose to one-third or more for the period 1946-1960 before falling sharply again to a little more than one-tenth from the mid-sixties.[56]

From this book and other sources on the industrial sector, the overall impression is of a complex pattern of gains and losses from the approach taken under Stalin. The gains seem to outweigh the losses, supporting an evaluation consistent with the 3:7 ratio for Stalin's mistakes and achievements attributed to Mao. As Wen Yi and Chen Zhihua, both contributors to the forthcoming *Sulian shigao* (Draft History of the Soviet Union), Volumes 1 and 2 (on the periods from 1917 to 1937), explained to me, there has been no great change in Chinese evaluations of Stalin since Mao's assessment of 1956, in contrast to the fluctuations in official Soviet evaluations. Yet, they added, on concrete issues, the changes in China have been considerable.[57] Chinese continue to credit Stalin with the great accomplishment of building socialism, while finding since the late 1970s new sources of error in the economic model he introduced. For the most part, they attribute these errors to circumstances, such as the world situation and existing interpretations of theory beyond a single leader's control, rather than to the personality or leadership style of Stalin.

REFORM OF STALIN'S MODEL

In 1980-1981, articles were still appearing that stressed the militarized nature of the Soviet economy with little or no indication of reform currents. In the first half of 1980, treatment of the militarized economy was coupled with references to Soviet ambitions to conquer the world. By late 1981, the tone had calmed somewhat; yet accusations still referred to the USSR as a "social imperialist" country and as the most important breeding ground of contemporary war, and they referred to the furious buildup of armaments as causing severe harm to normal development of the economy. One article in late 1981 justifies the military orientation of the economy in Stalin's time because of the German threat. It observes that after World War II, Stalin had not converted the economy back to a normal track of development in a timely manner; yet to a certain degree, this

---

[56] Ibid., 256-59, 543-44.
[57] Interview with Chen Zhihua and Wen Yi on January 8, 1985.

delay was necessary and defensive in nature due to the continued foreign threat. Only after Khrushchev and Brezhnev rose to power did the Soviet Union shift from a defensive military strategy to hegemonist policies. The military character of the economy became all the more prominent.[58] To some extent in 1981 and increasingly in 1982, this critical tone was replaced by a more positive outlook on the reform trends of the post-Stalin years.

After Khrushchev took office, the Soviet Union made many changes, greatly relaxing its planning and management system. The 1982 book on the Soviet economy edited by Jin Hui, Lu Nanquan, and Zhang Kangqin analyzes these changes. It traces the efforts to transfer economic management authority to the localities. The result was severe departmentalism and localism, leading to extreme disorder in the economy and eventually to new reforms designed to increase control over the localities. The reforms did not fundamentally alter management methods. While the Khrushchev reforms increased, local motivation to a certain extent, they failed to expand enterprise authority and did not stimulate motivation at that level; therefore the reforms' effectiveness was very weak. In fact, because of Khrushchev's impatience, which led to ordering one reform in the morning and changing it by evening, serious harm was done to the national economy, which, together with the mistakes of other economic policies, produced a clear decline in the speed of economic development. This was a factor leading to Khrushchev's ouster in 1964.[59]

Chapter 11 in the 1982 book is entitled, "The System of Labor Remuneration in the Soviet Union and the Standard of Living of the People." The first paragraph conveys the overall positive tone. "In the more than sixty years after the October Revolution, the labor remuneration system of the Soviet Union gave rise to very big changes, there were notable increases in the real living standards of the people. In the more than twenty years after Stalin's death, the Soviet leadership group in order to stimulate economic development, strengthened the use of wages, bonuses, and other economic mechanisms. At the same time, in order to stabilize domestic political control, it continuously emphasized the need to increase the living standard of the Soviet people, proclaiming this to be the 'highest aim of economic policy.' According to Soviet statistical materials, in 1965-1979 the Soviet per capita real income rose by 88 percent." The chapter notes that the Soviet standard is merely in the middle level of the world, ranking, roughly as tsarist Russia had, below the twentieth posi-

[58] Mei Wenbin, Lin Shuiyuan, and Chen Yunqing, "Sulian zai jingji shang jiajin wei fadong zhanzheng zuo zhunbei," *Hongqi*, no. 13 (1980): 45-48, 40; Yi Yu, "Sulian jingji de zhunshi tezheng," *Shijie jingji*, no. 10 (1981): 45-53, 59.

[59] Jin Hui et al., *Lun Sulian jingji*, 11-14, 70-75.

tion. This is mainly because the Soviet Union has for a long time devoted a relatively large part of its national income to the military.

The Chinese authors leave no doubt that Soviet wage policies have continuously emphasized the principle "to each according to his labor." Yet they point to four stages of interpretation of this principle to the time of Stalin's death: 1) 1917-1920, when policies reduced wage differentials, including restricting public service personnel and officials to wages corresponding to those of workers; 2) 1921-1926, when policies widened differences after Lenin called for opposition to egalitarianism; 3) 1926-1931, when policies favored more equal wages; and 4) 1931-1953, when the slogan "eradicate egalitarianism" led to repeated widening of differences (e.g. between skilled and unskilled workers and light and heavy industry). Party and government officials, enterprise directors, engineers with higher education, scientists, and some in the fields of culture and education received much larger incomes than ordinary workers. The Chinese book cites the example of medical personnel who earned nine times that of other public health personnel, of professors who earned twice as much as the well-off medical figures, of ministers who with their "special rations" received fifty times what some workers were paid.

In 1956, Khrushchev had criticized excessive egalitarianism as well as small numbers of people who received wages so high that they were inappropriate. He sought to make sure that workers performing the same job really did receive the same wage, to increase the role of material incentives for the individual. These objectives along with reform measures were repeated in the late 1960s and 1970s. There was no fundamental change from the wage policies of the Stalin period—egalitarianism continued to be opposed—but more attention was given to raising the lowest incomes. The high incomes of top officials and some intellectuals continued; yet limits were placed on special wages and rations. The minimum wage rose from 22 roubles in the mid-1950s to 40, 60, and finally 70 roubles in the 1970s. The average wage rose 3.3 percent per year over a quarter-century, from 75 to 168.5 roubles in 1980. The average income of the bottom 10 percent of wage earners rose from one-eighth to one-fourth of the average for the top 10 percent. Workers began to earn almost as much as engineering-technical personnel. Despite citing these examples of growing equality, the authors note that enterprise directors still made much more than ordinary workers; with their "special rations" the difference could be 10 or 20 times.

The chapter continues with a section on recent problems in the Soviet wage system. First, it says, the system is too complex, extremely inflexible, and unable in practice to follow the principles of equal pay for equal work and "to each according to his labor." Reforms may induce some increased motivation, but long before the next reform they are out-of-date. It is impossible for the center to establish, in a unified manner, a wage system to serve the many objectives that are supposed to be met. Second, the wage system is not beneficial for conserving labor and materials or increasing productivity and quality. This is due to the fact that before 1980, an enterprise could not retain funds in the wage allotment that were unexpended. Third, equalization of wages came too hastily, disrupting the rational proportion between the labor remuneration of workers and specialists, becoming disadvantageous for improving qualifications. In the past twenty-some years, incentives for skilled personnel have taken a back seat to raises for the lowest paid. The prestige of engineering and technical jobs has fallen among the youth. Among workers, there still exists the egalitarian tendency for little or no difference in reward whether one works well or poorly.[60] These are the inadequacies in the wage system that reformers had to address in the 1980s.

Liu Guoguang, Liu Suinian, and Zheng Li are the authors of the 1982 report (1983 book) on a tour of the Soviet Union from February to April to study the economic management system. They review Soviet economic reforms over the previous three decades. They describe the 1957 reform as causing confusion, leading to severe localism and fragmentation, and failing to solve the problem of relations between the state and the enterprise. They even quote Soviet economists as saying this was not a reform, but an unsuccessful experiment. The 1965 reform is credited by the Chinese travellers with restoring the principles of a socialist economy, reducing the role of local committees, and increasing the self-administration of large enterprises. Then the authors jump ahead to the 1979 reform, seeing it in the same vein as the 1965 reform, as a part of a continuous development to adjust the economic system.

What were the results of the reform process from 1965? The report submitted in 1982, in the midst of Chinese discussions over opening negotiations aimed at normalization, is, on balance, positive. Rapid economic growth continued; the Soviet average of 7.5 percent growth from 1950 to 1980 is more than double the American average of 3.5 percent and well above Western European figures too. (The authors only mention in passing the exception of Japan with a figure of 8.3 percent.) Basic industry was strengthened, with many products surpassing American figures. Defense industry and technology developed at a striking rate. Backward regions, especially areas settled by nonRussians, developed rapidly, many exceeding the figures for the Russian republic and some ahead of the living standards in that area. With the construction of the BAM line

[60] Ibid., 488-507.

into eastern Siberia and the Far East, the long-term prospects were improving.

The report also points to the relatively big improvement in the people's
living standards. Examples include per capita income rising by 95 percent
from 1965 to 1980, urban housing per capita climbing from 9 to 13 square
meters. The three economists observed that a huge amount of construction was in progress during their visit. They also noticed that women's
clothes on the street were much improved over the 1950s and that social
welfare had developed rapidly. In the Ukraine, they were told, in one dis-
trict they visited, no children lacked the basic means, nor did any parents
need financial aid over the past two years. The group listed four problems
to balance these many successes. The rate of economic development is
falling. Some sectors, especially agriculture and light industry, are relatively backward. Some types of market supplies of food are not up to the
level of the 1950s. High investment is not yielding a good return, and incomplete construction has been rising. Finally, the Soviet Union is
plagued by the slow application of scientific and technological findings
and the poor quality of goods.

Why are these results present? Success is attributed in the report to the
base built by Lenin and Stalin, to the rich natural supplies of raw materials, and to the long-term stable government. Problems are explained by
the high military costs and the foreign aid burden, the exhaustion of labor
resources, the need to shift eastward to replace natural materials and minerals that were running out further west, the growing costs of environmental protection, the excessively centralized political authority and aged
leadership, and a relatively strong conservative tendency. In addition to
these sources of problems, the authors see the economic management
system as the decisive factor.[61]

In the post-Stalin reforms, have trade unions better represented the interests of the working class? The answer provided in one Chinese article
is that they have not. There has been no notable change, only empty
propaganda that union activity already has the "character of the whole
people," that the functions of the trade unions widen in a "developed socialist society," etc. In reality, activities still follow the old forms and, in
some dimensions, controls have intensified. Especially as Soviet foreign
hegemonism has increased, extreme efforts have been made through the
unions to inculcate foreign policy thinking. For many years, the Chinese
article observes, not a few people inside the Soviet Union have criticized
the trade unions for merely attending to the activities of economic or-

[61] Liu Guoguang, Liu Suinian, Zheng Li, eds., *Sulian jingji guanli tizhi kaocha ziliao*
(Beijing: Zhongguo shehuikexue chubanshe, 1983), 169-91.

gans, for extreme formalism, for remoteness from the broad mass of workers. Acknowledging that historically the unions first played a certain positive role in the development of the economy, the article nonetheless faults this model for the fundamental shortcoming of not representing the workers. Unions have not developed into a school for workers to assume control over the state. Under this model, the vast majority of workers have little right to speak out on major matters affecting either the enterprise or the state. Union representatives as well as administrators and party leaders are seen by the masses as state representatives. Internationally, the Soviet trade union model has become known for its state-run unions.[62]

At the beginning of 1983, Jin Hui presented an overview of Soviet economic strategy and reform. Jin explains that the strategy of economic development is subordinate to and serves the demands of political and military elements. The first priority remains to strengthen the country's economic might, especially heavy industry. Jin adds, "In the Soviet Union, the development of heavy industry also means the development of military industry, the increase of military production capability." Furthermore, Brezhnev often declared that the Soviet Union sought simultaneously to develop consumer goods and service industries. To do so is a condition necessary in order to maintain political stability, to meet the requirements of stimulating worker motivation, to ensure that heavy industry and the entire economy develop steadily. Seeking to develop heavy industry and the military industry rapidly, the Soviet strategy also called for gradual improvement in living conditions. Jin concurs with Western critics that throughout the seventies, this was a strategy of "guns plus butter."

Soviet leaders also pointed out the principal means for realizing this strategy. Jin includes among them the raising of efficiency, the acceleration of scientific and technological progress, the raising of labor productivity, and the improvement of quality. Together these measures were referred to as the intensification of the economy. Jin continues, the main steps to assure these measures were: 1) preferential development of heavy industry, emphasizing the technologically advanced sectors of machine-building, energy, and metals—investment in heavy industry in 1980 was double the level of 1966-1970, while in light industry it had only risen by 54 percent, and heavy industry remained about 74 percent of industrial production; 2) preeminent development of the productive forces of the eastern region, where raw materials and energy for heavy industry could be exploited; 3) great increases in investment in agricul-

---

[62] Lu Wen, "Guanyu dongou guojia de gonghui gaige," 19-20.

ture; and 4) intensification of foreign economic ties. Jin observes that the
effectiveness of these reforms was not notable because of excessive centralization and bureaucratization, which suppressed the motivation and
creativity of localities, enterprises, and workers. Quality remained poor,
and capital was wasted on a large scale. As indicators kept falling, Brezhnev had to admit that the conversion to intensification in the economy
was proceeding very slowly.

Recounting the reforms of 1981-1982 from the time of the Twenty-
sixth Party Congress, Jin concludes that there has been no fundamental
change in the strategy of economic development. The most skilled workers and technicians continue to work in military industries. With the development of productive forces and scientific and technological progress,
the method of reliance on ministerial control increasingly reveals its
shortcomings.

After many years of economic reforms, the Soviets have yet to make
thorough improvements in production relations. They have not placed
the human element in the forefront. Workers and peasants have not secured democratic rights. Soviet leaders are now paying attention to the
activities of the working masses, but they focus only on work remuneration and incentives. As for management authority, not only ordinary
workers, but even enterprise leaders have very little. Some Soviet economists understand these problems, as Jin Hui demonstrates through quotations, but that has not led to sufficient reforms. The deleterious effects
of the current situation are visible in the limits on people's spirit of action,
killing their work enthusiasm, making them indifferent to the low efficiency, poor quality, and waste of production. Jin finds that while capitalist monopolies do not eradicate competition and the development of
new technology, the Soviet monopolies do. Consumers (both for production and individual consumption) have no scope for selection, which leads
to poor efficiency and quality. Failure does not lead to the enterprise's
closing or even to much pressure on the managers or the workers. The
result is that competition is frequently just on the surface. It is little more
than a method to induce enterprises to fulfill the state plan. Success does
not mean quality. Under capitalism, "natural selection" arises spontaneously. Socialism should use the plan to foster this through competition
among enterprises; only then can such phenomena as egalitarianism and
a "big rice bowl" be eradicated. Only then can the socialist principle of
"to each according to his work" be truly realized.[63]

A Shanghai journal reviewed a discussion in 1981-1982 on the pages of

[63] Jin Hui, "Sulian de jingji zhanlue he jingji gaige," *Sulian dongou wenti*, no. 1 (1983):
1-9.

the Soviet newspaper *Literaturnaia gazeta* entitled, "The Worth of Each Person." The articles and letters in this discussion showed that often the principle of "to each according to his labor" is not realized. When violations of it are common, the result is lowered discipline, increased turnover, and indifference to public property. When only task rates are utilized, individuals think solely of their personal bonus, damaging collective results. When time rates are used, the speed and efficiency of work decline. Participants in the discussion disagreed on how to make wages more effective and how to realize more fully the socialist principle of distribution. The Chinese article notes that due to the limitations of the present system, the result is the same whether workers work well or poorly; income is not affected. Enterprise directors lack the power to use profits for bonuses to reward superior workers.

A concluding article in the debate is described by the Chinese as pointing out the disquieting effect revelations of the egalitarian tendency in Soviet wages had on many people. Why does this tendency exist? There are historical reasons. Theorists thought it most corresponded to the distribution principle in a socialist system. For managers, equal division was also easier than calculation of each person's contribution to the collective effort in each situation. Moreover, some economic leaders welcomed the fact that egalitarianism made it easier to manage the collective, trying not to notice its harm on the collective spirit. The Soviet debate examined how to reduce egalitarianism. Participants pointed out that currently in the Soviet Union, workers do not take a sufficiently active part in controlling production; therefore they still have a subjective sensation of being hired and lack interest in the result of collective labor. Overall, the Soviet discussion supported making production brigades within enterprises economic accountability units. This would facilitate both payment according to the results of labor and a feeling of participation in management. Although differences in approach were evident, the majority of participants in the debate agreed on the direction that should be taken.[64] The Chinese author does not say so, but this direction is consistent with China's own efforts at increasing the material incentives of workers by opposing egalitarianism.

THE POST-BREZHNEV ERA

In 1984 a book appeared on the subject of the Soviet economy in 1982. It consists of a collection of twenty articles on the economic situation, eco-

[64] Zhang Jiaoling, "Yichang gongzi wenti de taolun," *Jinri Sulian dongou*, no. 6 (1982): 1-7.

nomic theory, economic reform, and economic strategy. The principal editor, Qian Junrui, announced that this is the first of annual volumes on the Soviet economy to be edited by the Chinese research association on the Soviet economy. It will have, more or less, the character of a yearbook, which after appearing for many years will be useful for systematic and deep understanding and research.

The first chapter, by Zhou Rongkun, objectively reviews many sectors of the Soviet economy from 1980 to 1982, ending with living conditions. Zhou observes that over the past ten or more years, the standard of living has continuously risen and the basic living needs have been defended, but market supplies have fallen far short of meeting rising consumer demand and, especially under the influence of recent poor harvests and consumer goods shortfalls, the people have not obtained many bounties. Consumer pressure in the Soviet Union is now increasing. Comparing statistics in 1982 to those of 1975, Zhou notes such changes as savings rising 91.4 percent, the social wage increasing 41.5 percent, personal wages rising 37 percent, collective farm incomes rising 36.3 percent, per capita real income rising 24 percent, the income of employees rising 21.6 percent, and retail prices rising 4.3 percent. Results for the single year 1982 were much poorer; per capita real income rose by only 0.1 percent.

Interpreting these results, Zhou points to two problems. First, there was severe egalitarianism; for example in industry, if a worker's wage was 100 in 1970, the wages of engineers and technicians were 136 and of employees 85, while in 1981 the engineers and technicians had dropped to 112.7 and the employees to 78. In 1981, at the Twenty-sixth Party Congress, Brezhnev acknowledged the problem of formalistic egalitarianism, where wages did not depend on the actual results of labor and their distribution had an extremely harmful influence on people's production psychology. Second, in some departments the average wage rose faster than the rate of increase of labor productivity. As a result, demands from the purchasing power of the people could not be satisfied. Market supplies were becoming tighter. Zhou also notes Soviet successes, such as housing improvements for 10 million people in 1982 and advances in education, science, and culture, as well as in public health and leisure.[65]

The next article, by Ge Linsheng, begins by listing three major events in the USSR in 1982 in the final months of Brezhnev's life after 18 years of comparatively orderly and stable leadership: 1) the repeated expression of willingness to improve relations with China, followed by the first ne-

[65] Qian Junrui, "Fakanci," and Zhou Rongkun, "80 niandai tousannian de Sulian jingji fazhan gaikuang," in Zhongguo Sulian jingji yanjiuhui, ed., *Sulian jingji (1982)* (Beijing, Renminchubanshe, 1984), i-ii, 1-25.

gotiations, bringing a hint of relaxation to the long-stagnant Sino-Soviet relations; 2) the establishment of a food program up to 1990 in order to guarantee stable food supplies in the shortest possible time; 3) the public approval and expression of the need to study the experiences of reform of the economic systems in Eastern European countries, and the mass-media debates on advancing the reform of the Soviet economic management system. Ge recounts many difficulties that the Soviet economy encountered in 1982, adding however that it is necessary to recognize that the Soviet economy continued to grow: finances were in equilibrium, prices were fundamentally stable, and the people's income and standard of living increased. Ge concludes that the Soviet economy has passed through severe difficulties created by three years of natural disasters and has begun to turn for the better.

Ge also discusses the early months of Andropov's leadership into 1983, when quick action was taken on labor discipline, the style of leadership, and enterprise autonomy. In January 1983, decisions were taken to reward good work and to cut the incomes of those who do poor work or violate labor discipline. Andropov especially stressed that discipline begins with ministers and leading cadres. Many high officials were fired or criticized. After reviewing many new developments, Ge observes that reform of the economic system and reform of the political system are intimately connected. Before the bureaucratic political system has been fundamentally changed, reform of the economic system cannot greatly advance. As for problems of worker motivation, there are even more limitations from social and political elements. Nevertheless, Ge emphasizes the positive economic turnaround in early 1983 and the new tendency for the Soviet economy to overcome its difficulties.[66]

Divergent Views on the Andropov Era

Many Chinese articles examine the reform currents of the brief Andropov era for their significance in resolving serious problems that plague the Soviet economy. For example, one study by Tang Zhuchang summarizes the reforms of the period, applauding the sharp criticisms leveled against longstanding problems and the many important resolutions and experiments designed to find a way out of these problems. Tang explains that because the time was short and barriers persisted, no complete reform program emerged. Nevertheless, he highlights two main elements: 1) the strengthening of macro controls, and 2) the increase of self-administration by management. To achieve the first goal, the Soviets established

[66] Ge Linsheng, "Sulian 1982 nian de jingji xingshi ji dangqian de jingji fazhan qushi," in *Sulian jingji (1982)*, 26-38.

some long-term programs, including the 1982 food program to last to 1990, the draft energy program presented in April 1983, and the plan for developing Siberia and the Far East. A 1979 resolution to achieve self-administration did not work, says Tang, and Soviets have become more serious about making this the first priority. He mentions a July 1983 decision to reduce the number of indicators sent down from above, 1984 experiments at decentralization, and efforts to expand the contract system. Brigades are to become the principal organization for workers. In some regions there are now household contracts. These contracts simplify management, reduce the need for managerial personnel, and increase the efficiency of production.

Soviet leaders, according to Tang, are coming to realize that a multi-formation economy is required; they are giving up the view that this is only a holdover from old, nonsocialist ways. Soviet articles are calling for studies of Eastern European experiences and for allowing private enterprises in services up to a certain scale, in order to resolve problems temporarily not handled by public and collective enterprises. Andropov proposed to break the egalitarian tendency in dispersing bonuses, to create a system of material incentives. Finally, Tang notes, there is the goal of democratizing management. Under Andropov, public opinion stressed the democratic principle in management as an important part of the strategy for economic development. Concrete steps to this end include permitting more participation of the working masses in the management of social affairs and making laws subject to the discussion of the whole people. Tang concludes that it is hard to predict the success of these reforms. There was a very big turn for the better in 1983 in comparison to the previous few years, but the long-term fundamental problems have not been removed. Many theoretical restrictions (e.g. on the relationship of planning and the market) remain. The Soviets have not yet abandoned their criticism of so-called "market socialism." Bureaucratism has barely been touched, while restrictions on the activities of the working masses remain. The economic reforms are at a crossroads; further vigorous steps are needed to break through the remaining barriers.[67]

Immediately following Tang's article appeared the report of a colloquium organized by the editorial board of *Sulian dongou wenti* on the economic problems of the Soviet Union in the Andropov period. Lu Nanquan led off the meeting with a statement that Andropov repeatedly pointed to the urgency of reform. He realized that because military expenses could not be decreased, because agriculture could not be expected

---

[67] Tang Zhuchang, "Andeluopofu shiqi de Sulian jingji tizhi gaige," *Sulian dongou wenti*, no. 4 (1984): 19-22.

to grow quickly, and because the Soviets were committed to vast capital expenditures in Siberia and the Far East, the best way to cope with the serious economic situation at Brezhnev's death was to make use of hidden economic reserves through reform in the system. According to Lu, Soviet scholars agree that the present management system cannot tap hidden reserves. The system was established at an earlier stage and, despite reforms in recent decades, still preserves outdated features.

In the report of the colloquium, Pang Chuan's remarks followed. He expressed his agreement with the view of some foreign scholars that in the 1980s in the Soviet Union and Eastern Europe a "second revolutionary wave" can appear. In the debates in the Soviet Union, he finds that the range of issues identified and the depth of treatment all go beyond the discussions in the Khrushchev period. Pang stresses the sharpness of the views, the sense of urgency, and the recognition that small changes cannot solve the existing problems. He adds that in Yugoslavia, where there is insufficient economic control and for many years economic results have been poor, new measures seek to increase central control. In Hungary, reforms seek simultaneously to increase control over the scale of investment and to strengthen enterprise self-administration by reducing the hold of ministries. In 1982, Poland began reforms, and in Bulgaria there is new emphasis on commercial relations. While the Soviet reforms are still experimental and there is not yet talk about changing the nature of the planning system, the views of Soviet scholars are leading in the direction of the Hungarian model. These are Pang's rather optimistic conclusions!

Li Renfeng's views appeared third. He finds it striking that after years of the Soviets regarding themselves as big brother who could set an example for others to follow and seeing no need to learn from the experiences of other countries, the Soviets are changing. Andropov accepted the many experiences of socialist countries, each based on concrete conditions, national circumstances, and traditions. Each country, he recognized, can make its own contribution to socialism. The Soviet mass media have also made an advance by criticizing the egalitarian tendency in wages. Eastern European countries are simultaneously launching their own anti-egalitarian reforms. Li discusses Soviet experiments to permit individual services where state services cannot completely satisfy living needs, an example of which is the recent growth of private construction brigades. Li is optimistic, arguing that the Soviets are contemplating a new, comprehensive, massive reform and that the Soviet Union possesses huge economic reserves whose use is currently blocked by its management system. Following the implementation of reforms, the Soviet economy can experience comparatively rapid development. Furthermore, reforms in 1983 already have exerted a positive influence. The contract labor use and intensification plan open vast possibilities. Li notes that in November 1983, TASS reported that Soviet economic development has entered a new stage, the importance of which can be compared to industrialization in the 1930s. Technical progress and reform of the economic management system are the means for speeding development.

Lao Baozhong, another participant in the colloquium, comments that under Andropov, the Soviet Union began to break out from the binds of more than fifty years of tradition. Under Brezhnev, there was just tampering and adjusting of the economic system, but not reform. Increasingly the system reached a dead end. While the theory stressed "to each according to his labor" and material incentives, leaders claimed that in a so-called developed socialist society there is a merging of mental and physical labor and a narrowing of wage differentials. High wages were frozen, while low ones rose. Bonuses and wage increases were not directly related to the quality of an individual's or a collective's work. This is the phenomenon of the "big rice bowl," says Lao. When Andropov took over, a broad debate opened on wage questions. In the Soviet Union many recognize that the present wage system is not working. The experiment begun in 1984 will tie wage increases to the growth of productivity and will give enterprises more autonomy in increasing and decreasing wages. Lao ends inconclusively that it is necessary to wait to see the results.

The final comments, by Jin Hui, concentrate on theoretical issues. Jin attaches most significance to the lively theoretical discussions of the Andropov period. They helped to liberate the economy from a tradition of rushing forward, and of optimistically viewing the socialist transition as very short, temporary, and simple. Andropov's caution represented a decisive rejection of Brezhnev's views of developed socialism. Jin regards the Soviet distribution system as a barrier to the development of production. Also, restrictions on personal ownership due to ideological errors damage the Soviet system. In these respects, Andropov's thinking brought some liberation. Jin stresses the need for more study of Soviet theoretical discussions, noting that Soviet problems are Chinese problems too. The Soviets are in the midst of intense, heated debates and views are changing. What the outcome will be, Jin Hui does not say.[68] In another article in the same journal, however, he has left no doubt that the problem with the economic system is the political system.[69]

[68] "Zuotanhui: Andeluopofu shiqi de Sulian jingji wenti," *Sulian dongou wenti*, no. 4 (1984): 23-30.

[69] Jin Hui, "Shilun zhengzhi tizhi he jingji tizhi de guanxi," *Sulian dongou wenti*, no. 4 (1984): 8-13.

232   CHAPTER FOUR

The Social Class System

One of the rare Chinese articles on the Soviet social class system appeared at the end of 1983 in *Sulian dongou wenti*. Written by Wang Dacheng, the article considers three themes: the main characteristics of the Soviet class system; the main manifestations of the merging of workers, collective farmers, and the intelligentsia; and some important questions about the class system disputed by Soviet scholars. Wang accepts the Soviet division into these three groups and argues that substantial changes in the class system have taken place since the 1960s as a result of the development of the economy, science and technology, culture, and education. He mentions first of all the continuous growth in the proportion of the population in the working class from 33.5 percent in 1939 to 49.5 in 1959 and 60.5 in 1981. Collective farmers dropped from 47.2 to 31.4 and finally to only 13.8 percent in 1981. The intelligentsia expanded rapidly from 18.8 percent in 1959 to 25.7 percent in 1981, after rising more slowly from 16.7 to 18.8 in the preceding two decades.

Wang points out that while workers have become ever more numerous, the rate of increase of this class has been falling. He divides this class into three groups: production workers (including those in construction and transport), agricultural workers, and service workers. As science and technology has developed, the intellectual level of work has risen steadily. This has changed the character of work. The number of mental laborers in the production sphere, as in the society as a whole, keeps rising. Deep scientific and technical knowledge is required to operate modernized equipment. "Differences in production are gradually being overcome between workers and engineering and technical personnel, manual and mental labor are increasingly merging, a stratum of 'worker intellectuals' has appeared in the Soviet Union. According to the statistics, in 1982 this stratum already had close to 5 million persons. Soviet scholars point out, the working class and 'the sum of physical labor in the national economy' and the traditional significance of workers 'mainly engaging in physical labor' are already viewpoints of the past."

Since the 1960s, merging trends are also evident in the sphere of distribution and in educational levels. Collective farmers have been catching up to workers and workers to the intelligentsia in income. Wang adds, however, that because skilled workers make as much or even more than specialists, some negative phenomena have arisen. As the prestige of specialists has fallen, some qualified specialists have turned to work that does not require specialized skill, leading to a high rate of mobility for specialists. Wang mentions a figure of about one million specialists moving each year. He notes too the continuously rising educational levels of all groups as universal secondary schooling becomes a reality. Nevertheless, there is still a big difference in higher education. In 1977, for each 1,000 persons, there were 116 workers, 39 collective farmers, and 303 members of the intelligentsia with higher education. Of course, Wang is utilizing Soviet classifications, which group together clerks, secretaries, scientists, officials, and others in the broad category of intelligentsia.[70]

Repeated discussions of economic reform make little mention of workers. An exception is Lin Shuiyuan's article in the same issue of *Sulian dongou wenti*. Lin concurs with the view that the Andropov era brought a major change after a long period of dead-end silence by theorists. Much of the new thought in the late fifties and early sixties was not included in the 1965 reform, and not long after came criticisms of "market socialism" that led to near stagnation in the reform process and declining growth in the economy. Finally under Andropov, discussions of economic theory grew livelier, and their theoretical depth, if not breadth, greatly exceeded that of the earlier debate. The Andropov debate greatly opened the field of vision of the Soviet people. At last the issue of reform was placed in the context of a discussion of fundamental contradictions in a socialist society, especially those between the relations of production and the forces of production. Soviets acknowledge that production relations remain much more backward and must be changed to remove barriers to rapid development.

According to Lin, the Soviet critics recognize that the bureaucracy represses worker motivation and enthusiasm. Referring to an internal report by the Siberian scholar Zaslavskaia, Lin notes that some Soviet economists are not satisfied with a one-sided stress on discipline and stricter control of workers. They are aware that the lack of discipline and work quality stems from the management system and cannot be resolved by tightening controls on workers. What is necessary is increased democracy, more mass participation in management. Lin mentions the June 1983 law on work collectives that leads in this direction. For him the key issue is promoting the worker's spirit of being master and increasing the worker's motivation. Prior reforms have been formalistic only, says Lin; how can they make workers feel that they are masters of their country? Lin concludes by expressing doubts that the reformers' theoretical views could prevail. He regards the conservative forces as very powerful (in theoretical circles too), and says that in the final analysis the Communist Party and state, not the current advocates of reform, determine policies and then theory.[71]

In the view of Li Yuanqing, recent Soviet policies have sought to ex-

[70] Wang Dacheng, "Sulian shehui jieji jiegou de yanbian," *Sulian dongou wenti*, no. 6 (1983): 60-63.

[71] Lin Shuiyuan, "Sulian jingji gaige lilun de yixie xin bianhua," *Sulian dongou wenti*, no. 4 (1984): 14-18.

pand the functions of worker collectives. There are five reasons: 1) to increase efficiency and quality in the economy; 2) to reduce commandism and bureaucratism as part of the drive to raise the autonomy of producing units; 3) to respond to improved scientific, cultural, and educational levels as well as rising aspirations to participate in management affected by changing mass awareness of the outside world; 4) to control vagrants, criminals, disorderly persons, and people affected by a consumer psychology or by pollution from the West such as notions of democracy and freedom; and 5) to respond to the impact of Poland's mass labor movement. At the Twenty-fourth Party Congress, Brezhnev attached great significance to widening the role of worker collectives. In the following years there was much talk of participation in management, the selection of talent, and the drawing together of workers to oppose unhealthy currents. Much attention centered on the increasing role of law in protecting workers. The Soviet constitution of 1977 stressed the duties and rights of worker collectives.

While Li makes clear that these developments in the seventies drew attention to worker collectives, his main focus is on the Andropov reforms of 1983. He explains that constitutional rights were made concrete and developed in that year. Now administrators had to take them seriously. Increasing worker participation in management and democratic rights somewhat reduced the distance between leaders and those they led. Over 120,000 worker congresses in two months, held to discuss the published draft of the proposed labor law, heightened worker consciousness. The 1983 reform brought a decrease in orders handed down to worker collectives without taking their own suggestions into account, widened the scope for the enterprise to devise its own internal procedures, increased the power of collectives in such areas as welfare, job security, housing, and culture, and increased participation in management. Li interprets these developments as a positive part of Andropov's economic reform.

On the final page of the article, Li turns his attention to revelations of shortcomings in the reported discussions on worker collectives. The first theme to which he draws attention is arbitrary authority. Decisive power was in the hands of officials who ignored the opinions of those at lower levels, arbitrarily flexed their power, and went around with bureaucratic airs. They interfered in union work, limited participation in management to a formal level, and rarely were punished for their misdeeds. Past measures to narrow the distance between the workers and their leaders had had little effect. Steps in 1983 to increase the Communist Party's supervision of administration had yet to bring significant results. Li concludes that as long as the system of appointments from above went untouched, the problem of the masses becoming the bosses could not be resolved well.

Also he argues that the concept of worker collectives is too broad, and that the laws are too vague, are difficult to apply, and provide for no concrete measures to secure the legal rights of workers. He sees bureaucratism and formalism still dominant in labor union work. The article ends inconclusively with Li suggesting that an increasing effect from the new law on worker collectives must await the entire economic reform advance.[72]

In early 1985, Chinese authors continued to criticize the slow pace of Soviet economic reform. For example, Jiang Shengfu concludes his overview of Soviet economic reform with the observation that the longstanding severe shortcomings of the Soviet economy have not been overcome, the rigid economic model has not been fundamentally transformed. Mere improvements are not the answer, reform is. The Soviets must recognize anew the economic laws of socialist society. Only by resolutely limiting leftist thought, eliminating traditional thinking, and discarding longstanding orthodox restrictions can the Soviet economic system experience a fundamental change.

Jiang's discussion of Soviet history traces the development of restrictive thinking. He begins by noting that after the October Revolution, the profound changes that occurred first revealed the great superiority of the socialist system. Only the long-term persistence of certain fixed ideas inappropriate to existing conditions, and the development of a rigid economic model that does not correspond to the needs for the development of the forces of production, have prevented that superiority from flowering as it should. This rigidity gradually developed in the process of socialist industrialization in the 1930s, when Stalin insisted that socialism means a highly centralized command economy.

Economic reforms began in the 1950s. Certain theoretical prohibitions were first broken after Stalin died. Khrushchev correctly realized that the center was stultifying the economy, but he went too far in 1957 in abandoning macroeconomic controls by transferring authority to the localities, and he did not realize that the main reform should have been to expand enterprise authority. His reforms failed. In 1966 Brezhnev began reforms: to improve the scientific nature of planning work, to increase material incentives and economic accountability, to advance the command economy through economic mechanisms, and to link the economic interests of enterprises and employees and workers to production results. These reforms did not resolve the basic problems in the economy.

After Andropov took power, he suddenly emphasized the necessity and urgency of reform. Not only did he introduce reform theories different

[72] Li Yungqing, "Cong Sulian 'laodong jiti fa' kan Sulian laodong qunzhong canjia guanli wenti," *Sulian dongou wenti*, no. 2 (1984): 44-48.

from the past ones, but he also launched a series of reform experiments. Nevertheless, in his very brief term, except to expand enterprise authority and to advance collective contracts in agriculture as well as certain other reform steps, treatment of other problems remained at the exploratory level. According to Jiang, the three main problems are the theory of the commercial economy and the law of prices, the economic functions of the state, and the form of ownership of the materials of production. All require decentralization. The Soviet economic model must change to realize the advantages of socialism.[73]

CONCLUSION

It is paradoxical that at the same time that most of the criticisms leveled against domestic conditions in the Soviet Union focus on the industrial management system, the history of Soviet industrial growth receives considerable praise. This praise extends to almost all periods. Reevaluations of Peter I and Catherine II credit them with spurring economic growth in the eighteenth century. Chinese historians note the rapid development of capitalist industries after 1861. The NEP is praised as a necessary reorganization to the correct path for moving forward to socialism. Stalin's industrialization is highly applauded, while his successors (especially Brezhnev) are commended for reforms that maintained a rapid growth rate. Criticisms must be understood against the backdrop of these positive impressions.

The criticisms emphasize recent Soviet difficulties, but also make some mention of earlier problems. Although there is no systematic overview of the pre-1917 legacy, some indications are presented that there were negative consequences. Labor relations had relied to an exceptional degree on personal dependencies. The state's hold over the economic arteries exerted a strong influence when only a narrow commercial market had developed within Russia. Prior to 1917, Russian workers experienced a doubly exploitative situation in which tsarism and capitalism combined in a system labeled military-feudal imperialism. One writer suggests that in its emphasis on the omnipotence of political power, War Communism was a continuation of Russian absolutism. Another source criticizes Stalin for rejecting commerce under the influence of the natural economy. Chinese also criticize Stalin's inattention to worker participation in management. Purges of union leaders put an end to debates on the role of unions and left union work lifeless. Theoretical errors— especially Sta-

---

[73] Jiang Shengfu, "Luelun Sulian de jingji gaige," *Shijie jingji yu zhengzhi neican*, no. 1 (1985): 22-25, 48.

lin's confusion of market exchange with capitalism—were made after Lenin's early death had left many questions unanswered.

Above all, Chinese find fault with the failure to reform Stalin's model of economic management sufficiently after World War II. Stalin resisted reform, Khrushchev bungled it, and Brezhnev approached it timidly. So-viet leaders do not learn enough from experience or take a scientific atti-tude to determine which changes will bring the best results. Theory stands in their way. They give priority to the military, seeking "guns plus butter"—which increasingly has meant that the butter is spread very thinly. A highly centralized system stifles initiative from below. Democratic rights are neglected. The human element is ignored. Reform voices also allege that the Soviet experience shows that political reform is essential to economic reforms; the Soviets keep trying the latter only to find that the political structure interferes with their plans. Most critiques, however, are more limited. The orthodox side seeks to confine the criti-cisms to specific, economic measures—including some decentralization within the context of central planning—and predicts that Soviet industry will reform and will continue to outpace American industry.

Implied in Chinese writings is that with sufficient reform and the right international environment, the Soviet economy could return to the boom days of rapid growth. While the very high growth rates of the era of ex-tensive development are behind, rates above five percent a year are within reach. Chinese estimates of what can be accomplished even in the absence of thorough reform have been creeping up. In the still somewhat hostile environment at the beginning of the eighties, much was made of an eco-nomic crisis in the USSR. By 1982-1983, the prognosis usually suggested a prolonged period of slow growth—perhaps three percent per annum. By 1984-1985, under the impact of the Andropov reform program and the prospects for a vigorous Gorbachev leadership, predictions were shift-ing upward to about four percent. By the standards of what could be ac-complished, even this figure was regarded as no major achievement, but by the comparative standards of the United States and Western Europe, the Soviet Union was judged to be narrowing the gap gradually. Within a few decades, according to one source, as the gap with the United States continues to narrow, a new situation will develop in the world.[74]

Comparisons with Soviet Views of China

Chinese criticisms of Soviet policies toward workers are not nearly as sharp as Soviet condemnations of China's policies. Many of the same

[74] Luo Zhaohong, "Lun Sulian jingji de changqi fazhan qushi," *Shijie jingji*, no. 1 (1984): 20; Lu Nanquan, "Dui bashi niandai Sulian jingji ruogan wenti de fenxi," *Shijie jingji*, no. 12 (1983): 68; Lu Nanquan, "Possibilities and Limitations of Soviet Reform in Its Economic System After Gorbachev Took Office," (unpublished manuscript, October 1985).

themes appear, but in a milder form. Chinese sources seem to concur with Soviets that workers have, on the whole, fared well in the Soviet Union, while Soviets regard Chinese policies for a quarter-century as a betrayal of the working class.

Soviet publications on China offer a much fuller sociological analysis of the working class. They examine the structure of that class prior to 1949 and its consequences in the period of transition to socialism and beyond. In contrast, Chinese virtually ignore the structure of the Russian working class both before and after 1917. Soviets write about the social psychology of various groups of workers, while Chinese largely confine their studies to the industrial (management) system. The workers themselves are scarcely in sight.

Both types of sources criticize the dearth of material incentives (related to excessive egalitarianism and insufficient democratic participation). State controls are excessive. Unions fail to give workers their rights as "masters" of their enterprises. Military needs take precedence over consumer goods.

Each side emphasizes the need for reforms in the other country. The Chinese place this call in the context of approval for many Soviet achievements of earlier periods, including substantial improvements in living standards and education. To a great extent, Chinese criticisms are drawn from Soviet self-criticisms of the 1980s; they tend not to probe further or to raise the most sensitive issues, such as worker alienation. Soviet sources, at least to 1983, reject the Chinese point of view. They do not credit China's leaders with any sincere interest in resolving worker problems or restoring the ideals of a socialist society.

In both sets of sources, one finds the orthodox position in favor of centralized planning and the reform side concerned with democratic participation. Reform and orthodox forces agree on the need for more material incentives, although the former group pursues this point more vigorously. It is the reform side that looks back more keenly on historical errors and seeks to draw more far-reaching lessons from history. We learn from this comparison that the lines between reform and orthodoxy are similar in China and the Soviet Union.

FIVE

THE INTELLIGENTSIA AND THE
EDUCATIONAL SYSTEM

Mao Zedong, as China's leaders in an earlier era, was preoccupied with the relationship between the educated elite and other groups in the population. The case of the Soviet Union loomed large in the background. Its purported successes in harnessing modern science and technology and in securing compliance had made Chinese enthusiastic about copying the Soviet system of higher education, socialist realism in literature, and much of the structure of the scientific establishment in the USSR. In the 1960s, perceived Soviet failures in maintaining revolutionary ideals in the schools and in controlling the younger generation of writers were among the factors that led Chinese leaders, especially Mao, to turn against the Soviet model. Examples from the Soviet experience kept being paraded before Chinese intellectuals as a justification for policies in their own country.

After Mao's death and especially from 1978, the Chinese leadership made a sweeping repudiation of the treatment of the intelligentsia and education in China over ten or more years. It virtually wiped the slate clean, leaving a vacuum that could be filled either by the preceding approach— the Soviet model and the only socialist alternative known—or by a new approach, drawing on nonsocialist countries such as the United States and perhaps creating a different framework that might still be labeled socialist. Perceptions of recent developments in the Soviet Union could still be influential in guiding China along its changing course.

THE MAOIST CRITIQUE OF THE SOVIET INTELLIGENTSIA

In the two 1956 official statements on Stalin and the dictatorship of the proletariat, the Chinese leaders said nothing about the Soviet intelligentsia. Following the Hundred Flowers Movement and China's antirightist campaign of 1957, at Mao's insistence the intelligentsia once again became a major preoccupation in ideological discussions. In late 1958, his comments on Stalin's *Economic Problems of Socialism in the USSR* indicate this interest. Mao criticized the Soviet Union for "walking on one leg." Not only did the Soviets stress heavy industry at the expense of light industry and agriculture, and the long-term interests of the people at the expense of their immediate interests, "Stalin emphasized only technology, technical cadre. He wanted nothing but technology, nothing but cadre; no politics, no masses." In other words, Stalin believed that technology and the experts, not politics nor the masses, decide everything. In 1961-1962, Mao's comments on a Soviet text showed continued distrust of experts. He wrote, "Some whose technical and cultural level is high are nonetheless neither diligent nor enthusiastic; others whose level is lower are quite diligent and enthusiastic. The reason lies in the lower political consciousness of the former, the higher political consciousness of the latter."[1]

In China's Ninth Commentary of July 1964, there is still no full-scale criticism of the Soviet intelligentsia, but much of the criticism against "bourgeois elements" and "political degenerates" appears to be directed against them. The article talks of reactionary elements that "sneak into the government organs, public organizations, economic departments and cultural and educational institutions so as to resist or usurp the leadership of the proletariat. . . . In the ideological, cultural and educational fields, they counterpose the bourgeois world outlook to the proletarian world outlook and try to corrupt the proletariat and other working people with bourgeois ideology." According to the Maoist critique, bourgeois influence is the internal source of revisionism. The Soviet leaders, beginning with Stalin, erred in stressing the homogeneity of socialist society, in not struggling against the inherently bourgeois elements, in paying them high salaries that had a corrupting influence, and in permitting scientists to publish works "attacking and smearing the socialist system." The answer to this problem is to build up a "large detachment of working class intellectuals," who are both "red and expert," to combine education with productive labor, to "struggle to promote proletarian ideology and destroy bourgeois ideology" among those engaged in science, culture, the arts, and education.[2]

In 1976, the official Chinese view of Soviet education remained unmistakably hostile. A typical article called Soviet education "decadent" and "capitalist." It referred to "bourgeois scholar tyrants" who occupy leading posts, while the working class is excluded. The schools instill bourgeois ideology. "They twist the meaning of studying communism and make it primarily a matter of mastering science and knowledge." They

---

[1] Mao Tsetung, *A Critique of Soviet Economics* (New York: Monthly Review Press, 1977), 129, 135, 83.

[2] "On Khrushchev's Phoney Communism and Its Historical Lessons for the World," in William E. Griffith, *Sino-Soviet Relations, 1964-1965* (Cambridge: The M.I.T. Press, 1967), 317-18, 321, 326-27.

lead young people astray by telling them that their task is "to acquire knowledge." They trumpet the idea of "giving first place to intellectual development," eulogizing "extraordinary talent" and creating special schools for "geniuses" who are regarded as the "elite" among students and "the future leaders of the Soviet Union." The same article contends that Soviet spokesmen classify middle-school students by origin much as German fascists had, placing those from the countryside in the category of "the indolent," treating children of laborers as " 'mediocrities' who should be barred from schools and are destined to be slaves, whereas only the children of the privileged are 'geniuses' who are entitled to a good education and are undisputed rulers."

Above all, the Chinese article criticizes Soviet schools for discriminating against workers, peasants, and their children. It says life for many of them "is so hard that they are forced to quit school before graduation," or they are thrown out on the charge that they are "backward in intelligence." "Children of workers and peasants of course have no access to higher education since they cannot even complete their primary education." The article quotes a Japanese journal to the effect that "practically all the children of the intellectuals pass the examinations while nearly all the peasants' children fail." Using both legal and illegal means, practically all children of parents with high political position can enter college if they so desire. They have access to supplementary classes, private tutors, political clout, bribery, and fraud. After these "sons and daughters of the privileged class . . . become 'experts' or 'scholars,' " they assume leading positions. This means class status is inherited in the Soviet Union, argues the article. Institutes of higher learning spawn "bourgeois intellectual aristocrats" who "constitute the social foundation of the Soviet revisionist ruling clique."[3]

In the mid-seventies, Chinese critiques of Soviet revisionism lumped together the upper intelligentsia (gaoji zhishi fenzi) in the spheres of science and culture with managers, engineers, and party, state, and military leaders as the privileged groups of Soviet society. On the pretext of the theory that the work of these people is more important, more responsible, and more skilled, Soviets claim that these groups deserve more reward as incentive. According to a 1977 book, it was the wage reforms of 1956-1961 that gave these privileged individuals wages much larger than those of ordinary employees and workers.[4] A 1978 book accuses G. M. Markov,

[3] "Reactionary and Decadent Education in the Soviet Union," Social Imperialism: The Soviet Union Today (reprints from Peking Review) (Berkeley: Yenan Books, 1977), 117-21.

[4] Xia Changan, Sulian jingji de tuibian (Hong Kong: Xianggang Chaoyang chubanshe, 1977), 67.

the first secretary of the Soviet Writers' Union, of receiving 192,000 roubles for a five-volume collection of his works published in 1972. This means that "writing is no longer done to serve the people, but has become a means by which writers rob the working people to enrich themselves."[5]

Chinese writings castigated contemporary Soviet literature and the arts for their service to the reactionary political line. Heroes had become mirror images of the new ruling class, living in high style and abusing those who work under them. The new kind of hero dresses fashionably, "reeks of expensive perfume, and flashes an engagement ring." Toward the workers, he uses "the ruble as a whip," and dismisses from their jobs the old and infirm as well as those he considers "unruly."

Chinese critics saw "poisonous weeds abounding" in Soviet literature. Their origin dates back to the fifties, when Khrushchev abandoned the struggle against revisionism. "By 'rehabilitating' discredited reactionary writers who had been criticized and expelled from the Writers' Union in the 1920s and 1940s," publishing these writers' works in great quantities and lavishing praise on them, the Soviet leaders "legitimized revisionism in literature and art." The leadership attracted and corrupted writers and artists with prizes and privileges, including the Lenin Prize and the State Prize. "These prizes go only to the most loyal hacks." They go to those already well-established in the artistic and literary "elite." A Chinese book mentions the examples of M. A. Sholokhov, K. M. Simonov, and S. V. Mikhalkov, who produced "much revisionist stuff." Sholokhov is called "the father of modern revisionist literature and art." Along with others, he was incited after Stalin's death "to expose the so-called 'seamy side' of socialist society and negate proletarian dictatorship. After the 20th Party Congress there appeared under the direct influence of Khrushchov [sic], the novels *One Day in the Life of Ivan Denisovich* and *Cruelty*, and the long poems *Stalin's Heirs* and *Terkin in Another World*, all directed against the dictatorship of the proletariat. They described the socialist system as 'an old wall nobody wants any longer' and clamored for its demolition."[6] Those are the harsh judgments that went unanswered in China until 1978.

THE LEGACY OF RUSSIA'S PAST

In comparison to the fascination with the milieu and extraordinary accomplishments of the nineteenth-century Russian intelligentsia shown elsewhere in the world, Chinese historians have remained rather quiet.

---

[5] Wei Chi, *The Soviet Union Under the New Tsars* (Beijing: Foreign Languages Press, 1978), 70.

[6] Ibid., 62-71.

The main exception is their interest in progressive writers, such as Chernyshevsky, who fanned the flames of revolution and, to a lesser extent, the great writers, such as Tolstoy, whom Lenin praised and the Soviet Union embraced as part of a progressive tradition. The revolutionary intelligentsia from the Decembrists to the Bolsheviks are, of course, subjects for historians, but original studies are not numerous, and the wider context of educated Russians and the emerging intelligentsia is little mentioned.

A history of the modern world, which first appeared in January 1982 and had its third printing in February 1984, describes peasants as the main opponents of the feudal system. The focus of attention in the first half of the nineteenth century was the abolition of serfdom. For a long time capitalist liberals opposed using revolutionary means to eliminate serfdom completely, urging reform instead. Gradually, however, contradictions with the feudal system mounted for the capitalists as capitalism itself developed. For their own self-interest, they demanded the abolition of serfdom. But because most Russian capitalists were incubated under the tsarist system and were closely linked to feudal power, they did not dare to split completely with tsarist absolutism. Also frightened by the proletarian revolutionary struggle against capitalists in Western Europe and guided by the assumption that tsarism is necessary for protecting the land ownership system and their own fruits of exploitation, they opposed the aim of revolutionary violence.

The Decembrists and some other aristocrats and capitalists did break out of this mold in the 1820s and the decades that followed. Herzen, Belinsky, Chernyshevsky, and Dobroliubov are also mentioned and given credit for many of their activities against the tsarist system. Yet they were long criticized for their capitalist romantic worldviews, which looked down upon the working masses. They could only become lone groups of revolutionaries, limited to the lecturn and periodicals, within the circle of a minority of intellectuals. The 1861 emancipation was far from being a complete capitalist revolution. Aristocratic land ownership and tsarist absolutism continued. Many feudal elements remained in the culture as well as in politics, economics, and other spheres.[7] The intelligentsia apparently had failed to provide sufficient guidance for the progressive development of Russia. This is the sort of overview available in general histories that, in fact, says little about the intelligentsia as a group.

Under the influence of the Cultural Revolution, all but the Leninist

[7] Lin Judai et al., *Shijie jindaishi* (Shanghai: Shanghai renminchubanshe, 1984), 318–24, 332.

wing of the Russian revolutionary and literary tradition were repudiated in China. A reevaluation had begun as early as the second half of 1977. In its first issue of 1978, *Hongqi* was already blaming the "Gang of Four" for completely rejecting Russia's revolutionary democratic thinkers, including Belinsky, Chernyshevsky, and Dobroliubov. The article appeals to Lenin's authority to rehabilitate these men for their revolutionary contributions, acknowledging at the same time that it would be inappropriate to worship them blindly. The backwardness of life in Russia prevented Chernyshevsky from rising to the level of dialectical materialism. Other articles followed in early 1978 in support of studying the writings of Russia's great nineteenth-century democratic figures.

By 1979, the scope of rehabilitation was widening. At first, a middle ground was proposed in opposition to the "Gang of Four," which had "completely rejected all the refined culture of human society," and the Soviet revisionists who "purposely propagated their capitalist class individualism." It was claimed that Chinese must judge literature from the standpoint of what is progressive at that point in time. The debate covered a wide range of literature, from how to evaluate Lermontov's hero, Pechorin, to whether to classify Mayakovsky as a futurist or a proletarian poet. Tolstoy figured prominently, especially as seen by Lenin and Gorky.[8] The result was a rediscovery of the "rich" and "largely progressive" literary tradition of the Soviet Union.

The 1983 *Yearbook of Chinese Historical Studies* reviews writings on modern Russian history in 1982. Peter I was the subject of a few articles. He is credited with initially changing Russia's backward appearance, including relying on capitalist elements. Merchants were among the beneficiaries. According to a 1983 article, by the end of the eighteenth century a system of urban self-government had been drawn up and the position of merchants had risen gradually, corresponding to their expanded economic activity. The 1983 yearbook points to articles that warn, however, against overestimating the development of capitalist relations in the nineteenth century and insist that in conditions of imperialism Russia's capitalist class completely transformed into a counterrevolutionary class. On the eve of revolution, they had problems with Nicholas II, but these were mainly due to the tsar's corrupt incompetence, especially his desire during World War I to come to an independent agreement with Ger-

[8] Ru Zhang, "Liening shi zenyang pingjie Cheernixuefusiji de?" *Hongqi*, no. 1 (1978): 74-77; Qi Tinggui, "Eguo de weida xuezhe he pipingjia," *Jilin shida xuebao* (zhexue shehuikexueban), no. 2 (1978): 70-74; Luo Ling, "Shilun Piquelin," *Wuhan daxue xuebao*, no. 3 (1979): 41-45; Fu Ke and Chen Shoucheng, "Cong weilaipai dao wuchanjieji shiren," *Wuhan daxue xuebao* (zhexue shehuikexue ban), no. 3 (1980): 12-18; Weng Yiqin, "Gaoerji lun Tuoersitai," *Fudan xuebao*, no. 6 (1980): 46-49.

many. Russia's capitalists thought of replacing him with a new tsar who would carry the war to completion and, with the aim of maintaining the system, would create a constitutional monarchy. Frightened by the victory in the winter of 1917 of the armed uprising of the masses, the capitalists became capitulationists, ready to take away the fruits of the revolution. The provisional government was reactionary; this was a message that Lenin succeeded in teaching the masses while organizing them against it.[9]

Chinese articles make it clear that the Bolsheviks were on the side of the working class. On the other side were the capitalists, who were counterrevolutionary and who expounded a false democracy. Their support for the parliamentary organs of the duma and for a constitutional party are described as part of a counterrevolutionary worldview. This negative appraisal leaves little room for recognition of the Russian intelligentsia as a vibrant force for change in the period before 1917.[10]

The exceptions to this general indifference to the intelligentsia in Russian history are examples of Chinese borrowing their socialist worldview from Russia complete with views of Russian history. By the 1950s in many fields of intellectual endeavor, Soviet specialists were tracing their scientific or progressive thinking back to nineteenth-century Russia. Much of Russian intellectual history had been reinterpreted as a positive force. Such Soviet-inspired traditions were borrowed in the 1950s and in some cases revived in 1980 or shortly afterwards. For example, in the field of pedagogy, the journal *Shanghai jiaoyu* in 1980 recalls the Russian child psychologist Ushinsky (1824-1870). It refers to him very positively as a distinguished teacher who taught with a progressive, democratic spirit and who highly appreciated the role of the teacher. The article notes that after the October Revolution, Soviet leaders such as Kalinin called on teachers to study Ushinsky's educational writings. The concluding sentence states for Chinese benefit that the viewpoints in these writings are still worth borrowing and studying.[11]

WAR COMMUNISM, THE NEP, AND THE STALIN ERA

The 1983 *Yearbook of Chinese Historical Studies* describes an article in 1982 by Sun Chengmu on how Lenin induced the intelligentsia to participate in the building of socialism. Starting from the fundamental inter-

---

[9] Chen Qineng and Yu Pei, "Sulian jinxiandaishi," *Zhongguo lishixue nianjian 1983* (Beijing: Renminchubanshe, 1983), 242-44; Zhao Keyi, "Shiqi zhi shiba shiji Eguo shangren de diwei yu zuoyong," ibid., 77-85.

[10] Ruan Darong, "Eguo guojia duma yu buershiweikedang dui duma de celue," *Shixue yuekan*, no. 6 (1982): 68-72.

[11] Fan Jiaqiong, "Ushensiji," *Shanghai jiaoyu*, no. 4 (1980): 47.

ests of the proletariat, Lenin repeatedly emphasized the important role of intellectual elements in the socialist revolution and socialist construction. Another article reviewed in the yearbook by Wang Shutong praises Soviet use of technical cadres in the period of industrialization. It mentions three positive measures: mobilization of the entire people to study culture and science and grasp technology, reformation of an irrational wage system, and development of technical education. As a result of these three measures, in a short time the Soviet Union trained a large group of specialists. The article approves of the slogans "technology decides everything" and "cadres decide everything," both of which had been attacked in the Cultural Revolution. At the same time, the article credits the Soviets with not underestimating political questions.[12] The Soviet Union, unlike China, achieved a healthy balance.

Actually, the two slogans favored by Stalin in the 1930s combined two separate themes that differed in their appeal to orthodox and reform advocates. The slogan "technology decides everything" was used by reformers in support of experts and against political interference in matters requiring specialized knowledge. The slogan "cadres decide everything" was reinterpreted to signify that experienced officials must be retained and may be promoted but not demoted. The situation is typical of many in the People's Republic, where the same slogan or concept receives differing interpretations from reform and orthodox groups.

In 1983 and 1984, several articles discussed the intelligentsia and education under Lenin. They credit Lenin with a positive attitude toward this stratum. Li Guidong divides his article, "Lenin and the Intelligentsia," under three subheadings, "in politics trust," "in work support," and "in life concern." These were Lenin's views, says Li. He trusted, supported, and showed concern for the intelligentsia. Lenin recognized that the intelligentsia is a part of the army of workers, not a separate class. In his plan to electrify the country, Lenin set up a commission, drawing wisely on scientists and allowing them to carry on their work. He was extremely opposed to arbitrarily ordering specialists and was very attentive to helping them overcome shortcomings and mistakes in their thinking. He hoped they would join with the workers and change their erroneous viewpoints. Lenin consistently supported their work and sought to create the necessary conditions for it, including allowing technicians to understand scientific and technological developments in other countries. Lenin realized that the Soviet people were very deficient in culture, and this was unsuitable for building socialism. He urged that teachers be paid more, that their living conditions be improved, and that their political status be

[12] Chen Qineng and Yu Pei, "Sulian jinxiandaishi," 247-48.

elevated. He understood that in an early stage of building socialism, a large number of intellectuals, including capitalist intellectuals, should participate. When he encountered strong opposition from the extreme left, he explained that these experts are not exploiters, but cultural workers who can serve society. They are a rich treasure that must be treated well. Some persons could not understand Lenin's favoritism for the intelligentsia in years of difficulty. They said it was unfair, and in some localities they reduced the housing or rations of this group. Lenin objected because the intelligentsia could make a great contribution to socialism.

Another article describes the contents of Lenin's thoughts on talented people (*renzai*). It praises his views, saying that capitalism wastes great numbers of talented persons among the workers, but socialism identifies and cultivates such talent. Able people are needed as managers. The talent left behind by capitalism must be used. Above all, the key is to select new persons of ability from the working class. Elsewhere, Lenin's approach to the intelligentsia is described as realistic. In response to backward science and culture and 68 percent illiteracy—the unfortunate legacy of old Russia—Lenin recognized the need to enlist the old intelligentsia in the tasks of socialist construction and to overcome the spirit of opposition to specialists. The Soviet Union followed Lenin's leadership, using specialists as managers, scientists, teachers, and engineers, even in leading positions in education. At the same time, Lenin stressed helping intellectuals overcome their erroneous views in order to establish sincere comradely cooperation with them. Lenin's Soviet policies are held up as a model for China.[13] Reformers have popularized the theme of Lenin's respect for intellectuals to attack Mao's legacy of mistreatment of this group and the continued orthodox attempts to maintain the control of officials over experts.

In the field of education, the Soviet Union under both Lenin and Stalin adopted many effective measures, we are told by Chinese sources. The cultural level of the broad mass of workers and peasants was initially very low in Russia. This was a huge obstacle to building socialism. It was also a feudal characteristic that created fertile soil for bureaucratism. Lenin understood this and established the theoretical base to overcome and wipe out bureaucratism through the development of education, including communist thought education. A Chinese article on early educational steps is totally laudatory, noting that new schools popped up like spring shoots after a rain and very great results were obtained. It calls Lenin's policies

---

[13] Li Guidong, "Liening he zhishifenzi," *Shehuikexue*, no. 2 (1984): 7-8; Ye Zhonghai and Chen Jiuhua, "Jianlun Liening rencai sixiang de jiben neirong," *Yangzhou shiyuan xuebao* (shehuikexue ban), no. 3 (1983): 8-15; Xue Muduo, "Liening shi zenyang kandai zhishifenzi zai jianshe zhong de zuoyong de," *Renwen zazhi*, no. 1 (1984): 26-27, 33.

correct and successful. Another Chinese article, also from 1983, on Stalin's thought concerning talent is no less laudatory. It claims that Stalin
was a great Marxist, that he continued the socialist task that Lenin initiated, and that he continued and developed the glorious thought of Marx,
which stresses the importance of people with talent in technology. As a
result, Stalin built up a strong force of such people, which was of decisive
significance for socialist economic development. In the party, a group of
people considered grasping technology to be a dangerous objective, requiring reliance on untrustworthy capitalist specialists. Stalin criticized
them, emphasizing the important position of technology in social production, the necessary functions performed by technicians, and the value
of the education that trains them. Under Stalin's leadership, the Stakhanovite movement brought forth countless talented people. The article says
not a word about Stalin's purges or negative policies toward intellectuals.[14]

Other publications praise the Soviet historical experience in the 1920s
and 1930s of attracting foreign capital and technology. They praise both
Lenin and Stalin for their policies of drawing on advanced, capitalist
countries to strengthen the Soviet potential to achieve self-reliance, and
for taking advantage of contradictions and competition among other
countries. The Soviets faced the threat of a small number of foreign capitalists who engaged in illegal activity; they were correct to tighten unified control over foreign capital. No mention is made of any Soviet mistakes in the handling of this policy.[15]

While the implicit comparison with China's neglect of education and
abuse of specialists places the Soviet Union in a favorable light, some criticism of the Soviet policy toward intellectuals in the Stalin and Khrushchev eras is also printed. One of the strongest condemnations appeared
at the beginning of 1979, in a brief interlude of relatively open discussion.
It discusses the life of Lysenko and his negative effects on the natural sciences in the Soviet Union. Early in the article, there is a discussion of the
sharp struggle in genetics (although the struggle was not limited to this
field) in 1929-1932. The majority of geneticists in one camp were driven
from the research system, individuals even being sent into exile. This use
of administrative methods to deal with a scientific dispute was harmful to
the development of science, the article indicates. This situation gave Lysenko his opportunity. Those who did not unconditionally support Lysenko and his co-leaders in the field were attacked; they were put in dan-

[14] Yu Pei, "Liening shiqi de Suweiai jiaoyu," *Jiaoyu yanjiu*, no. 3 (1983): 68-72; Wang
Yunming, "Sidalin de rencai sixiang," *Jianghai yuekan*, no. 4 (1983): 63-67, 18.

[15] Wang Side and Wu Rui, "Sulian zai er-sanshi niandai yinjin waizi he zhishu de lishi
jingyan," *Shehuikexue*, no. 1 (1984): 30-32.

ger of being called "enemies of the people" and forced on the rails of a political struggle.

Under Lysenko, science was distorted, biology became very backward. In 1948, a struggle began in the Soviet Union against foreign influence. Arguments appeared for just about everything having been invented on Russian soil, as if in the history of world science, only Russians had been creative. Lysenko cleverly used this political situation to extricate himself from a weakening position with the argument that genetics is a reactionary tool of American imperialism. Natural sciences have no class nature, but under Lysenko biology was divided into socialist and capitalist, progressive and reactionary. His Soviet opponents were accused of being the running dogs of the capitalists. The article describes a kind of inquisition in biology, agronomy, medicine, and other fields in which scientists had to announce their attitude toward Lysenkoism before a commission. Lysenko, the article adds, was not a scientist. He clothed unreliable or falsified discoveries in the garb of Marxism. Thus his deceptions not only damaged the natural sciences, they even stained Marxism.

How was this man's powerful hold on Soviet science possible? The article mentions Stalin's involvement in passing, but draws no critical conclusions about him. In contrast, it accuses Khrushchev of becoming Lysenko's protector in the mid-1950s, when the latter's power had begun to weaken. Khrushchev used administrative orders to resolve scholarly questions. Thus Lysenko's position was strengthened into the 1960s. Even in 1964, the article explains, Khrushchev was seeking to make gains in agriculture through Lysenko's methods and to thwart his political opponents. When scientists resisted his support of Lysenko, he rebuked them for interfering in politics; he even decided to abolish the Academy of Sciences. When Khrushchev was voted out of office soon afterwards, Lysenko also lost his position.

The historical lesson drawn by the article is to stop political interference in disputes within the natural sciences. History is like a mirror, the article adds. Scientists, philosophers, and even politicians should not forget Lysenko, the Chinese audience is told.[16]

In the late 1970s, the attack on Lysenko became a manifesto for the independence of Chinese intellectuals. The many internal circulation (*neibu*) articles on him reflected the numerous conferences on him. Translations circulated of the major foreign and Soviet evaluations of the rise and fall of Lysenko and the tragedy of his arbitrary and ignorant control over entire fields of science. This Soviet case evoked a sharp response because there were so many parallels with the even greater politicization

[16] Shi Xiyuan, "Lishenke qiren," *Ziran bianzhengfa tongshun*, no. 1 (1979): 224-33.

of science and scholarship in China. In the shadow of the Lysenko discussion, the natural sciences gained their independence as early as 1977-1978. Philosophy researchers tried to ride on the coattails of the natural sciences, pointing to the linkages between distortions of the two fields in the Soviet setting that gave rise to Lysenko, but by the spring of 1979, when Deng announced the four cardinal principles, they had clearly lost their appeal. Figures in the arts and literature in China conducted a longer struggle, finally at the end of 1984 enjoying some taste of victory with Hu Qili's speech to the Fourth Writers' Congress in favor of freedom of expression. Social scientists were also engaged in this struggle. Following Hu Qili's speech they were emboldened to try to move closer to the common goal of freedom of scholarship, but clearly no easy victory was in sight. Writings on Lysenko had been among the important early publications that launched the post-Mao quest for redressing the balance between intellectuals and officials.

On other subjects related to the social sciences and the arts, Lenin and Stalin are also given high marks. In one article published in 1983, the author writes that Lenin and Stalin, as Marx and Engels before them, were extremely concerned with problems of the urban economy.[17] Chinese should study the theoretical legacy of Lenin and Stalin on this issue as guidance for building the "four modernizations" and creating socialist modernization. The article regrets that Chinese political economists generally have not adequately studied the problems of the concentration of production in various industries. Study of this kind of question is just one way in which specialists can serve the cause of socialism. They should analyze the scientific distribution of the population, the formation of a national urban network and division of labor. Under socialism, the city still is the economic, political, and cultural center. As Lenin and Stalin understood, a correct strategy should be developed for urban development.

In China, as elsewhere, the most popular group in the Soviet intelligentsia are the writers. In the mid-1960s, Chinese authorities decided that Soviet literature in the previous decade had gone astray from its socialist ideals. Under the influence of Jiang Qing, the arts were depicted as a battleground where revisionist forces poisoned the minds of people. In scattered articles and lively behind-the-scenes debates, Chinese in 1979 reexamined these accusations against Soviet literature. As Chapter Two points out, by September a majority at a conference on literature recognized that Soviet literature is indeed socialist.

[17] Yan Ganwu, "Liening, Sidalin guanyu chengshi de jige zhongyao guandian," *Tianjin shehuikexue*, no. 2 (1983): 53-56, 47.

An article published in 1979 shows one facet of the reconsideration.[18] It focuses on Sholokhov's story "Fate of Man." Originally translated into Chinese in 1957 and acclaimed highly, the story was made into a Soviet film that was also translated in 1959 and shown in each of the large cities of China. Then, in February 1966, a conference (*zuotanhui*) in the arts called by Jiang Qing labeled the story as revisionist. A vast outpouring of critical articles followed, attacking "Fate of Man" for prettying up traitors and fascist bandits and for opposing revolutionary war. The 1979 article asks, what kind of a work is this after all? The answer it gives is that the Soviet people enthusiastically welcomed it. The author's treatment is realistic, deeply moving millions of ordinary Soviet people. This work describes how the Soviet people heroically refused to submit despite enormous losses. Filled with sadness, it does not make people pessimistic. The article notes that the work is not flawless and that it has the weakness of naturalism also found in Sholokhov's early works; yet on the whole, "Fate of Man" is a glorious, realistic work important for political consciousness and education. Here we see one of the early steps in the reexamination of Soviet literature after more than a decade of criticism.

LITERATURE AND THE ARTS IN THE POST-STALIN ERA

From July 31 to August 7, 1979, a conference was held in Beijing on Stanislavsky's system and the performing arts in China. Performers and theorists alike participated. In early 1980, an article appeared in a Chinese journal reviewing the discussion.[19] It says that the participants recognized that one cannot underestimate the severe damage done to the performing arts by more than a decade of an extreme leftist line. Now, through studying Stanislavsky's system, the realistic performing tradition can be restored and the results will have tremendous significance for raising the level of the arts.

In the uncertain days of August 1979, varied views were presented about Soviet literature. The article says that many differences of opinion were expressed in recent years about Stanislavsky; he has been called an idealist (*weixinzhuyi*), a mystic (*shenmizhuyi*), a revolutionary democrat (*geming minzhuzhuyi*). Since the "Gang of Four" fell and thought has been liberated, diverse views are being aired. The article reports that many comrades consider Stanislavsky's system to have its scientific side and its limited side. It is necessary to approach this system with the atti-

---

[18] He Maozheng, "Ping Xiaoluohuofu de "Yige ren de zaoyu," *Xuexi yu tansuo*, no. 5 (1979): 188-90.

[19] Gu Mingzhu, "Sitannilafusiji tixi yu Zhongguo huaju yishu," *Xiju yishu luncong*, no. 2 (1980): 161-65.

tude of "seeking truth from practice," adopting its fine points and discarding its dregs. Where there is disagreement, "let a hundred schools of thought contend" and through study seek a resolution.

One view expressed at the conference was that after 1949, Chinese completely accepted the Stanislavsky system, not permitting any disagreements. In 1958, the Chinese masses were stirred to criticize it, and the conclusion was drawn that the political tendency of this system is capitalist. From 1963, the label "revisionist" was applied to the Stanislavsky system, backed by the allegation that since the Twentieth Congress the system was used for Soviet revisionism. The ensuing politicization of studies of the system was a total error, says the Chinese article.

Everyone at the 1979 conference recognized that Stanislavsky was a courageous reformer of drama; his theory continuously advanced. Some previously had erroneously seen his system as isolated and unchanging when in fact Stanislavsky himself had reconsidered many of his early creative methods. Many comrades complained that research materials are needed. There should be a plan to increase translations, to introduce works, to remove confusion. Research should not stop at theory: China should have its own system of the arts, combining Chinese traditions and Stanislavsky's system and gradually forming a distinctive approach.

By mid-1983, the fruits of the reevaluation were appearing in print. Wu Yuanbian gives a detailed introduction of the new methods in Soviet art research, including systematic analysis and comparative, historical analysis. He points to differences of opinion over the use of these methods, but notes that they are seen in the Soviet Union as supplementary, not to replace Marxist philosophical methods. Soviets recognize the complexity and multi-sided nature of artistic phenomena. Fan Guizhen describes the generation of writers in their forties who burst on the Soviet scene in the 1970s. These young writers have aroused considerable controversy. They describe daily life in big cities with its complications. The scope of their subjects is small, e.g. love, marriage, the family, and the tensions of the intellectual stratum. Some Soviets praise these writers as a ray of light and the future of Soviet literature. Critics find them narrow, even sharply attacking their unclear standpόint, their avoidance of big themes, and their lack of respect for moral ideals. Yet most critics recognize the independent style, experimentation, and creativity of these writers.

The article by Fan elaborates on the perceived "shortcomings." It cites various Soviet critics and their views. One critic says that nothing of value is discovered in these stories. Another says they create doubts in readers, and every type of person is described, even a women giving birth to a child. The article mentions that at the Seventh Writers' Congress in

1981, Markov, the first secretary of the writers' union, was critical of many tendencies. It refers to articles, even as recent as early 1982, critical of unhealthy tendencies, such as the acceptance of Western modernist currents. Fan associates himself with many of the criticisms. Nevertheless, Fan sees these young Soviet writers as reflecting an age of latent social contradictions and quite stable social life. This contrasts with the situation that faced the previous generation of writers in the 1950s and 1960s.[20]

By the beginning of 1984, Chinese authors were expressing an unambiguous need to appreciate Soviet literature. Fu Xichun in the first issue of *Sulian wenxue* of 1984 discusses the aim of teaching Soviet and Russian literature. First the author discusses Chinese students, calling them enthusiastic but immature and easily influenced by social currents in establishing their favorite interests. In the 1950s they liked revolutionary Soviet literature, but had little interest in Russian classics. Many were stirred by the theme of individual sacrifice for collectives, while few talked about love. Recently that has changed. According to Fu, most Chinese youth now like Russian classics and do not much care for the revolutionary literature that appeared in the Soviet Union. Some youths like to talk about abstract human nature, about love that transcends social class. A small group for a time even was opposed to the revolutionary literature. Some say, "Let's not discuss Gorky's *Mother*," but nobody says, "Let's not talk about *Anna Karenina*." (The popular BBC television series "Anna Karenina" played in China in 1982 and aroused considerable discussion about conflicting value systems.) Individuals honestly ask if Gorky is considered a great writer and whether he is recognized in the West. A minority even raise doubts about the truthfulness of Soviet revolutionary literature.

How should teachers respond to youths' disinterest in Soviet literature? Fu's response is that youths are unstable, but can be influenced by the proper teaching methods. The answer is patience toward unhealthy interests and encouragement for healthy ones. The message for teachers is not to teach just what students desire. To give in to their demands is to harm the scientific character of teaching. Without surrendering, it is still possible to make literature lively. The problem is only the growing pains of young people.[21]

The journal *Sulian wenxue* has concentrated on translations and summaries of developments in Soviet literature. As an article by Cheng

---

[20] "Jieshao Sulian wenyi yanjiu de xin fangfa," *Wenyi lilun yanjiu*, no. 3 (1983): 37; Fan Guizhen, "Guanyu Sulian '40 sui yidai' zuojia de taolun shuping," *Sulian wenxue*, no. 5 (1983).

[21] Fu Xichun, "Jiaoxue mudi ji 'xinshang qingxu,' " *Sulian wenxue*, no. 1 (1984): 92-94.

Zhengmin reported in the summer of 1984, recently not a few contemporary Soviet literary works have been translated into Chinese, but there have been very few reviews of books and little creative scholarship. This situation had begun to change in 1983 when the journal began to accept letters and articles in the spirit of "let a hundred flowers bloom, let a hundred schools of thought contend." It said that different viewpoints would be welcome, adding that there is not complete agreement on some questions. The goal for all, however, is to improve the quality of teaching and research on Soviet literature.

In response to one letter, the journal editors acknowledge that the current system and contents of teaching Soviet literature are relatively old, knowledge has aged, and reform is necessary. The majority agree that Gorky's *Mother* should remain the focus of instruction. Yet the problem remains to figure out how to interest students so that they gain a deep appreciation of Gorky and representative proletarian class literature. Teaching that fills all the time of the students and gives students no motivation needs reform. Such reform, we are told, must serve to build socialism in China—both redness and expertise—and advance the socialist spiritual civilization. The editors explain that proletarian literature after the October Revolution is our good friend and teacher. It plays a great role in heightening the trust of young people in communist thought and in developing their morality. The editors say that due to erroneous currents and the propagation of the viewpoint of abstract human nature and humanism, some students blindly admire Western capitalist literature and the arts of the modernist school, and they are indifferent to proletarian revolutionary arts. They add, teachers have the task of struggling in the battle with various forms of spiritual pollution. Teachers must correctly guide the formation of students' views and interest in the arts, so that on their own, students will resist and oppose spiritual pollution.

Cheng Zhengmin criticizes Soviet literature during the decade beginning in the mid-fifties. It was a time when literature reflected the activity and confusion of a change of periods. Some young authors, asserts Cheng, departed from real life and tradition; they copied contemporary Western literature and no longer wrote anything good. In contrast, other writers started from their own superior tradition and added their own creativity. The deep realistic tradition in Soviet literature is still there, enriched by greater attention to the conflicts in contemporary life and changing morality and to the spiritual side of man in the conditions of the technological revolution. Cheng concludes his complimentary treatment of contemporary Soviet literature with the observation that the profound lessons of the Soviet experience are very much worthy of deep contemplation.[22]

As part of any wide-ranging reassessment of Soviet socialism, Chinese could not avoid the controversies of de-Stalinization that had first divided the leaderships of the two countries. For almost two decades, Chinese spokesmen had branded the Soviet system revisionist, in part because of its artistic and intellectual currents. The first onslaughts of China's own Cultural Revolution were portrayed as a struggle against similar revisionism. After the Cultural Revolution was repudiated and Chinese intellectuals were exonerated, were Chinese leaders prepared to grant the same treatment to Soviet arts and letters—to the Soviet intelligentsia?

The concept of revisionism when applied to intellectual circles has had many meanings in China. Three broad themes can be discerned: they are concerned with the importance, the independence, and the cosmopolitanism of intellectuals. Under Mao, Chinese leaders were critical of careerist intellectuals, whose authority, income, and reputation were considered to be inflated beyond what their true contributions to society warranted. It took little effort to extend these criticisms to the exaggerated self-importance of Soviet intellectuals. The issue of independence for intellectuals raises the questions of artistic freedom and the right to comment critically on social problems. Soviet writings critical of the Stalin era were inevitably regarded in China as taking an incorrect class standpoint and indicating defiance against the true interests of the party and the working classes. The winds of revisionism are also seen as blowing spiritual pollution from the capitalist world. Cosmopolitanism refers to the tendency of intellectuals to ride the currents of world culture. Interested in such themes as romance and personal psychology, Soviet artists were seen as spreading pollution into the lives of the Soviet people. In the process, they contributed to social problems—divorce, sex outside of marriage, crime, corruption, and, in general, social relations based on material calculation rather than altruism.

ASSESSING THE SOVIET "THAW LITERATURE"

In 1984, a collection of twenty-eight articles on Soviet literature in the 1950s and 1960s was published in Beijing. Following five years of journal articles and conferences on Soviet literature, this new collection summarizes the state of a rapidly maturing field. It shows that in the years after

[22] Letter to editor and response in *Sulian wenxue*, no. 4 (1984): 94-96; Cheng Zhengmin, "Sulian dangdai zuojia de sikao he tansuo," *Sulian wenxue*, no. 4 (1984): 88-91.

the majority at the Harbin Conference of September 1979 had expressed their view that the Soviet Union is socialist, much had been done to specify the exact character of socialist literature in that country. Many controversial questions about the exciting decades of the 1950s and 1960s in Soviet literature had been answered.

It should be noted that by late 1979, the Soviet "thaw literature" (covering the ten to fifteen years after Stalin's death) was circulating widely among Chinese intellectuals. Translated in the years of the "Gang of Four" in part because of its critical perspective on the Soviet system, but restricted only to officials of high rank and certain professors, these materials were available already and, following the arrest of the "Gang of Four," quickly reached a wider audience. Concern for the powerful impact of this literature in its encouragement for a process similar to de-Stalinization prompted Chinese spokesmen to restrict positive comments on it. This is the background for the literary criticisms of the "thaw literature" that appeared in the 1980s.

This richly informative collection, covering 613 pages, is easily the fullest presentation of Chinese views on the complex decades of the 1950s and 1960s in the Soviet Union. It is also a blend of detailed scholarship—specific identification of tens of authors, ample summaries of plots, etc.—and general interpretations. Despite the editors' acknowledgement that some of the views expressed by the many authors represented in the book are contradictory, there is, in fact, a general consensus. All of the authors accept the following overall perspective: 1) literary and artistic creativity had declined under Stalin by the beginning of the 1950s; 2) strong corrective action was necessary; 3) the two decades under consideration were a complex and important period, with many positive results; 4) serious negative tendencies, including the introduction of Western capitalist literature, threatened socialist realism and socialism; 5) in the mid-sixties Soviet literature overcame these tendencies, leading to positive developments in the following period.

There is also remarkable consistency in the list of authors, from chapter to chapter, who are associated with the negative tendencies. Among the names that appear over and over are Aksenov, Dudintsev, Ehrenburg, Kuznetsov, Pasternak, Solzhenitsyn, Tvardovsky, Voinovich, Voznesensky, and Yevtushenko. The book paints a consistent picture of socialism under threat by a considerable force of writers. It explains why the threat arose and the nature of the threat. Nonetheless, it is vague about how the threat was overcome. The relevance to China is rarely mentioned despite the fact that the book repeatedly discusses "humanism" in Soviet literature and went to press in March 1984, before China's anti-spiritual pollution campaign of 1983-1984, which focused on the meaning and dangers of humanism, had been halted. Yet on page 1 of the preface, the editors explain that this book on a subject previously neglected in Chinese scholarship will help China learn from the Soviet experience.

Little is said anywhere in the book about problems in Soviet literature before the mid-thirties. There is reluctance to suggest that the socialist system or socialist realism may in any way be at fault. All of the problems faced by Soviet literature are traced to the time of "late Stalin" or to causes beyond the control of the socialist system. A rare exception is the brief mention made in a chapter on the "positive hero" to the one-sided elimination of romanticism in the 1920s, but this is qualified by a general assessment of this period as a time of happy results for literature through the treatment of revolution as the central theme.[23] The chapter recognizes a short-term tendency to make the whole working class or the party the hero, leaving out the individual apart from the collective and cutting out the inner world of the individual on the assumption that the worker does not have a complex psychology. In the early 1930s Soviets successfully combatted the coarse sociological view that mechanically assigned positive and negative class character, confining the possibilties to two types and totally overlooking individual personality and the psychology of daily life. Such extremes were only minor aberrations in the light of the world-renowned achievements of Soviet literature and the outstanding results of socialist realism, the principles of which had been formally developed in the early 1930s.

The 1984 book returns frequently to the theme that Soviet literature deteriorated from the second half of the 1930s. Although no effort is made to show the stages or pattern of deterioration or to give examples, the Chinese writers explain why it occurred and describe the shortcomings of the resulting literature. They emphasize theoretical reasons. The 1936 Soviet Constitution erroneously proclaimed complete unanimity in politics and morality, and complete correspondence between the forces and relations of production in a socialist system. This meant that there were no more possibilities of contradictions and conflicts, said Stalin. As a result, some writers were led to wear rose-colored glasses. They saw the ideal and the reality in total agreement. Increasingly, especially after World War II, Soviet writers were guided by the "theory of no conflict." A false distinction was drawn between the old realism prior to the socialist revolution that demanded only criticism of reality, and the new one, which was applied to a socialist society, that called only for praise. The

[23] Liu Ning, "Wu-liushi niandai Sulian wenxue zhong de zhengmian renwu wenti," in Wu Yuanbian and Deng Shuping, eds., *Wu-liushi niandai de Sulian wenxue* (Beijing: Waiyu jiaoxue yu yanjiu chubanshe, 1984), 60-61.

new realism required heroes, optimism, and prettying up reality. The inability to introduce conflict was especially damaging to drama and films. Chinese also attribute leftist influences harmful to the arts in the postwar era to the theory of the intensification of class struggle and to an international factor, the influence of the Cold War. All inner doubts and conflicts could now be described as results of these factors. After World War II crude administrative interference was used to resolve artistic questions. Chinese refer to the erroneous tendency of treating artistic transgressions as anti-Soviet. Many good works could not appear, and some popular plays of the 1920s and 1930s were taken off the stage.

What literary works were able to appear under these difficult conditions? They were writings that praised, but did not expose—writings that conveyed simplistic, formalized, and dogmatic interpretations. Creativity was overlooked; art directly served party politics. Unbelievable heroes could not serve the socialist education of the reader. On the contrary, they led to a loss of belief. These are the harsh judgments of the late Stalin era that can be found in the Chinese collection on Soviet literature.[24] Yet there are also hints that good writings continued.[25] There is no systematic survey of what went wrong and why. Instead, through most of the book Chinese authors seem content to stop with the label "cult of personality" to explain dogmatism in the arts and a deteriorating situation.

When it comes to the literature of the 1950s and 1960s, Chinese find the key to success or failure in the treatment of Stalin and his period. They criticize both extremes, the glorification of Stalin during his own lifetime and the complete rejection of him following his death. The principal message of the book is that the main threat to socialism in the post-Stalin era is from the right. This danger, which was present in any sweeping attack against Stalin, was widely evident in literature of the 1950s and the first half of the 1960s.

The first chapter by Wu Yuanbian, one of the two editors of the volume, takes this position. Wu accuses some authors of attacking not only the cult of personality and violations of the legal order, but the entire socialist society under Stalin's leadership. He especially draws attention to writings on concentration camps, beginning with *One Day in the Life of Ivan Denisovich*, as going from the late Stalin extreme of prettifying to the opposite extreme of uglifying, from adorning reality to blackening it, from the "theory of no conflict" to its opposite. According to Wu, these authors forget that nineteenth-century critical realists did not limit

---

[24] Ibid., 62-63; "Bianyi shuoming," in Wu and Deng, *Wu-liushi niandai*, ii. Li Minghu, "Guanyu 'jiedong wenxue' de jidian kanfa," in Wu and Deng, *Wu-liushi niandai*, 104-105.
[25] Liu Ning, in Wu and Deng, *Wu-liushi niandai*, 63.

themselves to criticism, but also showed the character of future man. Wu rejects these writings of the post-Stalin era with the assertion that there never can be pure criticism. He adds that it was because of the complete rejection of Stalin that the wave of interest in humanism in the Soviet Union led to complex and contradictory ideas, including the dangerous views of abstract humanism or that humanism is a concept that transcends class. (This was the official view of the campaign against spiritual pollution raging in China when this book was completed.) Solzhenitsyn and others erred in treating the Soviet dictatorship of the proletariat under Stalin as the opposite of humanism.[26]

In a chapter on the literary dispute between *Novyi Mir* and *Oktiabr'*, Tan Sitong discusses views on Stalin in more detail. He notes that in the late Stalin period, under the influence of the cult of personality, the system of democratic centralism of the Communist Party and the principle of collective leadership were violated. As a result, a series of big errors were committed—for example broadening the purges to the point of wrongly accusing many loyal Communist Party members and good citizens, which caused severe losses. (Other articles also criticize broadening of the purges, but the purges as a whole are not criticized.) In addition, Tan mentions missteps in the early leadership of the war, not very satisfactory resolution of problems concerning the development of agriculture and the stimulation of the material interest of peasants, and many theoretical problems including those associated with stagnation in the arts. After Stalin's death, Tan affirms, it was entirely correct to expose and criticize his serious errors. But, he adds, the complete repudiation of Stalin's image incited the dissatisfaction of the people. In fact, it represented a repudiation of the Soviet socialist system, of socialist construction, of Soviet artistic achievements, and of the contribution of the Soviet people in the Great Patriotic War. Tan blames the Twenty-second Congress for publicly encouraging vilification of the Soviet system. Solzhenitsyn's *One Day in the Life of Ivan Denisovich* (the only work by this author mentioned in the volume) appeared in this political climate as did the poem *Stalin's Heirs*.[27]

The following chapter by Qian Shanxing on the Soviet novel divides authors into three types. One type, in which he includes such authors as Dudintsev, Nekrasov, and Trofimov as well as Solzhenitsyn, exaggerates the negative phenomena created by the cult of the personality and bureaucratism. Such authors make it seem that in all important stages since

[26] Wu Yuanbian, "Wu-liushi niandai Sulian wenxue sichao jianlun," in Wu and Deng, *Wu-liushi niandai*, 19, 33-34.
[27] Tan Sitong, "Jianping 'Xin shijie' yu 'shiyue' de wenxue lunzheng," in Wu and Deng, *Wu-liushi niandai*, 129.

1917 and in each area of society there was severe harm, a tragedy resulting from the cult of personality. Matters are almost hopeless. These authors show only the dark side of things; as a result they lose artistic realism. Everywhere they see bureaucratism—tyrannical, selfish, cruel
officials. Solzhenitsyn considers the prisoners all to be innocent, pitiable
victims of the cult of personality. In the view of writers of this type, Stalin harmed the Soviet Union and all of progressive mankind; now no one
believes in tomorrow. This viewpoint shows their subjective one-sidedness, and the absence of a comprehensive, dispassionate analysis, seeking
truth from facts.

Qian contrasts this view to a second view that although the cult of personality existed, it was neither widespread nor serious, and a third view
that does not deny the dark side of the cult of personality with innocent
victims and Stalin setting himself above the people, but sees it as serious
only in Stalin's late years, and even then the view is not extreme in rejecting the fundamentals of the system. Qian suggests that the third
view, which exposes without exaggerating, may have had the most support. It is not negative or pessimistic, recognizing that social conditions
have already changed and that earlier problems are being overcome. He
charges that a complete rejection of Stalin contradicts a scientific attitude
and leaves an impression of a dead-end society where there is no way out.
This view attributes all difficulties to the cult of personality as if it were
the only reality from the time of the October Revolution. It is an unhealthy view, harmful to the thoughts of the people. From this analysis,
one sees how much is at stake for socialism as a whole in the assessment
given to Stalin.[28]

There is even some indication by Qian and others in this volume that
Stalin before his death was active in the effort to revive literary creativity.
In 1952 *Pravda* attacked the "theory of no conflict," arguing that without
conflict there is no life and that one should not be afraid to reveal many
difficulties in life. Later that year the Nineteenth Congress carried this
theme on, calling for major changes in literature. Chinese authors do not
fail to note, however, that just as soon as it opened the door, the Congress
closed it by making everything in the arts a political question. Stalin's
death and even criticism of the cult of personality were necessary to overcome the many shortcomings.[29]

Above all, Chinese spokesmen keep alive Mao's judgment that the
Twentieth Party Congress was a tragic mistake. Its complete rejection of

[28] Qian Shanxing, "Wu-liushi niandai Sulian xiaoshuo chuangzuo fazhan de jige wenti,"
in Wu and Deng, *Wu-liushi niandai*, 139-41, 145-47.

[29] Ibid., 142; Wu Yuanbian, in Wu and Deng, *Wu-liushi niandai*, 4-5, 20; Liu Ning, in
Wu and Deng, *Wu-liushi niandai*, 64-66.

Stalin kindled doubts in many youth, leading them to reject revolutionary traditions and to plunge into spiritual emptiness. It confused social
thought, tearing down old beliefs and morals without building new ones
to replace them. Raised to revere and trust Stalin, young people were
shaken up and some of them became known as the fourth generation of
writers, rising to prominence in the second half of the fifties and first half
of the sixties. They were the ones who totally repudiated Stalin.[30]

It is worth noting that Chinese writers assign more blame for the dangers faced by Soviet socialism in the 1950s and 1960s to the Twentieth
Congress and to related policy errors in dealing with Stalin than to Stalin's errors. There is no praise for the Twentieth Congress, while Stalin
continues to be referred to as a "great Marxist."[31] Chinese recognize,
however, that Stalin had left a problem for his successors. A combination
of his mistakes (the cult of personality) and the legacy of the war left people in need of a new "humanistic" orientation in literature concerned
with people. It was necessary to expose real problems as well as to praise.
The simplistic, one-sided, dogmatic approach in literature to 1953, what
one author calls seeing only a rose garden, had to be rejected. Chinese
applaud many of the steps taken to envigorate literature and make it more
critical, but they often qualify this approval with rejection of much that
occurred in the name of reform.[32]

One finds in this 1984 book the reasoning of the campaign against abstract humanism as a form of spiritual pollution that was at the center of
attention in China early in that year. Qian Shanxing gives three reasons
why humanism became so popular in the Soviet Union in the 1950s: 1)
the memory of the great sacrifices and suffering of World War II; 2) the
previous insufficient interest in the material and spiritual life of the people due to the cult of personality and bureaucratism (including purges
that claimed good people); and 3) the weakening of traditional morality
and human feelings, as scientific-technical development and the impact of
Western civilization drove people to seek material pleasure. This combination of forces aroused a sense of urgency about restoring respect for
man and the importance of the value of war. The "no conflict" theory of

[30] Liu Ning, in Wu and Deng, *Wu-liushi niandai*, 75, 85; Fan Guizhen, "Wu-liushi niandai Sulian qingnian zuojia chuangzuo de mouxie qianxiang," in Wu and Deng, *Wu-liushi
niandai*, 350.

[31] Li Huifan, "Wu-liushi niandai Sulian shehuizhuyi xianshizhuyi de lilun tansuo," in
Wu and Deng, *Wu-liushi niandai*, 40; Qian Shanxing, in Wu and Deng, *Wu-liushi niandai*,
144.

[32] Wu Yuanbian, in Wu and Deng, *Wu-liushi niandai*, 7, 14; Gao Limin, "Wu-liushi
niandai Sulian wenxue lunzheng de jige wenti," in Wu and Deng, *Wu-liushi niandai*, 87-
88; Li Minghu, in Wu and Deng, *Wu-liushi niandai*, 115; Qian Shanxing, in Wu and Deng,
Wu-liushi niandai, 143-44.

the late Stalin years had deprived literary characters of rich and complex personalities, and even of human character altogether. This heightened the need for humanism that would place man at the center stage. It could combat emptiness and cruelty and be a force for truth, goodness, and beauty.

Wu Yuanbian's explanation for the rise of Soviet humanism follows similar reasoning. Under the influence of the cult of personality, Soviets had overlooked the motivation and creativity of the people and given insufficient attention to their material needs. Bureaucratism and recurrent political movements had wronged more than a few people. War losses had been enormous. Humanism was a response to these conditions and provided a basis for respect for the arts. It called for trust in man, interest in the common man, valuing man rather than treating him as a screw, and opposing one-sided emphasis on the responsibility of the individual to the society and state. Li Minghu also broaches the subject of humanism. He reviews its history in the Soviet Union, noting that it was rejected in the 1920s and 1930s for class theory. By the mid-thirties those who favored the concept of humanism were subjected to criticism. Humanism and class conflict were seen as opposites akin to fire and water. There was then insufficient attention to this concept, but in the 1950s it rose to become the focus of consciousness and the banner of Soviet literature. Abnormal relations among people due to the cult of personality drew attention to humanism as the guiding thought of the literary thaw.[33]

In the final analysis, the Chinese specialists on Soviet literature grant that the Soviet Union arrived at the correct decision about humanism, thwarting those who would use this concept against the socialist system. The threat, however, was not negligible. At a Soviet conference on humanism and contemporary literature, which helped to restore the concept of humanism onto a socialist foundation, the majority of discussants were correct to recognize that in the present world there is no unified, abstract humanism. They understood that capitalist humanism is seriously flawed; it cannot address problems of the liberation of man and the abolition of the entire private system. There was a minority, however, who erroneously advocated that no distinction be made between socialist and capitalist humanism. In their view, there is a natural character of man or an abstract human nature. Qian Shanxing finds this view exemplified by Pasternak's *Doctor Zhivago*, which goes so far as fundamentally to reject the October Revolution. Lending sympathy to the enemies of socialism—

[33] Wu Yuanbian, in Wu and Deng, *Wu-liushi niandai*, 25-30; Li Minghu, in Wu and Deng, *Wu-liushi niandai*, 106-109; Qian Shanxing, in Wu and Deng, *Wu-liushi niandai*, 153-54.

finding common human qualities in them—is the danger to which abstract humanism can lead.[34]

In the name of humanism, Soviet literary figures committed many other errors, say the Chinese analysts. Nekrasov even tried to show Lenin's humanism, seeing him as sympathizing with the enemy and thus betraying his principled nature. The view expressed by Soviets in 1961 that under the cult of personality Soviet literature could not be guided by humanism is another error. Li Minghu summarizes the excesses committed by Soviet authors due to abstract humanism. The authors discussed the nature of man, cutting out all reference to his class and party nature. They stressed society's concern for man, overlooking man's duty before society and the state. They only stressed the free character of man. They overemphasized the complexity and multi-sided nature of man's inner world. They rejected models and heroes for anti-heroes. We find Chinese commentators applauding the sharp Soviet criticisms of abstract humanism in the late 1960s as a departure from socialism and class principles.[35]

Chapter after chapter of the 1984 book on Soviet literature hurls charges against the fourth generation—the young writers of the post-Stalin era. Fan Guizhen lists eighteen young writers who wrote about such themes as the conflict of fathers and sons, criticism of the cult of personality, and the experiments of young people in life. These were the people whom Voznesensky (one of the group) dubbed the children of the Twentieth and Twenty-second—the two congresses that denounced Stalin. Fan finds that many of these authors were spiritually confused by the Western capitalist lifestyle. For example, Aksenov depicted the dark side of life, the daily troubles of the spiritually empty little man, the thoughtless life of urban youth, the incessant clashes of the older and younger generations. The main tendency of this fourth generation was to proclaim the anti-hero, who doubted everything and rejected past thought. These authors used opposition to the cult of personality as an excuse to reject the socialist system and admire the arts in Western capitalism. In another chapter we read of not a few novels that mechanically copy and blindly worship Western modernist literature. Fan finds no ideals in these writings. Authors raise the slogan "self-expression," only to pursue and copy Western modernism and formalism. They call for "reform" in order to reject the superior traditions of Soviet literature. Fan notes with obvious dissatisfaction that the authors cited by these young writers are Tolstoy and Dostoevsky, but rarely Gorky and never Ostrovsky. Among

[34] Wu Yuanbian, in Wu and Deng, *Wu-liushi niandai*, 25-26. Qian Shanxing, in Wu and Deng, *Wu-liushi niandai*, 155.

[35] Wu Yuanbian, in Wu and Deng, *Wu-liushi niandai*, 27, 31-34; Li Minghu, in Wu and Deng, *Wu-liushi niandai*, 111.

contemporaries they choose Pasternak, Esenin, Mandelstam, Tvardovsky, and Ehrenburg. Hemingway and Salinger are two Westerners high
on their list.[36]

Liu Ning's chapter focuses on the absence of the positive hero in the
writings by these young authors. They present anti-heroes who are always struggling with bureaucratism, with red tape; everywhere their
characters are full of doubts. These authors saw the Soviet drive to restore
positive heroes as a return to disregard for the common man. For them,
the common man is the victim of the personality cult and bureaucracy.
For instance, Liu criticizes Voinovich for treating parasites and deserters
as worthy of sympathy. Liu notes that even in recent years many Soviet
writers avoid positive heroes and that this is a problem that leaders in the
literary field regard as serious and are seeking to overcome.[37]

Almost never do Chinese analysts draw attention to intervention by
Soviet leaders, at least following the Khrushchev era (his name is left un-
mentioned), in the literary process. The excesses so extensively described
in this book are said to have largely come to an end, but it is never explained why. Only in the course of referring to Western interpretations
of the "thaw literature" do Chinese mention Sinyavsky's arrest in 1966
as a factor bringing this period to a close and launching an underground
literary movement.[38] Nothing further is said about *samizdat'*, and no
émigré writings are analyzed.

In contrast to the Western perspective on bureaucrats who were tightening controls on literature, the Chinese perspective stresses the dangers
of loss of control. Wu Yuanbian gives four examples of erroneous thinking under the claim of sticking to the truth. First, the author makes his
own subjectivity the guide, casting aside objective standards of literature.
Wu implies that the judgment of truthfulness should not be left to the
individual author, since he cannot be expected to recognize when he has
departed from it. Second, the author puts down everything felt and imagined. Wu calls this the old theme of naturalism, and he criticizes it for
disregarding past, collective experience obtained in the arts. Third, authors propose that there are no limits but their own true field of vision.
This too is opposed by Wu as one-sided. In fact, he insists, life is filtered
by the worldview and class position of the author; therefore, the author
does not just see the original reality, and art cannot simply mirror life.
Fourth, authors operate on the assumption that only if literature is per-

---

[36] Qian Shanxing, in Wu and Deng, *Wu-liushi niandai*, 169; Fan Guizhen, in Wu and
Deng, *Wu-liushi niandai*, 349-56, 362-63.

[37] Liu Ning, in Wu and Deng, *Wu-liushi niandai*, 60, 72-75.

[38] Pu Limin, "Xifang pinglunjie lun wushi niandai yilai de Sulian wenxue," in Wu and
Deng, *Wu-liushi niandai*, 594.

meated by a critical thrust can it convey real life. This, Wu alleges, is the opposite extreme of the post-war rejection of all criticism and is equally incorrect. It leads to hopelessness, failing even to distinguish between the despair of the Russian village in the 1890s and the state of the same village in the 1960s. In other words, it could even be seen as a call to revolution.[39]

Chinese analysts refer to the literature of the "thaw"—a term they associate with Western interpretations and are uncomfortable in using—as necessary to overcome the dogmatic ways of the post-war years. It broke down the old vulgar sociology. It overcame the tendency to prettify reality. Yet the new literature also brought what Chinese refer to as dangerous tendencies. The journal *Novyi Mir* is closely identified with these dangers, turning against the great achievements of past Soviet literature and seeking to repudiate the role and significance of socialist realism in its development and with it the guiding role of the Marxist-Leninist worldview. The journal *Oktiabr'*, by contrast, receives credit for supporting the socialist literary tradition and Marxism-Leninism, and opposing capitalist literary thought. Nonetheless, *Oktiabr'* does not receive a totally clean bill of health. Qian Shanxing charges it with a one-sided emphasis on praise, as if criticism in literature is not possible and there are no internal contradictions among the people. Qian says that literature should reflect the conflicts of life and reveal the dark side of life. Only through criticism will literature flourish. *Oktiabr'* did not do enough to overcome the negative tendencies of the late Stalin era. It excessively rejected the new works and authors of the 1950s and 1960s. It was too conservative.[40] In the context of repeated, sharp attacks throughout the book on *Novyi Mir* for threatening socialism, Qian's brief criticisms of *Oktiabr'* are relatively mild.

The contributors to the 1984 volume credit Soviet literature from the mid-1960s with overcoming the negative tendencies represented by *Novyi Mir*. Learning the lessons of the 1950s and 1960s, literature in the 1970s reached a new level reflecting social life and the contemporary spirit. Every indication is given that the authors made this transition of their own accord. Li Huifan writes that some authors had tried to discard socialist realism, but the vast majority disagreed. Gradually authors came to a unified view; by the early 1970s a modified theory of socialist realism had won their support. The theory was broadened to conform to changes that had already occurred in literary reality, explains Li. The discussion

[39] Wu Yuanbian, in Wu and Deng, *Wu-liushi niandai*, 10-12.

[40] Ibid., 24; Li Huifan, in Wu and Deng, *Wu-liushi niandai*, 40; Liu Ning, in Wu and Deng, *Wu-liushi niandai*, 70, 77; Tan Sitong, in Wu and Deng, *Wu-liushi niandai*, 130-34.

from the mid-sixties that led to this relaxed solution, which allowed each author his own creative path, had ranged widely. Li describes it favorably as open and systematic. Discussing the fate of poetry, Wang Shouren refers to a decline in the second half of the sixties, but then adds that in the seventies Soviet poetry became lively again. He even speaks of a "new renaissance." Gao Limin explains that the literary debate gradually quieted, although no clear conclusion was reached, because disputed problems were already resolved. He adds that unlike in the 1940s, administrative methods could not be used to settle problems of literary criticism. Wu Yuanbian even refers to a breakthrough in the theory of socialist realism beginning in the 1970s.[41]

Many contributors to the collection are critical of Western views of Soviet literature in the "thaw" period as well as of the contaminating effects of Western literature. At times the Chinese claim to be staking an independent position, siding with neither Soviet nor Western capitalist views; yet they fail to note their disagreements with recent Soviet interpretations. Li Minghu accuses the "thaw literature" of the first half of the 1950s of turning on the green light for the liberal tendencies of the capitalist class and creating conditions for anarchist tendencies and such errors as the anti-hero, blackening, abstract humanism, naturalism, and blind worship and copying of the West. Rice plants and weeds alike grew up from the new fertilizing of seedlings in this period. The capitalist and anarchist tendencies were manifested in doubts about the need and correctness of party leadership in the arts and by propaganda in support of absolute freedom of creativity and self-administration by artists. Li's balanced conclusion is not to reject the "thaw literature" completely because of some negative tendencies, while also not to underestimate the influence of and losses brought by these negative tendencies. He finds that the positive results continue in Soviet literature today. That which corresponds to the interests of society and the people has since the late 1960s occupied the leading place, and that which does not has been in decline. The close affinity of Chinese and Soviet literature is also brought out in Li Bengai's chapter on works about Lenin, where the high tide of "Leniniana" is described as a "pleasure for us." Li adds that Chinese, of course, do not want to see any distortions of a great leader.[42]

In the final chapter, Pu Limin reviews the treatment of Soviet literature

[41] Wu Yuanbian, in Wu and Deng, *Wu-liushi niandai*, 18; Li Huifan, in Wu and Deng, *Wu-liushi niandai*, 41-42, 45-49, 56-59; Liu Ning, in Wu and Deng, *Wu-liushi niandai*, 86; Gao Limin, in Wu and Deng, *Wu-liushi niandai*, 95-100; Wang Shouren, "Wu-liushi niandai de Sulian shige," in Wu and Deng, *Wu-liushi niandai*, 221.

[42] Li Minghu, in Wu and Deng, *Wu-liushi niandai*, 119-22; Li Bengai, "Jianlun Liening ticai zuopin," in Wu and Deng, *Wu-liushi niandai*, 367-92.

since the 1950s by Western critical circles. He accurately reports on some
of the views in Western books published in the late 1970s, but warns that
we cannot blindly accept their criticisms without using Marxism-Leninism-Mao Zedong Thought as a guide and following our own principles.
Many of the Western views, says Pu, are subjective and one-sided from a
capitalist class standpoint. They completely reject and denigrate the literature of the Stalinist period and the theory of socialist realism. They
approve the liberal faction that arose in the mid-fifties. Despite this subjectivity, Li credits the Western critics with some new viewpoints that
should be consulted on various aspects of Soviet literature. He contrasts
two different viewpoints. The first, found in books by Brown and Slonim,
sees creativity as coming from betraying and going beyond the scope of
socialist realism, and views the state of Soviet literature after the "thaw"
from the mid-sixties as hopeless. The second, found mostly in Western
European publications, sees the new critical realism as consistent with
and an enrichment of socialist realism, and views the state of literature
after the "thaw" as not bad. While the approach to literature was more
dogmatic than in Khrushchev's (his name is mentioned only in reporting
on Western views) time, it was less stagnant than in Stalin's time. Officials are depicted as moderate, turning a blind eye to much that goes on.
In an earlier chapter, Li Minghu criticizes Western views for underestimating the role and influence of most currents in the "thaw" literature
on Soviet literature as a whole and for taking a one-sided view of the anti-
Stalin currents in the literature. Western critics miss the mainstream,
while insisting that the "thaw" literature completely wiped out the past.
Li concludes, "We generally cannot agree with Western views."[43]

Later in 1984, Wu Yuanbian wrote about research in the Soviet Union
on Lenin's artistic thoughts. His message is unambiguous: socialism cannot advance if it departs from Lenin. Wu recounts the history of Soviet
treatment of Lenin's writings on the arts. Until the end of the 1920s these
writings were little emphasized. Wu notes that Plekhanov's contributions
to Marxist aesthetics deserve to be recognized, as they were in the 1920s,
but it was completely inappropriate to glorify his views. Worse yet, some
Soviets used Plekhanov to put down Lenin. Wu applauds the changes that
began around 1929 with publications of Lenin's essays on the arts and the
very positive influence on appreciating Lenin's theoretical legacy of the
establishment in 1931 of the Central Committee's Research Institute of
Marx, Engels, and Lenin. In 1938 the first book appeared on Lenin's aesthetics. Wu calls it historically significant in refuting the view that Lenin

[43] Li Minghu, in Wu and Deng, *Wu-liushi niandai*, 102-104; Pu Limin, in Wu and Deng, *Wu-liushi niandai*, 591-600.

left no important theory in this area. In the 1930s there were sharp criticisms of vulgar sociology, and a distinction was made between Plekhanov
orthodoxy and Marxist standards. Wu applauds the recognition that Lenin's aesthetics were an important development of Marxist theory, commenting on the happy results in the 1930s for social life and for the development of the arts. Vulgar sociology only saw aesthetics as the
manifestation of economics and class interests, even attacking Tolstoy as
defending his own class interest. According to Wu, Lunacharsky was entirely correct in his 1932 article, which drew on Lenin's appreciation of
Tolstoy as a great writer who could reflect the masses' lives and hopes.
Wu also praises some books of the late forties and early fifties, only
briefly noting a 1952 error that confused party spirit with adherence to a
model, but indicating that this error was criticized in 1955. Above all, the
article stresses the continuity in Soviet views from the 1930s to the present. Already in writings of the 1930s one can find a relatively systematic
and complete aesthetic interpretation based on Lenin. After 1945 (no dividing line in the 1950s is indicated) Lenin's thoughts were more fully
linked to current, pressing problems.

From Wu's article we get a sense of a battle in the arts world that was
won in the Soviet Union by the defenders of socialism. He mentions some
sharp criticisms in and out of the Soviet Union that party spirit drives out
creative freedom and that self-administration is needed in the arts. Critics
also attacked what Wu refers to as Lenin's indisputable view that the minority must follow the majority. In the face of these threats, Soviets reasserted their superior traditions. From the mid-fifties, articles struggled
against artistic theories of the Western capitalist class, such as modernism and formalism. Beginning around 1970 the scope of research
expanded, research became deeper and more systematic, and the number of works increased greatly. In comparison to the previous two
decades, the struggle against capitalist views intensified. Because Soviet
scholars followed the traditions of Lenin's thoughts on art, they obtained
continuous, deep development in the 1970s and 1980s. Wu describes the
rich harvest in aesthetics during this period.[44]

Li Mingbin stays close to the theme of the collective volume in an article he published in 1984 about cultural and literary creativity in the
1950s and 1960s. He repeats the idea that by 1954 culture was getting out
from under a long period of stagnant air. Favorable trends into the 1960s
were creating a livelier artistic world, more in touch with reality, and
granting a role to the individual. At the same time, Li argues, some peo-

[44] Wu Yuanbian, "Liening wenyi sixiang yanjiu zai Sulian," *Sulian wenxue*, no. 5
(1984): 23-30.

ple went to an extreme, using individual experiences to accuse society and attack socialism. What Li adds that is new is specific reference to Khrushchev and his political motives. He charges that Khrushchev was looking for support in his effort to reject policies of the Stalin era and therefore approved these critical writings. Li adds that although these publications were not numerous, they had a very pernicious influence, leading to the development of erroneous tendencies. Li insists that writings such as Solzhenitsyn's *One Day in the Life of Ivan Denisovich* were doubtlessly representative of the liberal tendency of the policies of the capitalist class. Nevertheless, Li takes a positive view of the new literature as a whole, seeming to limit rather narrowly the writings in the liberal camp and concluding that this period, despite the shortcomings, helped the development of literature. He sees advances in opposing excessive administrative interference characteristic of the past, in increasing respect for the arts, and in changing the one-sided stress on thought that overlooked artistry.[45]

The large degree of concurrence with current Soviet views of their own literary history is further disclosed in a review in *Sulian wenxue* of a 1982 Soviet history of Russian and Soviet literature, which is to be translated by Beijing Teachers' College.[46] The review applauds this book, rich in ideas, and its importance as a reference. It expresses agreement with Soviet interpretations of each period in the history of Soviet literature. The book succeeds in pointing out the creative force of the people that was liberated by the October Revolution without omitting treatment of problems due to "simplification" in the 1920s. It correctly points to the great advance in theoretical circles during the 1930s, when the Soviets completely overcame tendencies of vulgar sociology and formalism. The reviewer does warn, however, that the authors of the book are perhaps excessive in their estimation since these negative tendencies, especially formalism, are still present in Soviet literature. Treatment of the postwar harmful influence of the "theory of no conflict" and its correction in the 1950s and 1960s is praised in the review. Above all, favorable comments are made about coverage of the comparatively mature philosophical and psychological understanding of life in the literature of the 1970s. There is praise for the creative individuality of the diverse forms of recent Soviet literature. Various articles in the journal *Sulian dongou wenti* share this positive assessment of recent Soviet literature.

For a sympathetic description of a new literary tendency in the Soviet

[45] Li Mingbin, "Sulian wushi-liushi niandai zhongqi de wenyi zhengce ji qi dui wenxue chuangzuo de yingxiang," *Sulian dongou wenti*, no. 2 (1984): 52-59.
[46] Book review, *Sulian wenxue*, no. 4 (1984): 95.

Union, one can turn to a 1984 article on the political novel. It describes the rapid development of this form in the 1970s, citing for example the three-volume novel *Victory*, which appeared from 1978 to 1981 and won the Soviet state prize in 1983. The article praises the high level of creativity, the rising overall cultural level in Soviet society, the increasing diversity in the arts, and the more complex treatment of personal psychology. Why has this new art form advanced rapidly? It is, we read, for objective reasons. There are many readers of these novels, and cultural leaders have supported this form.[47]

EDUCATION

Chinese contrast the continuity in Soviet education to their own disruptive experiences in the 1960s and 1970s. Education has always been stressed in the Soviet Union. The prestige of professors has remained high. Heads of Soviet schools, Chinese note approvingly, are all university graduates. Pedagogy has attracted high-quality people such as Krupskaya and Makarenko. Chinese specialists also applaud the diversity of the curriculum: the stress on studying political thought, the inclusion of aesthetics, the grounding in science and technology, and the all-around development of the personality. While acknowledging recent problems that are discussed in the Soviet press such as the unwillingness of some graduates to take teaching assignments in undesirable locations, the Chinese specialists approve of the principle of sending manpower where it is needed. Even when they raise some questions about narrow specialization and other problems, their criticisms usually do not go beyond those voiced in the Soviet Union on the eve of the 1984 educational reform.

Bibliographies show that educational specialists in the People's Republic are fascinated with recent developments in Soviet pedagogy. After the complete bankruptcy of the educational policies of the Cultural Revolution was exposed in 1977-1978, specialists turned back to the theories of Makarenko and other Soviet pedagogues. They credit Soviets with showing that teaching is a science and with scientifically developing a theoretical system of pedagogy.[48]

Pavlov is one of the positive figures for the Chinese in the field of education. His teaching tradition is described in one article as a "golden

[47] Qian Xi and Zhang Jie, "Sulian zhengzhi xiaoshuo," *Sulian dongou wenti*, no. 2 (1984): 85-87.

[48] Jiang Rongchun, "Babansiji jiaoxue guocheng youhua lilun de jichu," *Shanghai shifan xueyuan xuebao* (shehuikexue ban), no. 2 (1984): 142-48.

tower," for building a large network of talented specialists. With Pavlov at the top, a vast base was constructed.[49]

In late 1980, a Chinese conference on Soviet education focused attention on Makarenko's contributions to pedagogy. During the following year many journals carried articles on Makarenko.[50] They were uniformly positive. They refer to his writings as the most valuable educational legacy after the Russian Revolution, as having a place of honor in the history of world education and literacy writings, as bearing a great responsibility for reforming vagrant youths into the new socialist man. At a time of extreme social disorder and urgent social problems left from the tsarist period, the Soviet Union needed a new approach to upbringing, which Makarenko helped provide. He formed cherishing, trusting, and respectful young people. His views encouraged them to reveal their inner secrets, to look forward to a beautiful future, and to begin to develop a sense of responsibility before the state. He also linked labor production with education.

After ten years of troubled times in China that had left a residue of juvenile delinquency and a series of social problems, the writings of Makarenko are of special significance, one Chinese article concludes. Because his theories are strictly scientific and draw on his extensive experience, there is no doubt that they can be of help, another article asserts. It explains that Makarenko made service to the collective the greatest demand and highest principle of his educational thought. A third article argues that China urgently needs to study scientific educational theory and to train talented people for the "four modernizations." For these purposes, Makarenko's valuable experience is especially useful. The reader is told that his theory completely expresses socialist humanism and optimism; it is the foundation for communist education. It is based on integrating the child into the collective. Another article discusses Makarenko's great stress on aesthetics—e.g. opposing the use of makeup by girls and approving the idea that discipline and military-like training can beautify a child's life. He favored creating traditions. All of the articles convey the same general message: China should again pay close attention to the socialist approach to education found in the Soviet Union as exemplified by Makarenko's writings.

[49] Gan Cheng, "Pafuluofu he ta de rencai 'jinzi ta,' " *Shanghai jiaoyu*, no. 8 (1980): 41-42.

[50] Xu Zuwu and Zhu Xieqing, "Makalianke he ta de 'jiaoyu shi,' " *Yuwen zhanxian*, no. 3 (1981): 42-43, 112; Zhang Fangxu, "Lun Makalianke yaoqiu yu zunzhong xiang jiehe de jiaoyu sixiang," *Zhongguo jiaoyu xuehui tongxun*, no. 1 (1981): 38-41; He Guohua, "Makalianke lun jiaoshi de xiuyang," *Jiaoyu yanjiu*, no. 7 (1981): 89-92; Ge Cai, "Makalianke de meiyu sixiang he shijian," *Shanghai shifan xueyuan xuebao*, no. 2 (1981): 33-35.

By 1981, Chinese articles were also evaluating changes in the Soviet educational system over the previous twenty years. The principal assessment apparently occurred at the Third National Conference on the Teaching of Foreign Education. A two-part article on Soviet education written by Zhang Tianen and Jin Shibo and presented at the conference was published in 1981.[51] The article points out that over sixty-odd years, Soviet education has had erroneous tendencies both of the extreme left and the extreme right, but not serious ones. The current system follows the basic model begun in the First Five-Year Plan period. There has not been much change in the guiding thought, the aims of education, the system of organization, administrative management, the distribution of capital, classroom methods, and the principles of education. Despite continuous reform, the original system has not been discarded. Given the chaos experienced by Chinese education and the years of accusations that the Soviet educational system had deteriorated into revisionism, this reassurance of continuity delivered an important message.

The article continues with a breakdown of Soviet education by period. The 1920s are described as a transitional period, when leftist errors such as abolishing entrance exams for worker and peasant youth were quickly defeated and when new currents were alive. The turning point began in 1928, leading soon to expansion of compulsory education, teaching of systematic knowledge, confirmation of the leading role of teachers, criticism of various currents of capitalist education, and the establishment of many institutes with independent specialization. The school became the main base for developing the state economy and providing vast numbers of scientific and technical cadres. Higher education developed very quickly. Great stress was placed on political thought and moral character education. The successes of political thought education in this period are given some of the credit for the patriotism and revolutionary heroism displayed during World War II. After wartime damage, there was a time of recovery and restoration. The 1981 article makes the criticism, however, that rote memorization study methods had become quite common.

The second half of the 1950s and the 1960s was a time when reform was at the center of attention. A big debate opened on pedagogy, and various reforms followed, such as the reduction from four to three years in elementary schooling. To the extent possible, emphasis was now placed on developing the individual's potential. Before commenting separately on some of the intermittent educational reforms through the 1970s, the au-

    [51] Zhang Tianen and Jin Shibo, "Dui Sulian jiaoyu zhidu de jidian kanfa: luelun zuijin ershi nianlai de gaige dongxiang," *Waiguo jiaoyu*, no. 4 (1981): 7-10, and no. 5 (1981): 26-31.

thors of the article concede that they are not prepared for a detailed discussion since they have only seen fragmentary materials and lack primary sources. Nevertheless, they characterize the 1958 reform as a response to two shortcomings: middle schools only prepared students for entrance into higher education, and in middle schools there was a general tendency to look down on labor. Even if the actual reforms introduced by Khrushchev, about whom the Chinese authors speak in harsh terms, were a response to genuine needs, they produced many additional problems. They lowered the quality of education and made physical work time excessive. The article does mention, however, that not every element of the 1958 reform was repudiated later. Treatment of the 1964 reform is more favorable; the Chinese source praises the return to quality while not failing to note a preference still given to a certain percentage of worker and peasant youth.

The second article by Zhang and Jin identifies three pillars of the Soviet educational system: the absolute leadership and strict supervision of the party over education; the continuous emphasis on communist thought education from kindergarten to university; and the important position of technical education. In identifying these pillars, the article is critical of the introduction from the 1960s of big-power chauvinism and hegemonist thought under the names of communism, proletarian internationalism, and patriotism. Other comments are favorable: that the educational structure and social structure are closely tied, that graduates of higher schools must serve the country for three years, that the level of schooling at each stage of the hierarchy largely corresponds to the needs of the state, and that the level of Soviet graduates of universities and institutes on the whole corresponds to the level of master's degree holders in the arts and sciences in Western Europe and the United States. Another striking feature, add Zhang and Jin, is the intellectualization of worker and peasant elements already visible in the 1930s. The vast majority of cadres at all levels by 1980 were experts with higher education. In leading posts throughout the society are educated persons. The authors applaud the very far-sighted Soviet policies of continuously emphasizing the educational system.

What are the shortcomings of Soviet education? The article by Zhang and Jin concludes by discussing six of them. First, the Soviet system relies on highly centralized control, management through commands. In the past, especially before the 1950s, political influence decided everything and differences of opinion were not tolerated. The mistakes of a central reformer can bring much greater losses than in a dispersed system, as was shown by the 1958 reform example. Second, control is excessive. The traditional Soviet viewpoint is to stress collectivism and equal distribution;

this can easily repress the personality, hindering its free development and frequently leading in a conservative direction. Under these circumstances students can lose their motivation to study and to reflect on problems creatively. In higher education, uniformity of training obstructs the development of individual interests. Third, the state runs everything, having completely abolished private courses. Although the Soviet Union has encouraged enterprises to arrange for supplementary study, they are far from promoting the motivation of the masses in this respect. Fourth, management is not effective, and the bureaucratic system is not efficient. Departmentalism blocks cooperation among schools. Schools are under many ministries and governments, resulting in big differences in quality.

Fifth, theory is removed from reality; for example great Russian nationalism can be seen everywhere in education. Russians are overrepresented in higher education. Youths in general have difficulty gaining entrance at this level. Recommendations from people with power are of first importance, next come achievements in study. Rural schools often are quite inferior. Students normally are indifferent toward politics, socialism, and their academic specialty, as shown in questionnaires of the 1960s. They do not want to serve, but to enter commercial fields that provide access to scarce goods. Problems of labor education are severe, leading later to high labor turnover. Sixth, training that is too narrowly specialized often ill equips the graduate for a changing job market in a changing economy. General education and basic courses tend to be overlooked as specialization is decided early. The lack of correspondence to manpower needs leads to a waste of able people. From the mid-sixties the system of specialization has not changed greatly.

These strong criticisms of current Soviet education appeared in 1981 and may have been delivered in 1980 at a conference. While many articles in the following years were more positive, Chinese continued to place some of the blame for shortcomings in their own educational system on the Soviet model, and these complaints continued to be echoed to some extent in articles on Soviet education.

The orthodox group finds it convenient to repeat American self-criticisms in order to criticize the American educational system. The *cankao* or reference journals in China carry many articles of this sort, but they do not seem to have had much impact. Chinese opinions of American education, especially higher education, are reported to be very positive. The influence of the Soviet educational model has been waning. Under these circumstances, persons educated in the Soviet Union have a personal interest at stake and are trying to make the case for the continued relevance of that country's system and the desirability of sending Chinese there to study. The articles on this subject, therefore, may tend to reflect an atypical viewpoint within China, although one that is known to be shared by influential national leaders such as Li Peng.

Cheng Youxin's article comparing Soviet and American educational levels appeared in 1982.[52] Already in 1982 Chinese writers were less ambivalent about Soviet education. It was no longer necessary to focus praise on Makarenko and the achievements of the 1920s and 1930s, while casting doubt on the policies of the Khrushchev era and remaining indefinite about the most recent years of Brezhnev's leadership. Cheng's comparison of Soviet and American educational levels begins with the assertion that Soviet education in the most recent twenty-odd years has realized important advances. There are many reasons for this, among which is the fact that the successes of socialist revolution and construction in the first half of the century created the material and spiritual conditions for further achievements. The most fundamental reason is what Cheng refers to as the beginning of the third industrial-technical revolution after World War II.

Cheng makes five comparisons between current Soviet and American schooling. First, the level of Soviet general middle-school education largely corresponds to or is higher than the American level. After elementary school was shortened from four to three years and middle school was extended from six to seven years, the Soviet level notably improved and clearly became superior. Despite the fact the twelve-year American system is two years longer, in a certain sense one can even say, notes Cheng, that the Soviet level is higher. The Soviet system gives great emphasis to rigorous, systematic training in the arts and sciences, while America deemphasizes scientific subjects. American pupils study math, foreign languages, and sciences for fewer years and do not select such subjects as algebra, geometry, and physics as electives. The article cites American studies that point to the superiority of the Soviet system, indicating for example that 98 percent of Soviet high-school students graduate in comparison to 75 percent of Americans. Second, Cheng finds that specialized middle-school education has been extended and greatly improved in the USSR, attaining a level clearly superior to American community college programs.

Third, Soviet general vocational schooling has also greatly improved, to the point where it is often comparable to the level of American vocational high schools. Fourth, Soviet middle-school vocational training has new contents, and it now often corresponds to the level of American community college schooling. America treats this type of schooling as higher

[52] Cheng Youxin, "Sulian xuezhi de fazhan he Su Mei jiaoyu shuiping de bijiao," *Waiguo jiaoyu*, no. 5 (1982): 25-28.

education, while the USSR regards it as middle school. If one includes Soviet students in technical schools and comparable programs, the matric-
ulation rate for higher education would be close to that of the United
States. Fifth, Cheng argues that Soviet higher education and post-grad-
uate education are very greatly improved. The level of a college graduate
now generally corresponds to an American master's degree recipient, and
the level of the Soviet candidate's degree resembles that of the American
doctoral degree. In engineering, Cheng also finds a rough equivalency or
superiority of Soviet college graduates to the American master's degree
holders. Cheng bases this and other arguments largely on the number of
years of schooling, noting that most Soviet higher education is one to two
years longer than American schooling.

In 1984, Zhou Qu compared American and Soviet higher educational
systems and their relevance to China's educational reforms. She had
graduated in 1956 from an institute in Moscow and was working in the
field of comparative education. Zhou explains the need for this study,
pointing out that the Third Plenum of 1978 declared that China's higher
education must borrow from the achievements of foreign countries. In
recent decades the American and Soviet systems have exerted the most
important influences on the development of Chinese higher education.
They are also very advanced systems, each with many achievements but
also with shortcomings and contradictions. Obviously it would be useful
to compare the strengths and weaknesses of the two systems in order to
better understand China's current system and its reform options. Zhou,
of course, adds that any new borrowing must take into account China's
own needs.

Which system is superior? Zhou refuses to answer, saying that it is
very difficult to decide. Each suits its own country. The two are different
due to differences in the political and economic systems and to differences
in cultural and historical background. Education cannot be independent
of these factors. Yet, Zhou explains, the two systems also have much in
common; since World War II, they have borrowed from each other in
their competition. She adds that she will concentrate on the differences in
this article. (Furthermore, Zhou says, Eastern European countries followed the Soviet model after World War II and then reformed it; each has
its own special features that differ from the Soviet system.) Zhou contrasts the first two years of higher education in the Soviet Union with
their emphasis on specialization to America's continuation of high-
school-style schooling at this level. She notes that far more people enter
higher education in the U.S. The system has more varied layers. Authority is also more dispersed in comparison to the centralized Soviet system.

Zhou's explanation of the Soviet system contains an unusual analysis of the continuing impact of tradition. Referring to the strong German influence before the revolution, which brought respect for the traditional intelligentsia and strict training, she says that this influence continued because it corresponded to Soviet needs. As the Soviet system became increasingly unified and centralized, the traditional elements became even more prominent despite some fundamental changes.

The Soviet system that developed in the late 1920s and early 1930s was not accidental, Zhou explains. The First Five-Year Plan created a tremendous need for specialists, especially engineers and technicians. These fields were given a prominent place in higher education. Each enterprise and ministry declared its urgent needs, and to meet them without delay, training had to be relatively narrow. The experts who graduated from these programs could get the job done. They made an enormous contribution to economic construction. To World War II, Zhou finds great development economically, militarily, culturally, technically, etc. The graduates of these programs also formed the backbone of advances in science and technology in the 1950s.

Zhou accompanies this praise of Soviet achievements to the 1950s with positive evaluations of Chinese achievements in the early post-liberation period. First she notes the planned, proportionate admissions and assignment of students in higher education that succeeded in meeting China's growing thirst for specialists. Eliminating private colleges, unifying leadership, and following the Soviet model in classifying types of schools and setting up specialized institutes meant that each step could be taken in accord with a national plan and could correspond to the needs of economic construction. Second, she commends the redistribution of fields; reducing some types of departments while expanding fields in such areas as agriculture and forestry enabled China basically to meet the needs of its First and Second Five-Year Plans. There was a huge quantitative jump in higher education, especially in the training of engineers and in the expansion of schools in the interior of China.

Third, Zhou praises the introduction of the Soviet curriculum, teaching methods, and organization. The formerly anarchic situation was replaced by a unified system of common quality. Numerous teaching materials were obtained from the Soviet Union. New courses in the field of political education are singled out by Zhou, including party history, political economy, historical materialist philosophy, and Marxist-Leninist political theory. She notes that the quality of students graduated from 1954 to 1957 is recognized as relatively good, and these graduates could immediately be used without retraining. To the time of the Cultural Revolution, the quantity and specialized training of graduates met China's needs

for constructing the national economy and culture. Without much spec-
ification, Zhou adds that there were not a few mistakes committed in
Chinese higher education, but her clear emphasis is on the positive influence of borrowing from the Soviet Union. As she explains, China's economic construction then resembled the Soviet experience of the late
twenties and early thirties. Although graduates were trained somewhat
narrowly, this was necessary. The proof is the great economic contribution made to China. Zhou adds that specialists trained under this system
remain the backbone of the Chinese economy today.

According to Zhou Qu's analysis, in the 1950s the Soviet Union entered a new stage. Curriculum errors of the past were becoming increasingly visible. The existing division of labor was too narrow. From 1954,
resolutions were announced in Moscow to address this problem; some
consolidation followed as more than 600 specializations in higher education were cut to somewhat over 300. Nevertheless, failure to reform sufficiently has continued to cause problems. The highly centralized Soviet
system has difficulty responding to local circumstances or arousing local
motivation. The ties of schools and nearby enterprises are not close
enough. The scientific basis for the unified plan of development is not
sufficiently complete to meet all needs for qualified personnel, while
some graduates are not used in their specialties.

Zhou explains that China has encountered the same problems. As
knowledge changes rapidly, many of its narrowly trained specialists face
the need for reeducation. Reform should broaden training without cutting its tie to China's economic development. Higher education has been
insufficiently flexible, failing to reflect local conditions. Lacking experience in the early fifties and having reason to admire the many achievements in the Soviet Union over the previous thirty or more years, including the rapid postwar recovery, Chinese had completely copied the
Soviet model. They had failed to make an historical analysis of it, to adopt
only its strengths while excluding its weaknesses. Insufficient attention
was given to linking Soviet patterns to the reality of China. In the 1980s,
Chinese were faced with the task of making a unified system flexible and
a collective system individualized (gebie).

The article points to five principal shortcomings in the Chinese system
that was modeled on Soviet higher education. 1) There is inadequate general training in the basic classes in engineering and agricultural institutes.
The differentiation into schools of three types—natural sciences, engineering, and agriculture—is also not advantageous for elevating the scientific and technological level. 2) Training is too narrow, especially in engineering, which reduces its applicability. 3) Essentially, only Russian
was taught as a foreign language. English was cut out in China under the

impact of the Soviet model. This influences a country's ability to absorb Western science, technological achievements, and culture. 4) Mechanical application of Soviet teaching methods leads to too heavy a burden for students and too many hours of classes for teachers. Student initiative and motivation are not promoted, and individual differences in the areas of concentration of the students are dealt with inadequately. 5) The qualities of the highest-level schools and special programs were lost during the implementation of the Soviet model, and their personnel was dispersed. Although these are not minor criticisms, the article also does not treat them as a major indictment of the Soviet system.

Perhaps the most interesting observations in Zhou Qu's article are her comments on what Chinese today think when looking back to Soviet education in China. She says that there are two opinions. One view holds that there were many shortcomings, but few gains. It contends that China's higher educational system now has many weaknesses as a result of borrowing from the Soviet educational experience. The other view stresses the important achievements that resulted from following the Soviet model. The results are clearly visible and should be approved, its proponents argue. Zhou distances herself from both views, accusing them of one-sidedness. She argues that it is not scientific to rely solely on the viewpoint from today, implying that these views are presented as justifications for current proposals. Instead Zhou calls for concrete historical analysis.[53]

Shortly after Brezhnev's death, Xu Zhiwen published an overview of changes in the educational system during Brezhnev's time. He notes two main goals of the period: universal secondary (ten-year) education, and satisfaction of the demand for specialists in the state economy. The first was realized in the 1970s; in 1970 only 81.7 percent of eight-year school graduates could continue to complete their middle-level schooling, while in 1975 the figure was 98.1, and in 1980 it was 99.3 percent. The second goal was also essentially met, according to a Soviet resolution quoted by Xu. In 1979 there were already employed in the state economy 13.5 million specialists with higher education. Xu explains that a reason for the comparatively fast growth of Soviet education was the stress given to its development; each year, 7.5 percent of the national income goes for educational expenses, which Xu terms the highest proportion in the world. A second important reason is the continuous introduction of educational reforms. The article dicusses the contents of reforms affecting successive stages of the educational ladder.

[53] Zhou Qu, "Mei Su gaodeng jiaoyu jingyan yu woguo gaodeng jiaoyu de gaige," *Zhongguo shehuikexue*, no. 3 (1984): 3-18.

Xu indicates that the most important change concerning preschool education was the development of educational theory as a result of long-term research. Noting that in 1980 only 50.2 percent of preschool-age children are enrolled in a nursery school or kindergarten, Xu points to a successful experiment with preparatory classes that can help those not enrolled narrow the knowledge gap and establish a common starting point for entering first grade at age seven.

Xu comments on the reduction in the primary school system from four to three years and the reform of the school program at the end of the sixties. He praises an academic research group for an important contribution, showing in their studies that primary schools were not sufficiently utilizing the intellectual abilities of their pupils and were actually artificially hindering their development. The reform built on this foundation helped deepen the contents of teaching. Dividing his discussion of middle-school education into reform of the contents of the lessons and reform of the system, Xu identifies a first stage from 1966 to 1975 and then a second stage that followed. He calls the big educational reform of 1958 fundamentally a failure because of its hasty implementation and unrealistic measures. After reverting to a general ten-year middle-school system in 1964 from the eleven-year program that Khrushchev had put into effect, the Soviet Council of Ministers in 1966 abolished the rule requiring labor training in general middle schools and then initiated changes in the curriculum to raise the level of modern science and to simplify studies. Electives were added beginning in seventh grade. Two problems that arose were the increasing time spent on homework from seventh to tenth grade and the lack of consideration for the effects of education on resolving employment problems. By the late 1970s, new resolutions were critical of inadequate labor upbringing, leading to various changes, including an increase in labor education at the beginning of the 1980s from two to four hours per week for tenth graders. Xu also notes the rapid rise of professional-technical schools in the 1970s.

On higher education, Xu applauds the many new contents and methods of teaching, including educational movies, television, slides, and tapes that greatly increase the effectiveness of teaching. He also mentions preparatory courses initiated in 1969 to raise the number of worker and farmer youths as well as soldiers in higher education. Despite the existence of as many as sixty-four separate ministries and agencies above Soviet institutions of higher education, Xu finds that a 1972 resolution strengthened the hands of the education ministries and served to overcome localism and fragmentation.

What were the results of the reforms? Xu says that it is difficult to determine because some are still in progress and some require a generation to show clearly. Yet he notes some problems. Most graduates of general middle schools cannot enter higher education, but they remain untrained for the factory jobs they fill; this is damaging to economic development. Another problem is the quality of middle-school education; yet Xu argues that scientific pedagogy, good teaching equipment, and a system of strict tests are important existing factors for maintaining the quality of education. Frequent changes in textbooks and teaching materials are regarded as a means used to raise the quality. Xu quotes the *Washington Post* of May 31, 1981 as saying that in some areas of math and science, Soviet ten-year education is equivalent to at least 13 years in American schools. He adds that the fact that the Soviet Union emphasizes normal schools and graduates a high proportion of its higher education students from them is important in raising its quality of education. The proportion of teachers with higher education has risen very rapidly, meaning that their professional quality has greatly increased. Xu adds, however, that in some regions and specialties, such as Russian, mathematics, foreign languages, and labor education, there are still serious deficiencies. It is difficult to attract enough students to normal schools, and many who enter do so without taking examinations. Many graduates do not obey their work assignments, especially to difficult outlying regions. Persons trained as teachers frequently switch to other occupations. Rapid feminization has influenced the "quality of upbringing of youths" and is a factor in high mobility. Low income and falling prestige also caused the quality of teachers to worsen. In the past decade, the images of teachers rose much slower than images of those in other sectors. In 1980, teachers' wages averaged only three-quarters of those of factory workers. Xu credits Soviets with noticing these problems, but not with taking any measures to solve them.

Finally, Xu focuses on the discrepancy between the aspirations of youths and labor needs. Too many without realistic hopes of succeeding want to continue schooling. The competition for higher education had intensified; however, in the past few years it has gradually begun to abate. Why? Xu quotes Soviet sociological research to the effect that this happened because of changes in the content of the labor of workers and peasants, improvements in working conditions and remuneration, the development of the system of professional-technical education, and especially the development of the professional-technical schools. He observes too that children of well-to-do, big-city families stand a much better chance to enter higher education. There is inequality of opportunity. This situation disturbs Soviets and has led to preparatory courses and other steps.

Xu contrasts very great success in middle-school education with problems in higher education. Intellectual training is too narrow, and specialists are finely divided into 449 fields. While this approach was needed to resolve quickly the demand for specialists in rapid industrialization, it is no longer suitable. Lately Soviets have recognized the problem and have called for expanding foundation training. The article concludes with praise of the 1979 resolution on training high-quality specialists, saying that it can closely link the training of specialists and the skills they will need to apply on the job.[54]

Articles in 1983 and 1984 on Soviet education often mention their relevance for educational reform in China. Qian Jingfang writes about a conference on Babansky's pedagogy held in Shanghai, June 7-13, 1984. It was sponsored by the Society for Comparative Educational Research and attracted thirty participants to discuss experiments over the previous two decades in Soviet teaching methods. Qian mentions that Chinese have already read about these new methods. The purpose of the conference is to introduce and more deeply analyze this approach and to relate it to China's own educational reform. Pointing to its relevance, Qian notes that Babansky's pedagogy uses Marxist historical materialism as its methodological base while adopting contemporary systems theory. The author says that there is still some uncertainty about what is new in this theory because not all of it has been translated. Conference participants await new translations that will appear in 1984 and 1985. The same issue of *Waiguo jiaoyu* carries an article on Sukhomlinsky's development of students' aptitude for thinking.

More than ten other articles in 1984 focus on the Soviet educational reform announced early in the year. They note that concrete reform measures do not completely correspond to China's circumstances and that it is not definite that they can be applied, but still suggest that some of the reform methods and points of view can be used in examining China's problems. In at least one article the message is more favorable. Chen Jia writes that the Soviet Union has had many reforms since the October Revolution, some in response to the need for political struggle, others for development of the national economy; some in order to advance science and technology, others to resolve problems of employment for middle-school graduates. Reform is a major matter with positive consequences for strengthening political authority, the social order, economic development, and productivity. China is now approaching educational reform; therefore, Chen adds, we are preparing to draw from the Soviet experience to make our reform faster and better. Among China's needs, he points out, are the goals of increasing patriotism, collectivism, interna-

[54] Xu Zhiwen, "Boliriniefu shiqi Sulian jiaoyu zhidu de yanbian," *Sulian dongou wenti,* no. 1 (1983): 50-57, 74.

tionalism, and communist thought education. Clearly Chen considers the Soviet experience important in guiding China to realize these goals.[55]

THE INTELLIGENTSIA AS A SOCIAL CLASS

Chinese articles on the Soviet intelligentsia tend to be factual with little or no evaluation of current social problems. Ji Hongjiang writes about the training of the intelligentsia without mentioning any present-day problems. He observes that the number of specialists rose rapidly, and that by the late 1930s, 80 to 90 percent were from families of workers and peasants, implying that the Soviet state did not have to rely heavily on holdovers from before 1917. While for a time former workers and peasants were promoted to leadership work or to engineering and other specialized posts without sufficient education or culture, this group gradually declined as a percentage of the total, until in 1977 it was under ten percent. Ji does mention that the percentages remain higher among some categories, such as engineers, teachers, and nurses. Mainly he surveys the accomplishments of the substantial Soviet educational establishment in training large numbers of specialists. Yang Baikui is equally positive in describing the increasing number of cadres who have specialized education. He observes, for instance, that in the Central Committee elected at the Twenty-fifth Party Congress, 94.8 percent of members and candidates had higher or specialized education, and the figure continues to rise. More than forty percent are professors, engineers, and artists. Yang also notes that 99 percent of government leaders had higher or specialized education. He attributes these successes to early attention to the recruitment and training of cadres under Lenin and Stalin.[56]

Wang Dacheng has reexamined Soviet debates about the intelligentsia, observing that as the national economy has developed, there have been big changes in the social-class system. He points to the growth of this stratum (broadly defined) to twenty-six percent of the population and to its expanding functions in the economy. Wang also notes that the 1977 constitution for the first time treated the intelligentsia, along with the collective farmers, as forming an unbreakable alliance with workers as part of the state of the whole people. Although on the whole the article is positive (e.g. in its comments on the intellectualization of work), it refers to some negative phenomena. For example, Wang points to wage trends

[55] Qian Jinfang, [title unknown], *Waiguo jiaoyu*, no. 6 (1984): 44-46; Chen Jia, "Sulian lizi jiaoyu gaige gei women de yishie qishi," *Waiguo jiaoyu*, no. 5 (1984): 11-13.

[56] Ji Hongjiang, "Sulian shi zenyang peixun zhishifenci de?" *Sulian dongou wenti*, no. 3 (1984): 31-36; Yang Baikui, "Sulian he dongou geguo ruhe shi ganbu duiwu zhishihua zhuanyehua de?" *Sulian dongou wenti*, no. 3 (1984): 37-39.

that have favored workers over specialists and to the declining prestige of specialists. Some educated people are turning to jobs that require less study in order to make more money, and labor mobility among specialists is high. Above all, Wang assesses the Soviet debate over how to treat the intelligentsia, emphasizing the common perception that socialist social classes are distinctive from capitalist ones and the generally positive view of the socialist intelligentsia.

Li Renfeng suggests that the Soviet Union may be following the most recent developments in Bulgaria and elsewhere in Eastern Europe to overcome egalitarian excesses. Bulgaria has promised great improvements in the attitude toward the intelligentsia, even calling for a distinction, at the most general level, to be made between the true intelligentsia and the employees. Li suggests that this new classification will have very great theoretical and practical significance for the entire process of economic development and social advance.[57]

SOCIAL SCIENTISTS

Chinese researchers recognize the existence of reform-oriented intellectuals working in the social sciences in the Soviet Union. They are intrigued especially with the writings emanating from Novosibirsk, including a secret report written by Zaslavskaia and delivered at a Siberian conference in April 1983, that was smuggled out of the Soviet Union. In 1983 it was published in the West and also, with two pages missing, in a Chinese translation that was distributed for internal circulation. When the journal *Sotsiologicheskie issledovaniia* finally mentioned Zaslavskaia's report at the conference, it was clear that the material circulating in China was genuine. Zaslavskaia's report reveals the emergence of a new branch in the social sciences, economic sociology. The report says that production relations have fallen behind the forces of production, that the economic model of the 1930s is no longer suitable. It calls for increasing democratization and decentralization to respond to new conditions.[58]

Writing about the history of sociology in the Soviet Union, Sun Yuesheng asserts that Lenin understood the importance of science in helping the party and state manage the society. It is necessary to rely on experts to accurately understand social conditions and the demands of the people. For these purposes, sociology is an indispensable instrument. Un-

[57] Wang Desheng, "Sulian shehui jieji jiegou de yanbian," *Sulian dongou wenti*, no. 6 (1983): 60-63; "Zuotanhui: Andeluopofu shiqi de Sulian jingji wenti," *Sulian dongou wenti*, no. 4 (1984): 26.

[58] Wang Jincun, "EKO zazhi yu Xiboliya pai," *Sulian dongou wenti*, no. 4 (1984): 92-96; [title unknown], *Sulian dongou wenti*, no. 3 (1984): 89-90.

der socialism, sociology is fundamentally different, serving as an instrument for awakening the class consciousness of the proletariat, Lenin recognized. In the 1920s, many Soviet sociologists followed Lenin's ideal of seeking truth from facts, in time budget surveys and social psychology surveys for example. Sun adds that, of course, in the first difficult years of the new socialist system, sociologists stressed the interests of the whole system, stressed the demands of the society on the individual, stressed tapping the latent production of workers and guaranteeing the individual's minimum social needs. Also, considering the objective situation of equality in the face of poverty, it was natural to focus on patriotism. Relying on this revolutionary spirit in adversity, Soviet society overcame many obstacles and set off on a correct course of construction.

In the 1930s, Sun continues, under the cult of the personality, step by step the healthy system of the party and state was encroached upon. A bureaucratic political tradition hundreds of years old was not overcome. Sociological research was prohibited. Objective scientific research was lost. Only a breath of sociology survived in historical materialism, later referred to as "theoretical sociology." This was an historical step backwards. Representative of this philosophical stage were men such as Konstantinov, Glezerman, and Fedoseyev. For twenty years, to the mid-fifties, the assertion that philosophy and sociology form a single theory posed a challenge. With the help of an East German and a Bulgarian in 1957, this challenge was met and articles on sociology sprouted like spring kites after a rain. They were a reflection of the Soviet reform group's struggle with the conservative group. The reformers wanted sociology to develop to study public opinion as a tool for managing society.

The article by Sun proceeds to describe the gradual emergence of sociology as an independent discipline, noting that although there is still a group of protectors of the old style of philosophy involved, one can foresee that sooner or later philosophy will become the basis for only one branch of sociological theory. Soviet sociology has followed a tortuous course and has lost a lot of valuable time. It has also done much to narrow the gap with international sociology. The level of motivation has been very high. This rapid speed of advance is due to social needs and the possibility of borrowing heavily from the West.[59]

Already in 1980, articles in Chinese journals were providing detailed introductions to Soviet sociology. For example, Tong Qingcai of the CASS Institute of Sociology writes about Soviet research in applied so-

[59] Sun Yuesheng, "Manhua Sulian shehuixue liushinian," *Guowai shehuixue cankao ziliao*, no. 1 (1983): 1-7.

ciology.[60] He notes that in the 1960s, Soviet sociology became an independent field divided into two subareas: general sociological theory, and applied or concrete sociological research. The latter was mainly to study social reality, that is, urgent problems facing society. Over twenty years, this subarea has developed rapidly, covering a broad range of research. Tong concludes that it has built a comparatively complete scientific system, in scope now comparable to America. Soviet scholarly circles evaluate the significance and role of applied sociology very highly, considering conclusions and suggestions by sociologists to be a guide for party and state organs as well as the entire working people.

Tong recounts the history of Soviet applied sociology, dividing it into five stages. From 1917 to 1924, Lenin greatly emphasized this work. In the decade from 1925 to 1934, both general sociological theory and applied sociological research experienced very substantial development. The only difference noted by Tong is some change in subjects of interest from the earlier period; for example, in the first period there was interest in problems of the working class and the intelligentsia, while in the latter period interest had grown in problems of religion, problems of culture, and criticisms of capitalist sociology. According to Tong, from the second half of the 1930s, applied sociology was severely restricted, and in the 1940s and 1950s sociology was completely rejected. It was incorporated into the scope of historical materialism, which was called Marxist sociology.

The fourth stage begins in 1960, Tong asserts, when the Institute of Philosophy under the Academy of Sciences established a research group on work and daily life. Afterwards, research groups and laboratories appeared in many cities and expanded—one was converted into a research institute in 1968. In the 1960s, applied sociology was still in its early stage. From the 1970s, it developed further. Tong singles out 1973 as the starting point for the fifth stage, characterized by quantitative methods and the use of computers. Applied sociology has become comparatively widespread. It is now found in party and state organs, social organizations, large-scale enterprises. Now in Moscow there are 300 factory sociologists, and in Minsk there are 100. Across the entire country about 30,000 persons work in applied sociology, and the figure is still increasing. Tong notes some disagreements in the Soviet Union about whether applied sociology is an independent field and about its relationship to historical materialism. These problems are being resolved, but large differences of opinion persist on the laws and scope of applied sociology.

[60] Tong Qingcai, "Sulian de yingyong shehuixue yanjiu," *Guowai shehuikexue*, no. 8 (1980): 32-36.

Chinese publications have shown increasingly detailed familiarity with the current state of Soviet sociological research. In addition to numerous translations, careful analyses are appearing of the debates in the Soviet Union. They point not only to attempts to improve and diversify scholarship, but also to efforts to resist one-sided viewpoints that diminished the role of Marxist-Leninist sociology. One article notes that Soviets basically recognize that such views are now a thing of the past.[61]

Han Wei, one of the deputy editors of *Sulian dongou wenti* along with Xu Kui and Jin Hui, wrote about Lenin's theory and practice of building a socialist civilization. According to Han, one of Lenin's important conclusions was that only in a socialist state can a truly high (both material and spiritual) civilization be attained. Along with economic construction, cultural development is a major goal; only through a cultural revolution can complete socialism be established. Lenin advocated wiping out illiteracy, establishing universal education, raising the cultural, educational, scientific, and technological levels of the masses of working people as well as their abilities to manage the state, and advancing their education in communist thought. Lenin also advocated political education with the aim of training true communists. At the same time, he opposed extreme leftist thought in culture, arguing that proletarian culture should be built on the entire heritage of the development of world civilization. Han adds that as Chinese today are building a high-level socialist spiritual civilization, Lenin's theory has great importance. It shows that the cultural sphere should not be neglected. It points to the need for building a socialist spiritual civilization, without which neither socialism nor communism could be established. With it the masses are prepared to participate in running the society, and they can overcome bureaucratism. Youths can study communist morality, self-discipline, a communist work attitude, collectivist and patriotic thought. Only in this way can capitalist thought be resisted and defeated. This is the concluding message of Han's appeal to the conservative theme of socialist spiritual civilization.[62]

THE SOCIALIST WAY OF LIFE

Already in 1981 educators were finding merit in the Soviet approach to aesthetics and its role in moral education. One article notes that as early as 1917, Soviet pedagogues affirmed the need for advanced education in

[61] Xu Wenyi, "Sulian shehuixue yanjiu jinkuang," *Guowai shehuikexue qingbao*, no. 11 (1981): 40.

[62] Han Wei, "Xuexi Liening guanyu jianshe shehuizhuyi wenming de lilun yu shijian," *Sulian dongou wenti*, no. 1 (1983): 40-45.

aesthetics, including literature, music, and spectator arts.[63] History
courses in the USSR are praised for devoting considerable time to culture
and the arts, including those in ancient Egypt, Greece, Rome, India and
China, America, and Arabia, as well as Europe of the Middle Ages. Ex-
tracurricular activities involve many youths, some at Pioneer Palaces and
specialized art schools. Specialized journals, broadcasts, and movies are
mentioned as serving the needs of children. The article stresses the ideas
of the pedagogue Sukhomlinsky on the goals of aesthetic education: to
recognize natural beauty, to appreciate beauty in music, to appreciate and
create painting, to appreciate and create literature, to beautify the school
environment, and to dress well. The relevance to Chinese interest in the
"four beautifications" is made clear by the insertion, below the article, of
designs (seals stamped) to show the different goals of beautification in
China—a healthy, green environment, polite speech, friendly behavior,
and a spirit of love of country, honesty, and sincerity.

At the initial meeting of the Chinese Association of Soviet and East European Studies in 1982, Lin Li spoke about research on humanistic theory
by Soviet philosophers. In early 1983, excerpts from her speech were
published. Lin explains that in Stalin's time, Soviet philosophers had not
rejected humanism, but merely had said that capitalist humanism is false
and socialist society is the only humanistic society. Hardly any research
was done on the humanistic viewpoint. After Stalin's death, when the
cult of the personality was being publicly criticized, lively propaganda on
humanism began. From the 1960s to the present, study and propaganda
on this theme has developed unabated. Examples of this interest are the
views that "man and the individual are the most precious capital," "the
system of communist thought is the newest, highest form of humanism,"
"the question of man is the most fundamental problem of Marxist philosophy." Soviets regard humanism as recognizing the value of man, recognizing man's rights to freedom, happiness, education and development
of his abilities, recognizing that the welfare of man is the standard to
judge a social system. They argue that Marxism opened a new stage for
the development of humanism, overcoming the abstract, incomplete, and
contradictory nature of thinking about the concept and providing a firm
theoretical base and a real political program for it.

Lin says that one important reason for Soviet interest in this concept is
as a response to Western capitalist attacks on the Soviet Union that point
to Marxist class struggle theory as evidence that Soviet humanist propaganda is false. Soviets respond that class struggle is an indispensable

[63] Huadong shida waiguo jiaoyu yanjiusuo, "Sulian xuexiao de meiyu," *Shanghai jiaoyu*, no. 5 (1981): 41-42.

means to resolve social problems (including anti-humanist ones) during the transition to socialism. It is revolutionary violence for the interests of the majority, and it suppresses the resistance of the minority. Some people say that alienation is the source of nonhumanist behavior and the aim of humanism is to eliminate it. This means that everything that discusses aspects of labor alienation can be seen as a manifestation of humanist thought. Some capitalist philosophers attack Lenin for not understanding Marxist humanism because he did not analyze the problem of alienation, but Soviet philosophers find in Lenin's early writings ideas about alienation and argue that Lenin developed Marxist humanism in new historical conditions. Lin explains that, as a matter of fact, there is no need for this proof since Leninism itself is the continued development of Marxism.

Lin argues that Soviets have consciously raised the banner of humanism for deep social, economic, and political reasons. Superficially the most obvious motive is to respond to the challenge of Western capitalists and dissidents with a counterattack that the Soviet system is the most humanist. Another reason is to obtain international allies among abstract humanists. There is also the deceitful motive of serving Soviet hegemonism by putting on an outer coat of humanism. But the most fundamental reason is to bring up a new type of man in so-called developed socialism. After the Soviet Union turned against Stalin, the spiritual support of the people was almost completely destroyed. In the confused thought of the time, youths worshipped the West and chased after pleasure, and crime rates rose; the situation in production was also unfavorable: productivity fell, the quality of goods worsened. Lin adds that all comrades who went to the Soviet Union in the late fifties know these kinds of circumstances. They cause problems of man to come to the center of attention, and they lead to the desire to train a new kind of man suitable to Soviet economic and political needs. This aim of bringing up a new man is reflected in many recent Soviet documents and speeches, Lin concludes.[64]

A popular Soviet concept from the 1970s was the Soviet or socialist "way of life." Xia Jie wrote about it in 1984, noting that it had a broad meaning and could be found in numerous Soviet writings across diverse fields.[65] "Way of life" refers to production activity, socioeconomic life, culture and consciousness; and consumption and family daily life. It includes relations among people such as marriage relations, the individual and the collective, and the individual and society. According to Xia, So-

---

[64] Lin Li, "Sulian zhexuejie guanyu rendaozhuyi lilun de yanjiu," *Sulian dongou wenti*, no. 1 (1983): 46–49.

[65] Xia Jie, "Sulian xueshujie dui 'shenghuo fangshi' gainian de biaoshu yu yingyong," *Sulian dongou wenti*, no. 3 (1984): 25–30.

viet writers stress its social psychological meaning and accuse capitalist sociologists of concentrating on the material level of life while overlooking the spiritual and qualitative sides. Socialist societies are distinguished by their collectivism, humanism, internationalism, socialist democracy (including worker participation in management and government), social optimism, and mutual concern of each toward the society. Xia notes that the term "way of life" was popularized by sociologists from 1972, and in 1978 indicators on the "way of life" began to be incorporated into plans on economic and social development. Sociologists claimed that along with changes in economic position and consciousness, increasing homogeneity across social classes and strata and nationalities was occurring in the "way of life".

Xia Jie assesses the vast Soviet research and numerous discussions on the "way of life" as achieving over a decade a certain amount of depth, and as developing a relatively complete theory. Although some concepts and structures remain unclear and questions continue to be disputed, there already exists a relatively scientific understanding. He sees the notion of "way of life" as, on the one hand, important in the struggle for consciousness, in opposing the penetration of the capitalist way of life and material culture that causes serious social problems. This notion helps clarify the tendencies of development of social relations and structures. On the other hand, it has not done much to resolve urgent social problems. There are still frequent violations of labor discipline, poor quality production and waste, and high labor mobility. These problems are at alarming levels, Xia finds, and they are a major reason why labor productivity remains low. He also points to serious problems of alcoholism, juvenile delinquency, and divorce rates. Recently, Soviet leaders have stepped up political education, labor education, and teaching about morality, law, and discipline to address these problems.

How can one explain the discrepancy between the theory of "way of life" and the actual conditions? Xia proposes that the theories of researchers are removed from real problems and that the economic and political systems account for some of the problems. Nevertheless, he suggests that Chinese can benefit from the Soviet research. They can clarify the scientific concept of "way of life," study Chinese forms of it to oppose the penetration of the capitalist class lifestyle, and make predictions and set policies on the basis of survey research.

In the minds of some Chinese, the Soviet Union has to some extent been succumbing to the destabilizing moral influences of Western culture and lifestyles. This view can often be found in the specialized literature, as in an article by Huang Aifan on the measures taken to combat the problem of unstable family relations in the USSR. Huang traces the problem to: 1) recent negative Western influences; 2) earlier bad moral influences resulting from two periods of massive numbers of male deaths, which led to skewed sex ratios and countless broken homes; and 3) weak propaganda work. The last factor results from mistaken theories and writings that fail to stress responsibility to one's family. The negative influence of education, the arts, and nonfiction writings has, Huang suggests, caused family consciousness to become very backward in comparison to economic and social conditions. Day-by-day family ideals are weakening; immature morality is spreading. The crisis deepens, as seen in increasing numbers of persons who do not marry or who fail to remarry after divorce, rapidly rising divorce rates, widespread illegal cohabitation, and a declining natural rate of increase. Huang links these problems to immoral behavior, such as males abandoning their families to form a separate family elsewhere. He contrasts the 1950s and 1960s, when economic problems such as poor housing were the main cause of divorce, to the early 1970s, when drinking and sexual incompatibility were listed as the main reasons, and finally to the late 1970s and early 1980s, when lack of trust between husband and wife and the existence of a lover were most cited. In this analysis he cites the main Soviet sociological journal, *Sotsiologicheskie issledovaniia*, as well as other Soviet sources.

Much of the article discusses Soviet efforts to strengthen the family. Huang mentions earlier laws to limit divorce and, after relaxation of restrictions in the 1960s, some recent retightening of the rules. He discusses marriage bureaus, family education of youths, new efforts to use literature and the media for moral education, and the introduction of rituals to foster family solidarity. Huang outlines recent programs to improve the working and living conditions of mothers, especially those with many children, and to help unmarried adults find mates, such as through introduction centers and newspaper advertisements. Finally he talks about the explosion of research on family questions from the 1960s. Observing some positive results from particular measures, Huang nonetheless concludes that the task ahead will be difficult.[66]

CONCLUSION

Positive assessments of Soviet policies toward the intelligentsia easily outweigh negative ones in Chinese publications. Considering the deep frustrations of Chinese intellectuals at the way communist officials have

---

[66] Huang Aifan, "Sulian gonggu hunyin jiating guanxi de cuoshi," *Sulian dongou wenti*, no. 4 (1984): 48-54.

treated them, it may seem surprising that so little critical analysis is extended to Soviet history. Several explanations come to mind. First, after the recovery from the depths of the Cultural Revolution, additional reforms for China's intellectuals remained more limited than those for peasants and also for many small-scale managers. Furthermore, recurrent reminders, such as the campaign against Bai Hua in 1981 and the anti-spiritual pollution campaign, set limits on freedom for intellectuals. As a result, censorship remained tight against criticisms of the Soviet experience from a reform perspective. Second, the legacy of Maoist criticisms of Soviet mistakes in the 1950s and 1960s endured in this area more than others. The "thaw literature" became inseparably linked in official rhetoric with Khrushchev's programs at the party congresses and with de-Stalinization. Third, China's historical experience was so inferior to the Soviet experience—in the development of education, the creativity permitted in the arts, and the recognition given to intellectuals—that reform and orthodox writers alike could appeal to Soviet examples in their efforts to affect China's domestic policies.

While all of the above factors seem to operate, censorship would appear to be the chief force at work. How else can one explain the great fascination with Lysenko in the late 1970s that was suddenly choked off without follow-up inquiries? Why else would so little interest be shown in the historic development of the Russian intelligentsia and this group be treated in such unambiguously negative terms, when Chinese have historically followed their own intellectuals with great fascination and foreigners have long directed attention toward Russia's remarkable prerevolutionary intelligentsia? Whereas the Chinese consensus in publications is largely on the side of Soviet domestic reformers concerning policies toward peasants and workers, it is fully behind Soviet orthodoxy with regard to the crackdown on literary dissent in the 1960s.

Apart from Khrushchev, Soviet leaders fare well in Chinese estimations of policies toward the intelligentsia. Of course, Lenin tops the list for his wise policies and pronouncements. He appreciated specialists, seeing them not as exploiters but as important contributors to socialism who deserve good treatment. On the whole, Stalin is also depicted favorably, although in his later years he damaged literary creativity with his theory that there is no conflict in socialism. The legacy of administrative interference led to such negative phenomena as Lysenko's powerful hold over genetics and related fields and unbelievable heroes in literature with whom young people could no longer identify. Reforms were needed at the time of Stalin's death, but his achievements were considerable. Chinese devote little attention to the problems affecting Soviet intellectuals that required reform in the 1950s and after.

Above all, the Soviet Union of recent years stands high in Chinese publications as a model (but not to be blindly copied) for its socialist policies toward education, literature, the social sciences, and intellectuals in general. Many articles sympathetically describe Soviet innovations—in educational pedagogy, in literary concern for conflicts in contemporary life, in expounding the "socialist way of life," etc. They credit the Soviets with preserving socialism—proletarian revolutionary arts, for example. Implicitly, and sometimes explicitly, they also find the Soviet experience of value for its continuity with the Stalin era and resistance to Western, capitalist developments. Acknowledging on occasion the great interest of Chinese youth in Western education and artistic currents, Chinese sources turn to the Soviet experience for a counterweight in order to protect the distinctive character of socialism.

COMPARISONS OF CHINESE AND SOVIET VIEWS

Actual differences in the history of China and the USSR account for a part of the contrast in their publications: the Soviets pile criticism upon criticism in their commentaries on Chinese policies (except for the period 1949-1957) toward intellectuals, while the Chinese find some fault, particularly in the two decades 1945-1965, in the midst of general praise. Perhaps a no less weighty factor is the greater severity of censorship in this area of Chinese scholarship. Reform voices have not been very audible in Chinese studies of Soviet intellectuals, while they could be heard with considerable force in Soviet studies of Chinese intellectuals. To be sure, Chinese had other outlets in the 1980s; even if criticisms of a socialist country were limited, they could proceed directly to borrow from Western countries. In contrast, Soviet writings on China during the Brezhnev era tried to keep alive the reform spirit when there was little prospect for immediate reforms.

Each literature rejects the most flagrant kinds of anti-intellectualism, such as Stalin's insistence around 1948 that Russia had been the seat of virtually all past great inventions. Each calls for the training of large numbers of experts, and each highly values education. On both sides, the orthodox view stresses the same set of concerns—first of all, the need for continued central controls and resistance to capitalist spiritual pollution. Orthodox writings accept the existence of a danger from the right, intimating that the highly educated are the principal bearers of this pernicious influence.

China's writers on the Soviet intelligentsia and the Soviet orthodox camp that writes on China each accept Lenin without reservation and Stalin to a substantial degree. Their principles of socialist realism and control over intellectuals remain the standards to apply. In turn, each side rejects the forces set in motion by Khrushchev's de-Stalinization movement and, more briefly, by the relatively open atmosphere in China in 1979 and (to a lesser extent) 1980. It is the Soviet reform camp and the largely silent Chinese reform camp that are excluded from this consensus.

SIX

OFFICIALS AND THE SYSTEM
OF GOVERNMENT

A key test for the strength of reform in a communist-led country is the degree of accuracy tolerated in reevaluating the mistakes of previous leaders and their causes. According to Western and Soviet reform interpretations, the Soviet Union in the post-Stalin period failed to delve deeply enough into the nature of Stalin's errors and their causes. Soviets used the expression "cult of personality" as if it offered a comprehensive explanation, without permitting Soviet citizens to elaborate on its meaning. They spoke of Khrushchev's speech at the Twentieth Party Congress as if it represented the culmination of a full-scale examination of the Stalin period, refusing to permit it to become the starting point for scholars to reexamine the past. After barely a decade, even these code references rarely could be found in print; silence reigned concerning official policies and class relations, even if the literary world continued to explore some of the implications for individuals in the Stalin years.

The Chinese response to de-Stalinization from 1956 to the present has been the opposite of Western responses. On this issue the Chinese side with the Soviet orthodox group, including Brezhnev. Both contend that Khrushchev erred in being too critical of Stalin, exaggerating his mistakes and forgetting his achievements. Rarely can one find a Chinese publication that calls for more evidence about Stalin's shortcomings or criticizes the Soviet Union for concealing the tragic consequences of some of his policies.

Of course, Chinese evaluations of Stalin remain inextricably linked to the treatment of their own country's "cult of personality." The refusal to examine in depth the nature of government under Mao Zedong and the relations of officials to other social groups is a fundamental reality in China during the post-Mao era. Chinese studies of Stalin and the entire Soviet political system operate in the shadow of the many remaining statues to Chairman Mao.

The inability of Chinese specialists to address many central themes of Soviet political history has not nullified the importance of publications on Soviet officials and the governmental system. Opportunities can still be found to analyze interesting issues, some of which have been too sensi-

tive for Soviets to discuss publicly. Chinese write about the struggle in
the 1920s between Bukharin and Stalin and about the excessive bureaucratization of the Soviet system. Reform voices have introduced, although usually obliquely, some deeper critiques of insufficient democracy. Because Chinese reforms since the end of 1978 have wavered on
matters of central party control, relations between officials and various
social groups, and Marxist ideology, there have been opportunities to
probe Soviet political history in an original manner.

What the Chinese have argued in their reevaluation of Stalin as well as
Mao is that a country's political system does not depend solely on the nature of its state and its political principles. The existence of socialism
alone is not a guarantee of just officials. The quality of government also
rests to a great degree on historical conditions, the level of economic and
cultural development, the ratio of forces in different classes, and the political thought and state of maturity of the art of management among
party and state leaders. With this general interpretation of what could go
wrong, the way is open to research on the Soviet political system. Persistent restrictions limit the range and depth of such research, but from
1980 with regard to the Soviet political struggles of the 1920s, and from
late 1982 with regard to current Soviet government, at least some topics
could be explored by Chinese specialists.

THE MAOIST CRITIQUE

On April 4, 1956, in the aftermath of Khrushchev's speech at the Soviet
Twentieth Party Congress, appeared the first official criticisms of Stalin
by the Political Bureau of the Central Committee of the Chinese Communist Party. Entitled "On Historical Experience Concerning the Dictatorship of the Proletariat," the article, based on discussions of an enlarged
meeting of the Political Bureau, appears to agree with the position of the
Twentieth Congress, but indirectly it begins to stake out a separate
Chinese position on Mao. It refers to what happened in Moscow as a
"courageous self-criticism." "In a very sharp fashion the Congress exposed the long existence of the cult of the individual which had caused
errors in work and bad effects on Soviet life." Then the article seems to
argue that Stalin's errors were largely inevitable and should not be exaggerated, as reactionaries are doing. "Would it be conceivable for the
first socialist state in history to practice the dictatorship of the proletariat
without committing errors of this or that sort?" The article notes that
"reactionaries throughout the world have been crowing happily about the
Soviet Party's self-criticism of the cult of the individual. They say: Good!
Just look, the Communist Party of the Soviet Union, the first to establish

a socialist state, committed serious errors and, what is more, it was J. V. Stalin, a greatly famed and honoured leader, who committed them. The reactionaries think they have something that can discredit the Communist Parties in the Soviet Union and other countries. But their efforts will finally prove futile."

The Chinese criticism of Stalin is placed in the context of strong praise. "Stalin made certain serious mistakes in his work, in the latter part of his life, as a top leader of the Party and the state. He became conceited and not circumspect. His thinking was subjective and one-sided and he made erroneous decisions on certain important questions, bringing about serious, harmful consequences." Nevertheless, "Stalin, as the chief leader of the Party and the state, creatively applied and developed Marxism-Leninism in the struggle to defend the legacy of Leninism against the enemies of Leninism—the Trotskyites, Zinovievites and other bourgeois agents. Stalin expressed the will and wishes of the people and proved himself an outstanding champion of Marxism-Leninism. Stalin won the support of the Soviet people . . . he defended Lenin's line on industrialization and agricultural collectivization. The Communist Party of the Soviet Union, in carrying out this line, brought the triumph of socialism in the Soviet Union and created conditions for victory by the Soviet Union in its war against Hitler. . . . However, after Stalin had won high prestige among the people, both within and outside the Soviet Union, by his correct application of the Leninist line, he indulged in inordinate exultation of his own role and posed his individual authority against collective leadership."

The Chinese article of April 4, 1956 accepts that both highly centralized power and a high level of democracy are needed in a socialist country. "Marxism-Leninism acknowledges that leaders play an important role in history. The people and their Party need outstanding personalities. . . . But when any leader of the Party or state places himself over and above the Party and the masses instead of among them, when he alienates himself from the masses, he loses over-all, penetrating insight into the affairs of the country. In such circumstances, even so outstanding a man as Stalin inevitably made unrealistic and wrong decisions on certain important matters." The article identifies the following examples: he "carried the problem of eliminating counter-revolutionaries to excess, showed lack of necessary vigilance on the eve of the anti-fascist war, failed to pay proper attention to the further development of agriculture and the material welfare of the peasantry, advocated certain erroneous lines in the international Communist movement especially on the question of Yugoslavia."

Why did these mistakes occur? Why was there undue emphasis on centralization rather than democracy? Why was Stalin subjective and one-

sided, divorcing himself from objective circumstances and the masses?
The official statement on April 4 answers, "The cult of the individual is a
putrid carry-over from the long history of mankind. The cult of the individual has its roots not only in the exploiting class but also in the small
producers. It is recognized that paternalism is a product of the small producer economy. After the establishment of the dictatorship of the proletariat . . . certain rotten, poisonous ideological remnants from the old society may still remain in the minds of the people for a very long period."
The article urges vigilance against dogmatic habits, "thinking by rote,
lacking independence of mind and the spirit of creation." While opposing
individual worship of Stalin, it calls for continued serious study of his
works. "All that is of benefit in his works, especially much of his writing
in defence of Leninism and in correctly summarizing Soviet experience in
construction, we should take as an important historical legacy." These
should not be studied dogmatically, but should be examined according to
circumstances. From 1927 to 1936, crude applications of Stalin's formula
on revolutionary struggle were a dogmatic error that badly damaged the
Chinese communist movement, the article adds.

The April 4 article concludes with a thinly veiled criticism of Khrushchev. "Some people consider that Stalin was wrong in everything. This
is a grave misunderstanding. Stalin was a great Marxist-Leninist, yet at
the same time a Marxist-Leninist who committed several gross errors
without recognizing them for what they were. We should view Stalin
from the historical standpoint, make an all-round appropriate analysis of
his rights and wrongs and draw beneficial lessons from it."[1] China would
not join in a blanket condemnation of Stalin. It would continue to talk
about his achievements, while criticizing his errors.

Eight months later, another enlarged meeting of the Political Bureau
issued a second official statement on Stalin and the socialist political system, entitled "More on the Historical Experience of the Dictatorship of
the Proletariat." The need for further answers is attributed to the "Hungarian Affair" of October 1956, which is described as a grave attack by
imperialists against the socialist camp, and to the November 11 publication in Chinese newspapers of an "anti-Stalinist" speech by Yugoslavian
leaders calling for power to workers' councils in Hungary and of the responses of communist parties to it. The article lauds the tremendous successes achieved by the Soviet Union since 1917, noting for example that
the working people "have become masters of their own country and society; they have displayed great enthusiasm and creativeness in revolu-

[1] "On Historical Experience Concerning the Dictatorship of the Proletariat," *Hsinhua*
(Xinhua), no. 4 (April 5, 1956): 54-59

tionary struggle and construction and a fundamental change has taken place in their material and cultural life." Then it mentions that "the Soviet Union also had its mistakes and failures. No country can ever avoid them entirely though they may vary in form and degree. And it was even more difficult for the Soviet Union to avoid them, because it was the first socialist country and had no successful experience of others to go by." But the fundamental experience of the Soviet Union was a "great accomplishment"; the basic path in revolution and construction was correct.

The December 29 article points out that people are asking how Stalin's mistakes happened. In the light of later developments, the April answers were insufficient. "It is necessary to further expound our views on this question." Again the first stress is on Stalin's "great contribution" and his creative application and development of Marxism-Leninism. There follows a discussion of his arbitrary method of work, which impaired democratic centralism and disrupted part of the legal system. Mistakes in two areas are singled out: the suppression of counterrevolution and relations with certain foreign countries. In each area, the article credits Stalin with major accomplishments. "Stalin, on the one hand, punished many counter-revolutionaries whom it was necessary to punish and, in the main, accomplished the tasks on this front, but, on the other hand, he wronged many loyal Communists and honest citizens, and this caused serious losses. On the whole, in relations with brother countries and parties, Stalin took an internationalist stand and helped the struggles of other peoples and the growth of the socialist camp, but in tackling certain concrete questions, he showed a tendency towards great-nation chauvinism and himself lacked a spirit of equality, let alone educating the masses of cadres to be modest. Sometimes he even intervened mistakenly, with many grave consequences, in the internal affairs of certain brother countries and parties."

The article takes pains to deny that many features of a socialist system are mistakes. It disagrees with bourgeois critics who say that "once the government takes charge of economic affairs it is bound to become a 'bureaucratic machine' hindering the development of the socialist forces. No one can deny that the tremendous upsurge of Soviet economy is the result precisely of the planned administration of economic affairs by the state of the working people, while the main mistakes committed by Stalin had very little to do with shortcomings of the state organs administering economic affairs."

Stalin's mistakes were not due to trying conditions, the article contends, since Lenin worked under much more complicated and difficult conditions and did not make these mistakes. Rather, victories and eulogies in the latter part of Stalin's life "turned his head." "He began to put blind faith in personal wisdom and authority; he would not investigate and study the complicated conditions seriously or listen carefully to the opinions of his comrades and the voice of the masses." Nevertheless, Stalin's achievements outweigh his errors. "In the nearly 30 years after Lenin's death, he worked to build socialism, defend the socialist fatherland and advance the world communist movement. All in all Stalin always stood at the head of historical developments and guided the struggle; he was an implacable foe of imperialism. His tragedy lies in the fact that, at the very time when he was doing things which were mistaken, he believed they were necessary for the defence of the interests of the working people against encroachments by the enemy."

In comparison to eight months earlier, the criticism of Khrushchev's negative attitude is more pointed. "If . . . one takes a completely negative attitude towards those comrades who made mistakes, treat them with hostility and discriminate against them by labelling them this or that kind of element, it will only help the enemy." "By adopting a negative attitude towards everything connected with Stalin, and by putting up the erroneous slogan of 'de-Stalinization,' some Communists have helped to foster a revisionist trend against Marxism-Leninism."[2]

On the ninetieth anniversary of Lenin's birth, *Hongqi* issued a new, more direct challenge to Khrushchev's leadership. The Chinese took exception to Khrushchev's optimistic assessment of world conditions at the Twenty-first Party Congress in January 1959 and his speech in Beijing in September 1959 on the eve of China's tenth anniversary celebrations. They associated with the authority of Lenin a series of "irrefutable truths": that war is an inevitable outcome of exploitation and imperialism, and that the proletarian dictatorship is essential for the continuation of socialism and for the success of class struggle against the resistance of the exploiting classes. *Hongqi* assumes that bourgeois influence remains an internal source of revisionism, which attempts to prove that Leninism is outmoded. The article continues by saying that in the name of opposing dogmatism, Tito (and by implication Khrushchev) opposes Marxism-Leninism. Elsewhere in the article one reads that "by its economic and technological leaps the Soviet Union has left the European capitalist countries far behind and left the United States behind, too, in technology." Yet, "in world history it is not technique but man, the masses of people, that determines the fate of mankind." Despite its upper hand in the development of techniques, the Soviet Union is veering from Leninism and will be unable to determine the fate of mankind.[3]

---

[2] "More on the Historical Experience Concerning the Dictatorship of the Proletariat," *Hsinhua* (Xinhua), no. 12 (December 29, 1956): 251-66.

[3] G. F. Hudson, Richard Lowenthal, and Roderick McFarquhar, eds., *The Sino-Soviet Dispute* (New York: Praeger, 1962), 78-79, 83-84, 90, 92.

Roughly at the same time, Mao turned his attention to theoretical analysis in the Soviet Union. He found it wanting in many respects. For instance, he found "no discussion of labor's right to run the state, the various enterprises, education, and culture." Mao calls this right to manage the superstructure "labor's greatest right under socialism." Mao faults the Soviet text for downplaying the need for struggle, erroneously regarding contradictions under socialism as reconciliable. The text errs in conceiving history "as something the planners rather than the masses create." It fails to emphasize political-ideological work. Mao finds the text hard to understand in its treatment of the state. It ought to be clearer on the continued need of the machinery of the state for suppressing opposition forces. Commenting on the general point of view of the Soviet text, Mao asserts that it contains a good many views that deviate from Marxism-Leninism. Two important themes, "politics in command" and the "mass line," are not stressed. The text does not proceed from concrete analysis, but always proceeds from general concepts or definitions. Mao adds, "Quite without foundation the book offers a series of laws, laws which are not discovered and verified through analysis of concrete historical development." Although Mao acknowledges that the basic framework for the text was set by Stalin, he applauds Stalin's writings as necessary for dealing with reactionaries and preserving Leninism. The first edition of the text had appeared in early 1955, and Mao welcomes the possibility that another text with an opposite approach will be produced in the Soviet Union.[4]

In 1963, the Chinese issued a response to an open letter of the Central Committee of the CPSU. In it they reject as a "big lie" the criticism that the differences in the international communist movement were started by the three articles published in China in April 1960 under the title of "Long Live Leninism." They say the truth is that the CPSU took the first step along the road of revisionism at its Twentieth Congress, violating Marxism-Leninism above all in "the complete negation of Stalin on the pretext of 'combatting the personality cult' and in the thesis of peaceful transition to socialism by 'the parliamentary road.'" ' "The criticism of Stalin at the 20th Congress of the CPSU was wrong both in principle and in method. . . . During his lifetime, Stalin made some serious mistakes, but compared to his great and meritorious deeds his mistakes are only secondary. . . . It was necessary to criticize Stalin's mistakes. But in his secret report to the 20th Congress, Comrade Khrushchov [sic] completely negated Stalin, and in doing so defamed the socialist system, the great CPSU, the great Soviet Union and the international communist move-

---

[4] Mao Tsetung, *A Critique of Soviet Economics* (New York: Monthly Review Press, 1977), 61, 71, 79, 82, 99, 107, 115, 109.

ment . . . he treated Stalin as an enemy and shifted the blame for all mistakes onto Stalin alone." The article calls much of Khrushchev's report lies, "charges that Stalin had a 'persecution mania,' indulged in 'brutal arbitrariness,' took the path of 'mass repressions and terror." ' The Chinese article adds that in April 1956 Mao told Mikoyan that Stalin's merits "outweighed his faults" and that over the next year Chinese leaders on many occasions complained about the total lack of an overall analysis of Stalin. In contrast, the Chinese articles of April 5 and December 29 "made an all-round analysis of the life of Stalin. . . [and] unequivocally criticized the erroneous propositions of the 20th Congress." Chinese criticisms were previously couched in the hope that the Soviets would improve, but instead their revisionism has deepened. At the Twenty-second Party Congress they renewed the concentrated onslaught on Stalin. They substituted humanism for the Marxist-Leninist theory of class struggle. And they first openly criticized the Chinese Communist Party. These are among the many Soviet steps toward revisionism.[5]

On July 14, 1964, China's Ninth Commentary, "On Khrushchev's Phoney Communism and Its Historical Lessons for the World," presented the fullest critique of the Soviet Union. Above all, this Maoist critique concentrates on the state under socialism. It attacks the "revisionist Khrushchev clique" for "declaring that the dictatorship of the proletariat is no longer necessary in the Soviet Union and for advancing the 'absurd theories' of the 'state of the whole people' and the 'party of the entire people.' " The article observes that "socialist society covers a very, very long historical stage. Throughout this stage, the class struggle between the bourgeoisie and the proletariat goes on and the question of 'who will win' between the roads of capitalism and socialism remains, as does the danger of the restoration of capitalism." Stalin erred in prematurely declaring that there were "no antagonistic classes" in the Soviet Union, that it was "free of class conflicts." Nevertheless, he continued the Soviet Union on the socialist course under the dictatorship of the proletariat.

The Ninth Commentary brands many state functionaries "bourgeois elements." They use their positions in factories to amass fortunes. They may work in state ministries or other departments and work closely with and shield managers. They have "men in the police and judicial departments who protect them and act as their agents." High-ranking officials are involved. The Chinese commentary calls these persons exploiters and oppressors, who share in the spoils and belong to the bourgeoisie. Even

[5] Editorial departments of *Renmin ribao* and *Hongqi*, *The Origin and Development of the Differences Between the Leadership of the CPSU and Ourselves* (Peking: Foreign Languages Press, 1963), 6-8, 11-13, 41-43.

before Stalin's death, high salaries were being paid to certain groups, "degeneration and corruption had appeared in certain Party organizations." The group interests of these organizations were setting them apart from the people. A privileged stratum was forming. After Khrushchev "usurped the leadership of the Soviet Party and state," the income gap widened, polarization was accelerated. Purges by the Khrushchev clique removed one group after another and brought in new bourgeois elements into ruling positions. They serve the private benefit of their small clique, appropriating the fruits of the people's labor. "Their sole concern is to consolidate their economic position and political rule. All their activities revolve around the private interests of their own privileged stratum." Claims that abolition of the dictatorship of the proletariat serves the development of democracy are attacked by the Chinese as a hoax to deceive the Soviet people and revolutionaries elsewhere and to cover up the betrayal of socialism. In short, the Maoist view is that the Soviet state is a repressive dictatorship over the masses by a small number who serve only the interests of their privileged stratum.[6]

More than a decade later, in 1976, numerous articles appeared on the nature of Soviet revisionism. One article describes the Communist Party of the Soviet Union as fascist. It claims to expose "the social composition of the party" trick played by the Brezhnev clique, which out of "a guilty conscience" keeps saying that "its party 'has tightened control over the growth of its membership' so that 'the working class has occupied a leading position in the social composition of the party.' ' Talk of "the democracy of the whole people" is solely intended to cover up a "barbarous fascist dictatorship." Khrushchev used "combatting the cult of the personality" as a pretext. He showed his true bourgeois colors by working to rehabilitate "old-line revisionists, counterrevolutionaries and bourgeois representatives of all shades, 'restore' their party membership and glorify them." Both Khrushchev and Brezhnev have led purges "directed first of all at party members who dissent from and resist the revisionist ruling clique."

The article adds that the fascist rule in the Soviet party "is even more brutal than that of Hitler's." "The nationwide Soviet spy system is even more closely-knit than Nazi Germany's Gestapo. . . . And in the Soviet Union today there are more and a greater variety of prisons, concentration camps and 'psychiatric hospitals' than there were in Germany under Hitler's rule. All the talks about strengthening the 'legal system,' 'order'

---

[6] "On Khrushchev's Phoney Communism and Its Historical Lessons for the World," in William E. Griffith, *Sino-Soviet Relations, 1964-1965*, (Cambridge: The M.I.T. Press, 1967), 340-41.

and 'discipline' by the men in the Kremlin are reminiscent of Hitler's out-
cry for people's submission to the regimentation of his Third Reich."
Controls were designed to force the working people "to docilely create
more surplus value for the bureaucrat-monopoly capitalists." Other
Chinese articles comment on "exorbitant taxes," the KGB and the police
making "their way into every nook and corner," " 'mass' organizations
exclusively controlled by secret and police agencies," the "ruthless fascist
reign of terror," and the more than 1,000 concentration camps with more
than a million prisoners, where there is "cruel torture and slaughter."[7]

In June 1977, two articles in *People's Daily* sustained the same basic
line of criticism against the Soviet Union as the previous year's campaign.[8] The first article responded to the distribution earlier in June of a
draft of the new Soviet constitution. Calling the constitution the first
since the Soviet Union restored capitalism, the article accuses the constitution of betraying the principles of Leninism and strengthening the fascist dictatorship of today's Soviet bureaucratic, monopolist, capitalist
class and the policies of social imperialism. The article criticizes the constitution for restating the view that the Soviet state has finished the tasks
of proletarian dictatorship and has already become a state of the whole
people. These ideas are called a complete revision and betrayal of Marxism-Leninism. If there exists a state, it cannot be above classes or of the
whole people.

Since it seized power, the Soviet traitor clique, the article says, has realized a Hitler-style dictatorship. All of social life is now controlled. The
working class is cruelly exploited and repressed. Polarization of rich and
poor and class struggle are intensifying daily. The notion of "developed
socialism" is nothing more than a self-deception. The state serves the bureaucratic monopoly capitalist class. State enterprises and collective
farms are not actually the property of the working people. A black line of
revisionism runs from Khrushchev to Brezhnev. Economic reform is
completely to enrich the bureaucratic monopoly capitalists. No other capitalist imperialism can compare with their control of the economic arteries. The Russian nationality is the first nationality. The constitution's
references to ethnic convergence and a common language are classic great
Russian chauvinism and forced Russification. While the constitution
writes of various rights and freedoms for Soviet citizens, it adds that these
must not harm the interests of society and the state, in other words the

[7] *Social Imperialism: The Soviet Union Today* (reprints from *Peking Review*) (Berkeley: Yenan Books, 1977), 80-81, 84, 89, 122-24.
[8] "Sulian xin xianfa de fandong shizhi," *Renmin ribao*, June 13, 1977; "Zai weida lingxiu he daoshi Mao zhuxi de lingdao xia Liening Sidalinzhei liangba 'yizi' women Zhongguo meiyou diou," *Renmin ribao*, June 14, 1977.

interests of the Soviet revisionist controlling groups. Although proposed and under discussion for close to twenty years, the new draft constitution was slowed by the ceaseless struggles within the Kremlin. Brezhnev fundamentally rejects Lenin's scientific conclusions on proletarian dictatorship and socialism and poisonously attacks the "dark ages" for the Soviet people in the period of building socialism under Stalin. Over the past twenty-odd years, the Soviet Union has experienced great changes in principle. Revisionism has been restored, the Chinese article insists.

The next day, June 14, *People's Daily* returned to the subject of Soviet revisionism. It recalled Mao's statement, "We have two knives: one is Lenin, one is Stalin. Now the Russians have lost this Stalin knife. Haven't some Soviet leaders now lost part of this Lenin knife too? In my view, they have also lost quite a lot of it." Mao's teaching, the article explains, reveals the extreme importance of the banners of Lenin and Stalin to the cause of the proletarian revolution. The traitorous Khrushchev clique began its betrayal of Marxism-Leninism with its complete repudiation of Stalin. Stalin was a great Marxist-Leninist and a very close ally of Lenin when Lenin was alive. He carried on an heroic struggle for the proletarian revolution. He was Lenin's successor. His entire life was of tremendous importance in the history of the international communist movement. At the Twentieth Congress, Khrushchev used the pretext of opposing the so-called "cult of personality" to fabricate a large number of lies in his secret report. His poisonous words were a shameless vilification and attack against Stalin. In fully repudiating Stalin, he actually rejected proletarian dictatorship, the socialist system, the world's first socialist state that Lenin had founded, and the international communist movement.

The very serious results of the Twentieth Congress and the total repudiation of Stalin were to damage the reputation of the Soviet Union and of socialism and communism. They fanned the currents of anti-socialism throughout the world, causing extreme confusion in the international communist movement and spreading revisionist thinking. The most striking event, indicative of the serious losses that resulted, was the Hungarian counterrevolutionary uprising. Brezhnev was Khrushchev's counterrevolutionary accomplice, and he developed revisionism further through the fascist "theory" of the Brezhnev doctrine, including limited sovereignty and an international division of labor. This was clear in the armed invasion of Czechoslovakia. Today the Soviet Union has become the most dangerous breeding ground for world war. These are the results of losing the two knives of Lenin and Stalin. The 1977 article comments that the recently issued Volume 5 of Mao's writings makes clear that China has not lost these.

Mao, it is argued, repeatedly pointed out that the fundamental direction of Stalin was correct, that a comprehensive evaluation of Stalin is needed, and that Chinese cannot agree with Khrushchev's complete repudiation. The two important statements issued in 1956 by the Chinese Communist Party on the historical experience of the proletarian dictatorship gave a complete analysis of Stalin and sharply refuted Khrushchev's poisonous attack. From the time of Mao's personally led criticisms of Soviet revisionism in 1963, China publicly undertook a complete attack against Soviet revisionism, especially evident in the Nine Commentaries prepared by the party under Mao's guidance. Chinese owe every victory to Mao. After his death, we need even more to raise high the illustrious banner of Chairman Mao, asserts the 1977 article. Chairman Hua enjoys the unlimited trust of Chairman Mao. He was selected as the best successor. Clearly, the article implies, he would never do to Mao what Khrushchev had done to Stalin. Stalin and Mao stand together. In this effort to wrap Hua in the mantle of Mao, the criticisms previously made by Mao of Stalin are ignored. Rather, Mao emerges as Stalin's defender, just as Hua is Mao's defender.

A book issued in English in 1978 expands on Maoist condemnations of the Soviet police state. It criticizes massive Soviet party purges, such as the one from March 1973 to February 1975 directed primarily against dissenters from the viewpoint of the ruling group. It describes the expansion of the Soviet spy system, whose "agents infiltrate into all walks of life." The book claims that great numbers of political prisoners are held in concentration camps and "mental hospitals." They are subjected to methods of repression that lack all humanity. Methods of mental and physical torture are cited, with one camp depicted as "a veritable Nazi 'death camp.' "[9]

For over a decade, Chinese commentaries talked of the "privileged class" (tequan jieji fenzi) in the Soviet Union. It enjoyed high incomes, vast power above the law, virtually hereditary status. It had special stores, villas, and a separate lifestyle, including imported cars and other Western goods. Members of this privileged group held leading posts in the party, the government, the military, and the police, as well as in enterprises, while others were high-ranking specialists, professors, reporters, and artists.[10] By 1979 this concept was dropped from discussions of the Soviet Union.

In January 1979, Mao's idea of the two knives could still be repeated as

[9] Wei Chi, The Soviet Union under the New Tsars (Beijing: Foreign Languages Press, 1978), 3-6

[10] Xia Changan, Sulian jingji de tuibian (Hong Kong: Xianggang Chaoyang chubanshe, 1977), 67-70.

an accurate reflection of Soviet revisionism. An article by Zhang Nian-feng on the philosophical thought of Deborin takes this position.[11] Zhang notes that in 1961 the Soviet Union issued the writings of the philosopher Deborin after thirty years of his silence. At the time of the revolution, Deborin had been a Menshevik. After it, his journal took a Menshevik position, separating theory from practice, philosophy from politics, rejecting the Lenin stage of philosophical development, distorting Lenin's party principles, and proclaiming Hegel. Zhang adds that at the beginning of the thirties, Deborin's systematic errors were criticized and purged by Stalin and Soviet philosophical circles. In "On Contradiction," Mao wrote that Chinese were very interested in this development because Deborin's ideas had exerted an extremely bad influence within the Chinese Communist Party. It was closely linked to the factional air of dogmatism. Stalin's struggle against the Deborin faction was, Zhang insists, a victory for historical materialism. Chairman Mao's study refuted Deborin's view that opposites unite, that contradictions can be ameliorated, that class struggle is unnecessary, and that classes should cooperate. Soviet revisionism now continues Deborin's viewpoint. It opposes the Leninist principle of party spirit. Zhang accuses Deborin of following Plekhanov and of regarding him as superior to Lenin as a theorist and as Lenin's teacher. Stalin was entirely correct in interpreting Lenin's philosophy, but the traitorous Khrushchev group found Deborin to their taste. The article concludes with the emphatic call to carry on to the end the struggle against the various philosophical factions of capitalism and revisionism.

THE LEGACY OF RUSSIA'S PAST

In most respects the new literature on the Soviet Union available from 1979 broke sharply with the Maoist views of the previous 15-20 years. In the area of foreign policy this was not the case. Some of the most obvious continuities can be found in writings on tsarist aggression and the state in Russian history. The Institute of Modern History of the Chinese Academy of Social Sciences, the History Department of Beijing University, and the Institute of Qing History at China People's University all were engaged in multi-volume projects on Russian expansion in the East or Sino-Russian border problems. The series volumes began to appear in 1976 and continued to be published to the end of the decade, while occasional studies along similar lines, such as a Heilongjiang volume on the

[11] Zhang Nienfeng, "Ping Debolin de zhexue sixiang," *Shehuikexue zhanxian*, no. 1 (1979): 54-59.

Russian conquest of Siberia, were still appearing as late as 1984.[12] The essential message in these materials is the militaristic, expansionist nature of the Russian state. Its aggressive conduct characterized relations with China as with other countries over several centuries.

Representative of the analyses of tsarist aggression centered at Beijing University in the period 1979-1981 is an article by Zhang Hanqing on Engels's opposition in his last years (1883-1895) to tsarist hegemonism. The article is mostly an exegesis of those writings by Engels that discuss Russian foreign policy. Engels shows, according to Zhang, that the material base for aggression was that it served the political and economic advantage of the feudal aristocracy and the capitalist class. The survival of the tsarist autocracy was at stake. Zhang insists that Engels's viewpoint was fully consistent with the principles of Marxism and was completely approved by Lenin. Zhang's method of analysis is a throwback to earlier criticisms rooted in ideology, and the absence of any mention of Stalin's contrary interpretations or of Soviet efforts to explain tsarist policies indicates a reluctance to directly confront complicating issues.[13]

Even a 1984 book speaks in harsh terms of Russia's march eastward. Concentrating on the takeover of Siberia from the second half of the sixteenth to the middle eighteenth century, the book refers to the alarming speed of occupation, the just struggle of resistance by the Siberian peoples against Russian annexation and expansion, the forms of exploitation used by Russia, and the colonial system of control. Insisting that the annexation cannot be spoken of as the "dissemination of culture" or the "promotion of the development of production," the book stresses that the Russians used troops to kill and plunder, they severely disrupted local economies, and the minorities continued to fight bravely for their freedom.[14]

Sun Chengmu's review article on historiography of Russia in 1981 begins by citing important recent research on the history of tsarist Russia's aggression and expansion. It compliments the two-volume Beijing University series for "comparatively completely, systematically narrating the aims and behavior" of tsarist aggression and expansion abroad, and

[12] Zhongguo kexueyuan jindaishi yanjiusuo, ed., *ShaE qinhua shi*, vols. 1 and 2 (Beijing: Renminchubanshe, 1976, 1978); Beijing daxue lishixi, ed., *Shahuang Eguo qinlue kuozhang shi*, vols. 1 and 2 (Beijing: Renminchubanshe, 1979, 1981); Zhongguo shehuikexueyuan jindaishi yanjiusuo and Zhonghua minguo shi yanjiushi, eds., *Ju E yundong 1901-1905* (Beijing: Zhongguo shehuikexue chubanshe, 1979); Xu Jingxue, ed., *Eguo zhengfu Xiboliya jilue* (Harbin: Heilongjiang renminchubanshe, 1984).

[13] Zhang Hanqing, "Engesi wannian lun fandui ShaE baquanzhuyi," *Beijing daxue xuebao* (zhexue shehuikexue ban), no 2 (1981): 38-46

[14] Xu Jingxue, *Eguo zhengfu Xiboliya jilue*, 3.

for criticizing the great-power chauvinist viewpoint of Soviet historians. The review also mentions many articles on tsarist expansionist policies, pointing to their scholarly contributions.

Sun acknowledges that while research on tsarist aggression was being conducted in the past several years, important historical personages were being ignored. In 1981 there was some change in this situation. Sun cites an article by Tao Huifen in *Shijie lishi* for its positive view of the progressive historical role of Peter I. The main accomplishments of Peter's reforms were his thinking in favor of service to one's country, his emphasis on studying and promoting talented people, and his courage in removing all obstacles in order to carry his reforms through to fruition.

The review article on 1982 publications begins with comments on another article by Tao Huifen—this time in *Lishi jiaoxue*—stressing the results of Peter's reforms for beginning to change Russia's backward appearance and fundamentally eliminating its economic dependence on the West, but also arguing that the aim of reform was not to abolish the serf system but to strengthen it. Its starting point was to strengthen the economic base for feudal serfdom, to support the landed aristocracy and the newly rising merchants. The fruits of the reform went completely to the serf owners, the new aristocracy, and the new merchants. The reform was carried out on the basis of cruel exploitation and oppression of the serfs. The review article also mentions Chen Lijin's article on Peter I, which contends that his reforms strengthened Russia's military power, accelerating its striving for expansion and world hegemony and increasing the exploitation of the Russian people.

Apart from its militarism, the tsarist state exerted a negative impact on the development of capitalist relations. While Peter I is now credited with a positive impact, the feudal autocratic system as a whole is still criticized. The authors of the review article for 1982 make this point very clear, saying, "In summary, controls by the feudal serf system and the feudal autocratic system were severely hindering the development of capitalist relations."[15] A world history textbook revised in 1980 links tsarist expansion to serfdom, arguing that after the Mongols were overthrown the tsars needed aristocrats to provide military service in order to expand their military power, therefore they divided a lot of land to give as appendages to the aristocrats. The lords in turn enserfed the peasants in order to squeeze more out of them and keep them on their lands. By the mid-seventeenth century, when the system was fully recognized by law, upwards of ninety percent of the country's population were serfs under

[15] Sun Chengmu, "Sulian jinxiandaishi," *Zhongguo lishixue nianjian 1982* (Beijing: Renminchubanshe, 1982), 225-26.

private, state, or court ownership. They lacked personal freedom; their owners could arbitrarily buy or sell them. In the second half of the seventeenth century, despite the very backward state of the agricultural forces of production, handicrafts began to be established and, as commerce grew, a national market gradually formed with Moscow at the center. The influence of newly risen merchants was climbing, but under the conditions of a continuously intensified serf system, crafts and commerce still developed very slowly. On this foundation, the controlling classes established the most reactionary and barbarous tsarist autocratic system. The tsar possessed unlimited power. His will was propagated as the will of "God," demanding complete obedience from the people.

The cruel control and oppression of this system provoked large peasant uprisings. In response, the landed class and the new merchants demanded stronger state control and foreign aggression. The textbook explains that Peter I responded to these demands, reforming along the lines of the West. Among Peter's reforms were many aimed at strengthening central authority. Combining direct control over local administration and the church and eliminating old aristocratic ranks, the tsar now had an unprecedented absolutist autocratic system. Technological, cultural, military, industrial and other reforms strengthened the hand of the tsar. Peter applied these new powers toward aggression, year after year advancing against one neighboring country after another. After Peter's death, class contradictions intensified as serf-owner exploitation increased and the peasant struggle became more heated. The tsarist government tightened its controls at home and sought more victories in its foreign aggression. In Catherine II's reign, Russia expanded its territory greatly, appeared as a conservative force on the European political stage, and tightened control at home. These are the main features of premodern Russian history as recounted in China.[16] The more positive image of Peter and Catherine in the 1980s was accompanied by continued, if less strident, references to the history of tsarist aggression.

THE SOVIET UNION UNDER LENIN AND STALIN

With a reevaluation of Mao underway and sharp disagreements emerging on how to assess Stalin, Lenin became the undisputed authority for Chinese socialism in 1979. In July, *Hongqi* carried an article on Lenin's system for combining collective leadership and individual responsibil-

---

[16] Ibid., 225; and Chen Qineng and Yu Pei, "Sulian jinxiandaishi," *Zhongguo lishixue nianjian 1983* (Beijing: Renminchubanshe, 1983), 242-43; Lin Judai et al., *Shijie jindaishi*, (Shanghai: Shanghai renminchubanshe, 1982), 298-310.

ity.[17] It conveys the message that in office Lenin provided all the right solutions. He established all of the highest principles. He emphasized that the Communist Party has the leading role in state management; without it the dictatorship of the proletariat cannot be realized. Lenin acted correctly by bringing the main directives and important resolutions to the party congress to decide. He recognized that it is the highest authority in the party. He also understood that party members must be motivated and creative, which requires involving them in discussions of all of the most important problems. When the party congress is not in session, the Central Committee and the political bureau take charge of everyday political work. Lenin totally respected their collective leadership. He emphasized party leadership over political organs, but opposed excessive interference in their work. The result of such intrusions would be bureaucratism, a reduced sense of responsibility, and an attitude that nobody is in charge, which would make everyday work difficult to perform.

With regard to restoring and developing the economy, Lenin stressed the necessity of respecting scientists and technical experts. Party committees frequently invited specialists and experts to discuss problems. Lenin also urged that the congresses demand that speakers report conditions accurately without long presentations and empty statements. The most important task, recognized Lenin, was not to issue orders, but to select able people, to create a system of individual responsibility, and to investigate the actual work performed. Without mentioning Stalin or Mao, the article appears to criticize implicitly the cult of the personality in disregard of party congresses and central committees, party interference in state government, officials who act without consulting specialists, barriers against frank speech, and failure to check up on the performance of officials. If Lenin succeeded in limiting these problems, the implication is that they are not natural to socialism and can be eliminated in the present period.

In 1979, Stalin's views were invoked for many purposes. His name could be used to help rally Chinese communists against the radical policies that had long prevailed. Stalin's views were cited to justify changes in policy toward intellectuals, education, wage inequalities, and the importation of foreign technology. On many issues his views were introduced in an effort to justify new policies or rally support behind new proposals. For example, in 1979 opposition was mounting against the group that remained in control of heavy industry. Called the petroleum group

---

[17] Lin Jizhou, "Liening zai goujia guanli zhong zenyang shixing jiti lingdao he geren fuze xiang jiehe zhidu," *Hongqi*, no. 7 (1979): 69-74.

because of its strong support from the Ministry of Petroleum, this group
was associated with the ambitious plans developed in 1977-1978 to draw
on foreign investment for huge steel mills and other large-scale projects
to modernize heavy industry. In October 1979, the journal *Gongren ribao* carried an article on Stalin's views about the goal of socialist production. It says that in 1952, Stalin criticized the idea that production should
be increased in order to increase production, arguing instead that it is to
satisfy the material and cultural needs of the entire society. The article
wonders if the ideas Stalin opposed had not also exerted a serious influence in Chinese economic work. It claims that the aim of socialist production is to give workers the most beautiful and richest life. Theory had
not been clear about the basic economic rules of socialism, leading to
long-term neglect of consumption, of improvements in people's lives, and
of consumer goods. For this reason, the article concludes, it may be useful
to look at Stalin's 1952 view.[18]

The debate about Stalin at the time of the one hundredth anniversary
of his birth served diverse purposes. Stalin's views were invoked for
many reasons: to reject the radical program of the Cultural Revolution in
favor of utilizing all possible resources for economic construction, to reassert centralized party and state control against the challenges of reformers, and even for a time in some articles to support reformers in their pursuit of more sweeping changes. The predominant pattern in the early
stage was to combine the first and second goals. Praising Stalin's theoretical contributions highly, authors argued that he was the leader who had
long experience with building the world's first socialist society, developing an advanced economy and culture, and strengthening the proletarian
dictatorship against the opposition of some Soviets who thought that
after the exploiting classes had been eliminated the state ought to wither
away.[19]

As economic reform currents swept ahead in 1980 and the reassessment of Mao was approaching, open critiques of Stalin became more visible in Chinese journals. Stalin was now widely blamed for the economic
ills that beset China before 1979. In one article, Shi Shiyin attributes the
tortuous course of China's thirty years of economic development to copying Stalin's thought in economic theory, especially his theory of the fundamental economic laws of socialism. Four examples are given by Shi.
First, Stalin failed to express the basic feature that the masses are the
masters of the socialist economy. He did not emphasize democracy, and

[18] Jiang Yingquang and Li Yue, "Sidalin dui Yaluoshenke wei shengchan er shengchan
guandian de piping," *Gongren ribao* (October 19, 1979).

[19] He Zikun, "Xuexi Sidalin guanyu jiancheng shehuizhuyi de lilun de yixie tihui,"
Zhongshan daxue xuebao, no. 1 (1980): 19-24.

thus he created a system of excessive control in production and bureau-cratism. As a result, the creativity and ability of the masses were re-pressed. Second, Stalin deemphasized the proportionate development of each economic sector. His approach was one-sided, leading to many neg-ative long-term consequences. Third, Stalin opposed profit and meeting social needs. His theoretical error of calling profit "capitalist" had harm-ful consequences. One of the main reasons, adds Shi, that Lin Biao and the "Gang of Four" caused great enterprise waste was the influence of Stalin's theory, which violates the law of value and does not encourage the necessary economic accountability. Shi refers to superstitious dog-matism along with blindly copying Stalin's theories. Fourth, Stalin did not express the mutually advantageous relations of socialist production and producers. Labor could not become the prime need of life; to a very great extent it remained a means. The worker must feel that work also serves his own needs, individual income must continuously increase, and living conditions must gradually improve. Under Stalin's theory it is easy for leading organs to concentrate on the needs of the state, society, and the public and not to care enough about individual living needs, which is reflected in the disproportion between accumulation and consumption. Shi presents a far-reaching critique of Stalin's one-sided theory that neg-lects democracy and individual self-interests.[20]

As criticisms of Stalin were mounting by early 1980, his defenders also became more active. Wang Yumin wrote one of the strongest defenses, focusing on Stalin's Marxist worldview. At the beginning of the article he notes that two kinds of opposing views have appeared in print.[21] First it was asserted that Stalin was a revolutionary at age 15 and a Marxist at 19, as if Stalin were born a Marxist. Later it was said that the terms "great" and "genius" ought to be discarded, even that his was a vulgarization of Marxism and that there is no point of speaking of a contribution. Wang declares that neither of these is a Marxist attitude corresponding to the facts of Russian history and Stalin's life. Wang goes on to discuss the formative years of Stalin's Marxist worldview, indicating that he was not born with it but went through stages of development. His argument shows Stalin deeply influenced by Lenin's writings in high school and al-ready in 1900 completely behind Lenin's position. Under the influence of Lenin's thought, Stalin traveled the revolutionary path, applying Marx-ism successfully to the problems of the revolution, including the nation-

[20] Shi Shiyin, "Dui Sidalin guanyu shehuizhuyi jiben jingji guilu lilun de yijian," *Xue-shu yuekan*, no. 9 (1980): 27-29.

[21] Wang Yumin, "Shilun Sidalin Makesizhuyi shijieguan xingcheng de jige wenti," *She-huikexue*, no. 2 (1980): 35-44.

ality question. Wang leaves no doubt that he finds criticism of Stalin's greatness about as scientific as the belief that Stalin was born a Marxist.

He Baolin and Liu Shaochuan wrote in early 1981 in defense of Stalin.[22] Their article begins, "The great Marxist Stalin . . . ." They note that after the Twentieth Congress, Chinese theorists popularized the view of totally rejecting Stalin's theory that in a socialist society there is no contradiction between the relations of production and the forces of production. Most recently there are still people who generate this view, laying all kinds of criticisms to this theory advocated by Stalin over forty years ago. Some claim it does not correspond to the facts, some that it does not correspond to dialectical materialism; even more, there are extremists who charge this conclusion with being not only theoretically false, but also harmful in practice. They attribute to this theory by Stalin the widened purges against counterrevolutionaries in the late 1930s, the slowdown in agricultural development, the "forced unanimity" (yiyan tang) in scholarly circles, the "theory of no conflict" in artistic works, and all other political, economic, scientific, and cultural missteps and short-comings. In our view, He and Liu assert, not only is Stalin's theory consistent with the basic principles of historical materialism, it also was in practice advantageous for the development of the Soviet economy and the elevation of the people's material and cultural standard of living. The real problem, they insist, was that because of Khrushchev's total rejection of Stalin at the Twentieth Party Congress and other unspecified reasons, this Marxist theory by Stalin was distorted. In China this theory was relegated to the "thirty percent error" side. After discarding it, the results in China were bitter, not sweet. In other words, China's problems are attributed not to Stalin's legacy, as the reformers suggest, but to departing from Stalin's approach and, presumably, the Soviet model as well.

By 1980 most overall assessments of Stalin balanced pros and cons and, in the final analysis, adhered rather closely to the formula of seventy percent good, thirty percent bad. Writings in the field of philosophy from the northeastern provinces of Jilin and Heilongjiang tended to accentuate the positive while remaining close to the approved formula. One article in early 1980 begins with the statement that for many years there have been many evaluations by philosophers of Stalin's *Dialectical Materialism and Historical Materialism*. Some deny that this book is a contribution to Marxist philosophy. Others deny that there are shortcomings in this work. Our view, say the authors of the article, is that both of these views are one-sided. Stalin's contribution to Marxist philosophy in this work

---

[22] He Baolin and Liu Shaochuan, "Zhengque pingjie Sidalin de 'wanquan shihe' lun," *Shehuikexue zhanxian* (zhexue shehuikexue ban), no. 2 (1981): 55-57.

cannot be eradicated. The article then describes the main contributions, concluding with Stalin's support and enrichment of the principle of party spirit in Marxist philosophy. Afterwards it identifies some shortcomings, including the incorrect conclusion that the relations of production and the forces of production are in total agreement in a socialist society. The article insists that the contributions are primary, the problems are secondary and can be explained as a reflection of the limitations of social practice at that time.[23]

Stalin's defenders searched for new explanations of his political theory after the Cultural Revolution view that Stalin had opened the way to Soviet revisionism by not recognizing the persistence of class struggle under socialism had been discredited. An article by Hu Zhaoyin draws attention to the debate following the second session of China's Fifth National People's Congress. He says that views changed after that meeting; some comrades consider that Stalin's declaration in 1936 that the exploiting classes were eliminated corresponds to Marxism, but that his estimation of the strength and influence of the remaining exploiting class was inadequate and led to excessive concern with class struggle and to the error of widened purges. Hu says that in choosing between the old view and the new one, we must recognize that neither fully corresponds to reality. He calls for research on Stalin's theories and on Soviet history in that period. Then Hu gives his own alternative explanation.

Hu insists that Stalin did recognize the existence of classes and class struggle under socialism, that he stood behind the theory of the dictatorship of the proletariat against arbitrary distortions by the Trotsky elements. When industrialization and collectivization incited class enemies to extreme opposition, Stalin led in the repression of enemies, especially rich peasants, to preserve the fate of socialism, but was met by opposition from the opportunistic elements around Bukharin. Repeatedly Stalin pointed out that the main danger for the party is the rightist opportunism represented by Bukharin. Hu concludes that the old view that Stalin was not alert to the intensification of the class struggle is incorrect. Stalin also was vigilant against plotters such as the counterrevolutionary group around Trotsky, Zinoviev, and Kamenev, who, a party investigation showed, had killed Kirov in 1934 and intended to assassinate other persons. Hu contends that the purge movement led by Stalin was completely necessary in these conditions, but because Stalin exaggerated the remnants of the exploiting class and the severity of class struggle and because

[23] Xue Wenhua and Li Shushen, "Quanmian pingjie Sidalin de 'Lun bianzheng weiwuzhuyi he lishi weiwuzhuyi,'" *Jilin shida xuebao* (zhexue shehuikexue ban), no. 1 (1980): 3-12.

of complex political and social reasons, the purges went too far. Many people were wrongly punished, and trial methods were secret and improper. Hu then says that this gave adventurists and opportunists a chance. Khrushchev was, Hu concludes, one who was responsible for very severe widening of the purges, and he managed to rise high in these conditions.

This article is one of the best examples of how the radical and orthodox positions were becoming fused in 1979-1980 in support of the overall justification for Stalin's purges and of attacks on his main political opponents and the intense criticism of Khrushchev.[24] However, the implicit judgment that revisionism arose in the Soviet Union was already passé when this article was published; the radicals would have no recourse but to accept the more positive, orthodox assessment of Soviet society.

One of the most forthright criticisms of Stalin by the reform group was published in 1981 by Wang Ruoshui.[25] Wang begins, "Lenin points out that 'development is the struggle of opposites' and 'development is the unity of opposites.' Stalin chose 'struggle,' but discarded 'unity'; from this was born an error in systemic theory and political consequences." Wang adds that the philosophical base of the leftist guiding thought of the Cultural Revolution was to admit struggle but deny unity. Although Wang claims that Mao differed from Stalin and followed Lenin in his thinking on this subject, he also suggests that Stalin's thinking was the base for China's Cultural Revolution. Stalin's theory did not recognize contradictions between the superstructure and the substructure, contradictions among the people. With this kind of reasoning, he attributed any difference of opinion to the influence of remnants of capitalist thought, which signifies a contradiction between the enemy and us. Wang explains that this is the ideological origin of the error of Stalin's widened purge (kuodahua sufan).

The Inner-Party Struggle in the 1920s

One of the themes that has attracted Chinese reformers is the Bukharin alternative to Stalin. In June 1980, Su Shaozhi went to Italy to participate in an international conference on Bukharin. Shortly afterwards articles on Bukharin began to circulate in China. The high point of this reevaluation may date to the year 1982. In May and June alone four writings on Bukharin appeared (two were translations, one from English by E. H. Carr and one from Russian by Roy Medvedev). A few months earlier, a

[24] Hu Zhaoyin, "Yingdang quanmiande yanjiu Sidalin de jieji douzheng lilun: jian tan Sulian sufan kuodahua de yige zhongyao yuanyin," *Lanzhou shehuikexue*, no. 3 (1980): 30-34.

[25] Wang Ruoshui, "Bianzhengfa de mingyun," *Shehuikexue zhanxian* (zhexue ban), no. 3 (1981): 1-2.

collection of articles on Bukharin and Bukharin thought was published without *neibu* restrictions in the out-of-the-way province of Guizhou. Su Shaozhi's introduction, written in July 1981, may have aroused some on the orthodox side for its almost unconcealed interest in "reversing the verdict" against Bukharin.[26]

Su writes that since Bukharin was executed in 1938, the Soviets have viewed him as an enemy of the people, a fascist agent and traitor, a counter-revolutionary plotter who even had plotted against Lenin. For a long time his name was not mentioned or was merely trotted out in time of political need as a negative example to criticize. He asks, why then should we study him and his thought now? His answer is that after 1953 the Soviets reversed the verdicts on some convicted dead persons, restoring their honor and proving that the cases against them had not been real. Yet Bukharin, Rykov, and other famous men of this type were not included. Despite an appeal in 1961 from an old Bolshevik who had worked with Lenin and a public declaration by an official at a 1962 all-union historical conference that Bukharin was not a traitor, despite appeals in 1961 and 1977 by his widow and son, no action was taken by the Soviet leadership. Su declares that world petitions have been sent, an international movement exists to reverse the verdict, and world opinion is on Bukharin's side. The need to act is not just for historical accuracy, but also for moral and political reasons. According to Su, the majority of Western scholars, and Chinese as well, see Bukharin thought as the only Bolshevik plan for socialist construction apart from Stalin's path. Since the 1960s in Europe, people who have searched for another path to socialism and have sought reform of the economic system could not avoid thinking back to the 1920s and Bukharin, the main theorist of the NEP. Although Chinese usually shun the term "Stalinism" (Sidalinzhuyi), Su uses it in this discussion. Su mentions that an article on the June 1980 conference even suggested that Bukharin is respected as the forerunner of Eurocommunism, and adds that this was disputed at the conference, which was against all dogmatism. He explains that the book on Bukharin aims to "liberate our thought, open our eyes, seek truth from practice."

In his 1984 two-page review of Soviet studies in China, Chen Zhihua identifies as one of the major themes after the economic history of 1917-1937 the history of the inner-party struggle in the 1920s. Researchers have emphasized this problem in recent years. Chen mentions his own 1981 article, which raised new outlooks about some theoretical viewpoints of Bukharin, indicating that this aroused a considerable reaction in historical circles. He notes also a 1984 article by him on Bukharin's

[26] Zhongguo shehuikexueyuan MaLiezhuyi Mao Zedong sixiang yanjiusuo, ed., *Lun Buhalin sixiang* (Guiyang: Guizhou renminchubanshe, 1982), i-iii.

thought regarding socialist economic construction. Comparing the two, he concludes that one can observe that research on Bukharin is gradually deepening. Researchers no longer simply advocate a reevaluation of the Bukharin question, but engage in concrete analyses of his theories, examining which are correct and which are in error. The great majority of comrades recognize that although Bukharin committed one kind of error or another, historically his work is an important contribution. His various theoretical viewpoints, whether in economics or in thought and culture, seen from today, all have quite a lot of things that are worthy of approval and further research.

Some researchers bring up other concrete questions of the inner-party struggle, such as the question of Trotsky's contributions to the October Revolution and the Civil War periods, the question of his role in the process of signing the Brest-Litovsk peace treaty, the question of his mistakes in the dispute over labor unions, as well as the errors of Zinoviev and Kamenev in the period of preparation for the October armed uprising. Recent articles have proposed outlooks not completely similar to traditional viewpoints. The opening of research on the inner-party struggle, Chen adds, will make research on Soviet history livelier and deeper. It will lead to a scholarly search focused on the advocates of diverse views, a completely different matter from following how the party and the state were represented in speeches to the outside. Chen says that restrictions should all be broken down, adding that although the problem has not yet been completely resolved, research workers feel more and more that scholarly questions and political questions should be separate in order to advance research on Soviet history and better draw on historical experience.[27]

Su Shaozhi on Reform

One of Su Shaozhi's strongest reform statements was written for the 1983 conference to commemorate the centenary of Karl Marx's death and has been translated into English.[28] Su argues that when Marxism stops developing, it becomes lifeless. Critics are to a certain degree justified in seeing Marxism as outmoded or in crisis because of the dogmatic attitude taken toward it. Sanctifying Soviet experiences and the personality cult, and closing the door to ideas from outside, impeded the development of Marxism. Su adds that Marxism must focus on current social problems in order to advance and better reveal the laws of development of human

[27] Chen Zhihua, "Sulian xiandaishi yanjiu de xin jumian ye yi xingcheng," in "Huigu sanshi nianlai de chengjiu kaishi shijieshi yanjiu de xin jumian," *Shijie zhishi*, no. 5 (1984): 5-6.

[28] Su Shaozhi, "Develop Marxism Under Contemporary Conditions: In Commemoration of the Centenary of the Death of Karl Marx," *Selected Writings on Studies of Marxism*, no. 2 (Beijing: Institute of Marxism-Leninism-Mao Zedong Thought, 1983), 1-39.

society. He makes clear that it is more important to apply the basic methodology of Marxism—to analyze actual conditions—than to cite "some relevant passages from classical Marxist writings." Stalin's death ended what Su seems to see as a lifeless period of "the domination of 'one centre, one road and one model.' " Marxists then began to proceed from concrete realities in their own countries; in Su's words, diversity replaced stereotype. What are the new historical events that Marxism must address if it is not to "suffer in prestige"? Su lists the expulsion of Yugoslavia, the criticism of Stalin at the Twentieth Congress, the Polish and Hungarian events of 1956, the Sino-Soviet polemics, the "Cultural Revolution" in China, the "Prague Spring" and its suppression, the Soviet invasion of Afghanistan, Vietnam's invasion of Kampuchea and the failure of the Kampuchean Communist Party, the military control of Poland, Albania's conflicts with other communist parties, "the nationalist movement within the Soviet 'community of nations,' " and Eurocommunism. Su calls for collecting firsthand data and analyzing on the basis of facts "instead of leaving a blank in the theory of Marxism as far as this eventful period is concluded." This is a remarkable list that virtually duplicates what non-Marxist critics see as the major failures in international relations within the communist bloc.

Su Shaozhi's reform agenda for research extends further. He urges researchers to expand their data base, to include for example deleted parts of the texts of the previous editions of Lenin's works, Lenin's will, and unspecified original data and unofficial histories regarding major events. He argues that this means reassessment of War Communism, the NEP, Stalin's "road of industrialization," Stalin's "revolution from top to bottom," "the truth of the magnification of the scope of the Soviet struggle against the counterrevolutionaries" (a stock phrase in Chinese writings), "the historical role of the Third International, Trotsky and the Fourth International, and the theories of Roza Luxemburg, Nikolai Bukharin, and Antonio Gramsci."

Su notes that Lenin saw defects in the Soviet system, "and that is why he raised the questions of democratizing the organs of the proletarian dictatorship and the Soviets, of opposing bureaucratism and overconcentration of powers, and of giving full play to the role of co-operatives. Stalin deviated from Lenin's thinking on these questions, and this led to serious tragedy for the Soviet party and state as well as for Stalin himself. Studies of what has been described above will not only help restore the true features of history but also have a direct bearing on the contemporary development of Marxism."

This remarkable article proceeds to treat Stalin and Mao together, mentioning their "outstanding deeds in guiding the practice of socialism" and their "gross miscalculations which find expression in their respective theories." It makes a plea for comparative studies of the socialist system. The first group of questions to be answered through comparisons pertains to politics: questions of the changes the Communist Party undergoes as a ruling party, of the succession of younger people to the party's leadership, of the respective powers and responsibilities of the ruling party and the state organs, of the relationship of party activities and the legal system, of the relations between the party and the mass organizations, of building a high level of socialist democracy, and of the relations among nationalities in the country.[29] These are among Su's many concerns in what might be called a reform agenda for comparisons of the Soviet Union, China, and other socialist countries, centering on the effects of ideology and politics.

In the still rather confused circumstances of 1979, Su Shaozhi and Feng Lanrui raised the question of the stages of social development after the proletariat seizes power.[30] The principle that seems to operate in general, and clearly in Chinese critiques of Soviet claims to be in developed socialism or some other advanced stage, is the lower the stage, the more necessity for substantial reform. A low stage implies that much more needs to be done to achieve the goals of communism and that the methods employed in the past may be discarded in accord with the further development of the forces of production. It also justifies combining so-called capitalist measures with socialist ones since the society is not ready for the purely socialist arrangements. Su and Feng emphasize that it is useful to identify stages in order to think clearly about appropriate policies. They recognize that socialism is not communism and that the transition to socialism is not socialism. They quote Lenin as saying that the transition to socialism is very long and that given Russia's backward conditions it would take longer. Su and Feng assert that in China, with its even lower levels of development, this transition had to require even more time. They explain that developed socialism implies mechanization, great wealth of material goods, vastly heightened communist consciousness, the prior elimination of the force of custom and the psychology of the small-scale producer. China will have to pass through a very long period of undeveloped socialism to reach that stage.

In the uncertain circumstances of 1979, not only revisionism but also socialism required redefinition. Reformers could avail themselves of many strategies in the attempt to stay one step ahead of the censors and the official pronouncements that closed off particular areas of inquiry.

[29] Ibid., 21-25.

[30] Su Shaozhi and Feng Lanrui, "Wuchanjieji qude zhengquan hou de shehui fazhan jieduan wenti," *Jingji yanjiu*, no. 5 (1979): 14-19.

The most direct line of attack would, of course, have been the examination of errors committed by the Chinese Communist Party and Chairman Mao, yet it was clear almost from the outset that ritualistic statements rather than research would be the only permissible way of treating this area. Writings about philosophical themes, such as humanism, that implicitly explored the relationship between socialism and capitalism became an indirect and generally tolerated mode of expression for reform ideas. In 1983-1984 these writings became the battleground in the orthodox assault against spiritual pollution. Particularly in 1979 and, to a diminishing extent, in 1980-1982, other paths of thought were explored. There was no lack of ingenuity among the advocates of far-reaching reform as they scrutinized each new slogan or policy initiative in the search for themes that could be turned to their advantage. Although acknowledging that the dictatorship of the proletariat is necessary, they criticize Stalin for interpreting it as the capacity to resist foreign aggressors.

Su and Feng raise the question, is China socialist? Their answer is that it is different from the Soviet Union in 1918. It has passed that stage because not only has the proletariat obtained power and established a proletarian dictatorship, but China has completed the socialist reform of the ownership of the means of production. But, the two authors add, one still cannot say we have established the socialist society (the first stage of a communist society) that Marx and Engels envisioned. The persistence of capitalist and feudal remnants, the predominance of small-scale producers and their customs and psychology, signifies that China is still an undeveloped socialist society, is still in the transitional stage of socialism. Our economic system, they inject, is also not developed or complete socialism. Confusion over stages, they conclude, leads to policies that are ahead of their times, that damage motivation, relations of production, and productivity. Although this article goes further than others in challenging China's readiness for socialist policies, its message about policies that rush ahead of what is appropriate for a society's stage of development can be found in many Chinese sources on the Soviet economy and its ideology of developed socialism.

In 1979-1980 the issue of how to maintain the dynamism of socialist economies was often discussed in rather forthright terms. The decision was reached that the old Stalin model of tight central control would have to be replaced. Steps by socialist countries to break away from this model were to be applauded. These steps often had political implications that Chinese could not easily examine in print. Yugoslavia had broken with Stalin and thus became the first country that succeeded in the 1950s in breaking away from the old model of economic management. Hungary's economic reforms followed the Hungarian uprising of 1956. The official

Chinese position remains that this uprising was an attack against socialism, in part provoked by the Soviet Twentieth Party Congress, but I understand that in at least one internally circulated article it was suggested
that the Hungarian events of 1956 were caused by mistakes inside Hungary related to the Stalin model and that the uprising had positive consequences for the substantial economic reforms that followed.

In an early 1980 article about the reform of the Hungarian economic
system, Su Shaozhi notes that after World War II all socialist states
adopted the Soviet-style centralized planned economy.[31] After Yugoslavia broke away, it gradually developed an independent socialist self-
management system. Su adds that after 1956 (an interesting choice that
highlights the positive consequences of the Twentieth Congress) and especially from the 1960s, each socialist state experimented with economic
reforms, giving birth to different models. Su credits Otto Sik during the
Czechoslovakian reforms of 1968 with dividing socialist countries according to three models: 1) reliance on some market principles in the Soviet
Union and Czechoslovakia; 2) only sprouts of market principles in Poland; and 3) relatively complete dependence on market principles in Hungary. Su also cites the Western economist W. Bruce as sharply distinguishing the Soviet Union's centralized (*jiquan xing*) type of economy
from Hungary's system of dispersed authority (*fenquan xing*). He adds
that Hungarian economists consider its economic system separate from
the Soviet centralized economy and close to the Yugoslavian dispersed
system. Su concludes by contrasting Hungary and Yugoslavia, arguing
that the latter with its system of socialist autonomy has completely broken out of the bounds of the Soviet economic system. The Hungarian
system has broken the bounds to a certain extent, but state planning remains the foundation. Such subtle references to 1956 and 1968 verge on
the limits of what has been possible, even in 1980 and in a *neibu* publication, in writing about the political problems associated with economic
reform.

Stalin Versus Lenin

Not much has been published that focuses directly on differences of opinion between Lenin and Stalin. An exception is a short review amid a series
of reviews of controversial issues in the journal *Xueshu yuekan* at the end
of 1983.[32] It examines opinions on the question of whether Lenin's and
Stalin's explanations of the nature of imperialism's imminent death are

[31] Su Shaozhi, "Xiongyali jingji tizhi gaige zhong de ruogan lilun wenti," *Jingji wenti
tansuo*, no. 2 (1980).
[32] Liang Bin, "Liening he Sidalin guanyu diguozhuyi chuisi xing de lunshu shifou yizhi,"
Xueshu yuekan, no. 12 (1983): 76-77.

the same. One opinion has it that whether in theory or policy, Stalin's views do not correspond to Lenin's. Lenin wrote completely from the historical position of imperialism and economic analysis, while Stalin focused on political analysis. Another opinion is that they are not fundamentally in disagreement; both think that imperialism will very quickly disappear. Lenin arrived at this conclusion from an economic standpoint, while Stalin did so mainly from a political argument. Finally the article cites one other opinion, that Lenin's and Stalin's thinking on this subject were not fundamentally different, and moreover Stalin's explanations completely followed Lenin's thought. They both started from the historical position of imperialism; only in their methods were there minor differences, such as Stalin combining economics and politics in the analysis. While this brief review is perhaps too abstract to understand the implications of the disputed issues, it at least gives the reader some evidence of the debate over whether Lenin and Stalin should be grouped together or whether Stalin should be separated from Lenin and treated critically.

Two Textbook Accounts

At the beginning of 1985 there had not yet appeared any Chinese overviews of Soviet political history or history in general. Nevertheless, the period of greatest uncertainty seemed to be drawing to a close. Over the previous six years Chinese views had gradually crystallized, not necessarily leading to agreement but at least establishing the limits of disagreement. Plans were already being announced to publish books that would represent the new consensus. Perhaps the first book of this type (although one that does not adequately represent recent scholarship) went to press in August 1984. Entitled *History of the International Communist Movement*, it is a textbook for correspondence schools written by a committee representing eight teachers' colleges.[33] The editorial group explains that the book is appropriate for political education classes in correspondence schools or all-day schools at the level of higher education. Cadres may use it in refresher courses; part-time and television universities may also find it helpful. Teachers of middle-school politics classes and graduates of upper middle schools can use it for self-study. Of the eight chapters, the first three treat Marxism from its origins to the beginning of the twentieth century. Chapter 4 focuses on the establishment of Russia's Social Democratic Party and the 1905 Revolution. Chapter 5 largely treats Lenin's views during World War I and the events of the

[33] Ba yuanxiao hanshou jiaocai bianxie zu, *Guoji gongchanzhuyi yundong shi* (Henan: Henan renminchubanshe, 1984).

Russian Revolution. Chapter 6 examines the Bolsheviks in power and the first stage of the Comintern. About half of Chapter 7 analyzes the struggle to build socialism under Stalin through the 1930s. The remainder of that chapter and Chapter 8 as well turn to the Comintern in the 1930s and 1940s, ending with the victory of the Chinese Communist Revolution. Over a quarter of this 435-page book is on Russian and Soviet history over a half-century to World War II.

This textbook shows how the controversies among Soviet and Marxist specialists are resolved in a volume designed for classroom use and a wide audience. The product leans to the side of orthodoxy without failing to mention some shortcomings in Soviet history that reformers have noted. The relative weightings are perhaps best revealed in the coverage given to three important issues: 1) Bukharin and the inner-party struggles of the twenties; 2) collectivization and the economic policies of the thirties; and 3) purges and Stalin's personal role in leading the country.

Coverage of the Russian revolutionary movement from the 1890s to 1917 offers no surprises. Since Chinese leaders—both Mao and his successors—have not allowed any reexamination of Lenin's interpretations of Russian history through 1917, the account in the 1984 textbook conveys a standard line. A new stage of capitalism had been reached around 1900. It was characterized by imperialism and monopolies. In these circumstances three principal contradictions intensified: 1) between the proletariat and the capitalist class; 2) between the imperialist countries and the colonial peoples; and 3) among the imperialist countries. Capitalism prospered, bringing enormous increases in production from the 1860s to the 1900s. Under these stable and peaceful circumstances revisionism spread. The textbook devotes a section to Bernstein's revisionism, including his rejection of class struggle and violent uprising. It accuses him and others like him of abandoning communism, attacking the basic principles of Marxist political economy, forgetting the basic nature of the capitalist system, proclaiming the "adaptability of capitalism," and becoming accustomed to using capitalist parliaments to wage a legal struggle. Advocacy of class cooperation and social reform were signs of the increasing influence of petty bourgeois thinking. Capitalists used a small part of their vast profits to turn some workers into a worker aristocracy, who became the main social foundation for revisionism. As monopoly capitalism developed, it drove great numbers of small producers to bankruptcy, forcing them into the ranks of the proletariat. Because they still maintained the narrow vision of the small producer and sought only the small gains that appeared before their eyes, they were attracted to revisionism too. To preserve their power, capitalists added "sugar-coated" policies to policies of the "whip." On the surface, "liberalism" appeared to shift from

force to tolerance, to widen political rights, to adopt miscellaneous reforms to increase worker welfare. Bernstein's revisionism corresponds to
the needs of imperialism and is its accomplice. It wears a Marxist cloak to
oppose Marxism. It consciously uses the viewpoint of capitalism to revise
the basic principles of Marxism. Revisionism is very deceptive and dangerous.[34]

Shortly after this section on Bernstein in Chapter 4, the textbook turns
to Lenin's success in counteracting revisionism in Russia. It notes that although politically and economically tsarist Russia was a backward, feudal
empire, after serfdom was abolished capitalism developed quite rapidly,
and Russia also entered the stage of imperialism around 1900. Economically, monopoly capitalism and remnants of capitalism mixed together.
Land was still concentrated in the hands of a small number of aristocratic
landowners who relied on a semi-serf system of exploitation. Monopoly
capitalists in pursuit of high profits often used noneconomic means, forcing workers to labor 14-16 hours a day, wages to be abnormally low, and
the broad mass of workers to live a half-starving life. The working masses
suffered cruel feudal control and thus had a higher revolutionary potential than in other countries. This is seen in the continuous development
of strikes. Nevertheless, conciliatory "economist" thinking directly
threatened the Russian workers' movement and the fate of the party.
Lenin recognized the danger and exposed the reactionary nature of many
revisionist views, such as the capitalist slogan of "freedom."[35]

After the victory of the October Revolution, Lenin followed Marx and
Engels, pointing to the need for proletarian dictatorship to replace capitalist dictatorship. Only in this way could the exploiting classes and their
remaining elements be resisted. Lenin recognized that proletarian dictatorship is the fundamental question of the proletarian revolution. It is the
essence of Marxist state theory, and the testing ground for separating real
Marxists from phony ones.[36]

The policies of the Soviet government in the first period of its power
are strongly endorsed. It wiped out the feudal system, enacted a universal
system of elections, established a system of mass supervision from the
bottom up, and strengthened the worker-peasant alliance through land
reform. Because many capitalists opposed worker control and supervision
and intentionally shut down, sabotaged, hoarded, and damaged materials,
or plotted to drain the enterprises of their capital, the Soviet government
enacted legislation and arrested people. The government closed the coun-

[34] Ibid., 181-89.
[35] Ibid., 193-94, 198-99.
[36] Ibid., 271, 276.

terrevolutionary capitalist papers, separated schools from the church, and established equality among nationalities. War Communism brought some emergency measures, such as requisitioning surplus grain, prohibiting private trade in grain, and centralizing factory management, but these were not measures of a socialist economy or of peacetime. The textbook explains that these measures exceeded the actual level of the forces of production and harmed the material interests of middle and poor peasants. The Soviet government of the time, because it lacked experience building socialism, subjectively regarded these as the basic measures for the transition to socialism, committing a serious error. Afterwards Lenin investigated this error, admitted it, and changed these policies. The NEP corresponds to the special conditions of Russia's transition, where small-scale commercial production and small peasant producers predominated. These conditions made it necessary to develop commercial ties between cities and villages, to strengthen the worker-peasant alliance, and to build a foundation for a socialist economy. The NEP is of great significance, for it shows the necessity in an economically undeveloped country to go through a set of special measures. Quickly the Soviet economy turned for the better; by 1924-1925 it was close to prewar levels.[37]

The most controversial sections in the textbook's discussion of the Soviet Union center on politics in the 1920s and 1930s. The basic viewpoint is that the new state organs were completely different from political organs of all governments under the control of exploiting classes. Yet the text also points out "because of various complex reasons" there still existed in state organs such phenomena as bureaucratism, suppression of democracy, even embezzlement and corruption. These problems influenced the close relations between state organs and the masses, even creating the danger of transforming the nature of the Soviet government. Lenin insisted on many countervailing measures, such as widely proclaiming socialist democracy, gradually bringing all of the working people to participate in management, and establishing a full legal system. After the party gained power, some connivers and bad elements tried to worm their way inside; therefore the party needed to cleanse its ranks. Lenin also called for education, democracy, and criticism, self-criticism in the party to change the workstyle. The textbook stresses Lenin's valuable guidance, not the mistakes made in the Soviet Union or the reasons for them.[38]

Political troubles of the 1920s are blamed on Stalin's opponents. Trotsky is characterized as a longtime opponent of Lenin who, although he

[37] Ibid., 285-86, 290, 297-99.
[38] Ibid., 303-305.

had a certain positive role in the establishment of the country, committed errors, such as rejecting the Brest-Litovsk Treaty of 1918 and provoking in 1920-1921 a dispute over trade unions. Lenin was dissatisfied with him on these occasions. Gradually Trotsky formed a leftist viewpoint, as in his "theory of uninterrupted revolution" and his advocacy of exploiting the peasantry to develop industry. Despite rebukes from the party Central Committee, Trotsky did not change. Moreover, he slandered the work of the Central Committee and publicly disseminated information without obtaining approval. The textbook makes it seem as if only after repeated provocation did the central leadership and Stalin act against Trotsky's petty-bourgeois tendencies. While the entire party and people were studying Lenin and following the Leninist path, Trotsky plotted to lead the party away from the Leninist path and to substitute Trotskyism for Leninism. He angered the old Bolsheviks who had been with Lenin.

Due to capitalist encirclement and domestic backwardness, Stalin was correct in seeing the necessity of rapid industrialization on the basis of the Soviet Union's own resources. His proposals were favorably received by party congresses, which resolved to root out capitalism from the economy and begin socialist industrialization. When Zinoviev and Kamenev rejected the possibility of building socialism in the Soviet Union and favored concentrating on raw materials and grain to exchange for foreign machinery, when they arbitrarily said that the NEP is a retreat toward capitalism and advocated freedom for factional activism inside the party, the party congress in 1925 rebuked their capitalist views. Soon the entire working people threw themselves into the high tide of building socialism. Zinoviev and Kamenev would not desist and in 1926 united with Trotsky in an anti-party alliance. Their expulsion from the party and punishments in 1928, 1929, and 1936 are fully supported by the textbook.

The decisions from 1927 to speed up industrialization and collectivization are praised as well. After research and discussion, leaders recognized that the small-scale fragmentation of production was the main cause of slow agricultural development. The basic task of the party in the village was to create large-scale collective farms and to follow the class line of firmly opposing the rich peasants, while relying on the poor peasants and uniting with the middle peasants. The state helped out, providing tractors and machinery for the farms and giving loans. The rich peasants were told to give up their surplus grain at state-determined prices, but instead opened an attack. This was the situation in 1929 that brought on all-out collectivization. The textbook does not hide the fact that leftist deviations occurred almost everywhere. Many places violated the principle of voluntary entry, even confiscating property, taking away election rights to force entry; some areas one-sidedly pursued rapid expansion and more public forms of ownership, even nationalizing dwellings and small livestock. These acts made middle peasants dissatisfied and caused agricultural production to fall. Stalin's name enters the presentation at this point. The textbook mentions his "Dizzy with Success" article of March 2, 1930, which emphasized voluntary membership and criticized the use of coercive measures. His speech was welcomed by the peasants. But Stalin's article laid the blame on the inexperience of local cadres and on enemy wreckers. He failed to make a self-criticism, and even more to point out the reasons for the errors. The leftist mistakes were now to a certain extent corrected; for example, the more one worked on the collective farm, the more income one received, and personal plots and livestock were permitted. The book refers to the "successes of agricultural collectivization"; to a certain degree it provided the supplies for socialist construction, it created the conditions for the mechanization of agriculture, it eliminated the rich peasant class, thus creating a dependable social foundation by changing the class system in the village. The book also notes not a few problems, including haste, coercive measures, falling production for a time, not-very-good solutions for the management system and the distribution according to labor, and long-term problems of motivation and productivity.[39]

Bukharin figures in the discussion at this point. His alternative approach is discussed. The book then asserts that Stalin considered Bukharin's views to be opposed to the party's industrialization and collectivization policies and a rightist line. The Central Committee supported Stalin and removed Bukharin from his party and government posts while warning Rykov. This is the extent of the discussion of Bukharin's fate and Stalin's actions against him.

The analysis continues with praise for the elimination of capitalist elements and the great success of industrialization in the first two Five-Year Plans. Stalin is repeatedly credited with wise decisions (e.g. his emphasis on technology and well-trained cadres). From 1928 the Soviet Union transformed quickly from a backward agricultural country to an advanced industrial country. Simultaneously, it eliminated unemployment and raised notably the material and cultural standard of living of the people. The real wages of workers rose five times from 1913 to 1940, and the cash income of collective farmers doubled, says this source. Housing conditions greatly improved. The superiority of the socialist system began to be revealed. The Stakhanovite movement showed the new socialist work attitudes of the masses of workers and their rising technical levels. Political consciousness and work enthusiasm rose continuously. These great

[39] Ibid., 343-56.

successes were of considerable significance in the victory against fascism that came later.

Politically, according to the textbook, the party was strengthened, factional activity was curbed, and the leadership nucleus with Stalin in the lead was unified. These steps strengthened party leadership for the construction of socialism. The party continuously recruited leading elements among workers, peasants, and the intelligentsia, thus making the party ranks healthier. In 1933-1934 there was a purge to cleanse the party, but it gave rise to missteps, removing some loyal party members. In building up the party, the emphasis was placed on supporting a Leninist work atmosphere, opposing bureaucratism, requiring diligent study of technology and science by cadres, and seeking truth from practice in guiding economic construction. This message to readers stresses the positive political results of the 1930s with only minor attention to the mistakes of the purges.

The acceptance of a new constitution in 1936 is also treated positively. It used legal forms to strengthen the victorious results of socialism and correctly proclaimed the establishment of a socialist society because all exploiting classes were eliminated. Stalin also correctly recognized a year later that remnants of the exploiting classes and class struggle still had to be taken into account. Having said this, the book adds that Stalin exaggerated the severity of class struggle, which resulted in the widening of the purges. Although the purges punished some counterrevolutionary elements that it was necessary to punish, it was a mistake to widen them. Many loyal communists and revolutionary comrades were wrongly accused as imperialist spies and killed. The party and state suffered severe losses. Later Stalin recognized that serious errors had been committed in the purges. This presentation mentions Stalin only as the one who recognized the mistakes already committed, neglecting to identify his role in launching the purges. Then it immediately follows with the remark that favorable conditions were created for the development of socialist democracy. The concrete provisions of the new constitution and the elimination of some past limitations on elections, leading to direct, universal, equal, and anonymous ballots, broadened socialist democracy, concludes the 1984 textbook.

Summing up the pros and cons of the Soviet experience, the textbook first praises the development of the socialist economy, including agricultural collectivization. Second, it compliments continuous improvements in the material and cultural living standards on this newly developed production base. In Soviet socialist construction, attention was always paid to raising the material welfare of the people, to improving housing conditions, health care, and scientific and cultural levels. These achievements show the superiority of socialism. Third, the book applauds maintaining the dictatorship of the proletariat and strengthening the worker-peasant alliance. The Soviet Union built up its defense and waged a struggle against all anti-socialist class enemies at home and abroad, also being careful to gradually develop socialist democracy. Fourth, the Soviets strengthened and improved party leadership. From beginning to end, socialist construction was carried out under the leadership of the Communist Party. Soviets paid attention to strengthening party discipline and unity. They preserved Lenin's theories in the struggles against Trotsky and other opposition factions. They also paid attention to strengthening political thought work, encouraging diligent study of revolutionary theory as well as science and technology.

On the negative side, the textbook explains that in the first country to build socialism there was no prior experience to borrow. If one adds to this the complex internal and external conditions and some subjective shortcomings of Stalin, it is understandable that there were mistakes. First, for a certain time, based on the historical necessity to develop heavy industry, there was one-sidedness that left disproportions unfavorable to agriculture and light industry and to meeting the increasing demands of the people. Second, agricultural collectivization went too fast for the level of development of the forces of production, leading to coercion, harm to the interests of middle peasants, and damage to the sense of responsibility and motivation of peasants. Third, some errors were also committed in political life, with serious results. Relations between the leader and the party were not handled correctly, the cult of the personality grew more serious, power was too centralized, the system of socialist democracy was not healthy, the purges were widened.[40] These negative conclusions appear to somewhat qualify—even contradict—the overall positive tone of the book's coverage.

In December 1983 another textbook, from Heilongjiang province, went to press, entitled *History of the International Communist Movement*. Volume Two treats the Soviet Union at length, covering from World War I to the post-war recovery. Treatment of the dispute between Trotsky and Stalin fully supports the latter. Trotsky is accused of trying to split the party, failing to heed party decisions, distorting Leninism, and trumpeting Trotskyism. Stalin is portrayed as acting in defense of Leninism and on behalf of the party. On all disputed points, Stalin was correct as he worked to make the party into a true Marxist-Leninist party. Stalin deserves praise, the book indicates, for his important role in defending Len-

[40] Ibid., 358-65.

inism and burying Trotskyism.[41] As in almost all Chinese writings, the term "Stalinism" is avoided.

On collectivization from the fall of 1929, the book argues that not only the poor peasants, but also the mass of middle peasants was attracted into the collectivization movement. There was much enthusiasm to join. For many years rich peasants had used various tricks to resist Soviet government restrictions. In 1929 they spread lies, incited people to leave home, engaged in anti-Soviet propaganda, poisoned livestock on collective farms, and brutally killed party and state workers and activists, even organizing anti-Soviet violence. It was necessary to repress them and to eliminate the rich peasant economy. The book acknowledges that some mistakes were made, especially because of confusion, and it claims that the enemies of the Soviet government, especially rich peasants, used these errors in the collectivization movement to incite opposition and cause great losses. The mistakes were soon corrected, however, and the collectivization movement developed anew.

Coverage of Bukharin is limited to five sentences. The textbook notes without comment many aspects of collectivization that he opposed, then says that Stalin and the Central Committee considered his views rightist opportunist and removed him from his posts. It adds that in 1938, because of conviction on the charge of "crimes against the state," Bukharin was sentenced to death.

The following section of the book praises the 1936 constitution. It lauds the constitution's worldwide influence on the struggle for liberation and its reflection of the great achievements already realized in the Soviet Union. The book refers to the new electoral system with anonymous ballots, the principle of voluntary federation for the various nationalities, and the equal rights and duties of the Soviet people. Briefly commenting on the purges that punished some counterrevolutionaries who needed to be punished but then widened to include many loyal communists and innocent citizens, the textbook concludes with a reference to Stalin's 1939 speech, which recognized that although serious mistakes had been made, they were difficult to avoid.[42]

The textbook sums up the pros and cons of the Soviet experience under Stalin. The favorable comments predominate, but three negative lessons are cited after being explained as caused by the lack of experience with socialism elsewhere from which to borrow and the "difficult and complex" internal and external situation. First, although high-speed indus-

[41] *Guoji gongchanzhuyi yundong shi*, vol. 2 (Harbin: Heilongjiang renminchubanshe, 1983), 694–708.
[42] Ibid., 709–717, 724–26.

trialization was necessary, there should have been an effort after the First
Five-Year Plan to restore equilibrium to the economy. Without it, the
people faced long-term shortages of consumer goods, and agricultural
production remained low. Second, collectivization was not voluntary and
occurred in a rush. Despite corrective measures, there were negative consequences for productivity. The biggest problem was that the collective
farmers bore too heavy a burden. The textbook quotes Mao's criticisms
of this Soviet approach. Third, in this concluding passage the text at last
notes Stalin's cult of personality, which led to excessively centralized
power. To a certain extent this damaged the principles of party democratic
centralism and collective leadership, harming socialist democracy and the
legal system and leading to the widened purges. With these brief comments—mostly clichés—the evaluation of the 1920s and 1930s ends.[43]

A PERSONAL RECOLLECTION

Reminiscences play a limited but perceptible role in Chinese thinking
about the Soviet Union. Wu Xiuquan's memoirs covering 1950 to 1958
are undoubtedly the most prominent publication of this sort. They were
excerpted in the popular journal *Shijie zhishi* and went to press as a book
later in 1983. Having served as a general in the People's Liberation Army,
Wu also studied in the Soviet Union prior to 1932 and later returned there
as a diplomat in 1950 and 1953. At other times he used his command of
Russian while in charge of Soviet affairs in the Foreign Ministry, and
from 1955 to 1958 as China's ambassador to Yugoslavia.

Wu recalls the meetings between Mao, Zhou Enlai, and other Chinese
visitors and Stalin in 1949-1950. He mentions that the victorious path of
the Chinese Revolution was chosen by the Chinese Communist Party
against the wishes of Stalin, but in meeting with Liu Shaoqi in 1949 Stalin admitted that he had interfered inappropriately and felt badly about
it. It was very difficult for Stalin to make this sort of self-criticism even if
it was in private. At the same time, the Soviets feared that China would
follow the Yugoslavian path, and they harbored doubts about representatives of the democratic parties and nonparty people serving in the government; therefore the Soviet attitude toward the Chinese was cold and
suspicious.

Wu also recounts that when he was with Zhou Enlai and Mao in Moscow during the winter of 1950, discussions, even disputes, went on for a
long time over the wording of a treaty. Setting forth the terms of the
treaty that was signed, he says only a little about the issues that were disputed. Wu concludes that the treaty maintained China's independent

[43] Ibid., 726-32.

sovereignty and advanced its economic construction. He notes some tendencies of Soviet national interest, but adds that the Chinese stressed the overall situation and did not quarrel about some specific problems. Stalin and other Soviet leaders were quite enthusiastic toward their visitors and were ready to help China's construction. Although the cult of personality had already formed, Wu finds that Stalin was quite friendly and not like the fearful "tyrant" depicted in Western propaganda. He was quite respectful and courteous to Mao and Zhou. The two sides were largely in agreement; there was no divergence on any matter of principle.[44]

After China's leaders had departed, Wu stayed behind for economic talks with Mikoyan. These talks did not go as smoothly. The two sides hotly disputed the relative values to be assigned to their respective currencies. Wu alleges that the Soviet side was adamant about giving the ruble a high value. All the participants were very unhappy. Only after the Chinese made some concessions and compromises, actually under quite unequal conditions, did the two sides agree on the ratio of currency values. Wu adds, "We felt comparatively clearly the great power chauvinism and pursuit of national advantage existing in the Soviet Union. For their own country's interests, they forced their will on others without considering the other country's interests. That the Soviet Union later became an expansionist superpower and pursued hegemonism is not accidental. In Stalin's time these sprouts existed."

Wu lists many agreements reached in 1950 and singles out the jointly run companies in Xinjiang, saying they were mutually advantageous at the time. China had no money, equipment, or technology, but it had rich raw materials, which in the 1930s the Soviet Union had already participated in developing. The Soviets also obtained many advantages. Thus both sides gained. China preserved its independence. The Soviets went all-out to help, but did not exploit. On the whole, Wu praises these accords, especially because only the Soviet Union and Eastern European countries helped his country to overcome the imperialist policies to close off China. Rumors from the West of Soviet annexation of North China or control over China are rejected by Wu, who says their relations were, on the whole, equal. For small compromises, China secured long-term gains. In the first half of the 1950s, while Wu was in charge of Soviet and Eastern European affairs, this spirit persisted although there were both friendship and contradictions. Wu mentions that the Soviets at one point tried to increase the scale of the oil fields they operated in Xinjiang. The

---

[44] Wu Xiuquan, *Zai waijiaobu banian de jingli: January 1950–October 1958* (Beijing: Shijie zhishi chubanshe, 1983), 1-16; and "Sui fang Mosike ji Zhong Su guanxi quji," *Shijie zhishi*, no. 16 (1983).

Chinese refused. On another occasion, the Soviet Union recommended a movie about a traveller who went to China, but the movie depicted the Chinese as completely poor and ignorant and showed small acts of charity totally within the framework of imperialists. Wu says this embarrassed the Chinese people, causing Zhou Yang to discuss it with the Soviet ambassador and ask that it be withdrawn as harmful to Sino-Soviet friendship.

Wu also recalls his experience at Stalin's funeral. He was deeply impressed by the mourning. Although Stalin had made mistakes and had killed very many people in the purges, Wu's group considered the sorrow to be sincere and from the heart. It is only natural that people cherish their leader when Soviet development and achievements under Stalin were striking. Stalin's sudden death was a great shock to the Soviet Union and the world. Despite awareness of Stalin's mistakes, Wu claims that in their hearts people were still full of respect and believed that Stalin was irreplaceable. A great many achievements must be credited to Stalin.

Then Wu adds that unfortunately in his late years, Stalin surrounded himself with adventurers, such as Khrushchev, and schemers, and he committed many errors. He left stains on his own history. Later Khrushchev exaggerated Stalin's mistakes and turned the Soviet Union into an hegemonist country that betrayed proletarian internationalism, provoking a split among socialist countries. Wu expresses dismay that a great person like Stalin departed from the masses and reality, fell into subjectivism, surrounded himself and closed himself off with some of the wrong people, and in the end created a tragedy for the state and the individual.

After Stalin's death, Sino-Soviet relations began to change slightly. Wu attributes this to Khrushchev's rise and other unspecified reasons. When in 1954 Khrushchev came to China, the two countries were still in agreement. The great majority of Soviet comrades were still very friendly. Wu mentions many positive steps, yet adds that unfortunately as time passed, the contradictions gradually intensified, finally leading to the break in relations. Khrushchev broke one agreement after another that had been reached after so much hard work. We are told that the elements for a split already existed in the early fifties, but they were overcome by China's central instructions, above all, from Zhou Enlai. Wu pays great tribute to Zhou for the successes that were realized.[45]

THE POLITICAL SYSTEM UNDER BREZHNEV

In the initial issue of *Sulian dongou wenti* at the beginning of 1981, the first five articles, following the opening statement by Liu Keming, con-

[45] Ibid., 17-32.

centrate on Soviet domestic and foreign policies and criticisms of the recently concluded Twenty-sixth Party Congress. The first article, by Xing
Shugang, discusses the global expansionist policy of the Soviet Union, regarding world hegemony as the ultimate aim of the Soviet strategy. The
second article, by Xu Kui, criticizes the Twenty-sixth Congress for its
continued support of hegemonist policies, its failure to change the priorities for heavy industry and military production despite concern about a
falling rate of economic development, and its tightening of domestic control in order to maintain the dominant position of the leadership group.
Xu explains that Soviet policies serve the needs of social imperialism. The
Congress sought to maintain domestic stability for this end. Brezhnev
concentrated power more fully in his own hands, having gradually moved
away from the troika form of leadership with which he began. While his
physical health was deteriorating, his power was reaching a peak. Xu says
this was needed to maintain domestic stability, but it cannot hide the
succession question, the power struggle, and other new contradictions.
An aged leadership remains unchanged to demonstrate the leading
group's solidarity, while the urgent political problem of succession persists. In the Central Committee the proportion of military officers, security officers, theorists and propagandists, and relatives and assistants of
Brezhnev rose. This shows the leadership's fear of any change and its eagerness to preserve its own controlling position. At the same time, the
Congress tightened control over political thought, ostensibly to prevent
the thoughts of the Soviet people from being corrupted.

Xu Kui sums up the meaning of the Congress as tightening domestic
control over the people and intensifying hegemonistic foreign policy of
social imperialism. From the Twenty-third to the Twenty-sixth Congress, the Brezhnev group strengthened its personal control, greatly developed Soviet military power, turned from defense to offense in the
struggle with America, and became ever more wildly expansionist. Despite the optimistic promises of Brezhnev's predictions for the end of the
century, actual conditions prove that if the Soviets stay on this course,
their contradictions and difficulties can only increase. Their prospects are
not, in fact, hopeful.[46]

Zheng Shi's evaluation of the Twenty-sixth Congress is that there was
no substantial change despite the difficulties the Soviet Union was facing.[47] Yet because of economic difficulties, especially the shortage of consumer goods, and problems brought about by the influence of the Polish
situation and other events, some measures had to be taken to strengthen

[46] Xu Kui, "Yici jixu jianchi baquanzhuyi zhengce de daibiao dahui—ping Sugong ershiliu da," *Sulian dongou wenti*, no. 1 (1981): 10-14.
[47] Zheng Shi, "Cong Sugong ershiliu da kan Sulian jiaqiang guonei kongzhi de jidian
qingkuang," *Sulian dongou wenti*, no. 1 (1981): 19-21.

domestic control. Zheng mentions renewed attention to labor union questions in the second half of 1980, criticisms of inadequate union autonomy for example, and insufficient responses to violations of the law and bureaucratism. Much emphasis in *Pravda* centered on unions and other mass organizations working in unison with the party, and on strict prohibitions against religious factions and other groups. Articles called for renewing the struggle against opportunist elements in unions and elsewhere. Underground unions were appearing, according to the Western press, and Soviet leaders also responded by stressing improvements in union work, caring for the living standards and welfare of the people. Just before the Congress began, *Pravda* said that not resolving problems in time can lead to increasing contradictions in the society.

Zheng next discusses the Congress's emphasis on political education in order to tighten control. This continues to be the center of Soviet ideological work, which has now been given a higher priority. In the late seventies, criticisms of shortcomings in propaganda became more widespread, and they continued at the 1981 Congress. Specifically the criticisms pointed to lax labor discipline, increased criminal activities in some areas, the attraction of youths to Western styles of life, the dissatisfaction with market shortages and the Soviet invasion of Afghanistan, and the activities of dissidents and religious believers. The Congress called for more effective propaganda work, especially by linking propaganda to urgent problems of life. Zheng also mentions that the Congress recognized problems in nationality relations and called for firm resistance to any nationalistic behavior. There was much talk in early 1981 of "international education." Because of Great Russian chauvinism in Soviet nationality policies, contradictions among the ethnic groups had become quite sharp.

Another theme at the Congress, Zheng observes, was the emphasis on reasserting party leadership in the world of the arts, criticizing authors who do not take a clear class position or who take a deviant path. In 1979 this concern had already become prominent, with criticisms of distortions of history and contemporary Soviet life at conferences on movies and ideology. Soviets were called on to take a principled stand and to carry on an uncompromising struggle. Finally, Zheng raises the theme of strengthening laws and supervision in many areas of life. This was aimed at increasing responsibility and tightening controls. Special emphasis was given to increasing the role of the KGB, as had been the case since the Twenty-fifth Congress.

In the aftermath of the Twenty-sixth Congress, an article analyzed the changing composition of the Central Committee from the time of the

Twenty-second Congress.[48] It contrasts Khrushchev's high turnover of members to Brezhnev's continuity of personnel, but also notes that primarily through higher turnover in the first congresses under Brezhnev and expansion of membership, eighty percent of the members chosen in 1981 were not holdovers from the Khrushchev-era committee. Who were the new members? The article finds an increasing representation of individuals with responsibilities in the security and ideological fields, and a big increase in military officers. Persons long close to Brezhnev were rewarded with the important posts in the party, state, military, and ideological areas. The article concludes by mentioning relatives and assistants of Brezhnev who had entered the Central Committee. While the impression it gives is critical, the article refrains from direct commentary on how these appointments contradict socialist principles.

Chinese analyses of the Soviet political system emphasize both its stability from the 1930s and the absence of qualitative change since the 1960s. They point to its highly centralized authority, multiple ministries, multi-functioned administrative control. Despite the formal division into republics, only the central government has real administrative authority. The central level has extremely broad powers, including control over planning and finances, as well as social and economic policies, direct management of important enterprises, and selection of numerous personnel at the republic level. Centralized authority developed early, the functions of the Supreme Soviet were not permitted much scope, and authority gradually was concentrated in the hands of a small group. What the constitution establishes is far removed from the real situation; for example, before 1977 the Soviet Council of Ministers had considerable power without constitutional backing. It could give direct orders to any republic or local administrative organ. The overall situation means very tight controls from above, stifling the self-administration of local organs and enterprises.[49]

One article points to the following features of the Soviet political system in comparison to other countries:[50] 1) It emphasizes ministerial control as primary, especially to control specialization and the development of science and technology, while relegating territorial control to a secondary role to resolve labor force problems, to provide the needed infrastructure, and to advance overall economic development of the area. 2) Following the tradition formed by the early 1920s, there is an enormous

[48] Xu Xiang and Zhang Pei, "Sugong sijie zhongyang weiyuanhui qingkuang jianxi," *Sulian dongou wenti*, no. 1 (1981): 21-24.
[49] Liu Yinchang and Liu Yanyu, "Sulian zhengfu tizhi qianzhe," *Sulian dongou wenti*, no. 6 (1983): 1-6.
[50] Ibid.

government structure with more ministries per capita than anywhere else in the world, which is finely differentiated into very specialized spheres of jurisdiction. 3) Because of the form of state ownership and economic planning, the government must control and organize the economy, so no matter what the sphere of activity, the economy takes precedence. Of 64 ministries in 1981, 56 concentrated on the economy, and only 4 on social and cultural activities and 4 on political administration; the government and the enterprise are not separate; administrative means of management have not been changed in any fundamental manner. 4) The state council, and within it the state planning commission, occupies an important position in the government structure.

Most studies of the Soviet system of government see little hope of major reform. Although minor adjustments have been made since the 1960s, there has been no qualitative change in the system of administrative authority, and the tendencies of development rule out major reform. Liu Yichang and Liu Yanyu describe the Soviet system as highly centralized, with many ministries and many functions. Despite the federated system, republics lack independent authority. Especially the intermediate level between the center and the basic local unit is very weak. Big questions are all decided at the center through both legislative and executive authority. Centralized powers include unified national planning, unified social and economic policies, direct control over important enterprises, control over foreign contacts, and determination over republic-level appointments and structure. The center's range extends almost to everything, the two Lius point out. A small number of people grasp administrative power at the top and very tightly control lower levels, often overlooking the autonomy of lower levels and enterprises.

The generally negative tone of the article is reinforced by a concluding paragraph that points to five principal manifestations of the political system's shortcomings. First, despite repeated stress on state management that would correspond to local conditions and encouragement of the creative spirit of localities and enterprises, and because of excessive centralization and administrative controls over the economies, problems in the relations between the center and local units have not been resolved. Second, orders from above have not been combined with democratic management from below. This means that citizens lack motivation and a sense of responsibility, while red tape and severe bureaucratism cannot really be overcome. Third, the massive, complex, finely differentiated administrative system does not clearly delimit responsibilities, which leads to low efficiency. Overlapping controls are extremely irrational. Fourth, each ministry has its own vertical system, leading to departmentalism. Although many approaches have been taken to secure horizontal cooperation among ministries, they have not achieved any fundamental solution. Tremendous waste of labor, material resources, and capital continues. Fifth, because of many complexities and never-ending changes, centralized planning cannot be scientific or effective. This greatly lowers the efficiency of administrative management. The political system, as other parts of the superstructure, must continually develop in correspondence to changes in the economic foundation; only in this way can it exert a positive rather than a negative influence on the development of productive forces. It is very natural, the two Lius explain, for there to be continuous reform in the government system. The key to carrying it out is reform of the entire state leadership system.[51]

Immediately following the article in *Sulian dongou wenti* by the two Lius was an article on the relations between the center and the localities by Zhang Zhengzhao and Liu Xiangwen.[52] The authors begin by examining the theoretical principles, asserting that Lenin's concept of democratic centralism established the theoretical basis for combining unified central leadership and local motivation and creativity. The primary manifestations of it are, first, elections of local authorities and supervision of local management organs by them in order to prevent the evil spirit of bureaucratism. Lenin opposed central or upper levels appointing local administrators as a practice that could destroy the takeoff of democracy. Second, Lenin wanted to parcel out power at each level so that each could take account of actual conditions to operate flexibly within its own area. This would permit each area to develop its initiative to the fullest degree. Third, Lenin sought to place local administrative management organs under dual control—horizontal and vertical. Fourth, he preferred to combine in local state organs a collaborative system under the responsibility of one executive leader. This could prevent a leader from hiding behind collective decisions, and it also could promote the role of collective leadership. Fifth, Lenin tried to start from democratic centralism and to take national elements into account. This meant local self-administration. The article says that these principles were established in early laws by Lenin and are written into the 1977 Soviet constitution, but after Lenin's death they were not actually put fully into effect. Relations of democracy and centralism, relations between the center and the localities have not been handled properly in all periods.

In practice, the theoretical principles are not fully applied. Despite repeated measures since 1965 to strengthen unified central leadership and

[51] Liu Yichang and Liu Yanyu, "Sulian zhengfu tizhi qianzhe," 1-6.
[52] Zhang Zhangzhao and Liu Xiangwen, "Sulian de difang xingzheng tizhi: tan zhongyang yu difang guanxi wenti," *Sulian dongou wenti*, no. 6 (1983): 6-12.

invigorate local functions, the existing administrative system remains highly departmentalized and centralized. Local autonomy is slight, Great Russian chauvinism has been strengthened, local motivation cannot burst forth, and the efficiency of local government is low. If the Soviet Union does not thoroughly apply Lenin's principle of democratic centralism, it will not be able to put the relations of the center and the localities in order and encourage incentives at various local levels, assert Zhang and Liu.

Specialists in China recognize the existence of a reform group (*gaige-pai*) that has recently become active in the Soviet political arena. They mostly write about the academic voices of the reform perspective, such as the Siberian journal *EKO*, and their interest in economic reform. They trace the roots of reform to Liberman's proposals in the early 1960s and find that while in the mid-seventies Liberman was often under pressure to engage in self-criticism, he is now publicly praised by the reform group as a "great scholar."

Who are the supporters of reform? Chinese specialists suggest that they are enterprise leaders, struggling to increase their own autonomy, and social scientists aware of the urgency of reform in historical and comparative perspective. An article by Wang Jincun explains that the clamor for reform rose dramatically after Andropov took office, and its advocates doubtless reflect Andropov's economic thinking and reform direction. While a few years earlier Soviet sources were criticizing "market social-ism," by 1983 many articles on the Yugoslavian and Hungarian experiences appeared without the critical language of the past. The clear message was to study the experiences of other socialist countries in order to find ways out of the Soviet Union's economic troubles. Soviet reformers see the reforms already initiated by 1984 as only a small part of what is needed to overhaul the excessively centralized Soviet system. In Wang's estimation in mid-1984, the reform view is not now the leading position in the Soviet Union, but its influence is growing. He suggests that *EKO* is a window to change in the Soviet system. In 1973 it had barely 300 subscribers, but by 1984 the figure had climbed precipitously to 110,000. The clamor for reform was growing.[53]

Critical of Soviet foreign policy in Asia and the economic slowdown at home, Chinese writers cannot refrain from tracing these problems to their source in the Soviet political system. By the second half of 1984 a Chinese author could take a deep look at the first decades of Soviet government to explain what had gone wrong. Li Yuanshu's overview begins with the theory of the state under socialism. He comments that although the proletariat seizes power, it cannot achieve complete mass direct

---

[53] Wang Jincun, "EKO zazhi yu Xiboliya pai," *Sulian dongou wenti*, no. 4 (1984): 92–96.

administration. This presents the danger of master-servant relations reappearing under socialism. Soviet theory after 1917 recognized this danger; it sought to reform state organs, to fight against bureaucratism, to expand close ties between officials and the masses. The solicitation of criticisms from the masses below and from inspection commissions comprised of workers and peasants helped in this struggle. From 1933 to 1936 the restoration of election rights to kulaks and their children and then to old whites and aristocrats on the basis of secret ballots and "one man, one vote" were important developments, according to Li.

The primary focus of this unusually forthright article is on errors committed in the Stalin era. These were made possible by the low cultural level and consciousness of the masses in the 1920s, which meant that a state completely managed by the "people" could not be set up. Furthermore, for some time after the proletariat seizes power, it needs to tighten repression of the exploiting classes and expand state organs. Under Stalin, however, these early requirements soon led to theoretical errors. Ignoring Lenin's analysis of bureaucracy and Stalin's own earlier writings, the Soviet Union overemphasized the function of a minority. Stalin adopted the slogan "cadres decide everything." A closed system of government removed from the masses evolved. Officials were in fact appointed, not elected, and although there was some need for this, the result was loss of supervision by the masses and by Communist Party members. Supervisory organs became the personal tool of the leader, indicating a lack of trust in the masses. There was no theory of high-level socialist democracy. Master-servant relations returned, even to the point of the arbitrary will of one man in charge of the people.

Rather than responding to the elimination of exploiters by reducing state repression and beginning to transfer state functions gradually to the society, Stalin continued to expand the dictatorial organs of the state, creating specialized branches in schools, enterprises, railroad stations, and other areas that had broad authority. Li describes a network of thousands of concentration camps for the targets of the big purge, which he dates from 1934 to 1941. He calculates that as many as 1.2 million Communist Party members fell victim to it. Theoretical errors were involved. In 1933 Stalin proposed that the eradication of classes comes from the intensification of class struggle, the elimination of the state from the strengthening of state authority. He claimed that the more socialism is victorious, the more class struggle intensifies. Even after the exploiting classes are eliminated, new enemies of the people appear. Spies and wreckers are all around. This theory justified an unlimited strengthening of state organs. Under Stalin, a gap widened between the longstanding anti-bureaucratic theory of socialist democracy and the newly proposed theory of class enemies, as well as the accompanying reality of state suppression.

Stalin widened wage differentials; in 1932 he eliminated the upper limit on salaries and allowed one man to fill multiple posts and increase his income accordingly. If one considers the entire income of high officials by the end of the Stalin era, Li adds, it amounted to forty or fifty— even in some cases one hundred times the bottom incomes in the country. New bureaucratism developed, with rapidly increasing numbers of bureaucrats eager to protect their high incomes and privileges, but not to seek out the truth or to criticize practices harmful to the state and the people. Li describes a bloated bureaucracy in which many officials were concerned not about the hardships of the masses, but with protecting their personal power. This led to corruption and to repression of the masses.[54]

Li Fangzhong has analyzed changes in the Soviet state administrative system. He finds its most striking feature to be the discrepancy between calls for simplification and the ever-growing complexity and scale. The number of personnel in the Soviet Union keeps growing: in fact, Li comments, by the 1970s there were Soviets who were even saying that continuous growth in the system of state administration corresponds to the laws of development, and people should not artifically hinder it. Why could the Soviets not simplify this system? The Chinese answer is, above all, because the economic management system is excessively centralized. The Soviets emphasized that the development of economic, scientific, cultural, health, social welfare, and daily services all must be pursued under a highly centralized system. As more and more systems have emerged, the result has been fragmentation of authority, weakening central supervision. Then attempts at merging and simplifying management followed, but when this could not have any clear results, Soviet leaders turned ever more to cooperative associations such as committees, at first temporary ones, and then gradually more permanent ones. The result of these developments has been to strengthen even more the system of excessive centralization.

Li argues that in the Soviet system, the position and personal interest of officials are closely linked. This leads to an increase in bureaucratic structures and officeholders. Simplification threatens the personal interests of officials and naturally leads to obstructionist sentiments and efforts to block it. Many attempts have been foiled. The author concludes that future reforms will continue to stumble over four factors: the highly centralized nature of the Soviet economic management system, the per-

[54] Li Yuanshu, "Sidalin shiqi Sulian zhengzhi zhidu jianshe de jingyan yu jiaoxun," *Sulian dongou wenti*, no. 4 (1984): 40-47.

sonal interests of officials, the problem of relations among nationalities that still require Russians to maintain controls, and the objective demands of economic and scientific development that call for new duties for administrators. It will be very difficult to make a notable change in the pattern of continuous expansion of the organs of Soviet administration.

Li also points to four lessons from the Soviet experience that China should consider. First, to reform the administrative system, it is necessary to recognize the limiting influence of the centralized power in the economic management system. If one country blindly follows another, trouble ensues. This was the case when in the late sixties the Soviets failed to restrain the growth of administrative personnel in an effort to follow the American automation of management, neglecting to take into account the restraining influence of its own economic management system. Second, reform is complicated; only moderate measures that can be sustained over a long time will be very effective. After Stalin's death, hasty measures failed to cut back personnel much, leading to a backlash. Brezhnev's comparatively conservative measures were influenced by the failures of the 1950s. Third, use of a large-scale political movement to bring about administrative reform and retrenchment in personnel is unmanageable. Fourth, the key to reform is the training of cadres. Success in reform presumes the presence of many cadres who are able to meet the new work demands. This can be achieved only gradually. With recent leaps in the development of science and technology, the Soviets have more and more stressed training officials in new advanced procedures. The article ends with this upbeat note on how China can benefit from the Soviet experience.[55]

Xiao Guishen's article on the training of cadres in the Brezhnev period claims that the Soviet Union, especially after the new economic system reforms began, paid tremendous attention to the training of party, state, and economic cadres. The Central Committee and council of ministers issued about twenty resolutions on specialists. Each party congress emphasized raising the professional ability and theoretical level of cadres, demanding advances in training too. The training system for leading cadres consists first of the system for training party and Soviet leaders in the Academy of Social Sciences of the Central Committee and its branch institutes, as well as numerous local schools, which together have as many as 500,000-600,000 students. Second, there are, overall, 1,000 refresher courses for economic cadres, with a new course required every five to six years, or even every two to three years in areas where the influence of the

[55] Li Fangzhong, "Dui Sulian guojia xingzheng guanli jigou bianhua de chubu pouxi," *Sulian dongou wenti*, no. 1 (1983): 58-63.

scientific and technological revolution is great. The article does not fail to mention some problems in the training system. Theory is removed from practice and life. The program of study is not often changed, and studies and experiences of the students are insufficiently coordinated. Many leading organs do not place much emphasis on training work despite the repeated stress of the Central Committee on the urgency of this. Some training units have a low level of teaching or exhibit formalism in their approach. Training units become in fact production conferences; theory is simplified. Some pursue more training, without making qualitative improvements in it. Recent efforts to address these problems have raised to some degree the quality of teaching.[56]

From Andropov to Gorbachev

Whether one was optimistic or pessimistic about the Soviet Union reflected to a large extent one's evaluation of the Andropov era. Assessments of Andropov in Chinese journals are uniformly positive, although some emphasize the brevity of the era in comparison to the long road to traverse while others compliment Andropov's ability and creative spirit as a force that will long remain in historical memory. The latter view appeared in August 1984 in an article on Soviet reform possibilities by Luo Zhaohong. Summing up the Andropov era, Luo identifies twenty major policy initiatives in fifteen months. On his list are an energy program, the experiment in expanding the authority of enterprises, a program to accelerate technology advances, a new legal policy on work collectives, the spread of the contract system, and a plan for increasing the availability of services and consumer goods. Luo argues that in no prior age did so much change occur in such a short period. Not only were policies greatly transformed, leading personnel were also replaced at an unprecedented speed and scale. Individuals in their forties and fifties replaced older and less able veteran officials.

Most of Luo's article examines the development of economic theory under Andropov's guidance. This was not an obscure debate, according to Luo, but very possibly will become the preparation of public opinion for a new economic reform. He adduces three points to substantiate this optimistic conclusion. First, Andropov reinterpreted the concept of developed socialism to indicate that the Soviet Union is at the beginning of a long-term historical transition. This big theoretical advance, as Luo characterizes it, opens the way for major reform in contrast to the earlier idea that the Soviet Union is already a mature socialist society with developed

[56] Xiao Guishen, "Sulian lingdao ganbu de peixun gongzuo," *Sulian dongou wenti*, no. 6 (1982): 41-45.

socialism in place for the foreseeable future. That in turn represented an advance over the view expressed in Khrushchev's time and engraved in the party platform that persisted until the Twenty-seventh Party Congress, which says that this generation will live under communism, that is, the transition to communism can be made soon and without great difficulty. The Andropov approach is described by Luo as more humble, less simplistic, and more supportive of social science research. Not everything is perfect and beautiful. Contradictions can be found under socialism. It is wrong to idealize past successes. Instead, what is needed is to recognize existing shortcomings, to gather the necessary forces, and to make improvements. Humility is the precondition for a realistic assessment of conditions and then reform.

Second, Andropov recognized the need for changes in the relations of production. Luo asserts that Soviets had been giving many explanations for the economic slowdown, including bad weather and shortcomings in personnel. Finally under Andropov, their consciousness took a leap forward when they conceded that the problems were more deep-seated. They abandoned their cover-up of contradictions, giving new life to theorists and opening the way for reform experiments. Luo cites Aganbegyan's view that because the contradictions between the forces of production and the relations of production were gradually intensifying, the economy was slowing down. In other words, the present economic system, which had been established decades earlier, is no longer suitable; it blocks the development of the forces of production. Specifically, debates focus on excessively egalitarian distribution and insufficient enterprise autonomy.

Luo's third point is that Soviets are at last realizing that their theory of property under socialism was in error. They had pursued "the bigger the better, the more public the better." Prematurely they had declared collective ownership a thing of the past. By 1983 Andropov and Soviet economists had begun to talk of the long-term coexistence of multi-sided property arrangements. Different types of management are acceptable as long as they do not lead to a change in ownership. The Soviet people, Luo adds, generally accept the necessity of reform in order to compete with the United States militarily and to keep up with the quick pace of the international technical revolution, among other reasons. We estimate, says Luo, that although Chernenko's commitment to reform is far less than that of his predecessor, the theory will continue to develop, leading to the possibility of reform. Luo predicts success, because only if there is a major economic reform will the system become more efficient.[57]

[57] Luo Zhaohong, "Cong Sulian jingji lilun kan gaige de kenengxing," *Shijie jingji yu zhengzhi neican*, no. 8 (1984): 1-5.

It would be a mistake to look only at the many Chinese articles on the currents of Soviet reform in the years 1982-1985 without noticing Chinese references to countercurrents. An article in *Ekonomicheskie nauki*, no. 7 (1983), was translated first in *Guowai shehuikexue dongtai*, no. 3 (1984), and then in *Shijie jingji yu zhengzhi neican*, no. 9 (1984).[58] It launches an attack on rightist revisionists and democratic socialists who confuse economic relations with market relations and treat centralized planning as if it contradicts economic democracy. The Soviet article accuses these revisionists of writing as if bureaucratism and alienation are the norm in socialist society. The accusation goes so far as to say that they seek to change the existing political and economic system. Although no Chinese commentary accompanied the translated Soviet article, its repeat translation in what may be the most important internal circulation journal on international affairs obviously indicates a high level of interest.

What were the theoretical innovations made under Andropov? Wu Renzhang and Jia Lianyi list many of them in an article written around the time of Andropov's death.[59] First they note that, in contrast to as recently as 1977, when Suslov spoke of building communism and said that the technological and material basis for building it already existed, the mood had shifted against policies that run ahead of the existing stage of development. Soviet leaders are now critical of rushing into the transition to communism. Above all, this signifies a critical attitude toward idealizing the achievements already made and a sober attitude toward existing contradictions within the socialist society. On this basis, attention can be concentrated on resolving these contradictions. Rather than dismissing them as nonantagonistic, discussions began to highlight them as contradictions between the forces and the relations of production. This terminology, harking back to the fundamental categories used by Marxists to argue the need for social change, indicates the seriousness of the matter. The term "reform" appeared more and more in Soviet writings in place of the less pressing concept of improvement (*sovershenstvovanie*).

Wu and Jia delineate many theoretical advances under Andropov. They point to changes in the theory of property from the simplistic view that one form of state property would automatically become all-inclusive (e.g. through conversion of collective farms into state ones) to a consideration of other routes and more complex combinations of property forms. Regarding the theory of distribution, Soviets reduced the emphasis on normative incentives in favor of more material stimuli. The rhetoric be-

[58] [Title unknown], *Shijie jingji yu zhengzhi neican*, no. 9 (1984): 55.
[59] Wu Renzhang and Jia Lianyi, "Jinnianlai Sulian fada shehuizhuyi lilun de xin bianhua," *Sulian dongou wenti*, no. 3 (1984): 20-24.

came critical of egalitarianism and excessive pursuit of a communist distribution system based on need. Another theoretical advance was the shift away from the idea that under developed socialism, no nonsocialist economic elements are allowed, which meant a rejection in theory of personal small-scale organization for production and distribution. The new approach, already signaled in the 1977 constitution, recognized the importance of individual economic elements and the contract system under socialism. In contrast to the tightening restrictions in Brezhnev's early years, in Andropov's brief term some individual crafts and services, such as a personally managed taxi and a family-run small restaurant, were permitted. Brigade contracts spread, especially in agriculture, and household contracts for raising livestock were approved on an experimental basis.

Wu and Jia draw attention also to the increasing theoretical discussion of self-administration under socialism. Before, this theme was largely set aside as a future goal under communism. Worker participation in management, which had long been neglected, became a matter of growing concern. Andropov talked of increased democracy, of unions more actively supporting workers' rights, of the Soviet state system gradually changing into self-administration. Chernenko asserted that contract units are an effective present-day form of socialist self-administration. The 1983 law on worker collectives was interpreted as a contribution to self-administration. Wu and Jia do not fail to note that there was also continued criticism of anarchism in self-administration, which they interpret as, to some extent, aimed at the Yugoslavian model. Acknowledging that the scope for self-administration remains limited mainly to worker collectives, they nevertheless consider it a step forward that Soviet leaders now recognize that the political system has insufficient democracy.

Perhaps the two most important theoretical breakthroughs, in the opinion of Chinese observers, are the move toward recognition of diversity in the models for socialism and the new humility in the theory of developed socialism. Soviet theorists recognize major differences among socialist countries, the existence of multiple forms, and the need to conduct detailed study and evaluations of other experiences. In March 1983, Wu and Jia point out, *Pravda* announced that a committee was being set up in the Central Committee to study other socialist countries, although the *Pravda* article warned against the danger of following the road of capitalist, reformist development. Despite these steps, Wu and Jia conclude, the Soviets have not yet recognized that there may be diverse models of socialism. From the second half of the 1930s, Soviet leaders have exaggerated the stage of their country's socialist development, from Stalin's proclamation of the transition to communism, to Khrushchev's twenty-year program of achieving communism in the main by 1980, to Brezhnev's 1967 announcement that the Soviet Union was a developed socialist society. Wu and Jia see Andropov backing off from such claims. They regard this as a further sign that under his leadership a real transformation in theory did occur, which may have a deep influence on the development of production. Yet their article concludes that theoretical obstacles remain, such as criticisms of the Yugoslav model and repression of those searching for internal reforms. In 1984 Wu and Jia perceived an intense theoretical struggle still underway within the Soviet Union.

Feng Shengbao wrote in the spring of 1984 about the sensitive subject of elections.[60] Looking back to the first elections to the local and national soviets, under Lenin, Feng explains that at that time a retreat from the principle of democratic elections was necessary in order to get party leadership of the masses. In Lenin's time, Soviet leaders were clear about the potential negative consequences of relying on appointments. Lenin always stressed the need to combat bureaucratism through democratization of the management of society. When foreign interference ended, the capitalists ceased to be a threat, and semi-proletarian party activists were no longer a factor, the practice of appointments unfortunately continued, adds Feng. Why? He mentions the backward culture of Russia, although he notes that the cultural level later rose sharply without bringing much change. He asserts that in the contemporary Soviet Union the legal requirements are not realized, elections occur in form only, and deputies to soviets have little to do. Authority has been very centralized within the Supreme Soviet, such as in the hands of Stalin or Khrushchev; this means the mistakes of leaders could not be changed until they were out of office.

Feng excuses the problem by explaining that it took about 200 years after the capitalist revolution to find the best government system, the capitalist democratic republic. One cannot expect an immediate solution under socialism. In his opinion, Soviet political history lessons show that putting executive, legislative, and legal power all in the Supreme Soviet cannot avoid problems. Nevertheless, he says that conditions have improved somewhat in recent decades. He sees it as a good sign that Brezhnev and Andropov favored strengthening the functions of soviets, even if they themselves combined communist party, government, and military authority in their own office.

CONCLUSION

In the late 1970s the concept of "revisionism" and the negative view of Soviet expanisionism made it obligatory to comment only negatively

[60] Feng Shengbao, "Lun Sulian Zuigao Suweiai zhidu de jige wenti," *Sulian dongou wenti,* no. 2 (1984): 38-43.

about Soviet government in the post-Stalin era. In 1980-1982, reform and orthodox voices vied to offer new interpretations. The reformers proposed a new set of negative assessments of Stalin, often developing criticisms that had been accepted in China as early as the authoritative 1956 articles that evaluated Stalin's pros and cons. They tried to reinterpret Lenin's views as conflicting with Stalin's and to cast doubt on Stalin's position in the intra-party struggle of the 1920s. According to their views, Stalin disregarded the individual's needs in favor of the state's, democracy in favor of bureaucracy. Severe critiques on these and other themes, however, were rare in the years 1983-1984. The orthodox side proposed instead a more positive evaluation of the Brezhnev era. Brezhnev offered stable leadership. He never neglected the training of new officials and political education. The Soviet Union was not government by an exploiting class but socialist democracy. In the eyes of orthodox figures, it was acceptable to criticize shortcomings in economic mechanisms, but not to criticize the Soviet political system.

In two relatively inaccessible internal circulation journals, the principal Soviet studies journal *Sulian dongou wenti* and the principal international relations journal *Shijie jingji yu zhengzhi neican*, a new set of reform criticisms were emerging by the second half of 1983. They centered on the post-Stalin political system. These critiques contend that economic reforms cannot be very effective without political reforms. They point to officials as an interest group whose personal interests are threatened by simplification of the bloated and complex state bureaucracy. Furthermore, these more recent articles regret the dearth of democracy in the Soviet Union, such as the absence of elections for local cadres, the absence of mass supervision over managers and officials, and even the absence of any theory of socialist democracy. These conditions contributed to low levels of motivation and initiative among the masses and the localities, and to unscientific and inefficient operations in the bureaucracy. Chinese observers call for continuous reform in the political as well as the economic sphere. They note too that in the Andropov era a Soviet reform group surfaced that pursues reforms that officials—particularly those at an intermediate level—continue to resist.

The Chinese sources on the Soviet political system are among the most pessimistic in their conclusions. They speak of the neglect of major reform since the 1960s, the resistance to reform among officials, and the difficult task of constraining a government that penetrates to the enterprise level so thoroughly. Nevertheless, there is an obvious reluctance to draw strong conclusions from this line of reasoning. It is not systematically linked to an analysis of Stalin's system of government, nor is it reflected in textbooks or many other studies of the Soviet Union. This reform appraisal has the potential to turn into an overall evaluation of socialist officials if linkages are permitted between the specific and fragmented articles on different subjects that now dominate in the field.

COMPARISONS WITH SOVIET VIEWS OF CHINA

In the 1970s Chinese and Soviets each showered abuse on officials in the other country. Each side wrote in accusatory terms of unworthy and incompetent power holders who were bent on corruption and who lorded it over the common people. Officials were divorced from the masses, who in turn responded with apathy or even hostility. The Chinese were the first to drop this line of criticism; the crackdown on the "democracy movement" in 1979 and the emerging consensus in 1980-1981 on how to limit criticisms of Mao brought with them a rapid reduction in negative statements about Soviet officials. Until negotiations were announced in September 1982, the Soviets showed no letup in their criticisms of Chinese officials. Then their pens fell abruptly silent. Soviet reformers were given no opportunity to portray China's debates about government reform; they had to rest content with their participation in the negative appraisals of how socialism could go astray. Chinese reformers continued to have some opportunity to assess Soviet shortcomings; however, most treatments of Soviet history were either silent about officials or gave subdued praise.

The Soviet political system served as an example for escaping from the ravages of China's Cultural Revolution. The Brezhnev period offered a model for stable government, continued leadership by the Communist Party, and recruitment of experts as officials. While the Soviet economy is seen as deteriorating, no such decline is ascribed to the Soviet government.

Despite the generally positive tone of Chinese writings on the Soviet political system, *neibu* publications continue to convey suggestions for moderate reforms. They essentially parallel the approved framework since 1979 for China's own domestic political reforms. Even a major cause given for China's deviation from socialist democracy—that the cultural level and consciousness of the masses were low—reappears as an explanation for Soviet neglect of popular participation in management. Soviets point to the same factor in China and, unlike the Chinese, who praise Soviet leaders for raising the level of Soviet mass education and political education, accuse Chinese leaders of failing to address the problem into the 1980s.

Chinese comments about Stalin's theoretical errors and excessive centralization of power follow some of the same lines as Soviet condemnations of Mao. The system stifled self-administration at lower levels, left the soviets or government organs too weak to exercise authority, failed to deliver on high-sounding constitutional principles, and led to red tape and bureaucratism. Each side said that the other should tone down its claims to have reached an advanced stage of socialism and should take actual social conditions more into account in order to make sure that initiative could be exercised from below. By 1985 each country had obliged the other in this way. The Chinese enthusiastically approved of the new currents initiated by Andropov, while the Soviets at first rejected Deng's efforts and then preferred silence. Under Gorbachev, positive impressions of China's economic reforms were gradually appearing.

SEVEN

CONCLUSIONS

In the 1980s China has become the pivotal country in the transition within the socialist world away from the tight controls established by Stalin and the intense suspicion of the capitalist West expressed by leading communist officials. Under the leadership of Mao Zedong, the People's Republic of China had carried these long-established modes of socialist conduct to an extreme rarely surpassed; yet just several years after his death, China had come to represent reform and accommodation on a scale that made the entire world take notice. The international debate on the future of socialist reforms and the ability of socialist and capitalist countries to overcome their differences has focused increasingly on China as a success story and, perhaps, as an example to the Soviet Union. As relations between Beijing and Moscow were improving in the mid-1980s and Moscow was launching its own substantial reform program, the possibility was rising that the situation of the 1950s, when China copied the Soviet Union, would be reversed, and the Soviet Union would begin to follow China's lead.

Many uncertainties complicate predictions about the future of China's domestic and foreign policies, and about the reform of Soviet socialism as well. Observers ask: Is China still socialist? After Deng Xiaoping leaves office, will the reform or orthodox camp win out? What is the prognosis for reforms under Gorbachev's leadership? How far will "normalization" between Moscow and Beijing lead? In the 1980s, questions about socialism abound; they draw attention to the need to understand Chinese thinking.

This book demonstrates that there exists a substantial literature in Chinese that can shed important light on how the Chinese worldview has evolved in the post-Mao era, that can reveal sharp differences between orthodox and reform thinking, that can offer an informed perspective on Soviet problems and possible reforms, and that can fill in the background on the development of Sino-Soviet relations. While the *neibu* system creates problems of accessibility, and censorship rules sometimes make the meaning of an article difficult to interpret, the evidence from the preceding chapters indicates that Chinese sources on the Soviet Union are largely explicable within a well-circumscribed Chinese worldview and in the context of a specific chronology of domestic and international policies. Publications on the Soviet Union in Chinese help us to understand the important problems facing the socialist world.

China's Evolving Worldview

Chinese discussions of Soviet revisionism lasted for twenty-three years. Beginning indirectly with the two *People's Daily* articles (*liang lun*) in 1956 on Stalin and the dictatorship of the proletariat and continuing through the force of inertia into 1978 and 1979 even after China's domestic policies were becoming reform-oriented, criticisms of Soviet revisionism reached a peak during the fifteen or so years from the time of the Nine Commentaries, attributed to the editorial boards of *People's Daily* and *Hongqi*, in the first half of the 1960s to the last outburst of radical campaigns in 1976-1977.[1] Mao Zedong remained the guiding spirit. Although Kang Sheng had formal responsibility for the Nine Commentaries which mapped the terrain of revisionism—beginning first with Yugoslavia and then turning directly to the Soviet Union—and the "Gang of Four" orchestrated the most intemperate condemnations more than a decade later, Mao's judgments are widely assumed to have prevailed throughout. Even after the theme of revisionism was dropped, certain of Mao's views were retained in the 1980s.

There are at least three continuities in Chinese interpretations of Soviet society from the era of Mao to the mid-1980s. In 1977 Deng Xiaoping said that Chinese would never do to Mao what the Soviets did to Stalin.[2] This consciousness of a parallel between de-Stalinization and de-Maoization helps explain one continuity: the official Chinese position has held steadfast to the ratio of 30:70 for Stalin's errors and achievements. Perhaps because this ratio was essentially worked out in 1956,[3] it is seen as a collective decision by China's leadership that does not reflect Mao's arbitrary exercise of authority when he stopped seeking agreement from other veteran communist leaders. Second, and also a consequence of the Chinese reaction to the Soviet Twentieth Party Congress of 1956, China's official line persists in condemning Khrushchev as a leader who brought

---

[1] Dozens of English-language books convey Chinese views during this long period of hostility, e.g., William E. Griffith, *Sino-Soviet Relations, 1964-1965* (Cambridge: The M.I.T. Press, 1967); and *Social Imperialism: The Soviet Union Today* (reprints from *Peking Review*) (Berkeley: Yenan Books, 1977).

[2] Georges Biannic, "Peking Wallposters Criticize Mao Tsetung's Critics," Hong Kong AFP, December 2, 1978, reprinted in FBIS, PRC National Affairs, December 4, 1978, p. E2.

[3] "More on the Historical Experience Concerning the Dictatorship of the Proletariat," *Hsinhua* (Xinhua), no. 12 (December 29, 1956): 251-66.

great harm to the Soviet Union and to socialism throughout the world. He is still faulted for completely repudiating Stalin, exaggerating his errors and ignoring his achievements.[4] Third, Chinese give Mao credit for the idea that China should not blindly follow the Soviet model of socialist development.[5] Consistent with the general restriction on criticisms of Mao beyond certain stock phrases, Chinese publications do not review, let alone take exception to, his ideas about the Soviet Union. It is sufficient to note briefly and only occasionally that mistakes in analyzing Soviet socialism were made before the Third Plenum of December 1978, and even to suggest that Mao Zedong Thought survives in China's independent view of this subject.

Views of Early Soviet Leaders

These continuities show that the old-time radical views have, in a limited way, endured and now lend support to the new orthodox views of the Soviet Union. They set rather strict limits on reform-minded critiques of Soviet history. As a result, reformers cannot be very harsh on Stalin and his decades in power—the focus of the most severe criticisms by students of Soviet history elsewhere in the world. Reformers also cannot say much that is positive about Khrushchev or his period in office. In openly distributed publications, Khrushchev is essentially a nonperson. The proscription on sympathetic explorations of the de-Stalinization process removes the possibility of comparisons with most of the politically or ideologically oriented reform steps in the Soviet Union from the 1950s on; this acts to stymie efforts to introduce far-reaching reform themes into writings on the Soviet system.

Perhaps the closest thing to a litmus test in the Soviet field is the way Stalin's purges are handled. Over and over again, one finds a stock phrase that dispenses briefly and almost noncommittally with the purges rather than exposing them to careful scrutiny. Chinese express approval of the purges, but regret that they were widened to claim innocent victims, especially those in the Communist Party. How many victims? What types of people were innocent? Who were the properly punished victims? These and other questions have been addressed in a few sentences only by a handful of bold, reform-minded authors, but normally they are ignored.[6]

---

[4] This was the consistent message in my interviews with Soviet experts in Beijing and Shanghai in the winter of 1984-1985, and I could not find a favorable view of Khrushchev in published sources.

[5] Su Shaozhi, "Jianchi he fazhan Mao Zedong sixiang," *Makesizhuyi yanjiu* (congkan), no. 1 (1984): 18-25.

[6] Su Shaozhi, "Develop Marxism Under Contemporary Conditions: In Commemoration

Deng Xiaoping may himself be motivated not to delve deeply into the Soviet purges. In 1957 he was a leading figure in carrying out China's repressive antirightist campaign. Later he looked back on these purges in almost the same terms employed in China for Stalin's purges: the campaign itself was necessary even if in many cases an incorrect judgment was rendered.[7] Reformers would prefer that the purges of China's Cultural Revolution be equated with Stalin's purges; this would open the way to Deng's unconditional condemnation and their own fuller critiques. In practice, they can only seek out small successes, such as slipping in a reference to Khrushchev or amplifying in a few sentences on Stalin's purges.

The verdicts on some of the more sensitive points have been subject to waves of closer, if on the whole indirect and partially concealed, scrutiny since 1978. At the end of 1979 and in 1980, articles on Stalin clashed rather openly in their interpretations of him;[8] the 30:70 guideline was attacked from both sides, but held when the same guideline was fixed for Mao. In 1980-1982 one finds evidence on discussions of Bukharin and the political struggle of the 1920s. By 1983 there was sharp debate over Soviet collectivization and the economic strategy adopted around 1930, and finally, in a more cautious manner, by 1985 there was some reexamination of the political system from the 1930s. In each debate different weightings were proposed for Stalin's rule. On selected themes some were apparently more negative than positive, even if the conclusiveness of the verdict rendered in 1981 on Mao's pros and cons made it difficult to reverse the overall verdict on Stalin.

In the middle of 1983, informal discussions on Khrushchev were bringing forward sharply varied judgments. A few apparently dared to propose that the balance lay roughly 60:40 in Khrushchev's favor, cognizant of the analogy between Deng and Khrushchev and wondering how Deng's reform course could be welcomed in China without, on the whole, approving Khrushchev's break from the model of Stalin's time. There were also a few among the most orthodox who, I understand, advocated a minuscule weight (even 0:100) for Khrushchev's achievements and, in the process, registered discontent with Deng's reforms. It was safest, naturally, to follow the well-travelled path, weighing Khrushchev's shortcomings somewhat more heavily than his accomplishments or, if one

---

of the Centenary of the Death of Karl Marx," *Selected Writings on Studies of Marxism*, no. 2 (Beijing: Institute of Marxism-Leninism-Mao Zedong Thought, 1983), 22-23.

[7] *Selected Works of Deng Xiaoping (1975-1982)* (Beijing: Foreign Languages Press, 1984), 279.

[8] Gilbert Rozman, "China's Soviet-Watchers in the 1980s: A New Era in Scholarship," *World Politics* 37, no. 4 (July 1985): 448.

were adventurous, perhaps making the ratio 50:50. Those who followed the established path could show that they were resisting any substantial tampering with the socialist political system and the dictatorship of the proletariat. Deng himself had criticized Khrushchev mostly for his methods—inconsistency, haste, extremism, etc.—not for his interest in reform.[9] The spiritual pollution campaign, however, interrupted the informal reexamination of Khrushchev, which had failed to make its way into print. In 1985 the debate resumed amid signs of greater openness.

Deng's caution about reassessing Stalin and Khrushchev as well as Mao may have stemmed from a fear that he might be treated in the future as Khrushchev had been treated in the Brezhnev era. Deng's awareness of parallels between the Soviet Union in the 1950s and China in the late 1970s and early 1980s both helped guide policy toward Mao and influenced views on Soviet history. Even so, as time passed, according to my informants, official party documents in China mentioned Stalin less and less. Quotations from him became less frequent in publications. Among intellectuals and the younger generation of officials a negative image of Stalin could be detected. Censorship alone kept this image from emerging clearly in Chinese writings.

By 1985, pressure was mounting also for a reassessment of Khrushchev. In theoretical circles some Chinese were proposing that his attack on Stalin's personality cult should be treated as a contribution. In the absence of a directive from the leadership, they could not state this in print. Also working against a strongly positive image of Khrushchev were foreign policy assessments, including lingering memories of the pressure he placed on Beijing to establish a joint navy and gain use of a Chinese port (goals later linked to Soviet gains in Vietnam).

The appeal to Lenin's authority in the 1980s in one important respect resembles the appeal in the 1960s and much of the 1970s: Lenin was the great leader who first grasped what socialism requires, but he died prematurely before he could firmly establish the policies and the theory that would make crystal clear to others what must be done. This is the seedbed for later mistakes in the Soviet Union. In Mao's times, these were mistakes, such as neglecting class struggle, that were attributed to Khrushchev's revisionism. Under Deng, Lenin's untimely death is linked to the later emergence of Stalin's rigid centralized economic model and bureaucratization,[10] which in turn led to the excessive rejection of funda-

[9] This was reported to me in several interviews, but I have not found a published reference.

[10] Chen Huijun, "Sulian guojia zibenzhuyi wenti chutan," *Shijie shi yanjiu dongtai*, no. 8 (1984): 24-26; Jin Hui, Lu Nanquan, and Zhang Kangqin, eds., *Lun Sulian jingji: guanli tizhi yu zhuyao zhengce*, (Shenyang: Liaoning renminchubanshe, 1982), 5-7.

mental socialist principles in the Khrushchev era. Either way, the problems of later socialism are never traced to Lenin's own policies, only to his shortened experience with the problems of building socialism that gave him inadequate opportunity to resolve the range of problems that would eventually be faced. The two Lenins in Chinese sources of different periods may scarcely resemble each other; yet each serves to legitimize the approved socialist worldview. Under Mao's shadow, there was but modest room even for Lenin to stand, while Deng has placed Lenin far higher on the most honored pedestal. Lenin is perhaps the strongest ideological bond between China and the Soviet Union. In China as in the Soviet Union, he is an unassailable figure in the history of Marxism. The apparently easy decision in 1978-1979 not to drop Leninism, keeping the label of Marxism-Leninism rather than Marxism for China's ideology, has had far-reaching consequences for writings on the Soviet Union. It limits the scope of reform-oriented criticisms. This common bond with Moscow is well understood in Beijing. People are known to refer to Lenin as the great god (*da sheng* or *da pusa*), as opposed to Mao who has become a small god (*xiao sheng* or *xiao pusa*).

Lenin means different things to orthodox and reform advocates. To the former he was deeply concerned about maintaining control. While approving the NEP and the introduction of capitalist elements, he insisted on controlling the arteries—economic, political, and military—of the system.[11] At any time, it would be possible to clamp a tourniquet on the flows of capitalism into the system without serious damage to the vital organs. This is apparently Chen Yun's reasoning as well as Lenin's. To the reformers, Lenin was a battler against bureaucracy and a man who came to appreciate the need for substantial market forces.[12] This may be Deng Xiaoping's reasoning.

One can detect a tendency in China to substitute "Marxism" for "Marxism-Leninism-Mao Zedong Thought." For some this may be nothing more than a convenient shorthand, while for others in the reform camp this may be practically the only permissible, if well-concealed, protest against the Leninist, Stalinist, and Maoist traditions.

The first three Soviet leaders represent the entire spectrum of socialist options in the post-Mao era. On the left is Stalin. On the right is Khrushchev. In the middle is Lenin. Only part of this spectrum may be advocated openly in the mid-1980s. The orthodox group does not stand fully

[11] Luo Gengmo, "Chongdu 'Suweiai zhengquan de dangqian renwu': jinian Liening danchen yibaiyishi zhounian," *Hongqi*, no. 8 (1980): 22-27.
[12] Li Guidong, "Liening he zhishifenzi," *Shehuikexue*, no. 2 (1984): 7-8; Xue Muduo, "Liening shi zenyang kandai zhishifenzi zai jianshe zhong de zuoyong de," *Renwen zazhi*, no. 1 (1984): 26-27, 33.

behind Stalin; it positions itself intermediate between Stalin's and Lenin's economic policy—with some criticisms of the former but never the latter. The reform group takes an intermediate position between Khrushchev's and Lenin's economic policy, stressing Lenin's anti-bureaucratic viewpoint and trying somehow to introduce Khrushchev's criticism of Stalin, in the hope, one suspects, of indirectly attacking Mao as well. Although Chinese might surmise that Deng's economic reforms have in many cases surpassed Khrushchev's, Deng's speech has been much more careful, and he has chosen to position himself on noneconomic matters largely in the center of a well-delineated socialist spectrum. Deng concentrates on China's economic reforms, agreeing to allow the orthodox position on politics and ideology and on interpretations of the first three Soviet leaders to maintain a central position.

Certain fixed ideas establish the framework for writings about the Soviet Union. They are not subject to direct assault except by Deng Xiaoping or a collective decision of the top leadership; yet there is room for maneuver. Whereas the overall evaluation of Stalin is an unchangeable 30:70, the concrete contents of pros and cons are changeable. Authors may demonstrate their compliance with the standard formula at the beginning or end of their presentation, then reveal their true leanings by the precise weight they give to one side in contrast to the empty words used for the other. Rarely is the ratio itself mentioned.

Should Chinese probe deeper into evaluations of various socialist countries and leaders? That was a question that was apparently raised in 1983, simultaneous with the discussion of Khrushchev. Some proposed that the four cardinal principles should be the standard for judgment. Others pointed out, however, that the inclusion of Mao Zedong Thought in one of the four principles creates an impossible standard for other countries. Some urged that a country's foreign policy be included as a standard. The debate failed to set theoretical guidelines before it halted with the spiritual pollution campaign. Statements by Deng Xiaoping and Hu Yaobang to leaders of nonruling communist parties proposed instead a "live and let live" view. "You don't criticize us and we won't criticize you."[13]

Broadly speaking, there were three alternatives for Chinese views of Soviet society: 1) to attack from the left; 2) to attack from the right; or 3) to accept the Soviet system as socialist. The first, which emphasizes the need for class struggle and continuous revolution, was the Maoist approach and had been discredited by its unsubstantiated application for a

[13] Li Ji and Guo Qingshi, "Uphold the Marxist Principle in Developing Our Party's Relations with Communist Parties of Various Countries," *Hongqi*, no. 2 (January 16, 1983): 10-14, trans. FBIS, PRC International Affairs General, February 24, 1983, pp. A1-A7.

period of fifteen or more years. Given China's reform program from 1978, this approach was inconceivable. The second is the Western approach to Soviet society and to socialism in general. Its stress on democracy and human rights threatens the Communist Party's hold on power. The fact that China's aged leadership at the end of the 1970s and through most, if not all, of the 1980s is comprised primarily of veterans of the revolutionary movement and high officials of the 1950s means that it has a huge stake in justifying earlier policies and sustaining communist control. How could these leaders adopt a capitalist worldview? In order to make the system work better, China moved to the right; yet officials did not talk in terms of left and right, nor did they apply these terms to the Soviet Union. It was sufficient to look for justifications in the original ideas of Marx and Lenin or in other reform periods (such as the NEP) in the history of socialism to legitimize reforms without indicating that China was embracing capitalist critiques of socialism. In the area of foreign policy, the Soviet Union could continue to be attacked from the standpoint of national interest without any longer mentioning that hegemonism was rooted in deviations from socialism found in domestic policies. China chose the alternative of recognizing the Soviet Union as socialist and confining its criticisms largely to foreign policy and to the need for reforms to reinvigorate the Soviet economy.

Leadership and Chinese Perceptions

To what extent has Deng Xiaoping played a direct role in Soviet matters? There are indications that just as Mao reserved Soviet relations as his own bailiwick, Deng remains the final arbiter of Soviet affairs. When the journal *Wenyi baijia* went public in the winter of 1979-1980 with the conclusion that Chinese regard the Soviet Union as socialist,[14] and about the same time a vice-president of Beijing University made a similar comment in public, Deng, one is told, took a direct role in criticizing these transgressions. On Soviet foreign policy, Deng has consistently taken the leading role. In late 1980 or early 1981, he is alleged to have led in shifting China's reaction to the Solidarity movement in Poland from condemnation of the Polish government and the Soviet role to a more neutral position. In early 1982 when a delegation from the International Liaison Bureau, led by Liu Xiao, a former ambassador to Moscow, returned from the Soviet Union, Deng was apparently influenced by their report in his decision to lead China into negotiations. Wang Youping, another former ambassador to Moscow and a likely member of the powerful Central Con-

---

[14] "Harbin Seminar Examines Soviet Literature, Society," *Wenyi baijia*, no. 2 (1979): 254-56, trans. FBIS, PRC International Affairs, Soviet Union, April 14, 1980, pp. C1-C4.

sulting Committee of which Deng is the chairman, has influence too. Yet
Deng has also been the architect of an open-door policy to capitalist countries and a chief critic of Soviet military expansion. He has carefully balanced reform and orthodox forces in the Chinese leadership, now leaning
to one side and then to the other.

Within China, ties with Washington and Moscow have been discussed
as tactical or strategic. The United States continues to be labeled "imperialist," ruling out a close association. Some officials have argued beyond
that, that relations with the United States should be tactical in nature, for
short-term advantage only. Others, however, favor the term "strategic"
to suggest the anticipated long-term character of Sino-American ties.
Deng sided with the latter group, recognizing this relationship as strategic.

One point of view is that Deng's judgment has been decisive; if he were
to leave the leadership scene, ties with the United States would stand in
peril of being downgraded to the tactical category. Another view is that
the reform forces have gained strength, and Sino-American, Sino-West-
ern, and Sino-Japanese ties are already deeply enough rooted to survive
Deng's departure. Perhaps a more widely held view is that Deng has stood
in the way of those in the leadership who are favorably disposed to Moscow, that he has strongly opposed Soviet hegemonism and fears that a
Sino-Soviet rapprochement could get out of control and lead to "leaning
to one side" again. It is a door Deng worries about opening. Even in 1979
that sort of worry may have been a factor in Deng's annoyance that the
reevaluation of the Soviet Union as revisionist had occurred prematurely.

Deng is the most powerful leader of China; yet he is part of a collective
leadership in which other veteran leaders with considerable prestige and
independence serve. Deng's primary attention has centered on domestic
economic reforms and the opening to capitalist countries. The orthodox
group has remained in the background on these matters, while Deng has
arranged for the promotion of other reformers, such as Zhao Ziyang, to
take charge of these policies. The power hierarchy dealing with the Soviet
Union appears to be different. Veteran party and heavy industry leaders
have a more prominent role. Second to Deng appears to be Chen Yun,
whose high office and vast experience entitle him to an important say on
both the economics and politics of the Soviet Union. Chen's ideas about
economic reform appear to differ substantially from Deng's. On economic relations as well as scientific and cultural exchanges, the most important figures in handling negotiations are Li Peng and Yao Yilin. Being
Zhou Enlai's stepson, Li is a new leader, but has not been identified with
economic reforms. Yao is closer to Chen Yun. Together they may make a
strong case for expanded Soviet economic ties, both to achieve balance

among trading partners and to reequip China's aging industrial plants as well as to build up the centrally managed heavy industrial sector. These views have been a driving force on the Chinese side toward "normalization" and may have been most openly reflected in December 1984 when Arkhipov visited China. As China's urban reforms ran into difficulty in 1985, anticipated Soviet aid for reequipping the centralized sector may have seemed particularly attractive.[15] In foreign policy the most prominent figure is Qian Qichen, who is in charge of the biannual negotiations. Some Chinese refer to Qian as "the Chinese Kapitsa." Similar to the Soviet deputy foreign minister, who has long been responsible for Chinese relations, Qian has important responsibilities for bilateral relations. Moreover, he is rumored to be a likely candidate for foreign minister, just as Li Peng is rumored to be a likely successor to Zhao Ziyang. On military matters, Yang Shangkun, who like Li Peng studied in Moscow, is second to Deng.

In the Soviet Union the central figures associated with China—Rakhmanin, Tikhvinsky, Kapitsa—have dual roles in policy-making and academic research. They have published extensively. In China there is a clearer dividing line between officials and intellectuals. Chinese specialists are further removed from decision-making. The intellectuals have long been excluded from policy-making, and the officials until recently could make little claim to academic learning. Intellectuals have tended to avoid giving concrete opinions. They have become accustomed to talking in abstractions that often only give a hint of their real concerns. Through philosophical discussions, Chinese specialists—on Marxism, on the Soviet Union, and in other social science fields—manage to participate in the debate about political and ideological reforms. The very term "political economy" used to identify the main field in the social sciences, conveys the close connection between economics and politics. In socialist countries, as Chinese are aware, one cannot strip politics and philosophy from economic principles. They are conscious of the interrelations between economic reforms and political and ideological reforms.

Three Countries in the Chinese Worldview

The Chinese worldview is primarily concerned with three foreign countries and three dimensions of social change and types of societies. The three countries are the Soviet Union, the United States, and Japan. The Soviet Union is the focus for the most open debate—the debate that

---

[15] David M. Bachman, *Chen Yun and the Chinese Political System* (Berkeley: Institute of East Asian Studies, University of California, 1985), 152-56; Huo Zhenyi, "Tianjin Plans to Increase Soviet Trade," *China Daily*, July 22, 1985, p. 2.

China's leaders see as most relevant to their immediate economic re-forms. It concerns the dimension of the old model of socialism versus re-form-oriented socialism. Although Hungary (and to a lesser extent Yu-goslavia) plays a part in this debate, it is seen as a small country, very different from China in its background conditions, and not a source of much that China can learn. The debate about the Soviet Union, which this book examines, is the most accessible and the least sensitive of the three great debates that interest Chinese intellectuals.

The United States is the focus of the debate on socialism versus capi-talism. The stakes for China on this dimension are much higher and the tolerance of leaders for diverse viewpoints is correspondingly much lower. The debate about the United States must therefore be less visible to the public, more focused on issues that seem to be peripheral, and more abstract. The term "ziyouhua" (literally "making freer") is a code for the American model.

Japan represents Chinese concern for the continuum: tradition versus borrowing from the outside. Japanese are thought to have borrowed heavily from foreign countries, yet preserved their own traditions. They have succeeded in modernizing rapidly without succumbing to many of the spiritual problems seen in the United States and elsewhere. Reform-ers ask, why can't China worry less about foreign influences and borrow more extensively, following the Japanese precedent? Traditionalists eager to preserve China's own value system and lifestyle look to Japan and to other East Asian countries, including Singapore, cognizant of their Con-fucian traditions. To simplify matters, we can surmise that young people are attracted to the debate over Japan as well as to that over the United States, while older persons and political figures have been concerned with the debate over the Soviet Union.

From the Soviet Union and other socialist countries (primarily Eastern Europe), China expects to learn much of relevance for reforming social-ism. This is the continuum that Chinese leaders want their people to be thinking about most. From the United States and the Western, capitalist countries, China is learning about modern science and technology, and seeking to obtain the economic benefits of an international division of la-bor. From Japan and other East Asian countries, China seeks guidance on how to maintain traditions while borrowing extensively from the West.

The Two Legs of Socialism

Chinese studies of the Soviet Union suggest the view that socialism has two legs in its domestic policy. One leg consists of economic policies. The other is a combination of political and ideological policies. The former is the primary problem in the Soviet Union, as it has been in China. The latter is not so serious. The orthodox position is that China has not broken very sharply from early practices—the Soviet socialist model—and does not need a sharp break. The orthodox group frowns on discussions that would call for reform in this second sphere. The reform group wonders if China really wants to go beyond the Soviet economic model or if it can afford to keep the Stalin ideological and political model for intellectual life. By now the economic model is different from those of Stalin's time and subsequent Soviet approaches; for reformers, the Soviet economy has become less interesting. Yet ideological and political reform topics have, if anything, greater appeal.

The discrepancy between the two legs is striking. Some Chinese ask, "How can we walk on two legs if the economic leg has grown long [*chang tui*] and the political and ideological leg remains short [*duan tui*]? How can China keep its balance?" Over a quarter-century earlier Mao had first talked of "walking on two legs" in order to achieve balanced economic development. Now the issue had resurfaced with noneconomic concerns. Another way of expressing the problem was also gaining popularity. Chinese summarize their leaders' policies as, "*Jingji yao kaifang, sixiang yao tongji, zhengzhi yao wending*" (We must open our economy, unify our thought, stabilize our politics). In other words, the economy should be reformed, but thought must be controlled to prevent deviations, and politics should also not be touched. Alternatively Chinese talk about the economic test being against the left (*fanzi*) and the ideological test against the right (*fanyou*). This is the leadership's basic model and the starting point for publications on the Soviet Union that reformers have challenged.

TURNING POINTS IN CHINESE VIEWS OF THE SOVIET UNION

Between 1977 and 1985 there were discernible changes in Chinese views of 1) Soviet history; 2) current conditions in the Soviet Union; and 3) contemporary Soviet foreign policy. On the whole, opinions of the Soviet Union were improving; yet paradoxically almost everything that is subject to strong criticism in 1985 occurred after this period of increasingly favorable views was in progress. Views of the Soviet Union became more complex, as they were differentiated to weigh pros and cons on many specialized topics.

Soviet History

Conferences and review articles have been concerned with many of the milestones of Soviet socialism: the transition from War Communism to the NEP, the political struggles of the 1920s including those between Stalin and Bukharin, the all-out collectivization and emergence of the Stalin

economic model, the significance of the "thaw literature" in the 1950s
and 1960s, and the economic reforms of the post-Stalin era. Other topics
are treated more indirectly, yet can also be analyzed, such as the overall
assessment of Stalin's leadership, the evaluation of Khrushchev's de-
Stalinization program, and the question of Brezhnev's legacy for Soviet
socialism. We can summarize the general consensus in China on these
matters and compare it to both recent Soviet and recent Western views.

The abandonment and, some would say, the repudiation of War Communism stands out as one of the most important developments in the history of Soviet socialism, according to Chinese writers. Lenin's theoretical
reevaluation of socialism at that time (late Lenin) also represents the single greatest contribution to the theory of the construction of socialism. In
official Chinese eyes, Westerners and Soviets since the time of Stalin have
both erred in dismissing the NEP too lightly as an aberration or a temporary retreat to capitalism when it has longstanding significance as a
foundation for establishing socialism in an economically backward country. War Communism symbolizes a coercive program without adequate
material incentives, while the NEP appears as a parallel to China's economic program in the 1980s: wide scope for market forces, household
management of agricultural resources, foreign investment, and reliance
on experts.[16] The wisdom of Lenin and the experience of Soviet history
are used to justify current Chinese policies.

Less openly and with more limitations, Chinese publications have examined the struggles in the 1920s between Stalin and his opponents, especially Bukharin, but also Trotsky. The suggestion that Stalin acted im-
properly in his struggle against Trotsky was easily rejected. The proposal
that Bukharin was treated unjustly and also was the true successor to
Lenin, seeking to preserve the NEP model and to maintain peasant support, was more tempting.[17] Nevertheless, despite reform-oriented translations and writings on Bukharin, the official position remains that there
should be no "reversal of verdicts." The issue was left in a state of limbo
with little direct analysis or refutation of the pro-Bukharin ideas, but also
little acceptance of them in the overall evaluations. Criticisms of Stalin
center on his later years, not his actions in the 1920s.

How do official Chinese views treat Stalin's collectivization, high-
speed forced industrialization, socialist realism, and purges? They acknowledge excesses and errors in timing, but criticize none of these policies in principle. Collectivization draws the most criticism in published

[16] Su Shaozhi and Feng Lanrui, "Wuchanjieji qude zhengquan hou de shehui fazhan
jieduan wenti," *Jingji yanjiu*, no. 5 (1979): 17-18.

[17] Zhongguo shehuikexueyuan MaLiezhuyi Mao Zedong sixiang yanjiusuo, ed., *Lun
Buhalin sixiang* (Guiyang: Guizhou renminchubanshe, 1982), i-iii.

Chinese sources.[18] Although sooner or later it would have been necessary, it was not carried out properly. Excuses are made for many of the
Soviet mistakes. The first socialist country lacked experience and had no
prior example from which to benefit. Enemies of the people could not be
placated and had to be dealt with through collectivization and purges.
Foreign imperialist enemies were becoming increasingly menacing, and
Stalin was right to adopt stringent measures to prepare his country for
the war that was to come. Set phrases are employed to close off discussion
of Stalin's serious errors. Chinese fail to explain what is meant by the
"widening of the purges" beyond that which was necessary. When they
draw attention only to the unjust treatment of loyal communists, it
seems as if the punishments meted out to anyone who was not in that
category are not being questioned. Brief mention of the excessively rosy
coloring in post-World War II Soviet literature also does not lead to any
analysis of what went wrong and how the principles of socialist realism
might bear some responsibility.[19] Chinese criticisms of the Stalin period
are limited rather than fundamental. Soviet choices were less-than-ideal
because of adverse circumstances, not because of systemic errors. Literary
conditions worsened, and the Soviet economic model became less suitable
after World War II. In other words, things had been fine earlier; the problem was a failure to reform. Chinese criticisms follow the Soviet example
of refering vaguely to Stalin's "cult of personality." Although they go
beyond Soviet writings (at least of post-Khrushchev times) in criticizing
some aspects of the Stalin era, such as collectivization, the overall rubric
and specific criticisms are similar, and the ratio of 70:30 in pros and cons
is probably not much lower than the implied ratio in Soviet publications.
Chinese specifically reject Western writings on the Stalin era as too negative and motivated by anti-communism.[20]

There is also close affinity between Chinese and Soviet treatments of
the Khrushchev era and the "thaw literature" that starkly contrasts with
Western writings. While the West praises Solzhenitsyn and others who
have pointed out serious shortcomings in the Soviet system, Chinese regard them as anti-socialist. This disapproval is accompanied by positive

[18] Wei Shaobo, "Sulian xiandaishi dierci taolunhui zongshu," *Shanghai shifan xueyuan
xuebao* (shehuikexue ban), no. 1 (1984): 118-22.

[19] Ba yuanxiao hanshou jiaocai bianxie zu, *Guoji gongchanzhuyi yundong shi* (Henan:
Henan renminchubanshe, 1984), 362-63; Li Mingbin, "Sulian wushiliushi niandai zhongqi
de wenyi zhengce ji qi dui wenxue chuangzuo de yingxiang," *Sulian dongou wenti*, no. 2
(1984): 52-59.

[20] This was a view often expressed in my interviews and is reflected in Zhou Xincheng
and Li Jun, "Shiying woguo jiakuai chengshi tizhi gaige de xuyao jinyibu kaizhan Sulian,
dongou guojia jingji tizhi gaige de yanjiu gongzuo," *Shijie jingji yu zhengzhi neican*, no.
11 (1984): 15-19.

comments about the literary policies of the Brezhnev period and the crackdown against the earlier erroneous tendencies of the "thaw literature."[21] Both Chinese and Soviets recall Khrushchev's blundering inconsistencies and hasty decisions while, for most purposes, making him a nonperson whose name must not be mentioned. He receives almost no credit for turning the Soviet Union sharply away from Stalin's practices and for condemning those practices. While in the West Khrushchev may be considered the best of Soviet leaders for giving a humane face to socialism, in China as in the Soviet Union he is treated as the worst of Soviet leaders.

The sharpest turnabout in Chinese thinking about Soviet history since the Mao era concerns the domestic policies of Brezhnev's time. Whereas as recently as 1977 these were harshly condemned, in the 1980s they are treated sympathetically, if critically. Some of the criticisms are exactly the opposite of what was earlier written: excessive egalitarianism rather than vast and unjust inequalities, timidity of reform due to rigid adherence to principles of the Stalin era rather than repudiation of Stalin's model.[22] Chinese criticisms are no longer sweeping condemnations; they recognize the continued superior functioning of the old system in comparison to American capitalism during much of the Brezhnev era and suggest that if reforms had been more comprehensive, the system would have been able to prevent the economic slowdown and other problems of the late 1970s and early 1980s. The problems faced by the Soviet Union are not treated as trivial; yet they are mainly discussed in the context of management shortcomings that can be resolved through reforms of the economic system with modest adjustments in the theory of socialism and in political institutions. One finds no echo of the severe Western attacks on the stultifying atmosphere and political corruption of Soviet life. As Brezhnev's successors, especially Andropov and Gorbachev, have been criticizing the inadequacy of earlier reforms, Soviet and Chinese opinions on the Brezhnev period have been converging.

Along with Soviet domestic policy, the history of Soviet foreign policy draws Moscow and Beijing together. The exception is pre-1917 tsarist policy, especially toward China. Soviets have concentrated on justifying the treaties Russia signed with China over a few centuries and other Russian activities in China. Although Chinese articles and books against Russian imperialism sharply declined in the first years of the 1980s, there has been no effort to revise the harsh condemnations of what is regarded as

---

[21] Wu Yuanbian and Deng Shuping, eds., *Wu-liushi niandai de Sulian wenxue* (Beijing: Waiyu jiaoxue yu yanjiu chubanshe, 1984).

[22] Jin Hui, "Sulian de jingji zhanlue he jingji gaige," *Sulian dongou wenti*, no. 1 (1983): 1-9.

one of the worst of the imperialist powers. Soviet foreign policy under Lenin and Stalin is another matter. If Stalin is depicted as making mistakes concerning the Chinese revolution, which meant that the Chinese under Mao independently worked out a successful revolutionary strategy, he is still viewed as a friend of China and as the defender of socialism in a world of hostile countries. Chinese sources largely praise Soviet foreign policy to the late 1950s and in recent years have become less critical of policies in the 1960s, such as the sending of troops into Czechoslovakia. Criticism now focuses on Soviet policy in the Third World, primarily during the post-Vietnam War era.[23] It is contemporary Soviet foreign policy of the past decade that bothers China, not the policies of earlier decades.

This perspective on Soviet history combines the pro-Lenin, largely pro-Stalin, and anti-Khrushchev thinking of Mao with the pro-NEP and pro-post-Stalin reform thinking of Deng. In late 1979, when the label "revisionist" was dropped from discussions of the Soviet Union, this overall perspective on Soviet history quickly took shape. Criticisms of the Soviet Union from a leftist viewpoint quickly disappeared. Over the next years attempts to move closer to a Western perspective critical of the Soviet Union from the right were deflected. By early 1982 the general outlines of the new consensus were in place.

Current Conditions in the Soviet Union

In recent years success or failure for the Soviet Union has been judged largely according to the standard of the economic growth rate. As the figures declined or remained very low for several years, the Chinese were switching from the negative explanation that the problem was in the Soviet system—its switch from socialism to revisionism—to constructive criticism concerning the need for reform. Already in 1981 and 1982 Chinese specialists were attentive to reform policies in the Soviet Union, suggesting that they are part of the same process in which China is engaged and hold some promise for alleviating Soviet economic problems.[24]

Andropov's early speeches and policies quickly heightened Chinese interest in Soviet reform prospects. From 1983 more optimistic predictions were appearing about the likelihood of substantial economic reforms, which would succeed in raising the Soviet growth rate. Andropov received a favorable press in China. Not only did his economic policies and experiments such as brigade contracts win praise; his revisions of Soviet

[23] Liu Jiangyung, "Sulian de dongya zhanlue ji woguo de duice," *Shijie jingji yu zhengzhi neican*, no. 2 (1985): 35-39.
[24] Zhou Xincheng et al., eds., *Sulian jingji gaige gaikuang* (Beijing: Zhongguo renmin daxue, 1981); *Sulian he bufen dongou guojia jingji gaige* (Beijing: CASS, Institute of World Economies, 1981).

ideology excited Chinese to react enthusiastically. Andropov is credited with many important revisions, most importantly moving the Soviet Union back to an earlier stage of socialism and opening the way to borrowing from other socialist countries.[25] It is true that Chinese articles continue to point to serious obstacles to reform and are reluctant to give a timetable in the 1980s or beyond for completion of the basic set of reforms needed to break out of the current difficult situation. Nonetheless, they have also been quick over the last few years to credit the Soviet economy with even small successes, while praising Soviet prospects in the long run. The Chinese position remains more wary than the Soviet one to proclaim success around the corner (after Brezhnev's death, Soviet caution approached the Chinese position), while it is more optimistic than the many American doubters who do not think that Soviet leaders are prepared for the drastic overhaul of the social system necessary to set the economy on a new, successful track.

While on economic reforms there is still considerable distance between the Soviet and Chinese positions, Chinese assessments of Soviet social conditions and academic debates suggest greater agreement. Many articles on education, sociology, city planning, and other areas convey a desire to learn from the Soviet experience.[26] Not only is the Soviet Union a model because of its more advanced modernization, it is also a model because it is socialist. Chinese use the term "socialist spiritual civilization" along with "socialist material civilization" as one of the two goals that guide the country.[27] This is directly opposed to capitalist civilization, which is described as corrupting and selfish. The Soviet Union is not devoid of spiritual problems, such as alcoholism and divorce, Chinese sources note, but on the whole, it is treated favorably for its noneconomic characteristics. By 1985 Chinese newspapers and journals were also reporting enthusiastically about the warmth of Soviet hospitality to visiting Chinese delegations.[28] All thought that the Soviet people were racist or that the leaders harbored strong resentments against China had apparently been cast aside. Lenin and Stalin had built a socialist spiritual civilization, and recent Soviet leaders kept adding to it through high-level educational programs, political stability, and the development of the natural

[25] Wu Renzhang and Jia Lianyi, "Jinnianlai Sulian fada shehuizhuyi lilun de xin bianhua," *Sulian dongou wenti*, no. 3 (1984): 20-24; "Zuotanhui: Andeluopofu shiqi de Sulian jingji wenti," *Sulian dongou wenti*, no. 4 (1984): 25-29.

[26] Zhang Tianen and Jin Shibo, "Dui Sulian jiaoyu zhidu de jidian kanfa: luelun zuijin ershi nianlai de gaige dongxiang," *Waiguo jiaoyu*, no. 4 (1981): 7-10; Tong Qingcai, "Sulian de yingyong shehuixue yanjiu," *Guowai shehuikexue*, no. 8 (1980): 32-36.

[27] "Liangge wenming jianshe bixu tongbu jinxing," *Liaowang*, no. 30 (July 29, 1985): 4.

[28] Ding Yiwei, "Fang Su yinxiang," *Renmin ribao*, June 22, 1985, p. 7.

and social sciences. Western specialists often find serious faults in the Soviet superstructure of government, academics, and the arts. Chinese are
reluctant to echo these criticisms, and when they do, they tend to narrow
the message (e.g. from denunciations of academic freedom to criticisms
of the slow rate of application of science and technology to the economy).

Contemporary Soviet Foreign Policy

Only in the sphere of foreign policy are Chinese and Soviet worldviews
fundamentally opposed. When the Chinese remark that despite considerable progress from 1983 to 1985 in improving Sino-Soviet relations
three obstacles remain, the message is that foreign policy alone stands in
the way of major gains that are vaguely referred to as "normalization."[29]
Chinese articles are not as vitriolic as earlier in the decade. The scope of
criticism has narrowed. Nevertheless, the Soviet presence at Cam Ranh
Bay and the Vietnamese military involvement in Kampuchea as well as
the Afghan situation and Soviet military buildups on China's northern
border are still strongly condemned.

To say that foreign policy is the number-one barrier to "normal" relations is not to say that Chinese thinking about Soviet foreign policy has
not changed significantly in the seven years following the Third Plenum
of 1978. It was slower to change than were views on domestic policy. The
Sino-Vietnamese war of 1979 and the reverberations in 1980 of Soviet
troops marching into Afghanistan delayed a new view of Soviet foreign
policy, but by 1982 it was emerging. The notion that an anti-Soviet alliance must be encouraged, with insinuations that the United States is too
soft on its superpower opponent, was the first to go. Increasingly Chinese
called for an independent foreign policy. Even so, they were clearly leaning to the American side for two or three years. Chinese stressed that
Moscow is the more dangerous of the two superpowers. It is on the offensive, while Washington in the post-Vietnam era stays on the defensive. Yet China's criticisms were becoming less one-sided. In Chinese
eyes the Soviet goal was a military impact on Europe, not on China. Under Reagan, Washington was seizing the offensive in much of the Third
World and in the arms race, while mired in Afghanistan, Moscow was becoming more defensive. The list of Chinese disagreements with U.S. foreign policy in the Third World was mounting, while the Soviet list became rather short: apart from the three obstacles, Soviet behavior in
Africa was the prime concern.[30]

[29] Shen Yiming, "Yao Yilin fuzongli fang Su," *Liaowang*, no. 30 (July 29, 1985): 27.
[30] Geng Dianzhong, "Chongxin renshi he pingjia Gu Su guanxi he Guba duiwai
zhengce," *Shijie jingji yu zhengzhi neican*, no. 4 (1985): 34-38.

By the end of 1983, a strong case for equidistance in Chinese foreign policy was being mounted in official circles within Beijing. Huan Xiang and other Western-oriented officials tried to ward it off with arguments that the Soviet Union remained the greater enemy.[31] Chernenko did not help matters in the first eight months of 1984, when Moscow adopted a tougher position toward China and the Chinese responded with renewed criticisms of Soviet foreign policy on a wide scale. Nonetheless, after the breakthrough at the foreign ministers' meeting in New York in September, Beijing moved somewhat toward a position of equidistance. Moscow and Washington are both hegemonists and dangerous to China, both superpowers and threats to world peace. The latter is also imperialist. America's Taiwan policy is regarded as no less serious than the Soviet Vietnam policy. Reagan's invasion of Grenada is portrayed as a parallel to the Soviet role in Afghanistan. Each superpower has regions of the world where it is the main aggressor. And each in its military presence and alliances in Asia poses a threat to China.[32]

Separately for history, contemporary domestic policy, and contemporary foreign policy, we can detect improving images of the Soviet Union from 1978 to 1985. Between 1977 and 1979 there occurred an abrupt change of course with the downfall of the radical viewpoint, which attacked the Soviet Union from the left. From late 1979 to 1981 there occurred another shift as Soviet domestic policies and Soviet history were interpreted more favorably. Gradual improvements continued to occur: by 1985 most official images were favorable, although there were sufficient exceptions to prevent great optimism about a sudden rebound in the Soviet economy or breakthrough in Sino-Soviet relations.

EXPLANATIONS FOR CHANGING OFFICIAL VIEWS

What happened during this seven-year period to account for China's improving impressions of the Soviet Union? To some extent, these impressions reflect actual conditions in the Soviet Union, above all the rise of Andropov and then Gorbachev, who are perceived as reform leaders whose domestic policies more closely resemble China's economic reforms. Another factor is the improving Soviet commentaries on China. Brezhnev's assertion that China is socialist helped establish a new bilateral atmosphere. Later, private Soviet interest in and implied approval of some of China's reforms for a time partially compensated for the absence of favorable press commentary in the Soviet Union. Intermittent prog-

---

[31] Huan Xiang, "Ouxing guangan," *Shijie jingji yu zhengzhi neican*, no. 1 (1984): 1-2.

[32] Wu Yikang, "Qian tan shijie jingji de duojihua qushi—jian ping weilai shi 'Taiping-yang shidai' de tifa," *Shijie jingji yu zhengzhi neican*, no. 4 (1984): 12-17.

ress in the negotiations that began in the fall of 1982 also gave momentum to more positive perceptions. The United States and Japan may also have contributed to China's partial turn toward the Soviet Union, particularly through America's Taiwan policies and the failure to meet China's expectations for foreign investment and open markets.

Although all of these factors are pertinent, there is little doubt that what has mattered most is China's own domestic considerations. China's leadership regards the country as socialist. It has sought to foster an environment of political stability and social control along with heightened economic development and individual labor motivation. Changing images of the domestic side of the Soviet Union have been seen as a means to these ends.

China's communist leaders have needed the Soviet Union to legitimize their social system and even their reform program. The history of socialism in China provides little to support Deng Xiaoping's programs. Soviet history is much richer in appropriate examples, such as Lenin's NEP, Stalin's expansion of the educational system and emphasis on technology, and even Brezhnev's support for the sociological (ideological) concept, "the socialist way of life." According to Chinese comparisons of socialist countries, China is not floundering in some limbo of unparalleled reforms; it is taking a middle path between Yugoslavia and the Soviet Union along the common course of socialist reforms away from the outdated Stalin model.[33] Proof of China's bona fide socialist credentials comes largely from the Soviet experience.

At least five purposes are served by Chinese publications on Soviet society. First, Soviet history, especially high rates of economic growth, demonstrates the superiority of socialism to capitalism. Second, Soviet history provides models to legitimize controversial reform programs in the People's Republic. Third, the Soviet Union is an example of a more modernized socialist country from which China can learn. Fourth, studies of the Soviet Union and Eastern Europe reassure the Chinese people that they are engaged in a common process of changeover and reform within the socialist world. Fifth, the example of the Soviet Union, particularly its superstructure in the arts, social sciences, government, etc., is a counterweight to excessive fascination with capitalist countries and their potential corrupting influence.

Chinese imply in the literature on Soviet society a future of Soviet and Chinese socialism standing together victorious over the capitalist countries of the world. The superiority of socialism will be revealed in a su-

[33] Ding Zeji et al., *Sulian he dongou guojia nongye jingji tizhi de gaige* (Beijing: Nongye chubanshe, 1982), 11-14.

perior material civilization, made possible by rapid economic growth, and a superior spiritual civilization, which is part of the inevitable contrast between socialism and capitalism. Chinese leaders want to show the superiority of socialism because they are veterans of the communist movement—most having served this cause for half a century or longer. They want to maintain their own power and the power of their networks of friends and associates. Many have noted with alarm the widespread admiration among the Chinese people of capitalist material life, music and literature, and even political principles. Positive impressions of the Soviet Union are an attempt to balance the one-sided fascination with the capitalist world.

To counter the enthusiasm with the West and capitalist East Asia, Chinese officials and certain academics have taken a selective approach toward praise and blame. They laud Western science and technology, seek to borrow extensively from Western education, and call for an open door for trade and foreign investment. Yet they criticize spiritual pollution in the capitalist world, point to Soviet successes, and seek to explain why socialist countries are behind in some areas.

While the course of China's economic reforms from 1978 to 1985 was, with short-term exceptions, a unilinear expansion in the role of the market and personal incentives, the course of political and ideological policies was almost cyclical. China's leaders would relax controls and then crack down or seek to set limits to debates. Renewed controls appeared in March 1979 (Deng's speech on the four cardinal principles), October 1979 (Li Xiannian's speech on socialist leaders), December 1980 and much of 1981 (the attacks on Bai Hua), October 1983 (the spiritual pollution campaign), and March 1985 (Deng's speech on the pernicious effects of capitalism brought by the urban reform).

Deng Xiaoping is China's foremost leader, and his speeches have initiated each major cycle of control as well as each major economic reform. Others in the leadership, however, are more often identified with the insistence on social control and the opposition to reforms of the political and ideological systems. It is primarily the old guard in the collective leadership, not Zhao Ziyang or Hu Yaobang, that has maintained the pressure to distance China from the capitalist countries and to silence domestic critics of the political and ideological systems.

Orthodox versus Reform Views

Debates on the Soviet Union and on Marxist ideology are the most open forums for following the clash of thinking in China over the nature of socialism. Those who seek to make far-reaching reforms in socialism turn back to early Marx, late Lenin, and Bukharin for a revised set of ideological precepts. They take advantage of each turn in the ideological cycle from control toward freedom to try to take a step forward in shifting the terms of debate. Early in 1979 they sought through theoretical discussions to move China back to a not-fully-socialist stage of development or to redefine socialism to emphasize freedom and democracy. In the 1980s they have drawn different lessons from Soviet history than have the voices of orthodoxy. They are also more critical of contemporary Soviet society.

The reformers who write about Soviet history challenge the excuses that are often presented for major policy errors. Their view of War Communism is not that it was a necessary response to the emergency of civil war, but that ideology had led Soviet leaders astray. On this topic reformers had some success, because Lenin had come to the same conclusion for the final year or so of radical policies before the abrupt shift to the NEP. The reform view of the political struggles of the 1920s is less visible, but in comparison to the Soviet Union, Bukharin became a subject of open discussion. Above all, reformers dispute the explanation that Stalin acted correctly in collectivization, the purges, and other major policy initiatives that expanded political control in the 1930s. A conference on collectivization in 1983 provided an opportunity for the reexamination of Stalin's economic policies,[34] but other more sensitive policies of the Stalin era (and the term "Stalinism") remain essentially off-limits.

Perhaps the most open expression of a reform position, apart from the numerous writings on humanism and alienation, occurs in criticisms of the Soviet economy in the 1980s. On this popular topic, it is possible to take a pessimistic position, demanding more thorough reforms, some of which extend into the political and ideological spheres.[35] Some critics manage to communicate the viewpoint that to motivate the people in a socialist system requires less control from above and new forms of voluntary participation from below. The themes of meritocracy (based on expertise rather than politics), material incentives, and democratic participation figure prominently in reform thinking about Soviet socialism.

The positive view of the Soviet Union in the 1980s generally expressed by orthodox thinkers is that the current reform process represents a "second revolutionary wave," a term attributed to foreign scholars.[36] The Soviet Union was on the reform track once from the 1950s to 1960s, but mismanaged the transition. As a result, it lost time. "It muddled through," again in terms taken from the West. After a delay of a decade

[34] Wei Shaobo, "Sulian xiandaishi dierci taolunhui zongshu," 118-22.

[35] Jin Hui, "Shilun zhengzhi tizhi he jingji tizhi de guanxi: jiantan Sulian zhengzhi tizhi dui jingji gaige de yingxiang," *Sulian dongou wenti,* no. 4 (1984): 8-13.

[36] "Zuotanhui: Andeluopofu shiqi de Sulian jingji wenti," 24.

or longer, it is now heading back on track. The transition from the 1970s to 1980s has the potential to accelerate Soviet economic growth. Moreover, economic problems are inseparable from other matters, including ideological and government reforms and even foreign policy. Not a few Chinese view the current transition as wide-ranging and capable of reinvigorating all spheres of Soviet life.

This research on Chinese views of the Soviet Union reveals persistent, sharp differences between reform and orthodox positions. These differences are not as easy to attribute to particular organizations and individuals as are Soviet differences of opinion on China. There are several reasons for this problem of identification. First, Chinese sources normally reveal less information about the differing viewpoints of individual authors. There are almost no footnotes or historiographical observations that place a particular study in a broader context. Review articles that summarize conference debates only mention that a few people hold one view, many hold another view, etc. No names are identified. Second, individual authors do not often write lengthy analyses. There are few interpretive books on the Soviet Union (indeed, no book-length study by a single author), and most articles are short. Finally, Soviet studies in China are much more decentralized than are Chinese studies in the Soviet Union. There are no counterparts to officials such as Rakhmanin, Tikhvinsky, and Kapitsa, or administrators such as Sladkovsky, whose own writings directly guide the work of most academics. China's officials who have a major role in Soviet policy do not write about that country, as far as bibliographies indicate, and senior advisors with longstanding ties to the Soviet Union, such as Wang Youping and Wu Xiuquan, are only identifiable through an occasional speech transmitted to a Hong Kong journal or a volume of memoirs. (Li Huichuan, who was active in border negotiations in the 1970s and remained prominent in 1981, is an exception.) Although Liu Keming and later Xu Kui have been the directors of the leading institute for Soviet studies, the Institute of Soviet and Eastern European Studies under the Chinese Academy of Social Sciences, neither has published many articles or ones that could serve to guide the field.

Certain factors obfuscate the division between orthodox and reform below the level of the top leadership. Frequent changes in Chinese views of the Soviet Union keep shifting the terms of debate. Cyclical factors, such as the rise and fall of the spiritual pollution campaign, create temporary pressures to adopt a point of view that may not persist. Furthermore, personal networks continue to operate in China, causing the individual's viewpoint to be subordinated to the views of someone higher in the hierarchy. All of these problems complicate the identification of groups of reform and orthodox advocates.

Despite these complexities, we can generalize about the general balance between reform and orthodoxy. On the whole, the orthodox position has prevailed in Soviet studies. It has done so because it is supported by most of the top leadership. Deng Xiaoping, apparently out of concern for political stability and as a consequence of the agreement reached from 1979 to 1981 in the handling of Mao Zedong's role in Chinese history, has accepted a largely positive assessment of Stalin and a negative one of Khrushchev. The Chinese leaders have agreed on Lenin's very positive place in the history of socialism. These evaluations are the foundation for the official Chinese viewpoint on Soviet history. Chen Yun and other Chinese leaders concerned with central control of the economy have helped boost the image of the contemporary Soviet Union. Deng Liqun, Hu Qiaomu, and other leaders eager to preserve ideological orthodoxy have created an atmosphere favorable to a positive image of the Soviet superstructure. The orthodox side has had formidable support from above.

On the reform side, there is support from both above and below. Above all, Deng Xiaoping's concern that political and ideological factors interfere with economic reform has been a vital force for a reform-oriented worldview. The general course of economic reforms from 1978 and the increasing opening to the West and Japan bore a momentum of their own. Moreover, the inherent contradictions in Chinese views of the Soviet Union, such as the praise for the NEP and the simultaneous praise for Stalin or criticism of Khrushchev despite the approval given to the post-Stalin economic reforms, open the door to reform interpretations. As seen in the remarkable demonstration of public opinion at the Fourth Writers' Congress in response to Hu Qili's call for "freedom of expression" and Zhou Yang's telegram (after he had been criticized a year earlier in the spiritual pollution campaign for reform-oriented ideas expressed at the conference commemorating the centenary of Marx's death),[37] Chinese intellectuals are struggling to reduce controls over them by officials. The Soviet Union symbolizes such controls, and criticisms of the Soviet political system, even if necessarily oblique, are a way of placing this issue on the agenda in China.

The reform viewpoint is welcomed by many in the younger generation—researchers, returnees from study abroad, students, etc. Positive thinking about the Soviet model of socialism worries them because it suggests that the outcome of China's reform process will only bring a Soviet style of socialism. Young intellectuals and many youths fascinated with

[37] "Zhongguo zuoxie disici daibiao dahui zaijing kaimu," *Renmin ribao*, December 31, 1984, p. 1.

Western materialism and youth culture are also worried about China's open door being partially shut.

Another factor making it difficult for Chinese official thinking to embrace the Soviet system tightly is the tendency, even among some orthodox thinkers, to associate that system, to some degree, with both Maoist radical controls and hegemonistic foreign policy. Some Chinese retain a critical view of the Soviet Union as a country stifled by central controls. Some apparently see all Soviet leaders, in the tradition of Russian expansionism or of Soviet social imperialism, as anxious to control China. These nationalist images, once fanned by Mao and reenforced by Chinese reactions to Soviet policies in the late 1970s and early 1980s, are not easily set aside. Given these barriers and the absence of "normalization" in Sino-Soviet relations, the Chinese are hesitant to assemble the pieces of their new view of the Soviet Union together. There is no overview of Chinese thinking, no attempt to summarize just how positive the new outlook has become. Many of the most positive as well as the most negative impressions have been somewhat concealed through the *neibu* system.[38] Chinese officials have not wanted the world, and maybe not even their own people, to grasp the general implications of their emerging understanding of the Soviet Union. This reluctance to generalize has also made it difficult in the preceding chapters to proceed from piecemeal interpretations to general conclusions.

IMPROVING SINO-SOVIET RELATIONS

In retrospect, what was the Sino-Soviet dispute about? Once the dispute gained momentum, so many themes were dragged into it that one has difficulty distinguishing what counted from what did not. Was it a dispute over boundaries? After all, the Sino-Soviet border is the longest in world history, and it was established from the seventeenth to the twentieth centuries through treaties the Chinese have characterized as unequal. Yet in the 1980s (and on other occasions over two decades), the Chinese insist that they have only been interested in minor adjustments, such as of islands where the course of the main river has shifted.[39] Once negotiations began they dropped the problem of boundaries without placing it on the agenda. Was it a dispute over ideology? In the first stages of the split, the chief combatants were Mao and Khrushchev, two leaders deeply concerned about ideology and directly opposed in their attitudes about de-Stalinization. Yet Brezhnev turned away from de-Stalinization without any effect on Sino-Soviet relations. The victory of Deng's prag-

[38] Rozman, "China's Soviet-Watchers in the 1980s," 437-39.

[39] Li Huiquan, "The Crux of the Sino-Soviet Border Question," *China and the World* (Beijing: Beijing Review, Foreign Affairs Series, 1982).

matism led quickly to abandonment of the term "revisionism" for the Soviet Union, while the shift to a reform course under Andropov and later Gorbachev caused Soviet specialists on China to discard the idea that China is led by "Maoism" or "Maoism without Mao."

Looking back to the 1950s, the Chinese continue publicly to blame the Soviets for the split. What is left from their earlier rationale is the idea that Moscow sought to control China. Mostly it was China's foreign policy that Moscow was bent on controlling. Moscow's developing relationships with Washington and Delhi were restricting Beijing's freedom to maneuver—especially on the Taiwan issue, which Beijing has always considered a domestic matter. The Soviets were restricting Chinese actions in East Asia. Soviet control also extended to what Chinese could publish about Stalin.

In the 1980s the Chinese insisted that they would maintain an independent foreign policy, and at home would reform their system according to the ideal of socialism with Chinese characteristics. These matters were stumbling blocks to better relations only insofar as the Soviets kept seeking reassurances that China's foreign policy was independent and not in collusion with the imperialists.

The problems that remained difficult to resolve from 1982 were no longer direct manifestations of Soviet control, but of Soviet intimidation and interference along China's borders. All of the problems dated from the post-Mao era, when, as the Chinese describe it, the Soviets went on the offensive while America pulled back for a time to a more defensive posture. Soviet "hegemonism" in Vietnam and Afghanistan are the transgressions that disturb the Chinese most.

Without putting it in writing, Chinese leaders seem to be communicating that little that happened before 1978 is any longer on their agenda with the Soviet Union. To be sure, there has been continued talk of a reduction in Soviet forces to the levels of the Khrushchev period and of the need for independence and equality within the international communist movement, but these issues can presumably be dealt with by Soviet declarations of goodwill and respect for Chinese interests. Chinese do not try to justify their past pronouncements or to hold the Soviets accountable for anything done or said. For instance, Chinese pay little heed to prior criticisms directed against their country's policies by Soviet specialists and officials. Even recent criticisms Chinese make no effort to refute in print. It is as if they acknowledge that for a long time Chinese themselves have been guilty of false accusations; so it would be wrong to hold the Soviets accountable for responding in kind to such provocations.

What more promising scenario could have been devised for preserving the wide divide between China and the Soviet Union than the situation in the Soviet Union from 1978 into 1982! In foreign policy, Moscow aided

Vietnam's march into Kampuchea, set up its southern fleet in Vietnam's Cam Ranh Bay, occupied Afghanistan, and carried out a huge buildup of powerful missiles along the Chinese frontier that could reach targets over a wide range of that country. The result was that almost all of the barriers to "normalized" relations that the Chinese identified after 1982 had been nonexistent only four years earlier. In domestic affairs, the Soviet economy went from bad to worse. In agriculture one severe shortfall followed another, while in industry the rate of growth slowed sharply without any sign that intractable problems were being solved.

Meanwhile, the aged Brezhnev leadership group failed to deliver on promised reforms and kept stifling the younger generation's hopes for change. In Soviet studies of China the tone remained hostile; some of the most threatening denunciations, such as Victor Louis's call, published in English, for the minority peoples from Manchuria to Tibet to rise up against the Chinese government and secede, were published in 1979 and later.[40] It was still common to hear the stock phrase "Maoism without Mao," in depreciation of China's reforms in the middle of 1982.

How little Moscow did until 1982 to win over the Chinese! The orthodox group in Moscow reigned supreme in the handling of Chinese affairs even if reform voices were growing bolder in publications on China that addressed—obliquely, to be sure—many fundamental issues of socialism. Yet the Soviet leadership still claimed to be beckoning the Chinese into negotiations, and Chinese officials may have found even the occasional overtures for better relations (e.g. a well-wishing telegram to mark an occasion) a signal that relations could improve.

What Moscow could offer both informally and merely by its very existence may have compensated for its lack of other blandishments. Informal contacts, such as the Foreign Ministry official Kapitsa's comments in annual meetings in Beijing beginning in 1980, were undoubtedly encouraging: Moscow was eager for better relations with a fellow socialist country. When Brezhnev made this view official in a series of short passages inserted into his speeches in 1982 and in authoritative articles in *Pravda*, it became clear that Moscow was bestowing a degree of legitimacy on China as a member of the socialist world.[41] Above all, what the Soviet Union was willing to provide was an end to China's outcast status and a working relationship with optimistic expectations.

The immediate gains—as limited as they appear—that the Soviet leadership promised China met many of the needs of China's communist

[40] Victor Louis, *The Coming Decline of the Chinese Empire* (New York: Times Books, 1979). This and other sources are discussed in Gilbert Rozman, *A Mirror for Socialism: Soviet Criticisms of China* (Princeton: Princeton University Press, 1985).

[41] Gilbert Rozman, "Moscow's China-Watchers in the Post-Mao Era: The Response to a Changing China," *The China Quarterly* 94 (June 1983): 215-41.

leadership. They needed the Soviet Union—Yugoslavia and Romania alone were insufficient—to reassert a socialist worldview in which the October Revolution is the turning point of history, and the remainder of the twentieth century is characterized by a fierce struggle between socialism and capitalism with the former gaining and eventually emerging victorious everywhere. Having repudiated Mao's radical version of socialist self-reliance and continuous revolution, they probably decided that the image of Chinese socialism standing alone would be hard-pressed to sustain their ideological and political needs at home. Somehow Chinese socialism had to be integrated into the inexorable march of world socialism in this century.

China's leaders needed to modernize the foundation they had established in the 1950s—not only the industrial foundation of Soviet-assisted factories, but more importantly the organizational and ideological foundations of management within a planned economy and education of socialist citizens. The Soviet Union and its allies provided experiences from which to borrow and with which to legitimize Chinese reforms.

In foreign affairs, renewed and improving ties with Moscow gave China increased leverage with the capitalist countries and at the same time helped stabilize the military environment in East Asia for China's concentrated attention on economic development. In the arts and education, these ties and the image of Soviet developments created a counterweight to the dangers of "spiritual pollution" from the West. In economics, the Soviet Union reemerged as a source of substantial assistance to China's heavy industry and as a promising trading partner.

All of these gains from "normalization" do not add up to a case for close Sino-Soviet relations. Chinese leaders and even more the Chinese people do not view Moscow as being in a position, even if it were sufficiently reliable and magnanimous, to meet China's principal needs. Moscow can help with China's economic program, but the Soviet weakness in modern science and technology and in world-class quality are obvious drawbacks. The Soviet Union is mired in its own serious economic difficulties and is not viewed as a long-term solution to China's economic problems. Chinese are benefiting so much from educational exchanges and sending students abroad to the West and Japan that they are also not tempted to place many of their eggs in the Soviet educational basket. Furthermore, as long as the Soviet military presence is formidable in Cam Ranh Bay, Afghanistan, and the northern border areas, China is likely to keep some military counterweight via ties to the United States. These are the chief limitations on the Sino-Soviet rapprochement. They indicate that a quadrilateral relationship roughly along the lines existing in 1985 will continue to be perceived in East Asia, in which the principal actors are China, the Soviet Union, Japan, and the United States. Yet there is

much opportunity for flux, and the main tendency in the 1980s of improved Sino-Soviet ties is still in progress.

The period 1978-1985 saw two contrasting trends in China: a consistent reform course for the economy and a roller coaster of inconsistent
policies affecting politics and ideology. The leadership agreed, on the
whole, about economic reform and opening to the outside world, but remained deeply divided on politics and ideology. Publications on the Soviet Union, because bilateral relations were in flux and the Soviet Union
represented the most important dimension of public or semi-public debate that Chinese leaders would tolerate, emerged in this period as perhaps the most lively forum for understanding the evolving Chinese
worldview and the struggle between orthodoxy and reform to shift that
worldview away from its current compromise position.

Our review of the Chinese debate over the Soviet Union presents one
additional set of evidence that in the second half of the twentieth century
the principal nonmilitary and noneconomic factor affecting the world balance of power has been China's initiatives brought about primarily out of
concern for: 1) domestic policy changes affecting economics, politics, and
ideology inside China; and 2) foreign policy along China's borders in
Asia. Chinese leaders took the initiative on three occasions: in the late
1950s and early 1960s when they broke with Moscow; in the early 1970s
when they joined with Washington against Moscow; and then in the first
half of the 1980s when they shifted part way toward a position of equidistance between Washington and Moscow. In each case, there were both
domestic and regional concerns that prompted Chinese leaders to act.
Moreover, the Chinese have preferred to leave the impression that the
other side in negotiations is the more earnest suitor. By examining the
debates within China, we gain a new appreciation for how carefully
China's specialists weigh the alternatives and how energetically they vie
in support of rival viewpoints as they seek to redirect China domestically
and within the world.

Chinese studies of internal conditions in the Soviet Union are written
by specialists on that country, yet they are widely perceived as a response
to and a commentary on domestic developments in China itself. To an
important degree, they are written with consideration of their impact on
the struggle between orthodoxy and reform inside China. Chinese publications on Soviet foreign policy are often the work of international affairs experts and more directly reflect the state of Sino-Soviet relations
and the general state of China's foreign relations. Different groups in
China have responsibility for these two types of publications. The first
group is more orthodox than the second and is less concerned with the
development of China's relations with capitalist countries. Turning
points in the two types of writings, as each has become less pessimistic

over the period 1978-1985, have not necessarily coincided. Views of the Soviet domestic scene have improved faster than those of foreign policy, but in both cases Andropov's leadership created new opportunities. His reform initiatives made it possible for the forces of orthodoxy in China to find new parallels between the two socialist countries, and his moves toward closer Sino-Soviet relations led to reassessments of Soviet foreign policy. In neither area did the brief Andropov era resolve all of the serious differences that divided the two countries. Chinese continued to be negative about Soviet military policy in Asia and doubtful about the Soviet commitment to major domestic reforms; but the tone of their writings on the Soviet Union became much less gloomy.

In Chinese writings on the Soviet Union, one finds the same six turning points that are treated by other schools of sovietology: 1) the switch from War Communism to the NEP; 2) the revolution from above, including collectivization; 3) Stalin's purges and his growing "cult of the personality"; 4) de-Stalinization, represented by the Twentieth Party Congress; 5) Brezhnev's stabilization and tightening of control from the mid-sixties; and 6) the Andropov-Gorbachev reform process of the 1980s. Writings on economics, literature, and politics all refer to many of these milestones in the history of the Soviet Union, evaluating them and sometimes drawing lessons for Chinese socialism. Intense debates have developed over each of these turning points; often both orthodox and reform views can be discerned. While differences of opinion are present, one finds in Chinese publications for most, if not all, of these key periods in the history of Soviet socialism a widely popularized consensus. By 1984 a clear understanding of the history of the Soviet system was emerging in China.

This consensus, which represents the official worldview, is positive about Soviet history, largely in agreement with the official Soviet perspective on Soviet history, and rather optimistic about the Soviet future. In the Andropov-Gorbachev era, there has been convergence between official Chinese and Soviet views of Soviet history, of Soviet reform needs, and of the nature of socialism. Both sides agree on the high priority of economic reform, while downplaying the need for political and ideological reform of a fundamental nature. Both agree on Lenin's greatness, on Stalin's overall successes despite serious mistakes, on Khrushchev's mishandling of the shift away from Stalin's model, and on the inadequacy of reform programs under Brezhnev. Since Brezhnev's death, the Chinese have found reason to see Soviet reforms in a more serious light, and the Soviets have looked more favorably on Chinese reforms. On domestic matters, a remarkable resemblance can be found in their views of Soviet history—all the more so since less than a decade earlier neither Chinese nor Soviet publications accepted many of the reform-oriented views that comprise this consensus.

While the similarities are striking, the differences should not be over-looked. As of late 1985, Soviet officials had not publicly acknowledged the wisdom of China's reform programs, and Chinese publications were not expressing optimism that Soviet reforms over the next several years would adequately address the serious problems facing that country. Nei-ther side was publicizing the growing consensus in the two worldviews. A continued barrier existed, preventing either side from expressing high optimism about the other's development and also blocking comparisons between the two countries. Given the widespread appreciation in both countries of strong similarities between the two, the absence of any com-parisons—historic or contemporary—was conclusive testimony to the existence of a firm barrier.

Two interpretations of the nature of this barrier to comparative schol-arship and positive mutual assessments readily come to mind. The first is that both Beijing and Moscow follow the practice of allowing foreign re-lations to determine evaluations of each other. They refuse to move ahead to praise and genuine optimism until their foreign affairs problems are clearly resolved. The second interpretation is that each side is awaiting the outcome of Gorbachev's consolidation of power. The signal awaited by China may be the decision by Soviet leaders to praise China's reforms and to comment directly about learning from the Chinese experience. The Gorbachev leadership may delay in doing so until it puts its own re-form agenda in order, but it also may hesitate because it is dissatisfied with continued Chinese criticisms of Soviet foreign policy in Asia. The challenge remained in 1985 for the Soviet leadership to launch a funda-mental reform program and to recognize an independent China within the socialist camp. The challenge was not new. What was new after Gor-bachev's accession to power and the appointment of many new members of the top Soviet leadership, and after the warming relations between the two countries in 1984-1985, was how likely it seemed that Sino-Soviet "normalization" and party-to-party relations could now be achieved on this basis. Even progress in relations, however, would not eliminate the potential for a continuing strategic rivalry between these countries within Asia and the pride Chinese have come to feel in their own independent place in world affairs.

During the first two-thirds of 1986 it became increasingly clear that Gorbachev had made improved relations with China one of his most im-portant foreign policy priorities. Soviet assessments of China's reforms and economic progress in the 1980s became decidedly more positive. As reform initiatives in the Soviet Union grew bolder, the relevance of

Beijing's prior reforms became more and more apparent. The Chinese evaluation of Gorbachev's domestic program could best be characterized as enthusiastic. This did not mean that Chinese were losing sight of the difficult reform process that still faced the Soviet leadership, but in calling attention to it they were scarcely being more cautious than the Soviets themselves.

On July 28 at Vladivostok, Gorbachev announced Moscow's readiness to take action on at least two of the "three obstacles" that Beijing had identified. He made concessions on a river dispute with China, indicated plans to withdraw a substantial part of Soviet troops from Mongolia, called for mutual withdrawal of troops along other parts of the Sino-Soviet border, and, concerning the second obstacle, announced a modest cut in the Soviet forces present in Afghanistan. In August the third obstacle was addressed when Gorbachev met with the Vietnamese party leader Truong Chinh and both pledged to work for better relations with China. The Chinese welcomed Gorbachev's statements although it remained clear that they were asking for more action, particularly concerning a Vietnamese withdrawal from Kampuchea. Nevertheless, at last the logjam on the "three obstacles" appeared to be breaking somewhat. There was every indication that 1986 would be another year of improved perceptions and relations. The Polish and East German party leaders visited Beijing in the fall, beginning the process of normalization of communist party ties with Moscow's close European allies. Much as the Maoist negative image of a revisionist Soviet Union created the momentum a quarter-century earlier for the Sino-Soviet split, China's increasingly favorable image of Soviet socialism in the 1980s has proved to be a driving force for reconciliation.

INDEX

Lu Nanquan, 92-94, 107, 215-22, 229-30
Lu Shoucai, 160, 180-81
Lunacharsky, A. V., 268
Luo Zhaohong, 344-45
Luxemburg, Rosa, 319
Lysenko, T. D., 248-50, 292

machine-tractors stations, 162, 167, 175
Makarenko, A. S., 270-75
management: comparisons of reform efforts, 222-26; pros and cons of Stalin-era system, 218
Manchus, 9
Mandelstam, Osip, 264
Mao Zedong, 6, 36, 45, 52, 65, 80, 103, 332-33, 376-77; assessment of role in history, 16, 42-43, 69, 72, 82-83, 88, 97, 310, 350, 358, 375; comparisons to Lenin and Stalin, 23, 94, 112, 247, 350-51, 355-57; views of Soviet revisionism, 4, 6, 18, 63, 86, 145-50, 190-96, 239-42, 260, 292, 296-307, 353-54, 359
Mao Zedong Thought, 15, 18, 22, 73, 90, 172, 267, 358; survival of, 54, 65, 358
market: historical development of, 8, 150, 164, 197-99, 236, 310; regulation of, 77, 156, 176; under socialism, 39-40, 51, 87, 100, 159-61, 166, 169, 173, 201, 236, 346
market socialism, 229, 233, 340
Markov, G. M., 241, 253
Marx, Karl, 9, 29, 197, 200, 216, 248, 250; centenary of death, 48, 112, 318; early views of, 47; reinterpretations of, 117, 152
Marxism-Leninism, 18, 20, 21, 23, 31, 162, 174, 267, 330; betrayal of, 84, 88, 192, 249, 265, 287, 300-301, 304; education in, 9, 111, 277; fundamental principles of, 16, 31, 73, 117, 157, 325; readiness for, 163; retention of, 13, 76, 90, 110, 288, 357
mass line, 22, 301
mass media, 77, 230
May Fourth Movement, 8
Mayakovsky, V. V., 244
Medvedev, Roy, 316
Mei Wenbin, 92, 168, 200
middle class, 20
Middle East, 115, 121

middle peasants, 146, 159, 163-65, 169-70, 174, 188, 204, 326-31
migration to cities, 149, 167, 177, 179, 183
Mikhalkov, S. V., 242
Mikoyan, A. I., 302, 333
military cooperation, between China and the U.S., 123
military feudal imperialism, 91, 199-202, 236
military role in Soviet leadership, 335, 337
ministries, number of, 338
models of socialism, 38-39, 59-60, 95-96, 211, 347
Mongolian People's Republic, 54, 85, 120, 135, 137
Mongols, 309
movies, 77, 134, 250, 258, 280, 288, 334, 336
multi-formation economy, 184, 229, 347

Nakasone, Yasuhiro, 123
national liberation movements, 105-106, 331
nationalities, 77, 83, 108, 222, 304, 308, 326, 331
nationalization, 209, 327-28
natural conditions, overlooked in farming, 174-76, 179
natural economy, influence of, 210-11, 215, 236
naval bases, 53-54, 135-36, 356
neibu publications, 34, 36, 43, 80, 110, 132, 142, 158, 350; a barrier to access, 26-28, 62, 97, 256, 349, 352; examples of, 36, 128, 161, 182, 249, 346
Nekrasov, Viktor N., 259, 263
nepmen, 208
new-born reactionaries, 111
New Economic Policy (NEP), 35; and Bukharin, 43, 317; a model for China, 4, 38, 158; significance of, 46, 157-61, 180, 204-208, 216, 236, 326, 357
New People's Democracy, 10
new socialist man, 271, 289
Nicholas II, 244
Nine Commentaries, 45, 63, 80, 86, 306, 353; Ninth Commentary, 95, 146, 192, 240, 302
nonagression pact, 140
normalization: barriers to, 91-92, 378;

LIBRARY OF CONGRESS CATALOGING-IN-PUBLICATION DATA

Rozman, Gilbert.
The Chinese debate about Soviet socialism, 1978-1985.

Includes index.
1. Communism—Soviet Union.   2. Soviet Union—Foreign opinion, Chinese.
3. Public opinion—China.   4. China—Foreign relations—Soviet Union.
5. Soviet Union—Foreign relations—China.   I. Title.

HX313.5.R69 1987   335.43'0947   86-25166
ISBN 0-691-09429-2